MY CULT YOUR CULT

My Cult Your Cult © Copyright 2025, Sean Prophet

All rights reserved. No part of this book may be used or reproduced in any manner whatsoever without written permission by the publisher, except in the case of brief quotations in critical articles and reviews.

Paperback First Edition ISBN 978-1-956872-56-9
Ebook First Edition ISBN 978-1-956872-78-1

AMIKA PRESS
2444 Pioneer Road Evanston IL 60201
847 920 8084 · info@amikapress.com
Available for purchase on amikapress.com

For updates and future resources related to this book, visit:
mycultyourcult.com

ExoProphet: *Notes from the Algorithmic Age*
exoprophet.substack.com

Cover illustration © Copyright 2025, Sean Prophet.
Illustration by Mouna Moumni. Cover design by Andrea Elder.
Author photography by Camille Gartrell. Designed & typeset by Beth O'Driscoll.

My Cult Your Cult

How Cults Destroy Truth and Bolster Authoritarian Power

By Sean Prophet

*To anyone who's ever been in a cult,
and to those who loved and missed them.*

"Every country has its own type of criminal. In America, we got the confidence man. Snake oil salesman, grifter.
He don't rob you as much as trick you into robbing yourself.
See, 'cause in America, people want to believe. They got that dream. And a dreamer, you can fleece."
—Loy Cannon, written by Noah Hawley, Enzo Mileti, and Scott Wilson, Fargo, Season 4, Episode 7

"The word 'cult' describes how humans without sufficient knowledge and coping skills adapt to abusive systems and grow to defend them, even at the cost of their lives."
—Sean Prophet, My Cult Your Cult, Chapter 2

"Power is the ultimate aphrodisiac."
—commonly attributed to Henry Kissinger

Contents

Foreword *by William Hamby* ....page 1
Prologue 4
Chapter 1: Meet My Cult 6
Chapter 2: What is a Cult? 16
Chapter 3: Fascism and Thought Reform 27
Chapter 4: No One Is Immune 42
Chapter 5: Betty Clare Wulf 55
Chapter 6: Existential Hunger 65
Chapter 7: Conspirituality 84
Chapter 8: Puritoxic Madness 92
Chapter 9: Theosophy, Race, and Christian Nationalism 101
Chapter 10: My Family Business 114
Chapter 11: Past Lives 128
Chapter 12: Survivalism 134
Chapter 13: Levers of Control 144
Chapter 14: Sanctity 152
Chapter 15: The Moral Landscape 163
Chapter 16: Totalitarianism 172
Chapter 17: MAGA 188
Chapter 18: Apophenia 197
Chapter 19: Seeding Mull's Vendetta 224
Chapter 20: Mother Under Oath 233
Chapter 21: Apologia 242
Chapter 22: Rumspringa 256
Chapter 23: Doubts And Dissent 266
Chapter 24: Reclaiming Your Power 276
Chapter 25: The Dweller on the Threshold 281
Chapter 26: War! 291
Chapter 27: Exit, Stage Left 303

Chapter 28: Healing: Beyond Deprogramming 315
Chapter 29: A Clean Break? 332
Chapter 30: Earthquake! 340
Chapter 31: Seeking Normal 351
Chapter 32: Alone 357
Chapter 33: Reconnection and Disconnection 363
Chapter 34: The Faith I Lost 369
Chapter 35: Who Am I? 379
Chapter 36: A Quiet Life 390
Chapter 37: I've-Got-Mine-Ism 398
Chapter 38: Neocons 404
Chapter 39: Dénouement 412
Afterword 425
Cult Documentaries 427
Acknowledgements 428

Foreword
By William Hamby, LCSW

I don't recall how I met Sean Prophet. I imagine it was the way a lot of people become "internet friends," through some shared forum or another. I admired his directness in challenging social mythologies rooted in abusive religious ideas. He was writing in depth about complex social systems, and he seemed to understand them better than the average layperson. When I learned that he was the son of Elizabeth Clare Prophet, a cult leader I'd actually heard of, that piqued my interest.

My first job as a psychotherapist fresh out of graduate school was at a community mental health and addiction clinic. The workload was smothering, and there were no "easy" cases. Poverty is a form of trauma and makes every other mental health condition worse, so almost by default, all of my patients had severe mental health issues. Within six months, I realized I didn't have the skills I needed to help them. They all had trauma symptoms on top of whatever else they might be experiencing. So I took every training I could find on treating physical and emotional trauma.

In the early 2000s, I was heavily involved in what would become known as the New Atheist Movement. I wanted to keep the separation of Church and State enshrined in US law and practice, and I wanted to challenge discrimination against nonbelievers and create safe communities where people who had left religion—or never believed—could be themselves in authentic ways.

This combination of professional training and activism gave me a powerful perspective: My atheist friends and colleagues seemed to struggle as much as their religious counterparts with—for lack of a better term—getting life right. For as much as I agreed with them that the universe appears to be godless, and as fulfilling as it was to have a community of like-minded people, it was obvious that something was wrong. The non-believers faced the same emotional issues, the same addictions, and the same dysfunctional relationship patterns as the churchgoers they chided for "getting the universe wrong."

Along the way, I became friends with Dr. Darrel Ray, founder of Recovering from Religion and the Secular Therapy Project. I've been a member of both since nearly the beginning. This connection allowed me to work with many patients whose experiences in religious settings left them with emotional scars, including crippling anxiety and depression. Having made my own journey out of an emotionally abusive religion, it was fulfilling to help others on similar paths. Concurrently, I became an expert in the pathologies of religious trauma.

Prophet and I interacted frequently over the years on our parallel paths of activism, developing a professional level of trust. We helped each other refine our understanding of fine points in our respective areas of expertise. When he asked me to contribute as a consultant on this book, I didn't hesitate. His story of escaping his cult is compelling. He had unhindered access to every facet of the organization, including detailed records of the private thoughts of his mother, who led the group for 26 years after the death of its founder, Mark Prophet. I felt confident from our history that he would do his best to accurately reflect cult psychology.

Perhaps it's counterintuitive to point out that Prophet is vulnerable and speaks plainly of his mistakes, but this is the step that most people who leave cults take only partially, if at all. In my life and practice, I have a saying: Sometimes we have to realize just how bad things are before we can get better. And that realization often involves things we were very wrong about. And being wrong caused us to make egregious errors. Only by accepting these errors for what they are can we move past them.

The best recovery stories are those that are honest about what went wrong and why. As long as we remain caught in the shame and defensiveness of self-justification, we will struggle to escape the situations that keep us from thriving. What drew me most to Prophet was his willingness to explore his own mistakes rather than taking the perspective of being coerced or manipulated—although that is a critical component of his story. Likewise, he has rejected the idea that there was some overriding justification that made it "okay" that things happened the way they did.

Prophet's story doesn't represent the typical cult experience. Very few cult members are born into godhood, and very few experience the dual responsibility and helplessness of being required to represent the cult while having no real power to direct it. As a result, I think Prophet has experienced a cult more completely than almost anyone, and as I survey my experience with cult survivors, I can't think of anyone who has made it as far out as he has.

He is eminently qualified to bring this critical message to light at what may be a fulcrum in history. The United States has just decided—again—to succumb to the cult of authoritarian personality. "Cult-like thinking" invades almost every aspect of Western society. He has painstakingly chronicled how his own cult embodied many of these patterns and meticulously connected them to larger, pervasive cultural mythologies.

Leaving a cult centers around purging the most egregious beliefs and then building new communities with healthy values and strong boundaries. This requires not only abandoning fantastic notions like being transported to other galaxies by aliens or channeling higher beings. It also involves examining the minutiae of how we believe the universe and humans work.

I want to emphasize that this book represents a first step. After reading it, if you find the motivation to leave your cult, I encourage you to find a trauma-informed, secular therapist to help with your next steps. There is no step as important as the first one. In my practice I often say, "We can't heal a trauma that is still happening." Leaving trauma means leaving trauma.

Recovery with a qualified secular therapist will help you feel safe to be who you are, think what you think, and feel what you feel. It will take time and patience, but the goal is to become a version of yourself that is deeply curious about the universe and unafraid of anything your brain might reveal. With time, you will come to believe that your mind is a beautiful and wonderful machine that is always trying to help you grow and thrive. Your body is yours to do what you want with whom. Your life path is to find what you love and pursue it how you want. Perhaps you have always believed that you needed someone else to show you the right path. There is another way. That road begins with leaving your cult, continues with therapy, and it ends with you knowing, at a deep emotional and intellectual level, that you are the one best qualified to decide your path in life—and that you have all the tools to make those decisions.

Prologue

I was the weird kid—on steroids. The year was 1969. I dressed oddly and didn't fit in with my classmates. I didn't know their music or their culture. I was ignorant of professional sports and even most childhood games. From the moment I enrolled in Broadmoor Elementary kindergarten at the age of five, I learned that my home and cult lifestyle had a bad reputation in our upscale neighborhood, which was nestled at the foot of Cheyenne Mountain in Colorado Springs. My family occupied an enormous 17,000-square-foot brick mansion called La Tourelle—by far the largest home in the neighborhood—along with 60 cult staff. Everyone knew I was from "that house." Further cementing my peculiarity, a young Black staff member named Leon dropped me off at school in a green Cadillac. To the other kids, I couldn't have been stranger.

The spectacle of my daily chauffeured grand entrance was enough to raise plenty of six-year-old eyebrows. Even kindergartners were smart enough to recognize there was a lot more going on there. Even *I* thought it was odd that my parents didn't drop me off. *Why couldn't I be like everyone else?* Why were they in on every joke, and what made me their target? When I asked my mother to explain why no one wanted to play with me, she blamed my "light." They were "of the world," and I was a "light bearer," destined for a superior path.

Of course it was a lie—among the first of a litany of falsehoods I was spoon-fed during my childhood indoctrination. The real reason I didn't fit in was that I was born into a classic *thought-reformed* cult environment—a princeling in bizarro world. My parents Mark and Elizabeth Prophet were self-proclaimed messengers of the "Teachings of the Ascended Masters." I had been sequestered in their enclave, only gradually catching snippets of external reality: Television, newspapers, films, music, travel. I learned to keep two mental ledgers for every experience—how it would be interpreted at home, and how it was viewed outside. Beginning my first day of school I struggled to master code-switching—adopting the dual identity required to alternate between the norms, behaviors, language, and values of disparate cultural environments. I didn't know the term. Only that I was moving in two worlds.

What set me apart was *how* we arrived at our beliefs—through divine revelation from my parents—our certainty, and our strategic rejection of society. Which made it impossible for me to fit in with my peers. I was separate, and chosen—a boy-messiah.

I soon learned that outsiders believed the people in my cult were "brainwashed," which seemed to inspire fear. Whatever brainwashing was, I had always been that way. As strange as our beliefs and practices were, I accepted them. "Normal" American culture was alien. It's taken most of my life to parse these differences and learn the mechanics of thought reform.

In early January 2024, I set myself the task of writing a book about the cult into which I was born. As I started pouring out my memories, I chronicled the many lessons I learned as the firstborn son of the founders and leaders of The Summit Lighthouse—which later became known as Church Universal and Triumphant. Over the next year, the book grew into something larger in scope, and perhaps more controversial. I came to recognize that the beliefs, tactics and abuses that suffused my cult could only be understood within a greater context that includes the world's religions, its politics, and how we derive our ethical norms. I also came to recognize important parallels between my own upbringing and the hyper-religious Christian Nationalist underbelly of the MAGA cult. Cult tactics have now become so pervasive that it is likely that you or someone you know has been or is currently a member of a cult. Hence the title, *My Cult Your Cult.*

CHAPTER ONE

Meet My Cult

In 1958 my father Mark Prophet founded our cult in Washington D.C. as an informal worship group called The Summit Lighthouse. In 1961 he met my mother, Elizabeth Clare Wulf, when she attended one of his meetings in Boston. They married in 1963, and I was born in 1964. In 1966 the pair moved their small organization into a stately brick mansion called La Tourelle, or "the little tower," in the Broadmoor neighborhood of Colorado Springs.

When dad died in 1973, my mother assumed leadership and relocated to a property in Santa Barbara she called the "Motherhouse." In 1974 we announced the formation of Church Universal and Triumphant, formally incorporated in 1975. The Summit Lighthouse became our publishing arm, also known as Summit University Press. In 1976 we moved to Pasadena, then in 1978 to Malibu. Our final move to Montana took place at the end of 1986. My mother led our cult until 1999, when she resigned due to cognitive decline from untreated epilepsy and early-onset Alzheimer's disease. She died in 2009. Since her departure, my cult has been without a spiritual leader. Rebranded as The Summit Lighthouse, it's now run by former junior staffers.

My cult is a classic *millenarian* movement, rooted in the long tradition of doomsayers who predict a purifying event that will uproot civilization, followed by a golden age.[1] My parents began their ministry with messages of spiritual world-transformation. Shortly before his death in 1973, my father began to forecast doom, kicking off a brief flirtation with survivalism which lasted two years. But my mother wasn't quite ready to head for the hills—and she soon set her sights on expansion. During our heyday while headquartered in Los Angeles from 1976 to 1986, we counted between 50,000 and 75,000 members, with teaching centers in most major American cities and on five continents.

My mother was fascinated with the Arthurian legends, which are deeply entwined with our theology. So she named our Malibu headquarters "Camelot." The 240-acre King Gillette Ranch[2] is located just three miles off the 101 Freeway. We were within commuting distance of most of Los Angeles, which gave members access to plentiful jobs and housing, while still providing an isolated retreat environment. Though many of our staff lived off campus in both Malibu and the San Fernando Valley, in our parlance, we were "in the world, but not of it."

Mark and Elizabeth Prophet with Sean Prophet. La Tourelle, Colorado Springs, Colorado c. 1966

The entrance to Camelot was a quarter-mile-long drive off Mulholland Highway lined with eucalyptus trees, leading to a spectacular mix of lush lawns, ancient California oaks, and a varied topography of scrubby knolls and farmland. We held Easter Sunrise services at the highest peak we dubbed "Ascension Hill." Our main facilities were the Gillette Mansion and two chapels with attached dormitories—built in the 1950s by the Claretian Order—one of which held our commissary. Amenities included three tennis courts, a swimming pool, and a soccer field. A small stream called Stokes Creek fed an idyllic artificial pond surrounded by drooping trees we called "Swan Lake."

Camelot bustled with activity. We repurposed dorm rooms as offices, a former horse stable became our graphic arts department, and the hay barn became our print shop. We ran a small farming operation that included sheep and goats. Our Montessori School, administrative offices, and audio-video department occupied the mansion annex. We modernized the larger "Chapel of the Holy Grail" with video lighting and sound equipment and built a 200-seat Summit University classroom. The smaller "Chapel of the Holy Family" often served as a wedding venue. For large conferences, we set up a circus tent in one of our parking lots. We planned to build more permanent facilities including a 3,300-seat auditorium and plenty of housing. But we lacked funding, and we were unprepared to navigate California's strict permitting process.

The former King Gillette Ranch and headquarters of Church Universal and Triumphant—known as Camelot from 1977-1986, Malibu, California.

As the Cold War escalated in the early 1980s, following President Reagan's "evil empire" speech and the Soviet downing of Korean Air flight 007, my mother's millenarian rhetoric swelled. In 1986 she published *Saint Germain on Prophecy*, quoting 16th-century seer Nostradamus to forecast a modern ride of the Four Horsemen of the Apocalypse. She admonished our members to expect nuclear war and "Earth changes," supporting President Reagan's "Star Wars" initiative for a defensive anti-missile shield. On October 3, 1987, at the Penta Hotel in New York City, she thundered: "…ere twenty-four months have passed, there shall be a confrontation and a reckoning if something is not done." She later clarified that our members should complete their war preparations, including bomb shelters, by October 2, 1989.

My mother had been preparing to withdraw from civilization since 1981, when we bought the sprawling 12,000-acre Forbes ranch in Park County, Montana, 50 miles south of Livingston. In July 1986, we sold Camelot, which is now again called King Gillette Ranch, and is a part of Santa Monica Mountains National Recreation Area. A convoy of semi-trucks moved our operation to the former Forbes property, which she renamed the "Royal Teton Ranch"—also dubbing it "The Inner Retreat," a name with survivalist undertones. By December, our pullout from Camelot was complete. As she sold our remaining urban real-estate assets, our Montana holdings grew to more than 33,000 acres, including the two 4,000-acre residential subdivisions Glastonbury North and South, the 13,000-acre Lazy W ranch, the OTO Ranch, the Big Spur Campground, and industrial property in Livingston.

Our lands were concentrated in Montana's Paradise Valley which extends from Livingston to the north entrance of Yellowstone National Park—a scenic marvel carved by the Yellowstone River, which meanders through lush meadows, past towering peaks of the Absaroka and Gallatin Ranges. From 1987 to 1989, thousands of members streamed into the valley. Many built underground bunkers ranging from single-family models to concrete and steel complexes that could hold hundreds.

In July of 1989, we made national news when my stepfather Edward Francis was indicted with staffer Vernon Hamilton for conspiracy to purchase heavy weaponry under an assumed name. Both did prison time. In March 1990, we conducted two dress-rehearsal drills, moving thousands of people and their belongings into the dozens of shelters spread across the Paradise Valley. That spasm of activity, along with a 32,000-gallon fuel spill in April at our Mol Heron Creek shelter site, brought intense national and global concern along with legal scrutiny.

By 1991, most shelters were completed and stocked. The fuel-spill cleanup took a year and cost $1 million. Unfinished bunkers in the Glastonbury subdivision remained open-pit scars on the land. Some members pulled out of Montana and moved back to cities. Our primary concern became financial survival—paying back the money we had borrowed while preparing for the end of the world. We fund-raised. We sold gold and land. We balanced our books.

Members believed their prayers, combined with our expensive steel and concrete tombs, had averted the apocalypse. While the shelter-building effort was an epic fiasco, we consoled ourselves that we had saved the world. We weren't broke fools who'd dug pricey hidey-holes in the ground. We were heroes.

In 1992 we held our largest-ever conference in a tent pitched on the picturesque Taylor Meadows adjacent to the Mol Heron Creek shelters, also known as "The Heart of the Inner Retreat." It was attended by nearly

5,000. Strengthened by that impressive audience, my mother turned outward, scheduling new lecture and book tours. But this time the crowds she had attracted through the 1970s and '80s failed to materialize. Notoriety over the bomb-shelter debacle and her husband's plea-deal on weapons charges had damaged her brand.

A satellite view of Church Universal and Triumphant's 756-person bomb shelter, located in Taylor Meadows by the pristine Mol Heron Creek, near Gardiner, Montana

As 1993 drew to a close, I was tired of trying to rationalize our messianic failure. And I began to see other cracks in our spiritual facade. I finally left my cult for good. I realized what the world already knew: 1989-1991 marked the end of the Cold War. The 1987 INF treaty eliminated an entire class of medium-range missiles in Europe. The Berlin Wall fell in November 1989. The 1991 START I treaty halved the number of nuclear missiles pointed at the United States. The Soviet Union collapsed in December 1991. We had misjudged history. We hadn't saved the world, or even ourselves. Instead of building a thriving above-ground community, we squandered our endowment on a subterranean boondoggle.

It's difficult to describe my disillusionment. What made our members embrace survivalism? Why were they so eager to reject civilization? I had an excuse: I trusted my mother. But what explains those who joined even *after* she announced a world-ending apocalypse? What convinces people to join cults—in general? There's no single answer. In this book I'll do my best to explore these vulnerabilities, which are as varied as the people involved. Understanding the basis for morality is critical. I will focus on Lawrence Kohlberg's theory of moral development, and touch on Jean Piaget's theory of cognitive developmental stages. My hope is to apply the lessons of my failures, and the failures of my cult, to the larger complications of the human search for meaning—and perhaps to achieve some harm reduction.

I'm highly attuned to cultic patterns on a national scale, because I grew up watching a smaller version unfold. If you didn't grow up like I did, you're unlikely to recognize the broad impact of cult-like thinking. These beliefs, tactics and abuses can only be understood in the greater context of the world's religions, politics, and ethical norms.

The difficulty is plain: Cults aren't easy to identify. Media perception tends toward caricature and sometimes limits public understanding. Dangers that may seem obvious while watching a Netflix documentary won't be obvious if you agree with a cult's dogma. Or when you're energized about some new group you found. You won't want to admit you're on the verge of being suckered in. Cults prey on your deepest longings and exploit your blind spots. This was as true of my cult as others.

Cult is a pejorative term that screams danger, fraud, and abuse of power. But if the dangers were obvious, cults wouldn't exist. They offer benefits to offset their high costs. These include social cohesion, belonging, a sense of purpose, plausible-sounding answers to big questions, and a refuge from boredom and the rough-and-tumble aspects of life. Lost people can feel very found in these groups. I knew thousands of them. But they got much more than they bargained for.

Most cults are also threads woven into the world's religious fabric, and they can tend to wield outsized political power. In the US, that power is concentrated under the rubric of Christian Nationalism—a term I'll be using frequently. According to the 2024 documentary *Bad Faith: Christian Nationalism's Unholy War on Democracy* (Amazon Prime), "Christian Nationalism is a political movement that believes America was founded as a 'Christian Nation,' privileging Christianity over all other faiths. Masquerading as religion, this ideology exploits scripture and sacred symbols to achieve extremist objectives." My cult was far removed from mainstream evangelical churches, yet it shared some of their theocratic doctrines and goals.

Words like "theocracy," "fascism" and "genocide" may seem hyperbolic, but there are aspects of cults we can't consider any other way. We can't protect ourselves from what we refuse to name. The authoritarian leadership of cults and religions—and less overt forms of tyranny hiding within spiritual movements—are fascist. When cults and Christian Nationalist churches clamor for the establishment of "God's law," or "God-government," that's an assault on democracy that should alarm us all. Many espouse an overly broad tolerance—in the name of religious freedom—of churches and "spiritual communities." Many dismiss the apocalyptic ravings of preachers and cult leaders as mere kookiness, rather than recognizing "end times" prophecies as calls for genocide.

Theocracy is a terrifying term for a brutal, exclusionary form of government that's incompatible with democracy or human rights—or even freedom of religion. Its leaders demand special reverence because they are "divinely" guided or chosen. It's rife with apocalyptic thinking that stands athwart civilization. In *Cults Like Us* social critic Jane Borden observes "The avatar of our country's founding was a doomsday group. We've been iterating on its prototype since"—referring to the Puritans, who established America's first theocracy in New England.[3] This enduring pattern in which communities prioritize rescue by a superhuman savior over the honest work of self-rule has been called "the American Monomyth." From those early colonial theocracies to modern examples like Iran, Afghanistan, and Saudi Arabia, the pattern is clear: Religious belief supplants laws and constitutions.

Fascism is another scare-word I use liberally throughout this book, to describe not just cults but Christian Nationalism, radical Islamism, political billionaires, and other anti-democratic movements based in order and hierarchy. It's not limited to 20th-century examples like Spain under Franco, Germany under Hitler, or Italy under Mussolini. That's *nationalistic* fascism. But Ur-Fascism, or "eternal fascism," is a subtler phenomenon that can fester within democratic republics—a morally vacuous strategy for seizing power.

In the 20th-century, the world endured numerous ethnic and political cleansings. The top three genocides were the Holocaust, the Holodomor, and the Chinese Cultural Revolution, which together claimed about 100 million lives. Lesser genocides have recurred in Cambodia, Rwanda, Bosnia, Darfur, Myanmar, Indonesia, Gaza and elsewhere. We say "never again." Yet in spite of widespread awareness, the world tends to sit on its hands.

Cults and religions routinely preach in favor of genocide, raising the specter of violent apocalypse in which "chosen people" will rise to heaven while non-believers perish. Sometimes these dark fantasies piggyback on real-world fears like nuclear war, Y2K, or stock-market crashes. They are hostile gambits by preachers, politicians and cult leaders to dominate society by stoking fear of mass death—usurping God's authority—to dole out "divine retribution." Since no one has a hot-line to the Almighty, we should recognize these doom-prophecies as power grabs.

Fascism is a growing danger, and it's not alarmist to say so. Over the past two decades, former secular democracies like Hungary and Turkey have succumbed to it, and more nations in Europe are leaning in that direction. With Donald Trump's re-election in November 2024, the United States has fallen prey to its own home-grown fascist insurgency—the MAGA cult.

How do cults differ from religions and political movements? How do they form? How do you avoid getting hooked? What is it like to be in one? What goes on behind the scenes? As a cult veteran, and former cult leader, I'm in a unique position to answer these questions. In 1987, I was ordained a minister and the next year became vice-president of my cult at age 23.

I will tell my own cautionary tale. My post-cult struggles drove me toward science, philosophy, and ethics. By revealing the steep price I paid for clarity, I hope to help others avoid becoming ensnared—and to help others escape, like I did. It's not enough to learn cult tactics. Cult abuses are real, and you should know what kind of distorted hall of mirrors a cult can be. But that won't keep you safe. Your best defense against cults is introspection, leading to well-examined, internally-consistent values. You must devote serious thought to existential questions, before someone uses your confusion against you. Cult marketing appeals to your fear of mortality, selling you made-up non-solutions.

Another wide funnel into cults is *conspirituality*—a portmanteau of conspiracy and spirituality. These have always been widespread. But they've become more entangled, especially since the early-2020s Covid-19 pandemic. You can explore this topic through the Conspirituality Podcast, and the bestselling book *Conspirituality: How New Age Conspiracy Theories Became a Health Threat*, by Derek Beres, Matthew Remski, and Julian Walker. In December 2021 I was interviewed on "Conspirituality 81: Praying for Fire," about my cult deconversion. There's a surprising link between my cult and one of QAnon's best-known proponents, retired US General Michael Flynn.

True to conspirituality form, no cult leader lets a good crisis go to waste. Millenarian cults thrive on political, economic, and personal malaise. I can't remember a day in 30 years when we weren't praying about some dire world condition, or against some dastardly politician or ex-member. It was a constant fight for global and spiritual survival. The nightly news blared at dinnertime, whether at home or in the commissary, and there was always urgency fueling our spiritual warfare.

Some concerns were legitimate. I grew up during the Cold War, the Vietnam War, Watergate, the 1973 and 1979 oil shortages, recessions, the Iran hostage crisis, Iran-Contra, the Soviet-Afghanistan War, and AIDS. Our outward focus wasn't bad in itself. Awareness of world events is essential for good citizenship. But we framed everything in stressful terms: We weren't just concerned citizens. We were *personally responsible* for averting calamities with our prayers. That's quite a burden!

There was little recourse for psychological pain. The answer was always to be more devout. If we weren't "out of alignment" with God, or our "divine plan," we wouldn't be suffering, would we? There were licensed therapists in our cult orbit, but the ones who were approved to see staff patients had to report back to my mother, violating doctor-patient confidentiality. Some staff gave their therapists permission to share information with their "guru," turning therapy sessions into a form of confession. This is typical—information is a cult-leader's lifeline.

As I grew up, I watched people I loved fall out of favor and disappear. One was my stepfather, Randall King. And there were other surrogate fathers I lost. Some were teachers, friends, and mentors who had failed to bend the knee to my parents' wishes. Sometimes it was a doctrinal dispute. Sometimes it was because they challenged my parents, had an affair, raised their voice or swore, drank alcohol, or violated some other rule. My mother had a policy that anyone being expelled had to be out by sundown, based on Jesus' words "let not the sun go down upon your wrath."

A lot of young, inexperienced, and idealistic people join cults for a few years and leave on their own. But they never get that time back. Far too many people become cult lifers. I was born into my cult, so I can't tell you what it's like to join one. But I've interviewed ex-cult members about what persuaded them. I'll discuss my 1984 Rumspringa, when I left my cult for two years at the age of 20. There's nothing quite like watching everyone you know turn against you. In spite of those betrayals, I returned to the fold in early 1987. A fateful decision with a steep price in lost career opportunities.

I've come to terms with my mistakes. Though my cult centered around spiritual teachings, it was a royal court, and I was the prince. In my early 20s, I was unprepared to assume ministerial duties or the responsibilities of being vice-president. My insecurity made me heartless—an object lesson in the pitfalls of nepotism. I casually mistreated and fired people who didn't deserve it. I supported my mother's decisions, even when I knew they were wrong. Still, I had discretion in some areas, and I bear significant responsibility for expanding the scope of our shelter project, as it became a runaway train. This book is a partial effort to atone for my complicity. I apologize to those I hurt. I hope to curb future abuses.

Cults appear to serve a range of human needs for belonging, personal development, and collective action. Finding wholeness, purpose and inner resolve on your own isn't easy. Many people can't—their chains are on the inside. So even if they manage to leave their cult, they can wind up right back in another one. There's no difference between a cult-lifer and a lifelong cult-hopper. Both abdicate their psychological freedom, and neither finds resolution of their traumas. The same unaccountable authority, information control and thought reform can be found within nations, religions and institutions. Your mind is the battlefield, and your only defense is rigorous self-knowledge.

I still carry leftover bad habits. One is my messianic sense of personal responsibility for world events. When calamities happen, like mass shootings, terror attacks, or the awful wars in Ukraine and Gaza, I drift toward cult crisis mode. For the past 25 years I've been compelled to write blog and social media posts, or produce podcasts—to *do something* to make a difference. Had I shaken off this burden, my life could have been happier and more focused. I could have had a more lucrative career, and I could have written this book 10 or 15 years ago. I'm not going to say "everything happens for a reason." That's just more cult-speak. But here's hoping my years of marinating on my experience might have produced a bit less anger, and a bit more insight.

---

[1] Wikipedia contributors. (2024, December 30). Millenarianism. In Wikipedia. Retrieved from https://en.wikipedia.org/wiki/Millenarianism

[2] Ventura County Trails. (2019, July 11). *King Gillette Ranch has a storied history*. Retrieved from https://venturacountytrails.org/WP/2019/07/11/king-gillette-ranch-has-a-storied-history

[3] Borden, J. (2025). *Cults like us: Why doomsday thinking drives America*. Atria/One Signal Publishers.

■■■■■■■ CHAPTER TWO ■■■■■■■

What Is a Cult?

"The real purpose of this trial was to destroy us," my mother said softly with a forced smile. She stood in front of her congregation at our Camelot headquarters on April 2, 1986, serenely detached from grim reality: Moments earlier, a jury had awarded $1.56 million in damages to San Francisco architect Gregory Mull, a former member of our cult. Church *Universal and Triumphant (CUT) v. Mull* was a grinding eight-week trial in Los Angeles Superior Court that marked an end to her impunity—and it shattered her. She put on her bravest face—repeating one of Roy Cohn's rules—"I do not feel that this is a defeat."[1]

But for a single juror, we might have ceased to exist, and all the harm we caused afterward might have been avoided. At the start of deliberation, the jury was poised to deliver a $20-30 million *coup de grâce*, with eleven out of twelve jurors ready to end us. But jury foreman Carole Snow, a USC sociology professor, convinced her colleagues to deliver a more measured verdict. Without her mercy, Church Universal and Triumphant (CUT) would have become Cult Obscure and Defeated (COD).

Though the lesser penalty spared us from ruin, it was still one of the most consequential events in our history. Perhaps thousands of people were damaged by their association with my cult, but Mull and his attorney Lawrence Levy were the first to hold us accountable. Their success lay in exposing the manipulations that flowed from our doctrine. Given the complex history of the case which spanned a decade, and dueling religious and secular frameworks at trial, perhaps there was never any simple justice to be found.

The outcome hinged on how the jury viewed our practices, which depended on testimony about our beliefs. Judge Alfred L. Margolis set the tone, "We are not going to litigate the validity of the beliefs of the church…

inescapably we are going to be talking to some extent about the content of the church's religious beliefs, practices, and teachings because that information is going to come into evidence and be relevant as it concerns Mr. Mull." The parameters of the trial were conflicted from the outset, creating an almost Kafkaesque courtroom dynamic: Our beliefs and practices *would be* examined, which led to frequent First-Amendment objections from our attorney Ken Klein, and tense bench conferences.

Church Universal and Triumphant defense attorney Ken Klein speaks at a post-trial video presentation at Camelot, Malibu, CA, April 2, 1986

I attended several days of the trial, which ran from February to April, 1986. But my understanding of the proceedings was limited. Few outside the courtroom were aware of its scope. It became a larger reckoning for our practice of using spiritual inducements and threats to secure volunteer labor. At some point, it dawned on us that we might lose. The fear among members was palpable. A large damage award could bankrupt us. After our loss, we still hailed Klein as a conquering hero for avoiding a death sentence. But the Mull trial remains a crucial case study of the complex legal, rhetorical, and theological smokescreens cults use to obscure their depredations, while claiming religious persecution.

The transcript runs 2,897 pages.[2] Reading it was revelatory. It includes key exhibits like Mull's personal letters to my mother and members of our board. Testimony reveals a pattern of duplicity and hypocrisy, and our full awareness of the consensual abuse our members endured. Some of my mother's testimony was plainly perjury.

The core of the lawsuit was a dispute over an informal contract: Mull logged 15 months of architectural design work for us from 1979 to 1980. Was it a donation of his time, or was he entitled to compensation? Promissory notes he signed for $37,000 added ambiguity. Were they valid loans or should they be treated as independent-contractor payments? There's a history of legal battles over such verbal agreements.[3] For example, in *Tex-*

aco Inc. v. Pennzoil Co. (1987), a handshake deal between Pennzoil and Getty Oil led to a $10.5 billion judgment against Texaco. In *Weiner v. McGraw-Hill, Inc.* (1979), an employee successfully enforced verbal job security assurances.

How did Gregory Mull, an architect with a comfortable home in San Francisco in 1975, end up a broken, unemployed man just five years later? Mull's descent into this mental and emotional quagmire was a slow erosion of self. A man who once steered his own course grappled with the abstract promise of salvation—a goal he couldn't measure but felt compelled to chase. The trial testimony and exhibits establish the symbiotic relationship between Gregory Mull's pre-existing spiritual beliefs and our carefully-curated dogma, which developed like a psychic spider web and trapped him completely. I'll return to Mull's story throughout this book, which will help further clarify the nature of cults.

San Francisco Architect Gregory Mull.
Illustration based on undated photo c. 1970s

But let's take a fresh approach. In 1964, US Supreme Court Justice Potter Stewart wrote, "I know it when I see it" to define hard-core pornography in his concurrence with the 6-3 majority in *Jacobellis v. Ohio*. The ruling nullified a $2,500 obscenity fine imposed for showing the French film *The Lovers,* affirming its protection under the First Amendment. Stewart's statement acknowledged the difficulty of defining obscenity, and defining cults can be harder still. Will you—to paraphrase Potter Stewart—know a cult when you see one? Your perception can depend on whether you agree with the group's goals and philosophies. And this provides a clue to expanding our working definition beyond stereotype.

A cult is not just a small group of religious wackos, holed up in a compound, in thrall to an abusive leader. That's one type of cult that's overrepresented on Netflix. Cults are a perverted tribe—hijacking the fundamental unit of human social organization toward an antisocial purpose. The word "cult" describes how humans without sufficient knowledge and coping skills adapt to abusive systems and grow to defend them, even at the cost of their lives.

Most of us inhabit overlapping identities without any of them becoming all-consuming. You might be a wife, a mother, a race-car driver, a Catholic, a Taylor Swift fan, a resident of Colorado, an American, an immigrant, and a Spanish speaker, all at the same time. Identity is a complex Venn diagram.

Humans evolved in villages of 150 people. When we isolated into the nuclear family, we lost our tie to community life. In 1992, Stephanie Coontz published *The Way We Never Were*,[4] debunking myths about this recent structure. It's a big piece of the cult puzzle. Most people crave ties to a more diverse group of people than live in a single household. And a Third Place other than home or work, such as a cafe, pub, park, library, or community center. Those who want communities of interest tend to seek out church and cult-like organizations, along with hobby and civic groups.

Cults form when one facet of identity becomes all-consuming. When that identity becomes a central organizing principle whose premises move beyond question. A cult doesn't require a leader. It doesn't need a brick-and-mortar location. It doesn't need a large group. Abusive relationships can be a cult of two. Corporations, multi-level marketing programs and ideologies can be cults.

The first stage of a typical cult is a small, insular organization, with a strange doctrine, strict rules, and a charismatic living founder. That describes my cult. Most cults die with their founders. Some survive a leadership transition. New leaders can broaden the appeal and expand their membership. Cults can splinter after the founder's death, as opportunists form offshoots and poach members. This skirts the most difficult period: Gaining the first few followers who form the inner circle. It also helps to rip off the original cult's dogma—which members already believe—because it's complicated to invent a new religion or cult and get people to accept it.

My father Mark Prophet followed this path when he founded The Summit Lighthouse. It was an offshoot of Theosophy,[5] Agni Yoga, the Mighty I AM, and the Bridge to Freedom, with a dash of Rosicrucianism thrown in.[6] In turn, former Summit Lighthouse staff members Monroe Shearer and David Lewis founded The Temple of the Presence cult and The Heart's Center cult, respectively. Monroe Shearer was vice-president of The Summit Lighthouse and "Archbishop of the New Jerusalem."[7] David Lewis worked in middle management. Both of them claim to be "messengers" of the Ascended Masters. Likewise, my parents followed in the footsteps of Guy and Edna Ballard, the leaders of the Mighty I AM cult. Christianity itself follows this pattern, with 200 major Protestant denominations and about 40,000 total sects.

To state the obvious, the major religions exhibit some characteristics of cults. And they've racked up plenty of abuses. But the larger the religion, the more it tends to be institutionally accountable and less totalistic.[8] Non-observant cultural Christians, Jews, Hindus, and Muslims lead secular lives. "Jack Mormons" identify as members of the Church of Jesus Christ of Latter-day Saints (LDS) but don't follow its beliefs or practices. Smaller and newer cults enforce higher commitment, demand tighter adherence to rules, and pose greater danger.

Differentiating a cult from a religion is a matter of semantics and point of view. Some Christians consider Mormonism to be a cult. But the LDS church isn't new, and it doesn't have a charismatic leader. It's large and wealthy, placing it closer to a religion. Presidents are still considered to be prophets, seers, and revelators. But they're constrained by accountability and succession. Churches like the Society of Friends (Quakers), Seventh-day Adventists, and Jehovah's Witnesses began as cults and gained mainstream acceptance.

What draws someone into a cult, and who is most susceptible? Anyone of any age can fall. *Important caveat:* Cult indoctrination is not transitive. It's *interactive*. It demands willing participation. In this it resembles a con. Seekers may be looking for meaning in a world full of chaos and randomness, undergoing life transitions, leaving home, graduating from college, enduring divorce, death of a spouse, unemployment, health crises, or just wanting group acceptance. Some are burdened by world suffering—seeking shortcuts that promise near-term spiritual world-transformation.

These are all healthy human pursuits. To avoid the pitfalls of destructive cult dynamics, these drives must be paired with a solid understanding of human psychology and the mechanics of power. Anyone who lacks coping skills to manage their emotions in alignment with their values is ripe for manipulation. If a cult leader understands power and history—and knows you better than you know yourself—you're in danger.

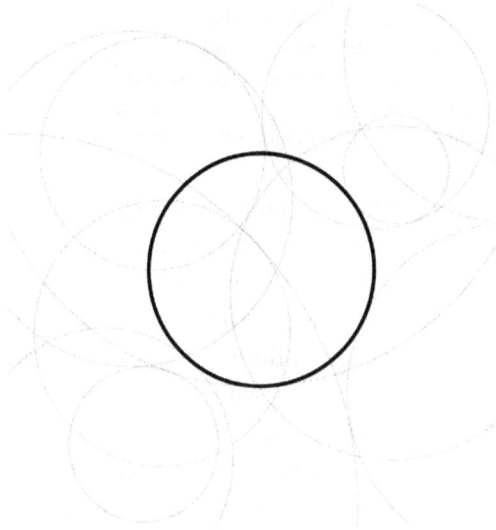

When someone joins a cult and becomes over-identified with one facet of their identity, the Venn diagram shrinks to a circle. Other identities and relationships fall away. This can harm the cult member, and damage the social fabric.

The tension between harm and freedom is key. With pornography, harm is in the eye of the beholder. Some people find nothing wrong with it, while others are convinced that even the mildest erotica undermines family and society, and they would gladly suppress First-Amendment rights for artists and pornographers alike. This highlights the difficulty of policing free expression.

If we're willing to run roughshod over the First Amendment, we could end destructive cults. Their beliefs and practices could be vetted by a body of psychologists, sociologists, and historians for their social impact. Any group deemed exploitative could be shut down, as they are in China, which lacks freedom of religion. The government recognizes only Buddhism, Taoism, Islam, Catholicism, and Protestantism.

I oppose such oppression. Meddling in religious practice deprives citizens of freedom of conscience. Religious beliefs don't need to make sense to outsiders. Mainstream religions hold core tenets preposterous to non-believers. Imagine putting Catholicism on trial for its doctrine of the virgin birth or metaphorical cannibalism—consuming the body and blood of Christ? Or persecuting Muslims for teaching that pork and alcohol are *haram*—or requiring cruel *halal* slaughter? Religious beliefs concern the metaphorical and the supernatural. By definition this makes them counterfactual. So they will always be controversial and potentially antisocial.

In her book *Cults in America*[9], anthropologist Willa Appel describes the difficulty:

> By their very nature cults alienate ordinary citizens, for they defy the existing social order. Seeing themselves as separate from the rest of the world, with a separate ideology and a different lifestyle, cult members stand in opposition to society, denying, in greater or lesser degree, its legitimacy. Believing themselves to be different from and superior to the rest of the world, cult members tend to ignore the rules that govern less exalted citizens. At odds with society in the first place, this antagonism can easily lead to confrontation.

Yet freedom of religion deserves strong protection. Policing religion is tantamount to policing thought. Some will always hold beliefs others find *insane* or that conflict with secular laws. The First Amendment's establishment clause conflicts with its free-exercise clause. Government is not supposed to either promote or burden any religion. But in practice, it always does. Courts frequently adjudicate these conflicts, which include government funding for religious schools, adoption guidelines, and religious exemptions to anti-discrimination and employment law. Some rulings threaten public health, like religious vaccine exemptions, and conscience clauses for doctors and pharmacists. There are also tax implications. In my cult for a time, we used the ministerial exemption to opt out of Social Security and Medicare payroll taxes.

Nearly a century of legal precedent enables cults and religions to skirt laws that apply to everyone else. In its landmark 1944 decision in *United States v. Ballard*, the Supreme Court ruled that the *sincerity* of religious belief grants First-Amendment protection.[10] Edna and Donald Ballard, leaders of the Mighty I AM cult, were convicted of fraud by a lower court for soliciting $3 million based on faith-healing claims. That's $52 million in 2024 dollars. The Supreme Court ruled that the Ballards sincerely believed in their healing powers and vacated their conviction. Recent cases, such as *Hobby Lobby Stores, Inc. v. Sebelius* and *Burwell v. Hobby Lobby Stores, Inc.*, have cited *Ballard* to gain exemptions to contraception and abortion insurance mandates on religious grounds.[11] The ruling remains a cornerstone governing the balance between state interests and religious freedom.

The 1997 mass suicide of 39 members of Marshall Applewhite's Heaven's Gate cult demonstrates the weakness of the US legal system.[12] Before Applewhite and his devotees donned their all-black clothing and black-and-white Nikes, before they ate their applesauce laced with an overdose of phenobarbital, before they drank vodka and put plastic bags over their heads—they had done nothing illegal. The recipe for their deadly cocktail came from a euthanasia website. There's nothing to prevent such a tragedy from recurring. Applewhite published videos encouraging members to "leave their physical bodies" to catch a ride on the Hale-Bopp comet. It was clear incitement to suicide. Under *Ballard,* such deadly teachings are protected.

The legal system is powerless to stop even the most extreme cults until they violate a secular law. That's dangerous. Paraphrasing Voltaire, absurd beliefs make people commit atrocities. *Important caveat:* Despite their strange beliefs, the vast majority of cults are non-violent. There's a key reason. Cults in stable, open societies are subject to external checks and balances and the rule of law. Which usually denies them power to commit large-scale atrocities.

In my cult, the worst that happened was that a few people died from refusing medical treatment. One woman died in a single-car accident driving from California to Montana. One man was shot by a sheriff, after he brandished a gun and ceremonial sword in front of his home. These deaths could have happened to anyone. The cult dangers I'm discussing in this book don't usually involve deadly violence. Cults are more insidious, committing subtle or unsubtle physical, sexual and psychological abuses, which in some cases cross over into criminal behavior. But only when cults reach the most advanced stages do people usually start dying. Here are a few more violent examples:

> **Jonestown Massacre (1978):** Led by Jim Jones, more than 900 members of the Peoples Temple died in a murder-suicide in Jonestown, Guyana. Some drank their cyanide-laced punch voluntarily, others were forced to drink at gunpoint, and some who tried to escape died from gunshot wounds.
>
> **The Cross and the Switchblade Church (1987):** In Philadelphia, an extremist religious group led by a woman known as "Mother Divine" committed mass suicide, resulting in the deaths of five children and one adult.
>
> **Branch Davidians (1993):** In Waco, Texas, more than 80 members of the Branch Davidian sect, including leader David Koresh, died in a fire following a 51-day standoff with federal agents.
>
> **Aum Shinrikyo (1995):** This Japanese doomsday cult carried out a deadly Tokyo subway sarin gas attack, killing 13 and injuring thousands.

The Order of the Solar Temple (1994-1997): A series of mass suicides, murders, and arsons in Switzerland, France, and Canada resulted in 77 deaths.

Movement for the Restoration of the Ten Commandments of God (2000): Approximately 778 followers of a Ugandan cult were murdered in a series of arson fires and poisonings. Some victims were trapped inside burning churches by leaders who nailed the doors shut. Others were found poisoned and dumped in mass graves.

Good News International Ministries, aka Shakahola cult (2023): 429 people died of mass starvation, suffocation, strangulation, and blunt force trauma, and 613 were missing, after Kenyan cult leader Paul Mackenzie instructed followers to go without food to "meet Jesus" and killed and buried some members alive in shallow graves.[13]

Like Heaven's Gate and others, cults can be inscrutable to outsiders. And that's why they have free rein. But they're not so obvious to insiders either, who might not recognize they're in a cult until something goes wrong. My cult spent a lot of time and money "proving" it was a legitimate religion. This included paying for a study called *Church Universal and Triumphant in Scholarly Perspective,* by James R. Lewis and Gordon J. Melton.[14]

It's best to be wary of *all* unaccountable structures run by authorities who set rules that can't be questioned. This covers a broad swath of humanity: Dictatorships, religions, privately-held corporations, drug cartels and organized crime syndicates, multi-level-marketing companies, pyramid schemes, militaries, terror cells, street gangs, motorcycle clubs, prison gangs, patriarchal families, and abusive relationships. All such groups have committed defenders. It's important to note that any group can become more or less cult-like over time.

There's also a blurry line between dangerous cults and communities of interest. We're a tribal species. Cosplayers, DIYers, fan clubs, classic car clubs, vintage collectors, foodies, and role-playing-gamers, to name just a few groups, can be cult-*ish*. So we're all probably in a cult to some degree, and most of them lack the power to cause significant harm. But they're only safe as long as they practice openness, low levels of commitment, and are held accountable. Whenever in-group commitment becomes an all-consuming identity, and external accountability declines, watch out.

It's a big challenge. We can't ban cults while maintaining freedom of conscience. So our goal must be containment. The first step is individual: strengthening our defenses by understanding cult tactics. The second step is societal: raising public awareness and defending the separation of church and state. The third step is diagnostic and requires cultivating self-honesty: developing the ability to recognize when we ourselves are caught in a dangerous cult. Each of these steps requires classification. Pay attention to a cult's size, level of commitment, and the virulence of its dogma. In particular, focus on cults that are too small to be on anyone's radar or so large they've been normalized. In other words, *non-obvious* dangerous cults.

Cults target those who lack psychological insight or struggle to manage their emotions in alignment with their values. Exploiting these vulnerabilities, they build strong followings by leveraging evolutionary traits that ensured our survival in villages. These traits serve us well in secure, open environments but backfire when we fail to distinguish healthy social norms from manipulative cultic structures.

---

[1] Roy Cohn, a controversial American lawyer and political fixer who rose to prominence as counsel to Senator Joseph McCarthy and later became an influential mentor to Donald Trump, is often associated with the rules "never apologize, never admit you're wrong, and never let anyone see you sweat." However, as illustrated in the film *The Apprentice* (2024), some accounts replace the final rule with, "no matter what happens, you claim victory and never admit defeat." This variant functions as a strategy to avoid taking responsibility or engaging in introspection by reframing setbacks—such as a lost lawsuit or criminal conviction—not as personal failures but as evidence of a corrupt process, reflecting a sense of royal superiority over laws and norms.

[2] Court transcript documenting Gregory Mull's legal proceedings against Church Universal and Triumphant. https://www.eprophet.info/gregory-mull-suit

[3] Key precedents for informal agreement enforcement include: Texaco Inc. v. Pennzoil Co. (1987) ($10.5B judgment for handshake deal interference); Weiner v. McGraw-Hill (1979) (verbal employment promises binding); Chern v. Bank of America (1976) (informal loan commitments enforceable); Vallone v. Vallone (1982) (community property rights without formal agreement). Sources: Justia U.S. Supreme Court Center (https://supreme.justia.com/cases/federal/us/481/1/), Oyez (https://www.oyez.org/cases/1986/85-1798), Casebriefs (https://www.casebriefs.com), Casetext (https://casetext.com/case/vallone-v-vallone), Quimbee (https://www.quimbee.com)

[4] Critical analysis of American family mythology and social memory. Coontz, S. (1992). *The way we never were: American families and the nostalgia trap*. Basic Books.

[5] Theosophy, founded by H.P. Blavatsky (1875), synthesizes religious unity, spiritual evolution, and esoteric knowledge. Core tenets include divine wisdom pursuit, universal brotherhood, and guided spiritual evolution, influencing modern New Age movements.

[6] Rosicrucian philosophy (17th century) integrates mysticism, alchemy, and Kabbalistic thought, emphasizing spiritual transformation through secret knowledge, ancient wisdom, and natural law alignment.

[7] CUT v. Mull, Superior Court of Los Angeles County C. 358191, (March 11, 1986) at 1983:1-6

[8] Totalism describes systems demanding complete ideological conformity through centralized authority, dissent suppression, and control mechanisms, characteristic of both political regimes and religious groups where individual autonomy yields to collective doctrine.

[9] Comprehensive analysis of American cult phenomena and recruitment patterns. Appel, W. (1983). *Cults in America: Programmed for Paradise*. Columbia University Press.

[10] United States v. Ballard, 322 U.S. 78 (1944).

[11] *Hobby Lobby Stores, Inc. v. Sebelius*, 723 F.3d 1114 (10th Cir. 2013), aff'd sub nom. *Burwell v. Hobby Lobby Stores, Inc.*, 573 U.S. 682 (2014).

[12] Vick, K., & Sawyer, K. (1997, March 28). 39 in cult suicide tied to Hale-Bopp. The Washington Post. Retrieved from https://www.washingtonpost.com

[13] Documentation of the 2023 mass casualty event in Kenya linked to a religious cult. https://en.wikipedia.org/wiki/Shakahola_Forest_incident

[14] Authoritative study of Church Universal and Triumphant's history and practices. Lewis, J.R., & Melton, G.J. (1994). *Church Universal and Triumphant*. Shewmaker LLC.

■■■■■■■ CHAPTER THREE ■■■■■■■

Fascism and Thought Reform

No one goes from zero to zombie in an instant. Cult recruitment begins with an attractive premise. But as thirsty seekers commit themselves, the leader demands increasing totalistic devotion in exchange for enlightenment. Willa Appel describes "the attempt to control the total environment of individual followers" through regimented activities like "prayer, chanting, meditation, group rituals, psychodrama and confession." Members come to believe they are flawed through "sin" or "engrams" or "discarnate entities" and can be "cleared" or "redeemed" through the cult's practices.

Most people believe they can spot a dangerous cult. They imagine compound walls, strange robes and rituals, and militant rhetoric. But cults that threaten your freedom can present themselves as something benign like yoga classes, wellness groups, martial arts, life coaching, success seminars, or new-age "love" and "transformation" projects. They don't require physical compounds—they'll reach you online. They come in all varieties, including spiritual channelers, identitarian groups, offshoots of traditional religions, and anti-democratic political movements like MAGA.

There are striking parallels between cults—especially the MAGA cult—and the fascist regimes that dominated Germany, Spain, and Italy in the first half of the 20th century. Fascism is a formula for seizing power—a transitional pathway to totalitarianism. It thrives on emotional narratives and archetypes, adopting and discarding ideologies. Italian intellectual Umberto Eco defined "Ur-Fascism" in a 1995 essay in the *New York Review of Books*.[1] He describes it as "Eternal Fascism," a framework which transcends historical contexts. These traits encompass fascist regimes and many cults, including my own.

1. *A cult of tradition and syncretism.* Reverence for ancient symbolism like hieroglyphs and runes. *Syncretism* combines disparate forms of belief or practice. If a message or scripture appears to contradict another, "all are alluding, allegorically, to the same primeval truth." In my cult jargon, "many paths lead to the summit." Eco cites the mashup of the Holy Grail legend with *The Protocols of the Elders of Zion*,[2] a classic anti-Semitic screed. And the New Age melding of Saint Augustine with Stonehenge. My cult hawked the "International Capitalist-Communist Conspiracy," which claims in part that biblical "Nephilim" came from an ancient alien breeding program.[3] The less coherent the juxtaposition, the more it represents Ur-Fascism.

2. *Rejection of modernism.* While fascists leverage technology, they subordinate modernity to mystical notions like "blood and soil." Ur-Fascism views The Enlightenment as "the beginning of modern depravity." My cult uses modern tools, and my mother embraced the scientific method when it suited her. But she was suspicious of technology, especially nuclear energy and genetic engineering. Our self-classification as "light-bearers" opposed to "dark forces" and "the power elites" was our version of "blood and soil." We viewed ourselves as the "salt of the Earth," the divinely-sponsored authority on the planet, while rejecting the "false hierarchy" of the "Nephilim" establishment.

3. *Distrust of intellectuals.* Eco cites Nazi Hermann Goering's disdain for academia and culture, "When I hear talk of culture, I reach for my gun." It's a metaphor for the authority of the cult leader, who sets the agenda and defines "acceptable" thought. Anti-intellectualism suffuses the MAGA cult, which savages universities for "wokeness" and "communism." My college-educated mother railed against the "intelligentsia" and said my father's failure to finish high school left him more receptive to God.

4. *No syncretistic faith can withstand analytical criticism.* "The critical spirit makes distinctions, and to distinguish is a sign of modernism. In modern culture the scientific community praises disagreement as a way to improve knowledge. For Ur-Fascism, disagreement is treason," Eco wrote. In my cult, we condemned the "carnal mind," meaning the brain and its reasoning abilities. My mother encouraged reliance on the "inner self," and the "mind of God."

5. *Fear of difference.* Differences are threats to unity. Nationalistic fascism employs racism and ideological absolutism, stoking fear of immigrants and disdain for lower classes. We feared outsiders, "dark" influences, or "discarnate entities" which might lead to questioning the spiritual path.[4] Appeals to reject the world and improve in-group conformity formed the bulk of our teachings.

6. *Individual or social frustration about the status quo.* Historical fascism appealed to a frustrated middle class which suffered economic strain or political humiliation. Cult members sequester themselves from society through a crisis of meaning or exhaustion from intractable conditions. Economic turmoil in post-World War I Germany created fertile ground for charismatic Nazi fascism, just as disillusionment with the establishment led to the 1960s counterculture movement in the United States and a new wave of cults. Twenty-first century populism repeats this history.

7. *Obsession with a plot.* Fascism uses scapegoating which leads to paranoia of internal and external enemies. This tears at the social fabric and softens up the political establishment for the strongman. Such demagogues promote conspiracy theories, such as "globalism," the "New World Order," "international bankers," "stolen elections," or racial "replacement." My cult embraced many of the same theories. We fixated on conspiratorial "plots of the sinister force"—fearing spiritual and physical enemies—and dangers lurking in our hearts and minds. We believed our only refuge was in God and, by extension, God's anointed messengers: my parents.

8. *Enemies are simultaneously too strong and too weak.* Eco wrote, "The followers must feel humiliated by the ostentatious wealth and force of their enemies… however the followers must be convinced that they can overwhelm the enemies." This aligns with my cult. We used the Christian Science affirmation, "Evil is not real and its appearance has no power." If true, why did "power elites" remain in control? Our struggle against "dark forces" fostered unspoken grievance. Though members rarely discussed their doubts, the question remained: Why were our prayers ineffective?

9. *Life is to be lived for struggle.* This affirms our millenarian outlook. Eco's "Armageddon complex" where a "final battle" leads to a "final solution" promising an era of peace in a "Golden Age." It's similar to the apocalypse in Revelation, which resolves to the Holy City. This is how we justified our shelter-building efforts. After nuclear war, we expected a cleansed world—which would have negated our purpose—a Golden Age removes the need for the fascist struggle.

10. *Popular elitism.* "Ur-Fascism can only advocate a popular elitism," Eco wrote. "Every citizen belongs to the best people of the world, the members of the party are the best among the citizens, every citizen can (or ought to) become a member of the party. But there cannot be patricians without plebeians." Likewise, "light bearers" must contrast with "fallen ones." Eco noted, "the Leader, knowing that his power was not delegated to him democratically but was conquered by force, also knows that his force is based upon the weakness of the masses; they are so weak as to need and deserve a ruler." My cult was obsessed with submission to divine authority.

11. *Heroism.* Our avenues for heroism included saving the world, judging fallen ones, and making our "ascension"—our final reunion with God—through self-sacrifice. Members overvalued heroic spiritual pursuits, devaluing earthly existence. In nationalistic and Ur-Fascism, heroism is linked with laying down one's life for the nation—which is certainly a matter of degree. Cults and fascism tend to valorize self-sacrifice, which normalizes imposing sacrifices on others.

12. *Machismo.* "Since both permanent war and heroism are difficult games to play," Eco wrote, "the Ur-Fascist transfers his will to power to sexual matters." Machismo implies disdain for women and intolerance of non-procreative sexual habits. Female leaders often enforce such norms. Though my mother's persona was dominant, she stood in the shadow of El Morya, an Ascended Master who became her male alter-ego and macho patriarch. Ur-Fascists tend to be obsessed with weaponry due to its phallic symbolism. True to form, during our two survivalist phases in 1973 and 1989, my cult was bristling with firearms.

13. *Selective populism.* Under Ur-Fascism, individuals have no rights. Eco observes that "no large quantity of human beings can have a common will." The leader pretends to interpret the will of the people, substituting their own dictates. This maps onto my cult's fascination with the "will of God," a rejection of popular democracy and secular governance. It concedes to rule by a virtual, invisible king—meaning his earthly representative.

14. *Newspeak.* George Orwell's 1949 novel *1984* established the totalitarian use of deceptive language.[5] Eco notes that textbooks under classical fascism "made use of an impoverished vocabulary, and an elementary syntax, in order to limit the instruments for complex and critical reasoning." My cult brimmed with jargon designed to reinforce in-group norms and shut down critical thought. I'll cite examples later.

Eco concludes with a warning:

> Ur-Fascism is still around us, sometimes in plainclothes. It would be so much easier, for us, if there appeared on the world scene somebody saying, "I want to reopen Auschwitz, I want the Black Shirts to parade again in the Italian squares." Life is not that simple. Ur-Fascism can come back under the most innocent of disguises. Our duty is to uncover it and to point our finger at any of its new instances—every day, in every part of the world.

The most dangerous disguise is divinity. Despite any religious pretext, the ultimate expression of cult power comes when leaders identify as gods. "Love Has Won" leader Amy Carlson called herself "Mother God." There's also Yahweh ben Yahweh, Father Divine, Shri Mataji Nirmala Devi, Sathya Sai Baba, Sun Myung Moon, David Koresh, Marshall Applewhite, Jim Jones, Shoko Asahara, and many others who claimed to be the "Messiah" or "God," or to have been anointed by God. My parents claimed to be the "Two Witnesses" from the book of Revelation. My mother called herself "Guru Ma," "Mother of the Flame," and "Vicar of Christ." Any claim to divine identity shuts down "human" dissent. One word sums up this gambit:

Authoritarianism.

No one forces people to believe or join. But those who voluntarily embrace thought reform are still radically changed by the experience. To understand how cults systematically transform followers, it's useful to look through an unfamiliar yet powerful lens: the *algorithm*.

In computer science, an algorithm solves problems or manages information: taking inputs, processing them through rules, and producing outputs. Over the past quarter century, rapid advances in computing power enabled more complex algorithms. They now approve loans, select military targets, and manage factory production—without human supervision. Algorithms shape what we read and see, influencing elections and forming a global shadow-government.

Consider the credit-scoring algorithm. The inputs are payment history, debt levels, and credit applications. The rules assess risk. The output is a single number determining who gets loans and at what rates. But this "neutral" process has profound social impacts. It can perpetuate inequities, trap people in debt, or grant life-changing opportunities. Its power lies in how the rules are written and what the system values.

The process is straightforward: supply data, apply rules, get results. But algorithms amplify and transform information. In his 2024 book *Nexus*, historian Yuval Noah Harari shows how information systems guided society long before computers.[6] He critiques two dominant views: the "naive view," which assumes more information leads to greater truth, and the "populist view," which casts information as a tool of power. Instead, Harari argues that the primary function of information is to tell stories, which hold enormous power to establish order—shaping norms, laws, and institutions. Without built-in corrective mechanisms, the most memorable and resonant ideas will overpower truth.[7] It's why emotional fascist narratives hold such power. When stories claim divine or mythic origins, they become impervious to correction.

History's first mass-information processor proves the point. The Gutenberg Press, invented in 1440, was hailed as a tool for spreading knowledge and literacy. Its first use was mass-producing Bibles. But in 1487, Heinrich Kramer and Jacob Sprenger printed *Malleus Maleficarum*, a manual for hunting witches that led to the death, imprisonment, and torture of tens of thousands across Europe. Though ideologically neutral, the printing press was the first engagement-boosting algorithm—a system for processing and amplifying information—that when abused can have devastating impact.

Modern social-media algorithms are still more dangerous. Like the press, they are content agnostic, promoting engagement. This favors outrage, hatred, and incitement to violence—connecting the limbic systems of millions of people, instead of their pre-frontal cortexes. Meaning that fast, emotional responses overwhelm slower rational thought. The results can be catastrophic, as seen in the 2017 Rohingya genocide in Myanmar[8] and the 2018 election of Jair Bolsonaro in Brazil.[9]

Cults are information processors of a different sort, taking in recruits, applying dogma, and producing transformed followers. Today they're embracing digital tools, but their core algorithm remains: *beliefs* that shape perceptions, *outcomes* that transform lives, *methods* that modify behavior, and *purposes* that concentrate power. For simplicity, let's call this the cult's BOMP. Each component corresponds to a part of its algorithm.

Beliefs are the algorithm's input parameters—attractive to new recruits. These aren't just curated public teachings. They include whispered folklore: past-life memories, dream visitations, miracle healings, psychic powers, levitation, bilocation, or masters appearing in physical form. They include rules—and whether members obey or buck against them. Where is the line between compliance, fear, and punishment?

Outcomes are the algorithm's result, which matter much more than intentions. A cult might earnestly try to "save the world," while destroying the mental health of its followers. Or produce wealthy, high-functioning members harboring psychological wounds. Some create codependents who can barely function outside the cult. These outcomes aren't accidents—they're baked into the algorithm.

Methods are the algorithm's processing rules, extending beyond recruitment tactics. They include schedules, organizational structure, norms, disciplinary procedures, publishing strategy, the design of liturgy and worship services, marketing, wages, housing practices and member diets. Does the cult operate like a corporation, with professional staff? Or is it a commune or ashram? Are members' needs properly met, or are they treated as disposable labor?

Purpose is the system objective, revealed through money flows and power structures—not theology or mission statements. Does the cult primarily support the leader's lifestyle? Is it building real estate empires? Supporting political movements? A "charitable" cult might function as a tax shelter or amplify extremist ideology. My cult's stated purpose is world transformation and the ascension, but we were embroiled in survivalism and right-wing politics.

The BOMP framework exposes how seemingly different cults run variations of the same algorithm. Their authoritarian structure guarantees they don't exist to serve the well-being of members. A self-help seminar might funnel into a pyramid scheme. A wellness influencer might sell fraudulent health products. An innocent-looking meditation group could support a foreign dictatorship. Consider two modern examples: The Chinese Falun Gong cult runs numerous US front groups including Shen Yun Performing Arts,[10] and publishes the extreme-right *Epoch Times*.[11] The Unification Church ("Moonies"), once tightly connected to South Korean dictator Park Chung-hee, publishes the right-wing *Washington Times*[12] and controls the US sushi market through True World Foods.[13] Both cults are intertwined with MAGA.

Let's examine my cult's membership structure to see how algorithmic processing works in practice. The Venn diagram shows levels of commitment. Some members read our publications from a distance. Others attended occasional conferences. Lower levels of membership did not follow strict rules imposed for staff and communicants of the church. Not everyone fully accepted cult dogma, and there was a wide diversity of opinion regarding acceptable lifestyle. However, disciplines imposed on staff and communicants were held up as the highest ideal of *chelaship*,[14] a Theosophical concept of submission, testing and training to which our members aspired.

Varying levels of commitment are built into every cult's algorithm, accommodating casual followers and the fully committed, applying different rules, expectations, and levels of influence. This tiered system is part of algorithmic processing—gradually increasing demands while maintaining flexibility to capture the maximum followers.

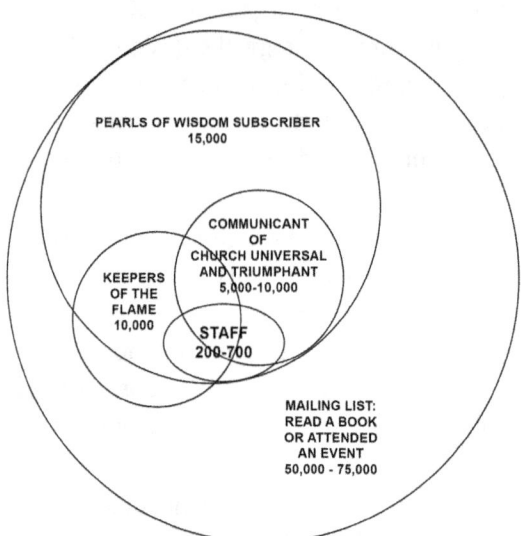

Democratic societies have structures in place to correct falsehoods and hold power to account. But religious freedom acts to sever cult algorithms from self-correcting mechanisms. This grants cult leaders impunity, so long as their actions can be justified under the *Ballard* test of "sincerely-held" belief. Framed as protected religious conduct under the First Amendment, the cult's BOMP becomes a black box, shielded from scrutiny.

The cult algorithm consolidates power in tyrannical leaders just as surely as it enforces submission among willing followers. Religious freedom is content agnostic, but rewards organizational success. So algorithms are tailored to the most vulnerable seekers, reinforcing extremist views of reality, including salvation, damnation, and deities who demand submission and sacrifice. These patterns are so consistent across cults and religions—they suggest an underlying psychological mechanism: thought reform.

The following analysis of my cult is based on the 1961 book *Thought Reform and the Psychology of Totalism* by Robert Jay Lifton.[15] It chronicles Chinese Communist indoctrination techniques. Lifton interviewed 1950s Cold War political detainees who were subject to thought-reform campaigns in Maoist China. He remains controversial to some scholars of cults and religions, because his subjects were held against their will and removed from their normal environment. There are other methodological concerns of varying validity.[16] However, the book offers a powerful exploration of the cult algorithm.

The term "brainwashing" is colloquial and imprecise, but it conveys a recognizable concept. Taken from the Chinese phrase 洗脑 (xǐ nǎo), meaning "to wash the brain," it implies a transitive act with a perpetrator and victim—a radical change in outlook caused by external influences. Lifton disclaims the term in his first chapter. But brainwashing-like effects are widespread, achieved through billions of dollars in advertising, political campaigns, and religious messaging.

Persuasion was the subject of the seminal 1928 advertising classic *Propaganda* by Edward Bernays, which explores methods for manipulating public opinion.[17] He suggests using symbols and media to influence unconscious desires and emotions, modifying behavior without conscious awareness—a classic fascist tactic. But he confirms that "brainwashing" must harness the target's brain to achieve the ends of the manipulator. Bernays focused on the emerging mass media of the early 20th century, which—for the first time—could reach millions.

I focus on the individual. We need to understand how cult leaders engage conscious and unconscious cooperation of their targets. How is this different from persuasion? Will you recognize thought-reform tactics before you succumb?

To explore these questions, I'll juxtapose Lifton's principles with the methods of my cult. My examples apply generally and specifically to the staff experience, and somewhat less so to communicants and our wider membership. Most citations of Lifton's work are clinical and detached from lived experience. I'll review both principle and practice.

1. Milieu Control

Milieu Control encompasses total control of communication and environment. In my cult, this meant systematically limiting contact between members and outsiders while monitoring communication—banning "negativity," "gossip," or "criticism." Even conversations with the opposite sex were capped at ten minutes. Control extended to members' internal world: we learned to regulate our "internalized communication" by avoiding the "carnal mind" in favor of our "I AM Presence"—another name for God.

Media control was absolute: banning "unapproved" materials while promoting cult literature and teachings. Geographic isolation reinforced this control through our Camelot campus in the Malibu Hills and our Montana Ranch Headquarters—far from population centers. Intensive programming—daily "decree sessions" of high-speed chanting, quarterly conferences, and three-month Summit University programs—kept members fully occupied. We cultivated antagonism toward the outside world. Our decree "The Flame of Freedom Speaks" drew on biblical sources: "come apart now, and be a separate and chosen people, elect unto God."[18]

2. Mystical Manipulation

Mystical Manipulation centers on the "planned spontaneity" of seemingly supernatural experiences. My parents served the *mystical imperative* as anointed messengers destined to save the world through the "Violet Flame" and prayers against apocalyptic threats. We identified as the "Great White Brotherhood" (referring to spiritual light, not race), representing the "mystical body of God on Earth." Members adapted to the "psychology of the pawn," policing each other and reporting doubts to authorities.

Experiences from *déjà vu*, to past life memories, to "angel" and "UFO" clouds, to sleep paralysis were all framed as spiritual validation. These appeared spontaneous but members were primed to expect them—coincidences became "signs," dreams became "visions," normal emotions became "divine contact." Though members knew my parents were human, as channels for Ascended Masters they became, in Lifton's terms, "more identified as God than any abstract notion of God."

3. Demand for Purity

The Demand for Purity sharply divides existence into pure (the cult) versus impure (outside world). Group actions become automatically "pure," while outsider behaviors are "contaminated." Rather than sin and Hell, we employed karma and reincarnation—break the rules, come back for more lifetimes to pay off your karma, or forfeit your reunion with God through the ascension altogether. Our purity focus justified harsh punishments and imprecatory prayers against enemies—asking God to strike down the "impure." The demand for purity manifested physically through strict diet and health regimes, each purification reinforcing dependency on the group as the sole source of cleansing.

4. The Cult of Confession

The Cult of Confession extends far beyond ordinary religious or therapeutic practice. While Catholic confession is private, cults can demand written confessions, auditing sessions, and group confrontations, as seen in Scientology and the Unification Church. The infamous Synanon Game exemplified how forced intimacy and mutual criticism create trauma bonds. Mutual criticism means "the more I accuse myself, the more right I have to judge you." Our Summit University applications required confessing personal, criminal, and sexual history—records that could be weaponized in counseling. The process never ends: selective confession creates escalating guilt. Public sharing transforms members into mutual monitors. Even without real change, confession offers symbolic cleansing, like being "washed in the blood of Christ."

5. Sacred Science

Sacred Science merges an ultimate moral vision with claims of absolute truth. Our *Science of the Spoken Word* established biblical authority through two verses.[19] Isaiah 45:11 states: "Ask me of things to come concerning my sons, and concerning the work of my hands, *command ye me.*" Job 22:28 affirms: "Thou shalt also decree a thing, and it shall be established unto thee." Since God gave humans free will, we were required to request divine intervention, making members personally responsible for saving or failing to save the world. Ex-member Talita Paolini describes her psychological state after three months of Summit University:

> More sinister was the change in my world view. Every morning I spent hours decreeing on a variety of world problems that were my responsibility, as a 'lightbearer,' to address. I saw the world through CUT's perspective. Every action around me was interpreted in terms of cosmic battle, Dark against Light. If my car didn't start, it was the result of psychic rays from evil forces. A rainbow was a blessing from the gods.[20]

Questioning this "sacred science" marked you as an apostate: Ask why prayers aren't working? Heretic. Wonder why decades of Violet Flame haven't saved the world? Doubter. The doctrine claims both moral purity and scientific accuracy. Any contradictions merely prove human limitation. Sacred science demands reverence for both the present bearers of the doctrine and the originators of the doctrine. For us this lineage ran from Theosophy's Blavatsky through the Roerichs who founded Agni Yoga, to the Ballards, messengers for the Mighty I AM cult, to my parents. This focus downgrades real-world knowledge, offering security through simplification—a "higher truth" with no rigorous study. Merging sanctity with "science" puts doctrine beyond questioning.

6. Loading the Language

Loading the Language employs what Lifton calls "the language of non-thought." Thought-terminating clichés shut down discussion: "It's all good," "not this again," "everything happens for a reason." Questions are deflected to "God's plan," or "the divine plan." These pervasive clichés confirm that we're all at least a bit cult-*ish*. More significantly, my cult assigned new, arbitrary meanings to words and coined its own clichés ungrounded in external linguistic reality:

- *"It is better to be harmonious than right."* Go along to get along. Don't argue, don't let your ethics interfere with cult agendas.
- *"Will of God."* The will of the cult leader.
- *"The Carnal Mind."* A pejorative term for rational thought.
- *"Order is Heaven's First Law."* A defense of hierarchy and discipline.
- *"Blue Ray."* A dressing-down or humiliation.
- *"Out of Alignment."* Being in mental rebellion or disobedience to cult doctrine.
- *"Animal Magnetism."* A catch-all term for mistakes, implying they're evidence of being "out of alignment."[21]
- *"Family mesmerism."* Suggests that family members or ancestors hinder spiritual progress.
- *"The call compels the answer."* Implies prayers are always answered, but if not, the person didn't pray hard enough.
- *"The Dweller on the Threshold."* The "dark" evolved animal nature or generalized uncertainty.
- *"There is no injustice in the universe."* Reflecting the just-world fallacy.
- *"Obedience is better than sacrifice."* Regardless of personal sacrifices, obeying cult teachings is paramount.
- *"The Tag."* A 24-hour prayer session, where a person must be relieved by the next person.
- *"Tool of the sinister force."* Someone making a serious blunder likely involving "animal magnetism."
- *"Human creation. Substance. Effluvia."* Unsanctioned "low vibration" or "human" behavior.
- *"The Path."* Following the Teachings of the Ascended Masters through self-sacrifice, purification, obedience, and enlightenment, balancing 51

percent of one's karma, leading to release from the "wheel of rebirth," and reunion with God through the ascension.

- *"Discarnate Entities."* Disembodied spirits who encourage vices, draining spiritual energy. Entities are said to have male and female counterparts—named after the vice.

Dope and Tobacco Entities	
COCAINE ENTITY, "CRACK"	
DELTA 9/CANNABIS SATIVA	marijuana entity
HEROICA	heroin entity
INHALA (f)	smoking entity
MORPHUS (m)	dope entity
NICOLA (f) / NICOLUS (m)	tobacco entities
PCP ENTITY	
Gossip Entities	
CARPIA (f) / HARPIA (f)	gossip entities
"Hallowe'en" Entities	
DRACULA (f) / DRACULUS (m)	horror entities
EXHORA (m/f)	entity that enhances horror
GUISA (f)	masquerade entity
MISCHIEVUS	mischief entity
SUSPOÓCIA (f)	suspicion and
SPOOKIA (m)	spook entities

A sampling of entity names from the 7.11E decree: "Names of Discarnate Entities and Possessing Demons."[22]

7. Doctrine Over Person—devaluing lived experience

Doctrine Over Person demands rewriting personal history to match group ideology. Members must claim authentic experience of prescribed *Truth* regardless of reality. Every issue in life must align with the group's "inner coherence." Questioning beliefs proves wrong thinking—that pesky "carnal mind." Personal experience, even positive pre-cult memories, becomes suspect. The group's doctrine supersedes individual reality, treating doubts as dangerous distractions that might knock someone off "The Path."

8. Dispensing of Existence

Dispensing of Existence establishes the ultimate ideological boundary between "being and nothingness." Those outside the group are evil, unenlightened, unsaved, without right to exist. As Matthew 10:28 warns: "Fear not them which kill the body... but rather fear him which is able to destroy both soul and body in hell." Our version replaced Hell with the "astral plane," like Christian purgatory but far more threatening—a realm where demons and fallen angels prey on "light-bearers" between lives.

The ultimate threat was the "second death," reserved for mass killers and "fallen angels" who betrayed God's messengers or led others astray. These faced a trial before the twenty-four elders at the "court of sacred fire."

If found guilty, they suffered the "second death" described in Revelation: "But the fearful, and unbelieving, and the abominable, and murderers, and whoremongers, and sorcerers, and idolaters, and all liars, shall have their part in the lake which burneth with fire and brimstone."[23] This final judgment dominated cult discourse, especially regarding enemies. Members feared straying from their path, dreading both the astral plane and the need to reincarnate to balance karma. Existence itself became tied to spiritual salvation, which depended on compliant behavior.

It's a complex labyrinth. While authoritarianism plays a central role, the power of thought reform stems from its supernatural precursors: gods, devils, angels, chosen people, fallen ones, sin, salvation, and divine destiny. These mythologies form the core of the cult algorithm, shaping *beliefs* that produce predictable *outcomes, methods* that enforce compliance, and *purposes* that concentrate power. Lifton's eight psychological principles—which echo Eco's fourteen fascist patterns—are crucial components of thought reform, and you should never underestimate their danger.

---

[1] Eco, U. (1995). Ur-Fascism. *The New York Review of Books*, 42(11), 12-15.
[2] Nilus, S. (Trans.). (1905). *The Protocols of the Meetings of the Learned Elders of Zion*. Znamya Press. A thoroughly discredited antisemitic text that nonetheless remains influential in conspiracy theories.
[3] The Nephilim: Referenced in Genesis 6:1-4 and Numbers 13:33 as offspring of divine and human unions. Modern interpretations, particularly within conspiracy theories and pseudoscientific narratives, link them to ancient alien hypotheses, though these lack support from mainstream biblical scholarship. See analysis: Hendel, R. S. (1987). Of Demigods and the Deluge: Toward an Interpretation of Genesis 6:1-4. *Journal of Biblical Literature*, 106(1), 13-26.
[4] Discarnate entities: Theosophical concept of vampire-like disembodied spirits said to torment humans toward vices, feeding on misqualified "light" energy. Elaborated in Blavatsky, H. P. (1888). *The Secret Doctrine: The Synthesis of Science, Religion, and Philosophy* (Vol. 1, pp. 233-235). Theosophical Publishing Company.
[5] Orwell, G. (1949). *1984*. Secker & Warburg.
[6] Harari, Y. N. (2024). *Nexus: A brief history of information networks from the stone age to AI*. Fern Press.
[7] Dawkins, R. (1976). *The Selfish Gene* (pp. 189-201). Oxford University Press. Memetic evolution describes how ideas spread and adapt through imitation based on their "stickiness" rather than truth value, as detailed in Chapter 11: "Memes: The New Replicators."
[8] The 2017 Rohingya genocide displaced over 700,000 people, with social media, particularly Facebook, playing a significant role in spreading hate speech and inciting violence. United Nations Human Rights Council. (2018). *Report of the independent international fact-finding mission on Myanmar* (A/HRC/39/64).
[9] The 2018 Brazilian election demonstrated YouTube's engagement-driven algorithm's role in promoting polarizing content and far-right narratives. Detailed in: Ribeiro, M. H., et al. (2020). Auditing Radicalization Pathways on YouTube. *Proceedings of the 2020 Conference on Fairness, Accountability, and Transparency*, 131-141.
[10] Shen Yun Performing Arts, founded by Falun Gong practitioners in 2006, has funneled millions in ticket revenue to the organization, accumulating over $250 million in assets by 2023 through unpaid labor and financial contributions from followers. Vick, K., & Sawyer, K. (2025, January 1). How

Shen Yun tapped religious fervor to make $266 million. GV Wire. Retrieved from https://gvwire.com/2025/01/01/how-shen-yun-tapped-religious-fervor-to-make-266-million/

[11] Kuo, L. (2019, October 9). The Epoch Times: How a pro-Trump empire built on Facebook has grown. *The Guardian*. https://www.theguardian.com/technology/2019/oct/09/epoch-times-pro-trump-facebook-advertising.

[12] The Washington Times, founded in 1982 by Unification Church leader Sun Myung Moon, is owned by Operations Holdings, a subsidiary of the church that manages its business interests. Curtis, B. (2017). *The Washington Times: Twenty-Five Years Closer to the Truth*. The Washington Times. Retrieved from https://www.washingtontimes.com/about/

[13] True World Foods. International seafood distributor specializing in Asian cuisine products. Company overview: https://en.wikipedia.org/wiki/True_World_Foods Additional information: True World Foods LLC. (2023). Company Profile and History. Retrieved January 29, 2025, from https://www.trueworldfoods.com/about-us

[14] Chelaship: From Sanskrit "cārya" or "chela" (disciple/student), a concept in Theosophy and Eastern traditions describing one who commits to a spiritual teacher for esoteric wisdom transmission. The process involves rigorous discipline, ethical living, and dedication to spiritual growth under adept mentorship, seen as crucial for transmitting hidden knowledge and attaining higher consciousness. Primary source: Judge, W. Q. (1893). *Letters That Have Helped Me* (pp. 45-48). United Lodge of Theosophists.

[15] Lifton, R. J. (1961). *Thought reform and the psychology of totalism: A study of "brainwashing" in China*. W.W. Norton & Company.

[16] Critical methodological issues in conversion studies: sample bias, overemphasis on coercion, simplification of complex processes, ethnocentric bias, ambiguous terminology, and oversimplified analysis of religious conversion. Analyzed in Richardson, J. T. (1993). *Religion and the Social Order* (Vol. 3, pp. 75-97).

[17] Bernays, E. L. (1928). *Propaganda*. Liveright.

[18] Biblical references (KJV) on divine selection and separation: 2 Corinthians 6:17: "Wherefore come out from among them, and be ye separate, saith the Lord"; 1 Peter 2:9: "But ye are a chosen generation, a royal priesthood, an holy nation"; Romans 8:33: "Who shall lay any thing to the charge of God's elect? It is God that justifieth"; 1 John 5:21: "Little children, keep yourselves from idols. Amen." Exegetical analysis in Carson, D. A. (1984). *Exegetical Fallacies* (pp. 123-125). Baker Academic.

[19] Prophet, E. C. (1983). *The Science of the Spoken Word*. Summit University Press.

[20] Paolini, K., & Paolini, T. (2000). *400 years of imaginary friends: A journey into the world of adepts, masters, ascended masters, and their messengers*. Paolini International LLC. p. 39

[21] Animal magnetism: Mesmer's discredited theory categorized influences as malicious, sympathetic, ignorant, and delicious. Original source: Mesmer, F. A. (1779). *Mémoire sur la découverte du magnétisme animal*. Modern analysis: Crabtree, A. (1993). *From Mesmer to Freud* (pp. 39-45).

[22] Prophet, M., & Prophet, E. (1999). *Prayers, Meditations, and Dynamic Decrees for Personal and World Transformation*. Summit University Press.

[23] Revelation 21:8 (KJV)

CHAPTER FOUR

No One Is Immune

Thought reform is a *voluntary*, interactive process through which the seeker and cult collaborate to establish a system of dominance and submission that defines their future relationship. The *CUT v. Mull* transcript verifies that no cult leader can control anyone without their consent. Gregory Mull's ex-wife Kathleen Mueller distilled the issue, "If Elizabeth Clare Prophet were in fact the messenger, this had to be the greatest thing that ever happened to this Earth, and if in fact she were not the messenger it had to be the biggest fraud ever perpetrated."[1]

The problem seems bald-faced obvious—a simple binary: Are the teachings true or false? Is the messenger authentic or a charlatan? If the messenger is a *bona fide* conduit to Almighty God, then submission is warranted and everyone wins: The chela achieves enlightenment, balances their karma, and makes their ascension. The guru serves the will of God by saving souls. But what if the teachings are false and the "messenger" is just an ordinary human? The chela is duped and sacrifices their life to a delusion. Through mass adulation, the guru becomes a mad monarch increasingly detached from reality, believing their divine righteousness justifies their dominance. With stakes this high, the guru's authenticity becomes the only question that matters.

This put our faith at the center of the trial. Despite weeks of testimony from loyal supporters, the jury was skeptical. Some jurors were petrified by my mother's authority and larger-than-life persona, and uneasy about our "decrees" which they knew mentioned their names. Other jurors thought we were strange and lacked human feelings. Most weren't sure about thought reform or how it worked, but they believed Gregory Mull suffered harm. They saw through my mother's spiritual pretenses—and refused to let her beliefs excuse her conduct.

Erin Prophet's 2018 book, *Coercion or Conversion? A Case Study in Religion and the Law: CUT v. Mull v. Prophet* serves as a useful study guide, though she and I hold divergent views of its implications.[2] Should Mull's involvement be seen as an authentic religious conversion involving voluntary self-sacrifice and a monastic vow of poverty? Or did our large, wealthy cult strategically subsist on free labor? Could sincere religious conversion be a path to exploitation? Examining my cult's practices requires an unflinching look at its theology of divine rewards and punishments, which I'll explore further.

Mueller's dilemma exposes the critical problem with *Ballard*. Courts can't judge "sincerely-held" beliefs—even when they're used to extract money and labor. The Ballards claimed divine healing powers. We believed our decrees alter physical reality. Those beliefs were off limits in court. But Mull's attorney Lawrence Levy took a different tack: Over Ken Klein's repeated objections, he explored how our beliefs might have caused Gregory Mull to act against his interests.

The trial thus focused on mechanisms of thought reform through testimony from cult experts, religious scholars, psychologists, and sociologists, including Margaret Singer and Rabbi Steven Robbins. Singer was a pioneering psychologist who systematically studied how cults indoctrinate individuals into accepting questionable beliefs. Her framework of coercive persuasion, initially adapted from military brainwashing studies, showed how cults manipulate members through isolation, control, and psychological pressure. While her theory was later criticized for lacking empirical grounding, Singer's work laid the foundation for understanding cult dynamics. Key patterns she identified—exploitative authority, thought reform, and emotional dependency—proved fundamental to understanding how cults operate.

The American Psychological Association eventually distanced itself from coercive persuasion theory, citing insufficient empirical support.[3] By 1993, US courts introduced the *Daubert* standard, requiring scientific rigor for expert testimony.[4] This effectively ended coercive persuasion testimony in legal proceedings. But Singer's core insight—that cults systematically manipulate their followers—has been validated and refined by decades of research.

Since then, more robust frameworks have emerged that build on Singer's work. *Religious Trauma Syndrome* (RTS) explains the psychological harm experienced by those leaving oppressive religious environments, leading to anxiety, depression, and struggles with reintegration. *Complex Post-Traumatic Stress Disorder* (CPTSD) focuses on the long-term effects of sustained trauma, including emotional regulation difficulties and relational issues. *Undue influence* recognizes how cults exploit personal vulnerabilities without requiring deterministic "mind control." Steven Hassan's *BITE* model identifies how cults influence members by controlling behavior, information, thought, and emotion.[5]

Each of these frameworks helps explain what the Mull jury sensed but couldn't quite articulate—how cults achieve their extraordinary level of control over individuals who never considered themselves susceptible. Most people believe such manipulation only works on the gullible or desperate, yet cults routinely recruit intelligent, capable members. For those on the outside, watching a loved one fall under such influence can evoke profound feelings of shame, helplessness, and grief. It's like a death—but the person you love is still very much alive—transformed by an alien worldview.[6] They will insist they're happy, healthy, and in control. Committed cult members are simply unaware of their peril. And some never get out.

To understand the danger, consider this: Could anyone talk you into withdrawing your life savings of $50,000, putting the cash in a shoebox, and dropping it through the back window of a black SUV that pulls up outside your home? No? That happened in 2023 to a seasoned professional financial adviser. And if you join a cult, it could cost you far more than $50,000. Cults want your money, yes—but you could also lose years of your life, your career, your freedom, and your dignity.

Depending on how you define cult, this phenomenon affects tens of millions to billions of people worldwide.[7] Any group that captures your sympathy is dangerous, if only because you are less likely to be skeptical. Mass thought reform is now accomplished through social media, YouTube videos, and Zoom meetings. You can become part of a dangerous cult without ever leaving your home.

If you're serious about getting yourself out of a cult, helping a loved one escape, or ensuring you never face that experience, start by understanding how they operate. Don't be disarmed by marketing appeal. Any successful cult will have a highly refined sales pitch that's recruited many others. They will insist they're not a cult, and that warnings about cult dangers don't apply to them. Like all salespeople, cult recruiters rely on human connection. Instead of being cajoled, *investigate* the BOMP: How is the group financed? What other groups or ideologies is it connected to? Who benefits? Pay close attention to hierarchical structures and especially to upsells requiring deeper commitments.

The word cult is considered a slur, and it rightly inspires fear. That's why it's so important to use it. Cults thrive in the darkness of our loathing and trepidation. Strange beliefs aren't the issue—destructive cults are defined by their algorithm: how they treat members and outsiders, with antisocial, authoritarian behavior and financial, emotional, or sexual exploitation. If the cult shoe fits, use the term freely. "Cult, *cult*, CULT!" Euphemisms like "high-demand groups," "spiritual communities," or "new religious movements" only normalize the predations of cult leaders and the consensual exploitation of followers.

Who joins cults? The demographic profile cuts across all ages, educational backgrounds, and socioeconomic levels. This diversity underscores the universal vulnerabilities that cults exploit. Intellectual acumen offers no protection. Like tobacco use or any other self-harming behavior, if it were a matter of intelligence, no one would succumb. Many cult members are highly educated, which also makes them better than average at motivated reasoning and rational self-justification. People don't tend to question what they want to believe—especially ideas that serve their emotional needs during a personal crisis or fulfill an especially deep yearning for meaning and belonging.

Cults prey on our investments in identity. A healthy identity is multifaceted, spanning the different life roles and characteristics we all inhabit. But cults don't target this complexity. Instead, they leverage what people believe about themselves: "I'm a loving person," "I'm a spiritual person," "I'm an ethical person." Or, "I'm a patriotic American," "I'm disgusted by X group/person," "My freedoms are under attack."

Cults are also cons—but vastly more complex and long-term. Both cults and cons appeal to greed and fear, but understanding which is more powerful provides insight into their tactics. Behavioral economics explains this through loss-aversion: it's more painful to lose $100 than it is pleasurable to gain $100.[8] To offset the pain of losing $100, you would need to gain $200 or more. This phenomenon is rooted in evolutionary survival instincts—losing essential resources could be life-threatening, while additional gains only provide incremental benefits.

Neuroscience explains why fear-based appeals are so effective. Loss aversion activates brain regions like the amygdala and ventromedial prefrontal cortex, triggering a rapid emotional response. In contrast, rewards engage higher brain regions, including the prefrontal cortex, which supports slower, deliberate, analytical thinking. Loss responses are instinctive and immediate, while reward processing takes more time. What's key to understand is that signals don't get into your brain without passing through the limbic system. Therefore, you cannot think about something before you have an emotion about it.

Research confirms this through studies of emotional priming. Participants shown happy or angry faces before cognitive tasks respond faster than those shown neutral expressions.[9] The effect is even stronger when emotional cues align—a happy face followed by a happy word generates quicker responses than a happy face followed by an angry word.[10]

If a cult is trying to recruit someone, the fastest route to capturing their mind is through priming with a negative emotional appeal that hijacks their emotional identity investment. This shuts down intellectual processing. Once a cult hooks into someone's identity, the next step is deepening that bond while amplifying the intensity of their investment—a strategy mirrored in scams.

Cults, like religions, typically start with your fear of mortality, compounded by fear of losing your "immortal soul." Their call to action insists that if something isn't done immediately, or if a threat isn't stopped, some irrevocable calamity will occur. Their millenarian apocalypse is always just around the corner. The greed-appeal of religious systems is some form of paradise, heaven, or eternal life. But due to loss aversion, Hell and the second death can be superior recruiting tools. The appeal of heaven is abstract—primarily about reuniting with loved ones. But hell is vividly salient, reinforced not only in weekly sermons but in dystopian Hollywood apocalypses that keep people primed for emotional reaction to any notion of doom.

Secular scams exploit these same psychological vulnerabilities. Get-rich-quick schemes appeal to greed, but the most successful ripoffs weaponize fear—posing as government agents, tech support, or bank fraud departments to extract passwords and sensitive information. The grandparent scam uses a voice actor pretending to be a grandchild in crisis, needing immediate bail money or hospital bills paid. Utility scams threaten to shut off essential services unless victims pay cash.

You may think you'd never fall for any of these. But thousands of people do, every day.[11]

It's not a sign of low intelligence or gullibility. Savvy, intelligent people can be victims too. The $50,000 cash in a shoebox was dropped into the back window of a black SUV in 2023, by *New York Magazine* financial-advice columnist Charlotte Cowles.[12] She said, "When I've told people this story, most of them say the same thing: You don't seem like the type of person this would happen to. What they mean is that I'm not senile, or hysterical, or a rube." This shows that well-educated people with good jobs and stable families are just as susceptible as anyone else—especially if they believe they're immune. In Cowles' case, the pitch was pure loss aversion: fear of having her bank accounts frozen and imprisonment. It was an elaborate, scripted scam executed by a team of voice actors impersonating corporate and government agents over the phone.

There were a dozen holes in the story, and plenty of easy outs that could have saved Cowles $50,000 if she had just hung up. But she didn't take those outs. It's a textbook illustration of the thought-stopping nature of fear. The scammers cleverly played on her fear of loss—not only of her money and freedom—but also of harming her husband's alleged criminal case, if she contacted him. None of us can say for certain that we wouldn't fall for such a scam—until it happens.

Your best defense is emotional regulation. Loss-aversion techniques work even when you know about them because your brain processes emotion before reason. Unregulated emotion beats your rational mind, every time. Cultivate reflexive awareness of when you're responding emotionally. Learn to pause, step back, think, and regulate your emotions before making important decisions.

This awareness extends to personal relationships, because abusive relationships are cults of two. If you reflect on your first meeting with an abuser, you'll realize they told you everything you needed to know about them to warn you away. But you didn't listen. Charming and charismatic people can make you fall in love quickly, or at least become infatuated, leading you to form an unconscious agenda toward a future involving them. There's a gauzy disorienting mental haze that hangs over such interactions, whether the gambit is a business opportunity, a romantic partner, or cult recruiting. To avoid falling prey to scams, abusers and cults, remain emotionally aloof and focus your rational mind. Because plenty of con artists, abusers and cult leaders are experts at disarming you with emotion. Their success depends on it. Which brings us to the Dark Triad.[13]

The Dark Triad theory of personality was first published by Delroy L. Paulhus and Kevin M. Williams in 2002. It combines three personality types: Machiavellianism, narcissism, and psychopathy. Found in roughly 1 percent of the population, the Dark Triad is disproportionately represented among authoritarians, crime bosses, billionaires, politicians, and cult leaders. Traits include extreme charisma, the capacity to spoof positive social cues, and a thinly-veiled drive for dominance, cruelty, and grandiosity. Other hallmarks are hair-trigger rage, self-centeredness, manipulation, lying, thin-skinned overreaction to insults, a chronic need for admiration, extreme cynicism, and violence. Not every Dark Triad individual exhibits all these traits, nor are they present in equal measure. Every trait exists on a bell curve that varies across the population.

Why are people swayed by charismatic leaders? It's a question worth exploring. My sister Erin Prophet offers insights in "Charisma and Authority in New Religious Movements."[14] First, her formal definition: "Charisma… refers to the attribution to an individual of extraordinary, superhuman, or supernatural powers by which the individual is seen as having authority to lead and to transform religious traditions." She references (but does not fully agree with) psychological theories. She also cites sociological theories from Max Weber, Émile Durkheim, David G. Bromley, and Eileen Barker, all of which confirm that—like thought reform—charisma is *interactive*, not transitive, requiring the cooperation of the target.[15]

Whether socially or psychologically based, charismatic authority is unstable and may tilt toward violence and chaos. Prophet reflects on Weber's phrase, the "routinization" of charisma, which also refers to the "institutionalization" of authority. This can help stabilize charisma, beginning to inject a measure of checks and balances—to help rein in its excesses. This occurs through the formation of what Weber calls the "charismatic aristocracy," which I refer to as the inner circle surrounding the leader. The charismatic aristocracy can be a stabilizing force. Depending on the strength of its loyalty, it can also be a powerful enabler reinforcing the leader's dictates.

Finally, Prophet notes that due to its reliance on an interactive relationship with followers, charismatic authority is "…neither absolute nor irreversible. The charismatic bond must be periodically refreshed and may deteriorate or disappear altogether. Charisma is unstable, like a radioactive isotope." She cautions that there are pressures on leaders to disrupt the process of routinization or institutionalization. Because they often "require the leader to relinquish control and hence status; leaders resist by introducing new teachings that disrupt routines, making increased demands on the members, and demoting or expelling middle management…Where that transition does not happen, the leader may continue to resist until illness or death precipitates crisis."

We're not going to contain charisma, or rid the world of narcissists, Machiavellians, and psychopaths anytime soon, so recognizing them is critical to your safety and well-being. An early tell for narcissism is a magnetic personality. Charisma can be authentic. But when someone is positively oozing it, so much that you can't look away, it demands extra due diligence. When someone is the center of attention in every room, their obvious social proof makes them less likely to be challenged. Cult leaders are masters at establishing the rarefied air of unquestioned authority.

There's a complex skill set involved in building a social group that will pay money and attention—and eventually devote their lives—to a cult leader. Magnetism builds over time, in step with the messianic ego required to support it. It revolves around a quick mind, a larger-than-life backstory, excellent public-speaking skills, and a sense of comedic timing. Any budding cult leader must develop a reflexive capacity to deliver withering putdowns to challengers without coming across as an asshole. This central part of the cult-leader persona frames all chastisements in spiritual terms and purports to be a deeper form of commitment to the well-being of the challenger.

It's a biblical approach: "For whom the Lord loveth he chasteneth, and scourgeth every son whom he receiveth."[16] While providing a framework to make sense of generalized misfortune, this quote is also often used to justify harsh punishments. It spiritualizes what would otherwise appear to be controlling behavior and makes the difference between the cult-leader being viewed as a bully—or further cementing the trust of the group. None of this is easy. But once accomplished, it's powerful. Sky-high confidence coupled with fluid sociality is strongly correlated with success. But there's a crucial difference between charismatic people who use their skill to build genuine empathy and accountable relationships, versus those who use it to build a messianic ego large enough to take advantage of others.

In my own cult experience, and from informally observing other cults, I've found that it's important to critically analyze charismatic messages. Not only what they're saying, but what they're implying, and what they're not saying. What tactics are they using? What are they trying to convince you to do? Are they threatening you, or trying to scare you? What are they selling? Is their message uplifting and inclusive? Or is it condemning and exclusive? Do they value hierarchy over fairness? These questions will help you comprehend the cult's BOMP—and act accordingly.

When you're hearing a sales pitch for a business, a romantic come-on, or a purported message of spiritual enlightenment, pay close attention to the person's tone. Don't be disarmed by humor. Every joke carries a serious message that reveals the character of the teller. A person's style of humor will tell you whether they genuinely care about others. Trying to make transgressive cruelty seem cool or edgy is a huge red flag.

Does the person listen more than they talk? Or do they interrupt and talk over you? Do they use the abusive pickup-artist tactic of "negging," putting you on the defensive by criticizing something small about you? Or are they polite, respectful, and genuinely interested?

How does the person treat people with less power? It's useless to observe how anyone treats their peers—those with some capacity to change their fortunes. To understand the person's ethics, watch how they treat subordinates including wait staff, ticketing agents, delivery drivers, and retail employees. This is the origin of the accurate "Karen" stereotype, proving that cruelty and self-righteousness aren't limited to any gender.[17] If you're not close enough to directly observe their behavior, look for conversational clues in their speeches or writings.

The narcissistic manipulator has one purpose: To get you to see the world as he or she does, by manufacturing a reality that exists to serve their ends.[18] It's the first stage of cultic indoctrination—to weave and dangle the alternate reality in front of their target using charismatic authority. The next step is to bring the target inside of it, by eliminating disconfirming influences. The "secret knowledge" gambit aids both. The cult leader can't abide you fact-checking their dogma using qualified experts. The essential part of their pitch is that their particular brand of exclusive understanding is not only "ultimate truth," but "can't be found anywhere else." If you accept that—you've bought into your own submission.

Cult leaders disqualify experts as "unenlightened." They dismiss doubts as "naïveté," "ignorance," "backsliding," or "human questioning." In the real, empirical world, all knowledge is probabilistic and uncertain. Qualified experts are keenly aware of the weaknesses in their disciplines, and know how to avoid overly broad claims. Charismatic authority projects supernatural certainty, which recognizes no such constraints. In the hall of mirrors of a narcissistic cult leader, every word, idea and glimpse of their dazzling divine visage is pure perfection. *Important caveat*: Cult leaders are skilled at projecting feigned humility.

While exploring the Dark Triad, it's crucial to recognize that these traits can manifest in many social and political contexts. Their presence does not align with specific political ideologies. Political extremists on the left and right exhibit similar pathological behaviors, although what represents "extreme" views on each side is a matter of some debate. Political affiliations are shaped by a complex interplay of factors, including moral foundations, cultural influences, and personal experience.

Most people genuinely believe in the merit of their perspectives for organizing society and sincerely aim to improve collective well-being. My focus is on recognizing manipulative behaviors and attitudes that signal deeper issues, regardless of political alignment. Here's the acid test: If someone fixates on attacking people beneath them in the social hierarchy, that's cult-level pathology.[19]

These methods for detecting a narcissist aren't foolproof. The best ones know how to avoid raising red flags. They don't lead with mean jokes, rudeness, cruelty, eternal damnation, or delusion. Instead, they sanewash their first impressions, holding back their true nature until trust has been secured. I watched this process unfold countless times with my own mother.

She was polished as she approached new recruits. People who met her for the first time were starstruck. She would flatter them, sometimes telling them they were "angels," or that she had known them in a "past life."[20] If they had money or property, she would make them feel special, emphasizing their important role in world salvation—and, of course, suggesting their funds were best used to support our cult. Once they committed their money and lives, she wouldn't hesitate to treat them spitefully or expel them if they crossed her.

Members also wrote letters or made appointments for personal counseling. They would ask questions like whether they should join our staff, or pursue their career or education outside the cult, or whether to marry a certain person. Many people claim—to this day—that she gave them good advice. But I saw a different side, in which her advice reflected what was good for the cult, and most convenient for her. She had no special insight to make life decisions for any supplicant.

Let's pretend you meet the perfect narcissist with perfect charisma, with no red flags you can see. The final warning is over-familiarity—the person wants to get too close, too fast. This can happen for different reasons, depending on personality type. Someone with borderline personality disorder might make you their favorite person because they want you to "save" them. A narcissist might try to become *your* favorite person, to control you. If you quickly feel like you've "known this person your whole life," take a step back from your swoon, and put up your guard. Especially if they pressure you to commit time, money, or your body.

Patience is your strongest ally. Vetting a person for a deep friendship, romantic relationship—or to avoid joining their cult—takes time. Rushing this process is exactly what manipulators count on. Trust, but verify. Check their reputation. Talk to their friends. Lurk on their socials. You can find out almost anything about anyone with a quick search. If someone comes up blank on Google, insist on getting their full, real name, and pay for a public records search. If it's an organization you're thinking of getting involved with, talk to members, read the online reviews *and* do a public records search. No safe person or group would object. It might be the best time and money you've ever spent.

No abuser or cult leader can gain your trust unless you give it to them willingly. And the more desperately you want something from them, the more likely you are to do that. Remember, no one is immune. When you encounter strong charisma, you need to determine whether it's Dark Triad, or just an amazing gift-of-gab coming from an authentic person.

To explore further:

Campbell, W. K., & Crist, C. (2020). *The New Science of Narcissism: Understanding One of the Greatest Psychological Challenges of Our Time—and What You Can Do About It.* Sounds True.

Shaw, D. (2013). *Traumatic Narcissism and Recovery* (Relational Perspectives Book Series). Routledge.

---

[1] CUT v. Mull, Superior Court of Los Angeles County C. 358191, (February 24, 1986) at 1086:15-22

[2] Prophet, E. (2018). *Coercion or conversion? A case study in religion and the law: CUT v. Mull v. Prophet.* Linden Books.

[3] APA's 1987 rejection of the Task Force on Deceptive and Indirect Methods of Persuasion and Control (DIMPAC) report, including Dr. M. T. Singer's research.

[4] The *Daubert* standard (*Daubert v. Merrell Dow Pharmaceuticals*, Inc., 509 U.S. 579, 1993) establishes criteria for admitting expert scientific testimony: testability, peer review, error rates, and scientific consensus.

[5] Hassan's BITE Model synthesizes Lifton's thought reform criteria through four domains (Behavior, Information, Thought, Emotion) for analyzing cult dynamics and supporting former members. Hassan, S. (2016). *Combating cult mind control: The #1 best-selling guide to protection, rescue, and recovery from destructive cults.* Freedom of Mind Press.

[6] Hill, F. (2024, July 30). The painful reality of loving a conspiracy theorist. The Atlantic. https://www.theatlantic.com/books/archive/2024/07/quiet-damage-qanon-jesselyn-cook-book-review/679235/

[7] Quantifying cult membership faces definitional challenges: https://www.peopleleavecults.com/post/statistics-on-cults

[8] Loss aversion. (n.d.). In Wikipedia. Retrieved January 29, 2025, from https://en.wikipedia.org/wiki/Loss_aversion

[9] Murphy, S. T., & Zajonc, R. B. (1993). Affect, cognition, and awareness: Affective priming with optimal and suboptimal stimulus exposures. *Journal of Personality and Social Psychology*, 64(5), 723-739. https://doi.org/10.1037/0022-3514.64.5.723

[10] Innes-Ker, Å., & Niedenthal, P. M. (2002). Emotion concepts and emotional states in social judgment and categorization. *Journal of Personality and Social Psychology*, 83(4), 804-816. https://doi.org/10.1037/0022-3514.83.4.804

[11] AARP. (2024, February 9). Americans reported losing a record $10 billion to scams and fraud in 2023. https://www.aarp.org/money/scams-fraud/info-2024/2023-ftc-consumer-losses.html

[12] Cowles, C. (2024, February 15). The day I put $50,000 in a shoe box and handed it to a stranger. *The Cut*. https://www.thecut.com/article/amazon-scam-call-ftc-arrest-warrants.html

[13] Dark Triad. (n.d.). In Psychology Today. Retrieved January 29, 2025, from https://www.psychology-today.com/gb/basics/dark-triad

[14] Lewis, J. R., & Bogdan, H. (Eds.). (2016). *The Oxford handbook of new religious movements: Volume II*. Oxford University Press.

[15] Charismatic authority requires follower recognition (Weber, M., 1968, *On charisma and institution building*, p. 20) and public opinion (Durkheim, E., 2001, *The elementary forms of religious life*, p. 160). Crisis enables charismatic authority when "cultural narratives no longer offer plausible interpretations" (Bromley, D. G., 2014, The *Bloomsbury companion to new religious movements*, p. 106). Barker adds that "charismatization" occurs through social reinforcement and unique leader-follower relationships.

[16] Hebrews 12:6 KJV

[17] The term "Karen" is a pejorative stereotype for white women perceived as entitled or racially confrontational, often linked to white privilege. Williams, A. (2020). The *"Karen" meme and the critique of white entitlement*. Journal of Cultural Studies, 34(2), 45-63. Retrieved from https://doi.org/10.xxxx/jcs.karen2020

[18] O'Connor, P. (2022, April 4). How a master manipulator creates their own reality. In *Philosophy: Stirred, Not Shaken*. Psychology Today. https://www.psychologytoday.com/us/blog/philosophy-stirred-not-shaken/202204/how-a-master-manipulator-creates-their-own-reality

[19] Devaluing and attacking those perceived as socially inferior is a recognized feature of cult psychology, reinforcing in-group superiority and control. Deikman, A. J. (1994). *The wrong way home: Uncovering the patterns of cult behavior in American society*. Beacon Press.

[20] Elizabeth Clare Prophet to Talita Paolini: "You know you are angels, don't you?"—illustrating charismatic validation. Paolini, K., & Paolini, T. (2000). 400 years of imaginary friends: *A journey into the world of adepts, masters, ascended masters, and their messengers*. Paolini International LLC, p. 32.

CHAPTER FIVE

Betty Clare Wulf

My mother ruled our cult as her personal fiefdom. Legally it was a non-profit 501(c)(3) charitable organization, but it was also a family business that was very much *for-Prophet*. Her personality suffused everything. Followers kept her picture in their wallets, in their cars and on the walls of their homes. She imposed her preferences, quirks and prejudices on community life: diet, clothing, sexuality, music, art, literature. Her need for that level of control—and the spiritual mythology that justified it—can only be understood in the context of her childhood and youth.

From an early age, my mother inhabited what I've come to call her "virtual world"—where challenges were interpreted as karma, spiritual attacks, or tests, and daily life took on cosmic significance. What began as a child's escape from trauma and isolation would eventually expand into a spiritual cosmology embraced by thousands of her followers. The seeds of both her power— and her vulnerability—were planted in her earliest years.

Elizabeth Clare Wulf was born on April 8, 1939, the only child of Hans Wilhelm Wulf and Frida Enkerli Wulf. "Elizabeth" was her grandmother's name and "Clare" came from Clare Weber, whom Frida had cared for as a governess. They called her "Betty Clare." Shortly after her first birthday, the family moved to their permanent home at 43 South Street in Red Bank, New Jersey.

As the only child of older parents who were recent immigrants, my mother experienced profound isolation that shaped her psychological development. Though she often told tales of childhood woe that bordered on martyrdom, they were interspersed with fond memories of the life-sized playhouse her father built in the backyard in a quarter-acre fairy-tale garden, swimming at the Jersey Shore, playing the piano, and caring for her beloved dog, Barry. There's no question that Frida doted on her only child, but in my mother's mind she failed to foster a happy environment or maintain a peaceful partnership with her father.

Hans carried his own deep wounds into fatherhood. Born in 1901 in Elmshorn, Germany, he was a U-boat captain during World War I. After the war, he joined the merchant marine and served as an oil tanker pilot. In the early 1930s, he settled in Maracaibo, Venezuela where he married a local woman and had three children, Blanca, Hans, Jr., and Iris. His younger two children, Hans, Jr., and Iris, died suddenly of tropical diseases. Heartbroken, he abandoned his family and moved to Port of Spain, Trinidad, where he acquired and managed a coastal plantation.

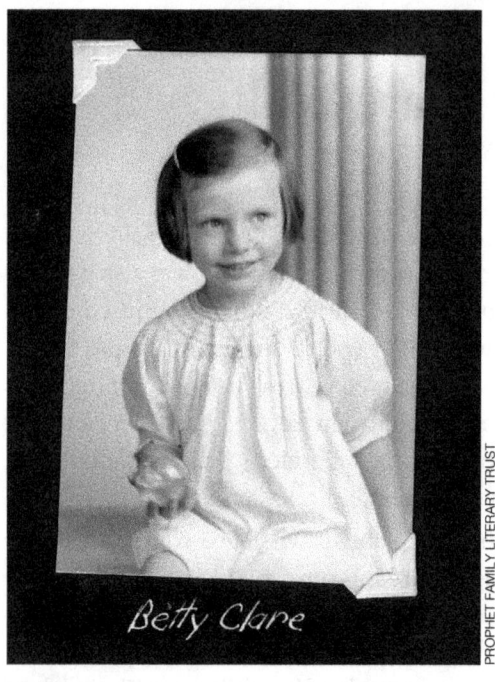

Betty Clare

In 1936, he met Frida, a Swiss governess working for the Weber family, wealthy New Yorkers on a bird-watching expedition to Trinidad. Hans soon sold the plantation, and in 1937 he and Frida moved to Red Bank, New Jersey. There, he purchased a defunct boatyard and started Red Bank Marine Works, producing wooden skiffs and runabouts under the brand SeaWulf. With the onset of World War II, the pleasure craft business declined, and in 1941 Hans pivoted to building military dories for the US Army, eventually completing 27.

During World War II, the US government targeted individuals of German, Italian, and Japanese ancestry under the Alien Enemy Act of 1798. Non-citizens deemed enemy aliens could be apprehended, interned, or deported. On March 3, 1942, Hans was arrested and held at Ellis Island due to his German heritage and military service. He produced numerous character witnesses and was released six weeks later. But the stigma of the charge hung over him for the rest of the war, along with strict military probation. Later, he became a US citizen.

Hans Wulf and Frida Enkerli at the Trinidad plantation c. 1937

A lack of capital and the new popularity of fiberglass boats forced Hans to sell his boat-building firm to his biggest competitor in 1951. This marked the start of a turbulent period for the Wulf family, as Hans' worsening alcoholism fueled escalating domestic discord. One day, in a rage over losing his business, he smashed the family's three prized aquariums, waiting for each mess to be cleaned up before destroying the next. My mother told this story often. It was a vivid metaphor for the emotional wreckage in the Wulf household—and a memory that fueled her lifelong disdain for alcohol. Emulating—or perhaps in response to—her father's explosive temper, my mother developed what we would later call her "Ram personality"—in reference to her astrological sign of Aries. It was a stern, unmerciful, authoritarian alter ego that emerged whenever she felt threatened or wanted to get her way. Like her virtual world, the Ram was a childhood defense mechanism born of necessity—that later grew into a potent weapon.

Betty Clare's relationship to Frida was fraught—from before she was born. In 1938, Frida tried to end her pregnancy at about three months, taking quinine sulfate, a drug known to cause miscarriage at high doses. It has neurotoxic effects on the fetus and can cause central nervous system anomalies.[1] The abortion attempt failed, but it may have contributed to my mother's lifelong struggle with epilepsy. This primal rejection would cast a shadow over their relationship and shape my mother's later views on abortion.

Hans Wulf pilots a Sea Wulf runabout, built by his company, Red Bank Marine Works, in Red Bank, New Jersey c. 1939

Epilepsy began to disrupt my mother's social life beginning in third grade. During a Christmas play, she had a petit-mal seizure, blacked out, missed her lines, and earned the cruel nickname "Spellbound." She awoke to her teacher shaking her violently. A year later, she blacked out again in her yard, putting her leg through the glass pane of a cellar door, requiring sixty stitches and narrowly avoiding amputation. But epilepsy wasn't her only burden. In first grade, her teacher asked all the girls who thought they were pretty to stand at the front of the class. Not feeling pretty, she stayed seated, later describing herself as an "ugly duckling."

This early insecurity was unsurprising given the turmoil in her home life—and her father's lingering wish he'd had a son instead. Years later, Hans described in an interview how the death of Hans Jr. had haunted him. He never told Betty Clare about his tragic loss, and my mother never got over the feeling that she had failed to meet her father's expectations. While growing up, my sisters and I never stopped hearing about her challenges with her father.

As my mother moved through her teen years, she played first-chair clarinet in band, and enjoyed some close friendships, but her growing preoccupation with spiritual matters along with her epilepsy kept her on the fringes of high school social life. She endured embarrassing moments, like blacking out when her boyfriend Dick Fontaine tried to teach her to drive. Frida often interfered, disapproving of slumber parties as "silly" and waiting up for her on the front porch after dates. She longed for the intimacy she saw other girls share with their boyfriends but abstained from sex, later saying, "I was in no way ready for any real sexual experience when I was in high school. I just was not. It was beyond me."[2]

Betty Clare, Frida, and Hans Wulf in their garden, Red Bank, New Jersey c. 1946

Betty Clare faced blackballing by a clique of mean girls in tenth grade. Instead of learning to navigate their cruelty, she spiritualized it, believing she may have harmed those girls in a past life. She concluded they were the "tares among the wheat" spoken of by Jesus. She recalled, "I felt left out of the 'fast' set, the cheerleaders and the football players." This foreshadowed her growing retreat from ordinary reality. Rather than building resilience and social skills, she found moral certainty by deeming the jocks inferior, which contributed to her difficulties with social belonging throughout her adolescence and into adulthood.

Her struggles at home persisted. She often recounted the toxic, codependent dynamic between Hans and Frida and how it shaped her young psyche. Frida engaged in parentification, leaning on Betty Clare as a confidante, disparaging Hans, and pulling her into the family's financial struggles. Meanwhile, Hans' womanizing exacerbated the tension, prompting Frida to guilt-trip her daughter with claims that she stayed in the marriage "only for her benefit." My mother described this period as feeling trapped between her father's betrayal and her mother's fear, "in the presence of mine enemies."[3] Her only solace came from reframing her struggles as karma and retreating into an inner communion with God—through nature, Christian Science worship, and her virtual world.

The virtual world wasn't just a coping mechanism. It became the foundation for the spiritual lens through which she interpreted her life's challenges. Her childhood burdens would later influence not only the doctrines she imposed on her followers but how she responded to her foes. She believed that real-world problems could be resolved through affirmations, which led her to embrace the "Science of the Spoken Word" and the "Violet Flame." She clung to Mary Baker Eddy's aphorism, "Evil is not real, and its appearance has no power"—a testament to the theodicy of denial and spiritual monism in Christian Science, which dismisses the material universe as an illusion. Despite the domestic turmoil, my mother outwardly remained a devoted daughter, obeying and serving both parents into adulthood.

Betty Clare Wulf c. 1957

College bound, my mother stepped out of her parents' shadow and developed the social skills, confidence, and poise she had once lacked. But the exclusion she faced in school, along with her childhood trauma, left a permanent mark. These experiences shaped everything from her understanding of authority to her complex relationship with sexuality—connections I'll explore in later chapters. In a foreshadowing of her destiny, she once had a painful experience as a camp counselor. She later recalled, "I knelt and prayed to God that he would never in my life put me in charge of anyone."[4] Her fear of leadership hints at a precocious understanding of the risks of unchecked power.

My mother's childhood patterns of escape and control were firmly established by her teen years, and she carried them into adulthood. One revealing moment came when she and I went to see a film in 1981. I was 17 and excited to drive her in my new Toyota Celica. It was a rare occasion—we normally spent precious little time alone together. The film was *Four Friends,* an innocent coming-of-age comedy about three suitors vying for the free-spirited Georgia—a young woman who claims to be the reincarnation of Isadora Duncan. Set in the early 1960s amid social upheaval, the film was rated R for love scenes and nudity. On the way home, my mother was silent at first. Then she broke into her Ram personality and pronounced God's judgment on Hollywood.

"That film is why California's going down!" she railed.

I was nonplussed.

"Mother, it's just a movie," I said. "Probably pretty realistic about the lives of young people."

"Such things are private," she retorted. "They should not be portrayed on film. This is the folly of the Cain civilization, and God will have His final word!"

"You're making too much of this," I objected. "The film was pretty tame. If you don't want to see people having sex, we shouldn't go to R-rated movies."

"No, Sean, this will not stand," she insisted. "God will not allow these abominations to continue. It's only a matter of time. We need to get out of this filthy city and get to the mountain of God."

I kept quiet and drove my mother home. At 17, I lacked any capacity to comprehend her reaction. We had recently purchased the 12,000-acre Forbes Ranch in Montana, signaling that she had already been planning to move beyond Los Angeles. I couldn't understand how seeing *Four Friends* had changed her outlook. I already knew she took a dim view of American culture. But years later while studying her life history, I began to recognize her reaction to the film was deeply rooted in her own experience—emblematic of her unresolved struggles with sex and intimacy. The self-possession and confidence of the Georgia character embodied what my mother might have wished for herself, if she hadn't withdrawn from sociality.

It wasn't just ordinary maternal prudishness about a risqué film. She had described having similar feelings decades earlier. In *Preparation for My Mission*, she mentions a summer of heartache and unrequited love in Beach Haven, New Jersey, in 1954. Walking alone one night, she heard the amorous sounds of couples in a beach setting—similar to the love scene in *Four Friends*, which was also set in the time frame of her youth.

> At night, the Coast Guard and military men would bring their dates down there for the purpose of being alone.... I could hear the sounds of what I could now identify as necking and love-making. I felt so isolated, wondering if I would ever have a boyfriend, and yet revolted by the easy way of these couples. Sensuality disturbed me. When I was in elementary school, I had gone on a trip to New York City and we passed by a bar that had its door open. There was an enormously fat woman in there, scantily clad, who was standing up and dancing. I was repulsed. I thought, "That is evil. I have just seen evil." But sensuality was all around me at Beach Haven. I told myself that God must not want me to have a boyfriend because I didn't have one, and that I would read my Bible and my *Science and Health*.[5]

I feel only sadness for the loneliness my mother must have endured as a young woman. Her response to *Four Friends* becomes clearer when viewed through key psychological frameworks: as Jungian shadow projection, where she attacked in others what she couldn't accept in herself, and perhaps even as Freudian reaction formation, where her extreme rejection of sexuality masked her own desires. These patterns emerged clearly in light of her teenage heartache. And her sense of isolation might even trace back before birth: My grandmother's abortion attempt was in effect a rejection of her daughter. I compare it to the psychological consequences of being put up for adoption, a core wound that impacts a child for life.

However, this doesn't fully explain how an elementary school girl came to internalize fatphobia, equating body size with moral corruption. Why would she call a voluptuous dancer evil, and what could have instilled such a damaging belief? Could this early sexual body shame also be at the root of her lifelong food obsession and *orthorexia*? These reactions might also be due in part to parentification, through which my mother was thrust into a confusing and unsafe adult world. It's no surprise she recoiled from the social complexity of young love, retreating instead into spiritual books. Her sex-negative outlook mirrored her spiritual escapism from her parents' dysfunction and the reality denial of Christian Science. In my mother's virtual world, these pieces fit seamlessly. But she was ill-equipped to fit into the real world.

Years later, my sister Erin would shed further light on our mother's tyranny and sexual conflict in *Prophet's Daughter*. She described a "clearance" session in 1992, a practice in which Erin acted as our mother's spiritual "seer" to obtain divine guidance and access past lives and karmic patterns. During one such session, Erin made a disturbing revelation that Mother accepted as true:

> I 'saw' for her a past life as a power-hungry and puritanical queen on Atlantis. I told her that she had begun with good intentions but ended as a tyrant, executing those who broke her moral code.[6]

At the time, my mother was preparing for a lecture series called "Nine Cats, Nine Lives," examining what she claimed were the past lives of several famous figures, including herself. In one lecture, she described a life where she murdered her first husband Dag in one of *his* previous lives in Denmark—one of the few times she publicly admitted to wrongdoing, even if framed in mythical terms. Privately, during the same tour, she revealed some of her own hidden sexual transgressions to Erin, my youngest sister Tatiana, and me, which shocked us. Then came the biggest bombshell: she casually dismissed the rationale for the harsh sexual repression she had long enforced, saying, "Sex is not that big of a deal."[7]

But it was a lie. Sex had been her obsession and torment, driving her to expel countless people for sexual infractions. I recalled her disproportionate rage about Hollywood's onscreen sex, which made her sudden reversal all the more jarring. But she was changing, and not simply having a change of heart. Her rigid sexual morality began to fracture, along with other cognitive shifts and memory loss that would later make tragic sense. None of us yet knew about her undiagnosed early-onset Alzheimer's disease. By the end of her ministry, she would often make humanizing admissions, only to revert quickly to her Ram personality and dispense harsh punishments. Notably, loss of sexual inhibition is a well-known early Alzheimer's symptom. At the time, I couldn't yet grasp her mental decline—or the childhood origins of her inner conflict.

---

[1] UK Teratology Information Service. (n.d.). *Use of quinine in pregnancy*. Retrieved from https://uktis.org/monographs/use-of-quinine-in-pregnancy/

[2] Prophet, E. C. (1993, July 10). Interview by T. Prophet.

[3] *Holy Bible* (King James Version). (n.d.). Psalm 23:5.

[4] Prophet, E. C. (1993, July 10). Interview by T. Prophet.

[5] Prophet, E. C. (2009). *Preparation for my mission* (T. Prophet & E. L. Prophet, Eds.). Summit Univer-

sity Press. p. 136.

[6] Prophet, E. (2008). *Prophet's daughter: My life with Elizabeth Clare Prophet inside the Church Universal and Triumphant.* Lyons Press. p. 247.

[7] Prophet, E. (2008). *Prophet's daughter: My life with Elizabeth Clare Prophet inside the Church Universal and Triumphant.* Lyons Press. p. 258.

■ ■ ■ ■ ■ ■ ■ CHAPTER SIX ■ ■ ■ ■ ■ ■ ■

Existential Hunger

As I grew up, I yearned for three things that seemed perpetually out of reach: escape from my cult, a normal middle-class American life, and the bright sci-fi future I anticipated for the 21st century. These distant "Middletown Dreams"[1] propelled my imagination far beyond the physical and mental barriers that confined me. From the moment I first heard "Tom Sawyer" in 1981, the music of Rush resonated with every longing I'd ever had—and created new ones. Their futuristic synthesizer sounds struck chords in me I didn't know existed, and their lyrics spoke to my struggle for independence:

No his mind is not for rent, to any God or government.[2]

"Boom!" I shouted, then laughed in sheer delight. The clarity and breadth of that line overwhelmed me in an instant. I have the same feeling about it today.

Rush kindled an optimism and determination I had never thought possible. Each new album marked a milestone in both their artistic evolution and my journey toward personal freedom. I can chart the timeline of my life after 1981 through the Rush discography, remembering precisely where I was when I first heard nearly every song: All-night drives between Los Angeles and Montana, the cramped freedom of my first apartment, an edit bay at Varitel or Stun Creative, even the college parking lot where I sat in my car, transfixed by the release of "Manhattan Project."[3] Each memory is tied to a particular moment when their music goaded me toward a better future. In 1984, at the age of 20, I snuck away from Camelot to attend my first Rush concert at the Inglewood Forum during the *Grace Under Pressure* tour.[4] I was transported to another planet. It was life-changing. That venue would later bookend my Rush journey in 2015.

As Chris McDonald documents in his 2009 book *Rush, Rock Music, and the Middle Class: Dreaming in Middletown*,[5] Rush stood apart from their rock contemporaries in a crucial way. While artists like Bob Dylan and Crosby, Stills, Nash & Young protested injustice and encouraged revolution, Rush reflected the skilled craftsmanship and forward-looking optimism of an educated middle class enjoying post-war prosperity. They valued self-discipline, scientific progress, and earned achievement. Their cerebral lyrics and musical excellence resonated deeply with listeners seeking integration rather than revolution—people like me—who wanted in rather than out. All three band members were from Willowdale, a suburb of Ontario, exactly the kind of place I wanted to live. Having been raised in my mother's world-rejecting cult, I didn't want to change society—I wanted to join it.

In 2012, Rush released their final studio album, *Clockwork Angels*, a meditation on time, existence, and meaning.[6] It marked the culmination of the Canadian trio's storied 40-year career. The scope of the album is breathtaking, reprising and transcending every one of the band's pioneering motifs. It begins with "Caravan," based on themes of adventure and risk-taking in the face of uncertainty.[7] It ends with a poignant send-off called "The Garden," which features tremolando strings and lush orchestration far removed from the band's heavy-metal roots. But it's the lyrics that truly shine, as virtuoso drummer and lyricist Neil Peart shared the wisdom gained from his extraordinary life—with satisfying finality. "The measure of a life," he penned, "is love and respect, so hard to earn, so easily burned."[8]

Three years later on the *R40* tour, I returned to the Inglewood Forum to see Rush play their last-ever performance on August 1, 2015.[9] That night, in a rare move, Peart stepped away from his kit after the encore. He joined frontman Geddy Lee and guitarist Alex Lifeson downstage for their last bow as the crowd roared with emotion—caught between joy and disbelief as some recognized Peart's farewell. I couldn't fathom that he would die just five years later from glioblastoma.[10]

Rush had played a crucial role in my cult exit and deconversion. In some of my darkest hours, their music kept me sane. At their final performance, I was overcome with gratitude for their "powerful visions," which had so influenced my life. Perhaps it's no coincidence that Rush affected me so deeply. Geddy Lee is the son of Holocaust survivors—a journey hinted in "Red Sector A."[11] He wouldn't have been born had his parents not managed to escape the Nazi death cult—a story of survival that he shared in his 2023 autobiography *My Effin' Life*.[12] I feel a special brotherhood with him in his narrow escape to a life of freedom and critical thought.

Peart also embodied superhuman dedication to his craft. Already recognized as one of the world's top drummers, he became a student again in the 1990s, retooling his technique under the tutelage of jazz legend Freddie Gruber. Then he branched out from music, publishing seven nonfiction books documenting his bicycle and motorcycle travels, his literary and musical evolution, and his grief journey following the sudden 1997 and 1998 deaths of his wife and their only child. Though he had written powerful anti-religious songs like "Faithless"[13] and "BU2B (Brought Up To Believe),"[14] Peart was wary of the atheist label, favoring doubt and inquiry. A devotee of Ayn Rand's anticommunist individualism in his early years, he later became what he called a "bleeding-heart-libertarian"—embodying compassion and a love for the mysteries of the natural world.[15] Years after leaving my cult, I followed his philosophical and political trajectory.

It wouldn't be hyperbolic to call Peart a "god" of time. The precision of his drumming was measured in microseconds. He carried on in the face of tragedy that would have broken lesser men. He never wavered from his humanism, describing the allure of faith as "blind men in the market, buying what we're sold." He leveled the peaks and valleys of existence, recognizing that, "The joy and pain that we receive, each comes with its own cost. The price of what we're winning, is the same as what we've lost."

Without leaning on false certitudes, perhaps no one has better vanquished their existential hunger than Neil Ellwood Peart. He set an example of excellence and fortitude, not only for me but for countless fans of his music and books. Peart channeled his angst into an embrace of uncertainty, finding the currency of life within an infinite series of metered instants, composing an eternal now. He embraced his mortality, cared about humanity, and always remained vulnerable. His final lyrics from "The Garden" offered no appeals for salvation, only graceful acceptance: "The future disappears into memory, with only a moment between. Forever dwells in that moment, hope is what remains to be seen."

In the starkest of possible contrasts, Gregory Mull and other members of my cult quelled *their* existential hunger with grandiose illusions—

embracing the path of self-abdication that baits every such spiritual trap. While Peart faced the unknown with resolve, Mull grasped at hollow assurances, losing his agency in the process. His longing for transcendence drove him to surrender his autonomy, unraveling the boundaries that might have otherwise protected him.

Alex Lifeson, Neil Peart and Geddy Lee say goodbye to over 12,000 fans after their final performance as Rush, August 1, 2015, Inglewood Forum, Los Angeles

So let's explore how Mull fell prey to my cult's siren song. In an October 1974 letter, he reports having read *The I AM Discourses*,[16] establishing him as a student of the Mighty I AM cult. As a young man, Mull followed Christian Science and read works by Alice Bailey, a student of Theosophy. After he learned of The Summit Lighthouse through a member of his meditation group, he played my mother's tapes in his home "for weeks." He describes a harrowing aircraft landing, writing that "The I AM Presence brought us in safely. I invoked out loud." It was a seductive conceit of immunity from physical laws, delivered without a trace of irony. Such delusions of grandeur were pervasive in my cult.

A February 1975 letter reveals Mull's hunger for spiritual guidance about what should have remained personal choices. He asked my mother whether his use of the name "Gregory" instead of his birth name "Gaylord" was spiritually acceptable, or whether he should revert to his given name. This placed his core identity in her hands. He also wondered whether getting a vasectomy "did harm to my spiritual being." Then he agonized over fantastical details from a past-life regression and over-committed himself to sacrifice, "May I always give of myself to the service we hold so vital."

Mull's letters confirm that he was already wounded by his spiritual longings. His state of mind was sadly typical of the kinds of people who flocked to my cult during the 1960s and 1970s. Erin believed at the time that Mull was "just one more of my mother's sycophants."[17] When I asked my mother why we attracted so many unstable followers, she would quote the Bible, "They that are whole need not a physician, but they that are sick."[18] Still—our theology couldn't heal anyone. It only tightened the ligatures of their magical thinking.

Mull was also rudderless. In later letters, he sought answers about practical matters and the conduct of his business. He trusted my mother to make decisions for him. In a 1977 letter he wondered whether his girlfriend Kathleen Hammond (whom he later married, then divorced) should attend Summit University, saying, "I leave this decision entirely up to you." Mull's submission to my cult was unwise, and our board should have recognized his lack of boundaries as a danger sign. But my mother was well-accustomed to such fanaticism, and she encouraged it. She, too, tended to pray out loud on airplanes, believing herself capable of commanding God to bend the laws of physics. And she, too lacked boundaries—being all too willing to play guru and dispense personal advice to her followers. After attending Summit University, Mull was asked in court, "would you have done anything that she told you to do?" He replied "Yes, I believe I would."[19]

Gregory Mull ignored his own interests because my cult offered him a prize he valued more: the promise of the ascension. But that carrot came with a stick: the threat of being cast into outer darkness and facing the prospect of endless re-embodiments and the second death. He was willing to do anything to achieve the former and avoid the latter, including walking away from his business and working more than a year without pay, signing promissory notes after the fact for expenses we advanced to him, and finally writing a check for his last $5,000 on June 6, 1980 as a partial settlement for those questionable loans. Mull placed his trust in my mother not because he was coercively persuaded but because he believed that as the messenger of God, she controlled the fate of his soul. And that made him a sitting duck.

The diminished man who wrote that check was nearing retirement age without a means of support. Yet despite knowing it was Mull's last money, my mother cashed it. It was a tragedy for both parties. For Mull, it represented financial ruin—he and his daughter Linda Witt both testified that they scavenged for food in grocery store trash bins.[20] For my mother, it seeded a costly chain of events that led to her public humiliation at trial and helped motivate her millenarian prophecies. What if my mother had shown more empathy? What if Mull had better boundaries? What if she had settled the lawsuit before trial? My mother's air of spiritual infallibility, combined with Mull's fanaticism, trapped them both in mutually assured destruction.

Mull's existential hunger led him to kneel at my mother's feet, grasping at illusions of permanence while relinquishing his hold on selfhood. Yet existential hunger doesn't always cower in compliance. For some, it ignites defiance. Such rebellion forms the beating heart of the classic 1982 film *Blade Runner*, an allegory for our struggle with mortality.[21] The replicant Roy Batty confronts his maker, Dr. Eldon Tyrell, voicing the rage many of us feel: "I want more life, fucker!" When Tyrell couldn't comply, Batty crushed his skull. Given his four-year lifespan, most of us can hard-relate to Batty's anger about his impending death.

But is it so different for us? In cosmic terms, four years, four decades, even four centuries are nothing. Our lifespans are barely longer than the flash of a firefly. Our planet is but a speck, a dust mote, Carl Sagan's "Pale Blue Dot."[22] Our bodies are tiny compared to our planet, which is tinier still compared to our galaxy, which is one among billions of galaxies. We can be forgiven for feeling a bit—small.

The slow speed of light puts us millions of years away from our nearest galactic neighbor Andromeda, making travel impossible. Light seems fast until you're waiting for a photon to get from the Sun to the Earth, which takes eight minutes and 20 seconds. To reach the edge of our solar system, it's more than four hours. Our Sun takes 250 million years to orbit the Milky Way. On a cosmic scale, everything moves at a snail's pace. But the speed of thought has no such limitation. To see Andromeda, at a distance of two million light-years, or GN-z11, a faint red-shifted galaxy 13.4 billion light-years away, is to be able to travel to either one instantly—by imagination.

We evolved in mammalian bodies, clinging to a fragile biosphere. But our minds are capable of being everywhere at once. Contemplating this vast universe and our very small place in it gives rise to powerful feelings, which many frame as spiritual experiences. Described in terms of awe, wonder, or oneness, they contrast with our dark animal fears of mortality, purposelessness, and isolation. These feelings drive our desire to explain existence and represent the core allure of religion and cults. Some avoid groups and cope by withdrawing into nature, ritual, meditation, or whatever else can temporarily make their sense of isolation disappear.

I spoke with sociology of religion expert Dr. Lorne Dawson in 2011 at the University of Waterloo. He challenged Maslow's hierarchy of needs, arguing that for some, the drive for meaning can surpass even survival instincts.[23] And Dawson was eerily prescient, anticipating movements like QAnon and the rise of online cults:

> When people need meaning, they need meaning more than anything else. People's lives are not as important as having meaningful lives, and we always forget that—yet our history is full of it. Every man that ever died in a war, died in part because they thought they were sacrificing their individual life for a greater cause or purpose... Charismatic authority can only gain prominence when other forms of authority, like traditional and legal, rational authority, are in crisis. Under those conditions, people will want to fill the vacuum with something. And they will turn to what will seem to us very strange ideas.

Sociologist Peter Berger's concept of societies as "enterprises of world-building" provides additional clarity. Shared frameworks shape human behavior, but individuals often fail to recognize their own roles in constructing or dismantling these systems. In Chapter 2 of his book *Comprehending Cults: The Sociology of New Religious Movements*, Dawson draws on Berger's analysis:

> Berger proposes, we are eternally trapped between a biologically given imperative to secure a stable and safe environment through culture and the inherent instability of the cultures we create. This is the human predicament. Religion is the ultimate response to this predicament. The success of a culture in providing a stable environment for human development 'depends upon the establishment of symmetry between the objective world of society and the subjective world of the individual.'[24]

Berger uses the term *nomos*, signifying a meaningful world order, as derived from the Greek "law" or "custom." Every society is built on systems that offer practical and psychological reassurance. But when external crises or personal traumas disrupt this stability, individuals experience *anomie*, a sense of rootlessness that can drive them toward religion and cults. Religion portrays the social order as divinely ordained—blending nomos with cosmos. This integration offers a powerful antidote to anomie, making chaotic events appear meaningful. Yet it can also deepen alienation, as individuals surrender their role in shaping society, ceding power to religious authority. Unchecked, this can lead to totalistic theocracy.

Can we ever find a sweet spot between anomie and alienation? Achieving that balance is elusive. As Dawson pointed out, meaning can be more important to some people than life itself. In my journey out of my cult, I gave up on objective meaning altogether. Don't misunderstand me—I'm not saying life is meaningless. I am saying that we are *each solely responsible* to create it for ourselves. This in turn forces us to clarify our values, and strive to connect them to our behavior. Our internal sense of meaning can't be derived from the democratic nomos alone. Nor can it be derived from any man-made construct describing the purported personality, wishes, or agenda of a supernatural being—or of the cosmos itself. Everything we've observed about the universe since The Enlightenment confirms that it's indifferent to our struggles. As Neil Peart observed, we ask, "What is the meaning of this? And the stars look down."[25]

So here's the work: When you're in personal crisis, or feeling a crushing sense of anomie, recognize that there is no external solution. You're feeling what we can all sometimes feel: that dark stew of anxiety and fear of death that's like a black hole, which never stops tugging at your gut. One ex-member of my cult called it "free falling." It's terrifying to realize you have no control over your ultimate fate. Religious and cult marketing exploits this terror by posing largely unanswerable questions, including:

Where do we come from?

Why are we here?

Where do we go when we die?

Terror management theory proposes that drawing attention to these questions ramps up anomie, driving people to seek comfort in cultural beliefs.[26] Many follow that drive into an intense focus on cosmos over nomos: the proposed existence of an immortal soul, salvation, preparation for the afterlife, and a higher purpose. Likewise, soldiers are willing to die because the "righteous cause" blunts the terror of war.

To avoid the terror-management trap, challenge yourself to find reasonable, firmly-grounded answers to those nagging questions. Here are a few strategies that I learned the hard way:

- Don't be rattled by strange coincidences, portents, dreams, visions, or distant natural disasters.
- Avoid superstitions and conspiracy theories at all costs.
- Try to make peace with what you can't explain, or at least set it aside temporarily.

- Recognize the central role of science in discovering the nature of reality.
- Accept that the universe is full of mysteries that may never be solved.
- Develop well-examined, internally consistent core values and an inner sense of direction and purpose, so you're not seeking answers outside yourself.
- Cultivate skepticism.

Effective skepticism is not questioning everything. It requires a nuanced understanding of probability and statistical significance while differentiating causation from correlation. It demands familiarity with the scientific method and the role of empirical evidence and replicability in testing hypotheses. Philosophy of science[27] is crucial for navigating these foundational principles, such as falsifiability,[28] and how science may be degraded by institutional corruption and groupthink, funding biases, and flaws in the peer-review process. Cults and religions never stop attacking science for its caveats and institutional biases. Understanding what science can and cannot do can help insulate you from anti-science broadsides.

Most people are easily tripped up by existential questions, which all came roaring back for me as I struggled to regain my footing after I left my cult. My science education helped ground me. But I've also spent a lifetime in reflection that gave me an internally-consistent framework. What worked for me, might not work for you. So follow your own process of contemplation where it leads.

Where do we come from?

The Big Bang was our creator—a truth more awe-inspiring than any myth.

This theory explains the observed features of our universe, including Cosmic Microwave Background Radiation and expansion. Gravity in the early universe pulled hydrogen atoms together into the first stars and lit the match of fusion, producing helium and heavier elements up to iron. Later, stars exploded or collided, forging elements heavier than iron—like gold and uranium. Leftover gases and dust from prior supernovae formed our Solar

System, including Earth, 4.6 billion years ago. Aside from hydrogen, every atom in your body was formed in the heart of a star. We are all stardust—observing starlight.

Some 4.5 billion years ago, the protoplanet Theia slammed into proto-Earth in an ultra-violent collision that liquefied both bodies, spinning off our Moon and tilting the Earth 23 degrees off its axis of rotation, giving us the seasons. The Moon contributes to our tides and transfers gravitational energy to Earth's molten iron core, which generates the magnetic field that shields life on our planet from high-energy cosmic rays.

Water came to Earth through a combination of comet and asteroid impacts, along with contributions from Earth's mantle outgassing. Asteroids brought organic compounds like methane, ammonia, and amino acids. Complex organic compounds also formed on Earth from lightning, hydrothermal vents, and other natural processes. About 4 billion years ago, RNA and other complex organic molecules interacted with proteins to begin a process of self-replication, eventually forming ribozymes. Those more efficient at replicating were naturally selected in the competitive chemistry of early Earth.

Proto-cells formed between layers of lipids, enclosing precious chemical resources, allowing cells to differentiate themselves, and to interact more precisely with the environment. The evolution of ribosomes allowed protein synthesis from RNA, leading to the evolution of a complex, ancient organism called LUCA (Last Universal Common Ancestor). We continue to learn more about the complexity of LUCA, and the sheer brilliance of ancient Earth biology.[29]

From LUCA came the three great domains of life: archaea, bacteria, and eukaryotes. Those cells began the evolutionary chain first described by Charles Darwin and Alfred Russel Wallace, that led to the Tree of Life, uniting all organisms on Earth.[30] We are descended from LUCA, and from the stars. That understanding represents a solid-gold key to self-knowledge—and peace of mind. For further reading on this fascinating topic, I recommend *Shadows of forgotten ancestors: A search for who we are*, by Carl Sagan and Ann Druyan.[31]

Why are we here?

This question speaks to our ravenous hunger for meaning. With understated petulance, it both demands and asserts a purpose, a plan, and a reason behind our existence. But what if there isn't one? In 1991, Neil Peart defied the question with a declaration, "Because we're here, roll the bones!"[32] Every proposed purpose for existence, or *teleology*, reflects an agenda or speculation. True to his lifelong embrace of uncertainty and risk, Peart's advice is clear: Don't worry about it, seek your fortune, and make the best of your life.

There are two kinds of purpose: universal and individual. Finding universal purpose would require understanding not available to us, including the origins of the Big Bang. But since the Big Bang marks the beginning of spacetime as we understand it, any concept of "before" the Big Bang is nonsensical. The most common solution to such mysteries has always been "God." Yet this merely shifts the question: "What caused God?" People often respond, "God is eternal and has always existed." But if we're speculating, why not propose that the universe has always existed—through a cyclical process or multiverse? These reflections can lead to further philosophical challenges like "Why is there something rather than nothing?" While the question is profound, we cannot conceive of nothingness, and if it existed, we wouldn't be here to discuss it.

Science is not equipped to answer these questions. Yet philosophy and religion keep trying to sidestep its rigor, sometimes claiming, "God is outside of space and time." But this only moves the question back a step: "How did God's realm outside of space and time come to be?" Perpetuating the mystery in a different guise. Like Kurt Vonnegut's two yeast organisms—pondering the meaning of their lives while unknowingly crafting a bottle of champagne—we must accept that any larger purpose to our existence may be forever beyond our grasp.[33] The only resolution is to make peace with limited knowledge. That may be frustrating, but it's better than making up non-answers—and it leaves us free to explore what we *can* understand.

Individual purpose is more accessible. Given a diverse, enriching environment, people gravitate toward specific interests and occupations. But your purpose is not what you do for a living—that's your function. Purpose is a drive that will define your legacy. In peacetime, most people's lives are mundane. Paying bills, taking care of a family, being a good citizen, helping others where possible. On one level, that's good enough! Take credit where it's due. But existential hunger makes people restless. Living a good life doesn't get you into the history books. What does? Creativity, discovery, conquest, and ruling over others. Everyone in history who you've heard about, every last one, did one of those four things, even if they were a peacemaker or reformer.

Will you know your purpose when you find it? Choosing one path means you'll never know the road not taken. Every decision comes with risk and opportunity costs. If you're religious or spiritual, you might seem to hear the voice of God telling you what to do. But it's safe to conclude that there are probably only two sources for that inner voice: the original thoughts of your brain, or some external human source which planted those thoughts in your head. Wondering about God's plan is a passive approach and hard to distinguish from failing to plan at all, which as the cliché goes, is planning to fail. It can lead to fatalism in crisis. "Well, God must not have wanted me to get that job after all." It's a reversion to childhood simplicity, freezing your moral development at Kohlberg stage 1, when your parents decided everything for you.

Religions rarely agree on purpose. Depending on your culture of origin, you might have been taught a very different idea than your neighbor about what God wants. Conflicting visions of God's plan don't just lead to personal confusion—they're a recipe for social division—channeled into nationalism, wars, politics, cults and religious sectarianism. And preferably, friendly competitions like sports.

Purpose can hide narrow agendas. In 2002, Pastor Rick Warren published a bestselling book called *The Purpose Driven Life*.[34] Which isn't about finding *your* unique life's purpose at all. It's telling people their purpose is to be *more Christian*. Worship, fellowship, discipleship, ministry, and mission. But what if you're not Christian? There are Muslim purpose books, too. Like *The Road to Mecca*, by Muhammad Asad.[35] If you're Hindu, you might read *The Laws of the Spirit World*, by Khorshed Bhavnagri.[36] For modern Jews, maybe it's *To Heal a Fractured World: The Ethics of Responsibility*, by Rabbi Jonathan Sacks.[37] These books all contain sound moral principles, but they also assert cultural hegemony over the domain of ethics.

Stripped of sectarian content, what are the commonalities? Altruism and reciprocity. Virtuous behavior and self-reflection. Honesty and justice. The value of community participation. Empathy, mercy and kindness. Reason and responsibility. Seeking knowledge and wisdom. Diversity and tolerance. Peace and conflict resolution. No need to ask why we're here, or what Yahweh or Jesus or Muhammad or Vishnu might want. Just follow a universal recipe for the betterment of humanity, reducing conflict and recognizing how much human beings everywhere share the same concerns.

In conclusion, I want to briefly address the "fine-tuning" hypothesis,[38] which is often presented as a rationale for "intelligent design." This idea rests on retrospective determinism—assuming the universe's constants were "meant" to produce life—and survivorship bias, which ignores the trillions of possible outcomes where life never arose. The fact that we exist to observe these constants does not imply intent or purpose. It simply reflects that, in this universe, the conditions happened to align to make life possible. Viewed in hindsight, the probability of our existence in such a universe is 100 percent, but this does not mean it was predetermined. It's just what happened.

Is Earth the only winner in the cosmic life lottery? That's unlikely. Out of the thousands of exoplanets discovered by looking at a tiny sliver of our galaxy, a few dozen have been found in habitable zones around their stars—defined by conditions which could support liquid water. This means they harbor the common physical processes that gave Earth life: volcanic activity, the formation of organic molecules, and hydrothermal vents, to name a few. It defies logic to believe that because we're here, in a universe with at least 200 billion galaxies and countless planets, everything was tailor-made for only our tiny speck of cosmic dust to sprout life. The whole proposal reeks of arrogance and collective human narcissism. A universe just for us? Even if intelligent fine-tuning were somehow found to be true, it would explain *how* we are here, but it would offer no insights into the larger *why*—leaving us, as always, to grapple with that question ourselves.

Where do we go when we die?

We dissipate. Our awareness ceases, our identity dissolves, and our atoms return to the Earth—dust to dust in biblical terms.[39] We came from the Earth through physical processes, and we return to it the same way. Our consciousness is composed of physical neural firing patterns, and our "meat computer," called the connectome, is more than just our brain.[40] It consists of 200,000 miles of neural fibers that permeate every part of our body, sensing pain and damage and controlling all its systems. The 100 trillion connections between neurons are what make you—you. Everything else in our bodies provides nutritional and oxygen support and locomotion. The spidery, tree-like network of our connectome is the substrate for everything it means to be human. Every shiver of fear, every frisson of pleasure, every thought, memory, emotion, aspiration, longing, love, hate, joy, pain, anticipation, and satisfaction—even feelings of spirituality—are emergent properties of our connectome.

Upon death, our connectome begins to disintegrate as cells decompose. Our neurons are eaten by their own enzymes (autolysis), and later by bacteria (putrefaction)—a process as humbling as it is universal to all living beings. Decomposition is like removing the motherboard and hard drive from a computer and dropping them into a vat of acid. After dissolution, the computer could never function again, and no data could be recovered. The same is true with the connectome. By the law of Conservation of Information, information cannot be destroyed, but it becomes randomized and entangled with the environment in a way that is irretrievable. This dissipation is an irreversible process according to the Second Law of Thermodynamics, which increases the entropy, or disorder, of the universe.

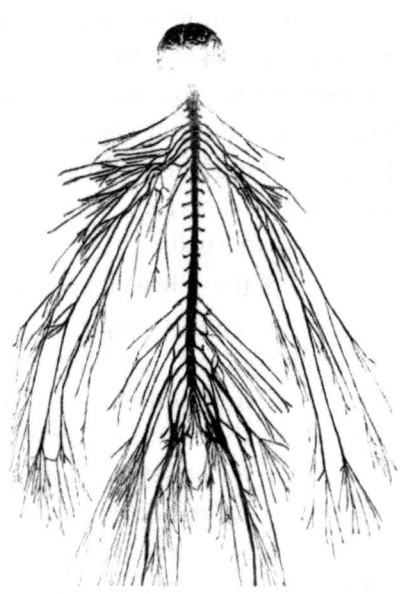

Schematic illustration of the human neural connectome, the source of our identity and experience.

Therefore, to an extremely high degree of probability, death is final. This is supported by all we've learned about physics, chemistry, and biology. It's vanishingly improbable for our 100 trillion neural connections to reconstitute themselves or "go" anywhere after they've broken down. It would take nothing short of pure magic. Most people rebel against this conclusion. No claim is more controversial than the finality of death. Resistance to mortality, with all the mental contortions that entails, is a natural part of our survival instinct. Like Roy Batty, we all "want more life, fucker," even while knowing we almost certainly won't get it. If you're interested in a more detailed scientific exploration of death, there are two highly entertaining books I would recommend: *How We Die: Reflections on Life's Final Chapter* by Sherwin B. Nuland, and *Stiff: The Curious Lives of Human Cadavers* by Mary Roach.

The near-death experience (NDE) is another topic over which barrels of ink have been spilled. Here's what's crucial to remember: People who have NDEs *have not died*. Their neural connectome remains intact. So NDEs tell us nothing about death. They represent highly abnormal brain states in which people see tunnels and light. They imagine traveling to the far reaches of the universe, feeling love and acceptance, often gaining life-changing insights. But these experiences are produced by extreme physiological stress, including oxygen deprivation and the release of endorphins and neurotransmitters. What else creates such experiences? Psychedelic drugs. Dreams. Delirium. This further underscores the neurochemical nature of all our perceptions. No matter how far our thoughts may seem to travel, we never leave our minds, and our brain never leaves our skull.

The idea of a soul separate from the body originates from ancient dualism, refined over centuries by influences like Plato, Aristotle, and Christian Platonism. René Descartes formalized this perspective in the 17th century, proposing that the soul and body are distinct substances.[41] At a time when people couldn't fathom how the body and mind worked, such ideas offered a comforting story of continuity to manage the terror of death. It's impossible to imagine not existing. If you contemplate your own funeral, you'll realize that to be there, you must adopt a third-person perspective. It would take someone alive to look down at your corpse and mourn the loss of your existence. You can't imagine the first-person perspective of death either, because being dead is like nothing at all. You won't be at your funeral, you won't know you're not there, and you won't grieve the loss of your existence.

Grief is for the living.

In this chapter, I've explored three central existential questions. My brief reflections won't satisfy everyone. Predictable objections will involve scientism, logical positivism, reductionism, the hard problem of consciousness, and specious claims about quantum physics, along with the argument from ignorance—an enduring diversion.

The argument from ignorance, or *ad ignorantiam*, is a logical fallacy that occurs when one claims something is true because it has not been proven false, or conversely, asserts something is false because it has not been proven true. This fallacy overlooks the possibility that the evidence may be unavailable, undiscovered, or insufficient to prove a proposition either true or false. It improperly shifts the burden of proof, suggesting a lack of contrary evidence is equivalent to evidence of truth or falsity.

Science continues to unlock the mysteries of the universe, offering profound insights into the forces that led to our existence.[42] What remains unknown is far greater than what we know, but within that uncharted frontier lies infinite potential for discovery.

I've come to trust the answers science provides—answers that evolve over time, tested through experience. Fundamental principles like gravity and evolution are *theories*, but they are also *facts*, supported by overwhelming evidence.[43] These theories are not going away. They will be refined but are unlikely to be replaced.

Two challenges often cited as weaknesses of science are worth addressing. Some argue science may never fully explain consciousness, suggesting *panpsychism* could reveal it as a fundamental property of the universe, akin to matter, energy, space, and time.[44] While this is possible, it would *still* leave consciousness as a physical property, with the neural connectome as the specific arrangement giving rise to self-awareness.

The second challenge involves dark matter and dark energy—constructs we've never directly observed, yet essential to our current cosmological model. If they don't exist, we might need an entirely new framework for understanding the universe. Far from undermining science, these challenges illustrate its strength: the capacity to evolve and refine paradigms in response to new evidence.

We may never grasp the totality of objective reality, but science allows us to describe parts of it with *functional accuracy*—illuminating how the universe works and our place within it. Science focuses on what can be proven and predicted, delivering concrete results: much longer lives and better health, images of our universe going back almost to the beginning of time, and artificial intelligence that is beginning to rival our own. That bright 21st-century sci-fi future I imagined while listening to Rush all those years ago is closer than ever, yet cult-like thinking has thwarted much of what we could have already accomplished.

What have religions and cults achieved, and what revolutionary spiritual advances have they delivered? Their methods have remained unchanged for centuries, exploiting fear and uncertainty while cloaking fabrications in authority. During the 14th-century Black Plague, religion blamed sin and divine wrath. Today, faiths promote vaccine exemptions that undermine public health. Faith systematically attacks the foundations of scientific thinking, beginning with childhood indoctrination and extending through every level of education and discourse. Faith thrives on what science hasn't explained—or science people refuse to believe—preying on existential dread. Don't let these diversions knock you off balance.

Inside my cult, I grew accustomed to weak, made-up answers from people pretending to know things they didn't know. No cult leader knows God's plan or your purpose. Their advice—on parenting, health, or politics—lacks any grounding in expertise. If their doctrines held any truth, their "sacred science" would be taught at universities. Clarifying your relationship to these big existential questions is critical to your safety. Take as long as you need. Because unless your answers bring you inner peace, they won't stick.

The competition between intellectuals and holy men is eternal. Outside of peer-reviewed science, anyone who claims to have the answers is either mistaken or lying. If you don't know who you are, where you came from, and how to determine what's true, you're vulnerable to being gaslit by charismatic figures. Without a well-examined sense of purpose, you'll find people eager to impose one upon you.

But you already have something better. Science offers no comforting illusions but gives you the freedom to ask questions and the tools to find answers—not handed down from "on high," but through testable conclusions you can reach yourself. The existential questions used to scare you—Where did we come from? Why are we here? Where do we go when we die?—represent frontiers you can explore. In doing so, you create your own purpose, grounded in the sheer wonder of existence. And that's not just enough—it's everything.

---

[1] Peart, N., Lee, G., & Lifeson, A. (1985). *Middletown dreams* [Song]. On *Power windows*. Anthem Records.

[2] Rush. (1981). Tom Sawyer [Song]. On *Moving Pictures* [Album]. Anthem Records.

[3] Peart, N., Lee, G., & Lifeson, A. (1985). *Manhattan Project* [Song]. On *Power Windows*. Anthem Records.

[4] Rush. (1984). Grace Under Pressure Tour [Concert tour]. Various locations.

[5] McDonald, C. (2009). *Rush, rock music, and the middle class: Dreaming in Middletown*. Indiana University Press.

[6] Rush. (2012). *Clockwork angels* [Album]. Anthem Records.

[7] Lee, G., Lifeson, A., & Peart, N. (2012). Caravan [Song]. On *Clockwork Angels*. Anthem Records.

[8] Peart, N., Lee, G., & Lifeson, A. (2012). *The Garden* [Song]. On *Clockwork Angels*. Anthem Records.
[9] Rush. (2015). R40 Live Tour [Concert tour]. Various locations.
[10] Hiatt, B. (2020, January 10). Neil Peart, Rush Drummer Who Set a New Standard for Rock Virtuosity, Dead at 67. *Rolling Stone*. Retrieved from https://www.rollingstone.com/music/music-news/neil-peart-rush-obituary-936221
[11] Peart, N., Lee, G., & Lifeson, A. (1984). *Red Sector A* [Song]. On *Grace Under Pressure*. Anthem Records.
[12] Lee, G. (2023). *My effin' life*. Harper.
[13] Lee, G., Lifeson, A., & Peart, N. (2007). Faithless [Song]. On *Snakes & Arrows* [Album]. Anthem Records.
[14] Lee, G., Lifeson, A., & Peart, N. (2012). BU2B [Song]. On *Clockwork Angels*. Anthem Records.
[15] Greene, A. (2012, June 12). Neil Peart on Rush's New LP and Being a 'Bleeding Heart Libertarian'. *Rolling Stone*. Retrieved from https://www.rollingstone.com/music/music-news/qa-neil-peart-on-rushs-new-lp-and-being-a-bleeding-heart-libertarian-234779/
[16] Ballard, G. W. (1935). *The "I AM" Discourses*. Saint Germain Press.
[17] Prophet, E. (2018). *Coercion or conversion? A case study in religion and the law: CUT v. Mull v. Prophet*. Linden Books. p. 15
[18] Luke 5:31 KJV
[19] CUT v. Mull, Superior Court of Los Angeles County C. 358191, (February 11, 1986) at 108:15-17
[20] CUT v. Mull, Superior Court of Los Angeles County C. 358191, (February 24, 1986) at 958:4-14
[21] Scott, R. (Director). (1982). *Blade Runner* [Film]. Warner Bros.
[22] Sagan, C. (1994). *Pale blue dot: A vision of the human future in space*. Random House.
[23] Maslow's Hierarchy of Needs (1943): Five-tier psychological framework categorizing human needs in ascending importance. Base level contains physiological needs (food, shelter), followed by safety needs (security, protection). Social needs (belonging, love) form the middle tier, followed by esteem needs (respect, recognition). Self-actualization crowns the pyramid, representing the achievement of full potential and creative fulfillment. The model demonstrates how basic needs must be satisfied before individuals can effectively pursue higher-level growth needs.
[24] Dawson, L. L. (2006). *Comprehending Cults: The Sociology of New Religious Movements* (2nd ed.). Oxford University Press. p.15
[25] Rush. (2002). The Stars Look Down [Song]. On *Vapor Trails* [Album]. Atlantic Records.
[26] Terror Management Theory (TMT): Developed by social psychologists Solomon, Greenberg & Pyszczynski (1980s), drawing from Ernest Becker's *The Denial of Death* (1973). Theory explains how awareness of mortality creates existential anxiety, which humans manage through cultural beliefs and values providing meaning and immortality concepts. Shows how death anxiety fundamentally influences human behavior through cultural worldviews, self-esteem maintenance, and pursuit of symbolic or literal immortality.
[27] Philosophy of Science: Studies foundations, methods, and implications of scientific inquiry. Examines nature and validity of scientific theories, processes of scientific investigation, structure of scientific explanations, and ethical dimensions of scientific practice. Analyzes how scientific knowledge is generated, justified, and applied, exploring the complex relationship between science and society.
[28] Falsifiability (Popper): Fundamental principle in scientific philosophy stating that for a theory to be considered scientific, it must be possible to conceive an observation or experiment that could prove it false. This criterion distinguishes scientific theories from non-scientific ones through emphasis on testable, potentially disprovable claims.
[29] Moody, E. R. R., Álvarez-Carretero, S., Mahendrarajah, et al. (2024). The nature of the last universal common ancestor and its impact on the early Earth system. *Nature Ecology & Evolution*. https://doi.org/10.1038/s41559-024-02461-1

[30] Darwin, C. (1859). *On the origin of species by means of natural selection, or the preservation of favoured races in the struggle for life.* John Murray; Wallace, A. R. (1858). *On the tendency of varieties to depart indefinitely from the original type.* Journal of the Proceedings of the Linnean Society, 3(9), 53-62.

[31] Sagan, C., & Druyan, A. (1992). *Shadows of forgotten ancestors: A search for who we are.* Random House.

[32] Rush. (1991). Roll the Bones [Song]. On *Roll the Bones* [Album]. Anthem Records.

[33] Vonnegut, K. (1981). *Palm Sunday: An autobiographical collage.* Delacorte Press.

[34] Warren, R. (2002). *The purpose driven life: What on earth am I here for?* Zondervan.

[35] Asad, M. (1954). *The road to Mecca.* Simon & Schuster.

[36] Bhavnagri, K. (2007). *The laws of the spirit world.* Jaico Publishing House.

[37] Sacks, J. (2005). *To heal a fractured world: The ethics of responsibility.* Schocken Books.

[38] Fine-tuning hypothesis: Proposes that life exists because fundamental physical constants fall within extremely narrow ranges necessary for matter, astronomical structures, and life to develop. Suggests either deliberate intelligent design of these precise parameters or the existence of multiple universes where our universe happens to have life-supporting constants.

[39] Genesis 3:19 KJV

[40] Neuroscientists increasingly recognize that the connectome extends beyond the brain, incorporating the spinal cord and peripheral nervous system in a complex, interconnected network. Irimia, A., & Van Horn, J. D. (2021). Mapping the rest of the human connectome: *Atlasing the spinal cord and peripheral nervous system. NeuroImage,* 225, 117478. https://doi.org/10.1016/j.neuroimage.2020.117478

[41] Robinson, H. (2020). *Dualism.* In E. N. Zalta (Ed.), *The Stanford Encyclopedia of Philosophy* (Fall 2020 Edition). Stanford University. Retrieved from https://plato.stanford.edu/entries/dualism/

[42] Noble, D. (2024, February 5). It's time to admit that genes are not the blueprint for life. *Nature.* Retrieved from https://www.nature.com/articles/d41586-024-00327-x

[43] Fact vs Theory in Science: Facts are observations consistently confirmed and accepted as true (objects fall toward Earth). Theories provide well-substantiated explanations incorporating facts, laws, inferences, and tested hypotheses. Gravity exemplifies both fact (objects attract) and theory (general relativity explains space-time warping). Evolution similarly demonstrates fact (species change over time, share ancestors) and theory (natural selection explains mechanisms). Both supported by extensive empirical evidence explaining diverse phenomena.

[44] Stanford Encyclopedia of Philosophy. (n.d.). Panpsychism. Retrieved from https://plato.stanford.edu/entries/panpsychism/

CHAPTER SEVEN

Conspirituality

What would it take to create a viral online movement that could convince left-wing anti-establishment hippies and social-justice progressives to espouse the tenets of right-wing authoritarianism? Seems like a tall order. Yet it's already been accomplished through the QAnon conspiracy theory that burst onto the scene in 2017 and the broader conspirituality movement.[1] To understand why this worked, I'll identify the connections between progressivism and fascism—its polar opposite.

The ancient Chinese *Taijitu* symbol connects dualities with their counterparts. The key overlap between authoritarian cults and organic alt-health spirituality is their shared fascination with purity. On the left, it's body, mind, and environment. On the right, it's order, nation, and race. Pure food and clean drinking water? Very good. Pure bloodlines? A precursor to ethnic cleansing.

Purification contains the seeds of toxicity, because no matter how pure you might be, you can always be more pure. This connects purity to its counterpart, perfection. It's an anti-science combination because nothing in the universe is pure or perfect. The closest we ever get is through "God" mythologies, or metaphysics like Plato's theory of forms.[2] Nature and the human condition are defined by imperfection and entropy. Biology and evolution are "just good enough."[3]

Conspirituality traps progressives into adopting conservative values by exchanging the ideal of purity-perfection between physical and moral domains. This can lead people to confuse beauty with goodness, health with virtue, and order with morality. Such notions pervade the world's scriptures, prompting 18th-century theologian John Wesley to declare, "Cleanliness is next to godliness."[4] People lacking modern sanitation might have embraced the corollary: filth is of the "devil."

The drive for purity taps our primal disgust reflex. While this protects us from pathogens in sewage, rotting flesh, and vomit, disgust is also triggered by swarming insects, slithering snakes, blood, bile, or any smells and textures that suggest danger. It's a base emotion that triggers the amygdala and easily transfers from the physical to the moral domain, targeting "contaminating" ideas like socialism or race/gender equality, fostering hatred of "contagious" immigration, loathing of gay or gender non-conforming people, and condemning modern art as "degeneracy."

The prosocial lefty-hippie drive for purity targets "disgusting" pollution, pesticides, GMOs, and preservatives. Yet it's the same poisoned false dichotomy. Pesticides and GMOs increase crop yields and nutrition.[5] Preservatives prevent natural pathogens from spoiling food. Focusing solely on the absence of genetic modification—or succumbing to chemophobia—ignores these tradeoffs.

Disgust over perceived violations of bodily purity united the MAGA right and alt-health left in vaccine and mask refusal. Both promote body fascism, victim-blaming people with "unfit" or "impure" bodies, and both view the spread of disease as a moral failing. Their shared hatred of the medical establishment—with its "contaminating" vaccines and dismissal of natural immunity—extends to broader distrust of science and institutions.

This culminated in baseless accusations about the origin of SARS-CoV-2 (COVID-19)—from a "lab leak" in Wuhan, to conspiracy theories about "big pharma" engineering the virus. But genetic evidence points firmly to a zoonotic origin.[6] In January 2025, the CIA waded into the highly politicized controversy with a new assessment favoring the lab leak theory. But it hedged its claim as "low confidence," and provided only fragmentary intelligence to support it.[7]

The best evidence that COVID-19 came from animals is that it shares 96 percent of its genes with a bat virus called RaTG13 and is even closer to BANAL-52, a virus from Laos.[8] The virus has a furin cleavage site (FCS) that helps it infect cells, but there's no sign it was artificially inserted. If COVID-19 had leaked from a lab, scientists would have found clear genetic markers, such as restriction enzyme sites (cut-and-paste marks from genetic modification) or unnatural codon usage (signs of lab-based synthesis).[9] The FCS would also show insertion scars, which are absent. Additionally, early cases clustered at the Huanan Seafood Market, not near any lab.[10] These facts, combined with decades of research showing that coronaviruses frequently jump from animals to humans, overwhelmingly confirm a natural origin for COVID-19, with no evidence of a lab leak.

After the December 2020 rollout of Pfizer-BioNTech and Moderna vaccines, notions of bodily purity fueled conspiracies about vaccine contagion—that vaccinated people could "infect" the non-vaccinated. Florida's Centner Academy threatened to fire vaccinated teachers under this pretext.[11] Described as a cult by former teachers and parents, Centner spread alt-health disinformation, ignored Covid protocols, and stoked fears about radiation from 5G towers. Such stories are depressingly common.

Those rejecting conventional medicine and vaccines rarely succeed at keeping themselves pure. They often take unregulated alt-health nostrums made from contaminated or dangerous ingredients. Many drink raw milk, which is teeming with pathogens.[12] "Natural" does not mean safe. Some plants produce toxins, which can be especially dangerous when herbal extracts are concentrated. Countless unregulated "natural" supplements have been found to contain heavy metals or even pharmaceutical drugs.

Toxic purity culture seems to dominate despite its terrible consequences. Post-Covid, these effects are stark: Growing vaccine refusal is now hardening into a political identity. Viruses we conquered *last century*, like measles and polio, are surging in the United States. The erosion of herd immunity for preventable diseases marks a new public health crisis—a deadly infodemic spread through the novel disease vector of online disinformation. In the second Trump administration, anti-vaccine extremist Robert F. Kennedy Jr. wields broad authority to reverse decades of public health progress.

The book *Conspirituality: How New Age Conspiracy Theories Became a Health Threat* by Derek Beres, Matthew Remski, and Julian Walker explains why conspirituality skews right.[13] The reasons include failures of global institutions, pandemic fears caused by lockdowns and millions of deaths, and rampant disinformation. The authors' collective cult experience parallels my own and expands on it, with copious examples of the madness of popular alt-health influencers. It's essential reading if you want to understand the connection between new-age fundamentalism and fascism.

Traditional cults are *authoritarian*, built on the deification of the leader and enforced through Lifton's eight principles of thought reform: doctrine, discipline, purity, confession, and so on. Yet a softer path has emerged. Extremism researcher Marc-Andre Argentino describes "Pastel QAnon," new-age cults that lead with unconditional love, acceptance, nurturing, meditation, yoga, and health, wrapping their message in pastel, feminine colors.[14] These seemingly opposite approaches confirm the *Taijitu* paradox of conspirituality.

Pastel QAnon cult Love Has Won was founded by Amy Carlson who called herself "Mother God." She preached unconditional love and world transformation but delivered authority, punishment, hypocrisy, delusion, idolatry, and thought reform—leading to her death. The 2023 HBO documentary, *Love Has Won: The Cult of Mother God*, directed by Hannah Olson, was culled from hundreds of hours of behind-the-scenes and live-streamed footage. Members included ex-military, ex-cons, meth addicts, abuse survivors, and people with eating disorders, all fixated on unconditional love while projecting their inner turmoil onto an imaginary "5D" galactic conflict.

Love Has Won was a level-ten reality-distortion engine. Despite its feminine branding, this cult's embrace of QAnon paralleled right-wing Christian QAnon cults. Both walk the same path of escalating absurdity. Members believe Carlson was the nineteen-billion-year-old creator of the universe and oracle for "galactics" like Saint Germain, Robin Williams, John Lennon—and notably *Donald Trump*. In reality, she was a 28-year-old mother of three who quit her job as a McDonald's manager in 2007, left her third husband, and abandoned her children to form a small, nomadic commune of about twenty core members, who gained an online following of thousands.

Carlson and her acolytes offered online counseling sessions and sold skin-care and alt-health products, including colloidal silver, which they treated as a religious sacrament. "Mother God" took a series of lovers she called "Father Gods" and lived a hard-partying lifestyle with escalating use of alcohol, cannabis, and tobacco. Followers dropped their names for spiritual identities like "Commander Buddha," waited on Carlson hand and foot, funded her hobbies, logged her words in handwritten journals, and enabled her worsening addictions. Carlson became increasingly abusive, punishing followers for minor mistakes.

As her health failed, Carlson developed skin lesions, extreme anorexia, and was paralyzed from the waist down. She continued increasing her colloidal silver intake, which turned her skin blue. In August 2020, members brought her to a Kauai beach condo to recuperate. Despite her condition, Carlson's grandiosity was reaching its zenith. On a live stream, she declared herself to be the Hawaiian fire-goddess Pele, enraging indigenous people. Angry demonstrators chased her entourage from the condo, and they needed a police escort to reach the airport.

In April 2021, Carlson died in an Ashland, Oregon hotel. She had so indoctrinated her followers that they refused her final request to go to the hospital. Their drive for purity was highly selective—and deadly. Members brought her body to their Colorado headquarters, where it was kept in a sleeping bag, wrapped in Christmas lights, and placed in a makeshift shrine. Police later discovered her mummified remains. Members believe Carlson never died but physically "ascended." After her death, some rebranded the cult as "5D Full Disclosure," insisting that their Mother God, in league with the "galactics," is still working to transform Earth into a planet of love.

Even after Carlson's death, her members clung to QAnon-inspired dogma, especially its fixation on powerful elites raping children. This reflects another *Taijitu* paradox: the greater the trauma, the more likely someone is to embrace both unconditional love and paranoid hatred. But how can you claim to "love everyone" while obsessing over an "evil cabal?" It's an insanely gross generalization—and false—to claim that anyone with money or power is a pedophile. But it's unsurprising that people who've suffered sexual abuse imagine it's part of an organized plot. The alternative is far worse: accepting that their abuser was likely a trusted family member or friend who escaped justice.

Violence, sexual abuse, natural disasters, attachment disruptions, chronic stress, environmental toxicity, and health issues can "freeze" cognitive[15] development—which remains stuck at whatever developmental stage was not passed successfully. For example, children molested during Piaget's pre-operational (ages 2-7) or concrete (ages 7-11) stages may live in very small worlds. If *their* world is filled with child abusers, it's as if *the* world is filled with them. It takes formal operational cognitive skills formed after age twelve to understand that one's own childhood world was quite small and may not generalize to the entire world.

Trauma also freezes moral development, creating another purity paradox: the more someone yearns for perfect love, the more likely they are to remain trapped in simplistic moral frameworks. Many victims focus on "unconditional love" because they crave what they never received from abusive families and partners. Their pursuit of purity keeps them locked in perfectionist thought patterns linked to Kohlberg's stages 1 and 2 of moral development.[16] Stage 1 focuses on obedience and punishment (ages 4-7), while Stage 2 emphasizes self-interest and recognizing that not all adults agree (ages 7-10).

Very young children often get unconditional love from parents and caregivers. Adults frozen in these early stages by abuse or neglect may idealize a state of total dependence, retreating into childlike magical thinking: "If mommy loves daddy, and daddy loves mommy, and they both love me, the world is okay." This infantile model of moral absolutes is all-or-nothing, explaining why conspirituality movements combine universal love with universal paranoia.

This childlike model of morality stands in stark contrast to mature moral development. Kohlberg's stages 3 (ages 10-13) and 4 (ages 13-16 and up) move into a world where reciprocity replaces unconditional love. At these stages, people recognize that relationships require give-and-take, and that laws and norms exist because they benefit everyone. Stage 5 (ages 16 and up) introduces the social contract, where differing values and individual rights can coexist, while Stage 6 represents morality based on universal ethical principles.

Humans are hard-wired for reciprocity, rewarding those who help others in close, tribal communities of 150 people or fewer. Reciprocity doesn't function well on a national or global scale, though many wish it did. That longing often surfaces in quotes like Martin Luther King Jr.'s: "Hate cannot drive out hate; only love can do that." It reflects Christianity's "turning the other cheek," and Gandhi's nonviolence. But without accountability, unconditional love becomes a deceptive form of magical thinking. People with unresolved trauma desperately want it to be true.

The more someone has been traumatized, the more likely they are to believe that their thoughts, feelings, and expressions of love can curb violence, heal others, and improve the world. Such magical thinking mirrors Piaget's pre-operational stage of childhood development (ages 2 to 7). A child at this stage can make perceptual errors, such as believing that if they cover their own eyes, no one can see them. It's equally immature to believe that loving everyone could ever stop violence.

Moving beyond magical thinking requires practical experience with real social dynamics. Let's consider healthy moral development in post-pubescent teens, as they learn to navigate larger social systems with competing cliques. They know they can't just love their enemies. Instead, they learn functional strategies. The nerds might never beat the cool kids in a popularity contest. But they can develop the skills to move from Kohlberg stage 4 to stage 5, forming stable arrangements where it's in no one's best interest to antagonize the other group beyond a certain point. This involves transcending conformity and compliance and giving up on perfection. No one can force their moral standards onto their rivals, so they learn to accept messy solutions, because those still work better than all-out war. This is relevant beyond middle-school competition.

Compromise is crucial to adult conflict-management and international diplomacy. Even nuclear deterrence and arms-control treaties rely on non-zero-sum collaboration.[17] The fantasy of pure love solving all conflicts must give way to negotiated coexistence.

Love represents one of the most powerful emotions in the human experience, making it ripe for exploitation and abuse. Unconditional love can be an avenue for this dark side—representing a lack of boundaries. It means you'll treat a violent abuser, criminal, or assailant the same as you would treat a cherished partner or responsible friend. How is that fair to the responsible friend? How is that not enabling to the abuser? How does that keep you safe? The only force that ever stops evil is accountability. The erroneous goal of "loving unconditionally" plays right into the *Taijitu*: it's the stereotypical caricature of the feminine as a passive doormat. A personality type which is the polar opposite of—and partner to—patriarchal dominance, and authoritarian cult leadership.

---

[1] QAnon, a popular internet conspiracy theory that's a modern version of the 1,000-year-old anti-Semitic "blood libel," claims that a "cabal" of global elites, sometimes described as lizard-people, engages in widespread sex trafficking and extraction of the blood of children.

[2] Plato's theory of Forms posits that the physical world is not "real" in the fullest sense, but rather consists of imperfect reflections of perfect Forms that exist in a higher realm of reality. Retrieved from https://plato.stanford.edu/entries/plato-metaphysics/

[3] Evolutionary "satisficing" explains why natural selection favors traits that are merely sufficient for survival rather than optimal. Constraints from genetics and the environment result in trade-offs rather than perfection. Orzack, S. H., & Sober, E. (2001). *Adaptationism and optimality*. Cambridge University Press. https://doi.org/10.1017/CBO9780511609084

[4] "Cleanliness is next to godliness." Commonly attributed to John Wesley (18th century), though the

precise source is unverified.

[5] Golden Rice, a genetically modified rice engineered with daffodil and *Erwinia uredovora* genes, was developed to produce beta-carotene and combat vitamin A deficiency in developing nations. Clinical trials confirmed its effectiveness as a vitamin A source, demonstrating that its beta-carotene is efficiently converted to vitamin A in humans, though it continues to face regulatory and acceptance challenges. Ye, X., Al-Babili, S., Klöti, A., Zhang, J., Lucca, P., Beyer, P., & Potrykus, I. (2000). Engineering the provitamin A (β-carotene) biosynthetic pathway into (carotenoid-free) rice endosperm. Science, 287(5451), 303–305. https://doi.org/10.1126/science.287.5451.303 Tang, G., Qin, J., Dolnikowski, G. G., Russell, R. M., & Grusak, M. A. (2009). Golden Rice is an effective source of vitamin A. *The American Journal of Clinical Nutrition*, 89(6), 1776–1783. https://doi.org/10.3945/ajcn.2008.27119

[6] Analysis of COVID-19's origins demonstrates the persistent spread of lab leak speculation despite robust scientific evidence for zoonotic emergence. See Holmes et al. (2021). The origins of SARS-CoV-2: A critical review. Cell, 184(19), 4848-4856. https://doi.org/10.1016/j.cell.2021.08.017

[7] Barnes, J. E. (2025, January 25). C.I.A. *now favors lab leak theory to explain Covid's origins. The New York Times.* https://www.nytimes.com/2025/01/25/us/politics/cia-covid-lab-leak.html

[8] Zhou, P., Yang, X.-L., Wang, X.-G., Hu, B., Zhang, L., Zhang, W., ... Shi, Z.-L. (2020). A pneumonia outbreak associated with a new coronavirus of probable bat origin. Nature, 579(7798), 270–273. https://doi.org/10.1038/s41586-020-2012-7

[9] Andersen, K. G., Rambaut, A., Lipkin, W. I., Holmes, E. C., & Garry, R. F. (2020). The proximal origin of SARS-CoV-2. *Nature Medicine*, 26(4), 450–452. https://doi.org/10.1038/s41591-020-0820-9

[10] Worobey, M., Levy, J. I., Malpica Serrano, L., Crits-Christoph, A., Pekar, J. E., Goldstein, S. A., ... Lemey, P. (2022). The Huanan Seafood Wholesale Market in Wuhan was the early epicenter of the COVID-19 pandemic. *Science, 377*(6609), 951–959. https://doi.org/10.1126/science.abp8715

[11] Wright, C., & Nehamas, N. (2021, April 26). Miami private school Centner Academy won't employ vaccinated teachers, staff. Miami Herald, republished in *Tampa Bay Times*. Retrieved from https://www.tampabay.com/news/education/2021/05/01/inside-the-florida-school-that-told-teachers-not-to-get-vaccinated/

[12] Support for raw milk has switched parties, an important indicator of the Conspiritualist realignment. Novicoff, M. (2024, March 10). *How raw milk went from a Whole Foods staple to a conservative signal*. Politico. https://www.politico.com/news/magazine/2024/03/10/the-alt-right-rebrand-of-raw-milk-00145625

[13] Beres, D., Remski, M., & Walker, J. (2023). *Conspirituality: How New Age Conspiracy Theories Became a Health Threat*. PublicAffairs.

[14] Argentino, M.-A. (2021, March 17). Pastel QAnon. Global Network on Extremism and Technology. https://gnet-research.org/2021/03/17/pastel-qanon/

[15] Piaget's cognitive development stages: Sensorimotor (0-2 years) sensory experience and object permanence; Preoperational (2-7 years) symbolic play and egocentrism; Concrete Operational (7-11 years) logical thinking and conservation; Formal Operational (12+ years) abstract reasoning.

[16] Kohlberg's stages of moral development: Stage 1 (ages 2–7): Punishment and obedience. Stage 2 (ages 7–10): Individual instrumental purpose. Stage 3 (ages 10–16): Mutual interpersonal expectations, relationships, and conformity. Stage 4 (ages 16–early adulthood): Law and order. Stage 5 (adulthood, if reached): Social contract. Stage 6 (rarely reached): Universal ethical principles.

[17] Non-zero-sum scenarios allow mutual gain or loss for all participants, contrasting with zero-sum situations where gains and losses must balance.

CHAPTER EIGHT

Puritoxic Madness

When I was five, my dad took me to a health spa and gym in Colorado Springs. It had weight-lifting machines, vibrating-belt machines, saunas, steam rooms, and whirlpool tubs. I thought it was neat. But soon, my mother insisted we become vegetarian, and Dad reluctantly gave up meat and anything with cholesterol. He was just past 50 and had suffered from high blood pressure, ulcers, kidney and bladder stones, and at least one heart attack. He also read *The Miracle of Fasting* by Paul Bragg,[1] and other health books. Before then, we used to go out for hamburgers, and buffets like Furr's cafeteria. His wellness kick, driven as much by necessity as my mother's resolve, brought all that to an end.

When my parents changed their diet, our family and staff followed suit. Fasting and vegetarianism were only the beginning. There were endless vitamin and mineral supplements, tinctures and tonics, and lines of multi-level-marketed products like Shaklee. We dove into Dr. Bronners, Dr. Jensen, and Bragg health products. In June 1972, Dad launched The Four Winds Organic Center, a health food store, restaurant, juice bar, and bakery in downtown Colorado Springs. It was a nice, upscale eatery with a decent-sized banquet room where we hosted family and cult events, some even featuring live music. In his final months, Dad spent considerable time at the Four Winds, chatting up customers and introducing them to his spiritual ideas.

The store featured a commercial bakery and gave us wholesale access to bulk health foods, appliances, and products. This meant we always had the latest thing, including water-purification systems like distillers, de-ionizers, and reverse osmosis units. We had juicers—first Acme, then Champion, and eventually a commercial-grade Norwalk hydraulic juicer. We made ourselves willing guinea pigs for any health fad.

Many of our members suffered from chemophobia—an irrational fear of substances based solely on their chemical names. You might be afraid to drink "dihydrogen monoxide," until you realize it's just water. Chemophobia often targets "ultra-processed foods" with their long lists of chemical ingredients. While ultra-processed foods can contain harmful additives like nitrites, dyes, and trans fats, most chemophobes lack the expertise to distinguish between safe and toxic ingredients. It's easier to categorically reject processed foods than to understand what's actually in them. That's why I'm grateful for the FDA and its generally-recognized-as-safe (GRAS) guidelines.[2] But conspiritualists often scoff at three-letter government agencies, ranking them only slightly above Satan. Two humorous examples of chemophobia in my cult were our irrational fears of monosodium glutamate (MSG), which is on the GRAS list, and aluminum chlorohydrate, a category 1 ingredient deemed safe and effective by the FDA.

MSG is the sodium salt of glutamic acid, a non-essential amino acid naturally produced by the human body. The glutamate ion enhances flavor by stimulating umami receptors on the tongue. MSG occurs naturally in many foods like tomatoes, miso, seaweed, peas, corn, broccoli, soy sauce, parmesan cheese, and fermented foods. Growing up, we were wary of restaurant food, especially Chinese food, fearing it might contain MSG. Caregivers would scrutinize food labels, and if MSG was listed, we weren't allowed to eat it. Meanwhile, we consumed soy sauce, Braggs Liquid Aminos, and the Nestlé condiment Maggi—all brimming with glutamic acid, which releases the same free glutamate ion as MSG. Apparently, ignorance of chemistry was bliss.

Aluminum chlorohydrate is used in antiperspirants to temporarily block sweat ducts. When I was old enough to need deodorant, I was warned to avoid products containing aluminum, which my caregivers insisted was toxic. Meanwhile, many people in my cult used "crystal salt" deodorant, believing it to be a natural alternative. Years later, I discovered that crystal salt is potassium alum—an aluminum compound! Potassium alum inhibits bacterial growth rather than blocking sweat ducts, but the chemophobes in my cult didn't grasp this distinction. They prioritized their self-concept as users of pure and natural products—avoiding worldly contamination. Understanding takes effort, while knee-jerk chemophobia offers a frisson of false superiority.

Concretizing his health kick, Dad eventually had a sauna and steam room installed in our basement, along with a high-colonic machine. Yes, I was forced to endure colonics. We also had a Diapulse machine that emitted pulsed electromagnetic fields that were claimed to speed the healing of wounds.[3] After I broke my leg at age eight, I got Diapulse treatments by the hour. There was a "Z-ray" machine that produced electric arcs and ozone—a toxic form of oxygen. It smelled like burning insulation with a hint of bleach and left a metallic taste in my throat. My parents also had a "Violet Wand" high-voltage generator attached to a glowing argon-filled tube for electrical skin stimulation.

Our home was a mecca for alternative therapies, including staff chiropractors who practiced muscle testing.[4] For a year or two, my mother insisted that everyone fast on water for their birthday. Of course that meant no birthday cakes. I was grateful that practice didn't last. When I was about ten, my mom took my sisters and me to see Dr. Jensen, a Los Angeles iridologist. He diagnosed disease by examining the iris and then prescribed dietary changes. In my case, orange juice and French fries were *out*.

The diets and alt-health treatments did not prolong my father's life. About three years after starting his health regime, he died instantly of a massive stroke on Saturday morning, February 24, 1973, at age 54. While I played with friends, his body lay in the hospital on a ventilator. By that afternoon, I realized that both my parents were missing. Someone mentioned that my father had fallen ill, and my mother was with him. I figured he'd get well soon. But he never came home. On Monday, February 26, my mother turned off his life-support equipment, marking the official date of death.

My sisters and I saw her car pull into our circular driveway and ran outside. She hugged us tightly—much longer than usual. Then she led us to our playground at the south end of our property, and sat us down on the edge of our sandbox. That's when she told us dad was dead. She crumpled a dry leaf in her hand, explaining that his body would return to the Earth just like the leaf, but his spirit would always be with us. She then explained that our father had ascended. We cried, but we didn't understand. We only knew that he was gone. His body was kept on ice for three days, then cremated after his March 1st funeral.

Elizabeth Clare Prophet speaks over the casket of Mark Prophet, draped in an American flag at his funeral, to honor his military service. Colorado Springs, March 1, 1973

After mother completed the memorial service, my sisters and I followed her into the crematory. She opened the casket, which was covered in a gray-patterned velvet. She took my hand tenderly and placed it on his chin through the opaque plastic shroud. "Can you feel daddy's chin?" she asked. "Yes," I replied weakly. It was ice cold. I never got to say goodbye to him. I wanted to rip that damn bag open to see his face one last time, but my mother closed the casket. The moment has haunted me ever since. Why couldn't I see him?

Then the attendants rolled what was left of my father into the scorching incinerator with a deafening whoooosh, and the door slammed shut with a finality that also marked an abrupt end to my childhood. Soon, dad began speaking to us as the "Ascended Master Lanello." It was pretty tough to recognize my mother's words as his. He was gone, but somehow still with us? I was intrigued by the dictations, and I wanted to believe it was really him. But his continued ersatz presence never gave me a chance to grieve. How could I mourn a man who hadn't truly left? Well into my teen years, my mother still gave me birthday cards with a personal message in her handwriting from my ascended father, signed "Lanello"—or simply "Dad."

Following his death, cult members began to wear talisman "scapular" necklaces, with pictures and pouches containing a lock of both my parents' hair. That freaked me out. *Why did they have his hair? Why was my mom's hair in there too? Was she also going to die?* I was simply too young to make sense of my parents' macabre personality cult. If anything was going to happen with my father's remains, wouldn't that have been private to our family? I felt so profoundly violated that I couldn't bring myself to ask my mother why she did it. Nothing about cult life made sense.

Despite the fact that our extreme health practices had failed to save my father's life, they became even more pervasive after his death. We tried everything from raw-food diets to macrobiotics[5] to rejuvelac[6] and wheatgrass juice—even the total elimination of sugar. Then there were the intestinal cleanses: Master Cleanse, Seidlitz Powder, psyllium husks, and frequent enemas. We also embraced William Donald Kelley's "gall-bladder cleanse" from his book *One Answer to Cancer*, which involved fasting for three days on apple juice, followed by Epsom salts and eight ounces of olive oil mixed with lemon juice—which was supposed to trigger the passing of gallstones.[7] Thankfully, I never attempted that regime, which the medical community considers hazardous and ineffective. Among other non-evidence-based "cures" my mother promoted were bentonite clay, dilute sulfuric acid, and even urine.

Yes, *urine*.

Our bizarre urine experiment was inspired by a 1944 book called *The Water of Life: A Treatise on Urine Therapy*, by John W. Armstrong.[8] In addition to the obvious ick factor, drinking urine is dangerous and has no health benefits. I can't fathom a thicker irony—or *Taijitu* paradox—than a purity-focused health dogma that embraced the drinking of bodily waste.

Once, when I was very sick with the flu, my mother insisted that I try the "urine cure." I was disgusted, but I trusted her advice. So I peed in a glass, taking only the "middle stream" urine as recommended by the book. Then I held my nose and downed it, trying not to gag. It was terribly salty and tasted as wretched as you might expect.

But I was unprepared for the physiological effects: my body wanted nothing to do with its waste. I felt a shot of adrenaline, my heart started racing, and I began to hyperventilate and convulse as my system rebelled against the poison. Unable to vomit, I ran to the kitchen and gulped down several glasses of water. I felt miserable for hours. *Fuck!* My mother had failed at her basic parental responsibility to keep me safe. It was a betrayal and a turning point. I swore to myself I would never again trust her health advice.

Later, I came to recognize that my cult's puritoxic madness was a genuine mental-health crisis. My mother endured a lifelong struggle with the eating disorder *orthorexia nervosa*,[9] In a 1993 interview, she remarked that as a young woman she had experienced profound dietary guilt, even before meeting my dad: "I wasn't pure. I ate meat, I ate butter, I ate potatoes, I ate pork... I think spiritual attunement comes when you totally get off all meat, except fish."[10] She was obsessed with her diet, convinced that it directly affected her behavior and state of mind. Food wasn't just nutrition. It was a moral force. She categorized foods as either healing or harmful and felt shame whenever she consumed those she believed would make her ill.

This dichotomy gave her another way to appeal to transcendence while providing yet another lever of control over her staff, whose diets could never be sufficiently pure in her eyes. On one occasion, she gave a "blue ray" (a dressing down) to the entire kitchen staff because someone put raisins in a batch of oatmeal. If anyone caught a cold or flu, she considered it evidence of a wrong diet—and a spiritual failing. She refused to accept that people with functioning immune systems occasionally get sick. And she would victim-blame, saying things like, "You need to get off sugar and get back on a strict macrobiotic diet to build up your immunity. Next time, don't wait to take care of yourself."

Mother subscribed to a form of pseudoscience known as *sympathetic magic*, which posits that objects or beings that resemble each other can influence one another. Regarding food, sympathetic magic involves the transfer of either physical or behavioral characteristics to a person when the food is consumed. This pseudoscience underpins various dietary philosophies she adhered to, such as the macrobiotic diet and Ayurveda.[11]

At the first sign of any respiratory illness or nasal congestion, my mother would demand we cut out all eggs, cheese, yogurt, and milk products, claiming they were "mucus-forming."[12] This false belief was probably based on the physical texture of dairy foods—which sometimes resembles mucus. Likewise, mother believed that eating pork could pass on the behavior of pigs, saying, "I think it's the same grouchy temperament that pigs have... I think that people who eat pork get real grouchy and nasty."[13] Of course, biochemistry debunks such outlandish notions.

Mother believed in the "law of similars," which underpins Samuel Hahnemann's 18th-century practice of homeopathy. Hahnemann taught that substances causing symptoms in a healthy person could be used in highly diluted form to treat similar symptoms in a sick person. Homeopathic "medicines" are not only ineffective, but they are often diluted to the point where not a single molecule remains.[14] It's basically spiritual medicine. It relies on the claim of a non-physical memory in matter that's loosely connected to the Theosophical concept of the akashic record and potentially tied to Mesmer's claims about a vital fluid surrounding living beings. These quasi-spiritual notions trace their origins to other ancient superstitions including animism[15] and vitalism.[16]

I was grateful to my mother for one thing: she never let us become officially anti-medicine or anti-vax. While she embraced a great deal of pseudoscience, she still mostly believed in evolution and the scientific method. It was a paradox that defined much of her worldview: trusting science when it was convenient, and discarding it when it clashed with her spiritual ideals.[17] She always told people to try the alt-health stuff first, and if it wasn't working, to go to a real doctor or hospital. A few people died from refusing cancer treatment in favor of natural cures, and she was not pleased.

My sisters and I had all our childhood vaccinations, plus inoculations against cholera, yellow fever and smallpox—required for world travel at the time. Our mother never denounced vaccines. But that didn't stop cult members from drifting into anti-vax territory on their own. Many of them had crunchy conspiritualist backgrounds, and the low levels of vaccine uptake within my cult allowed epidemics to spread. Talita Paolini was one such member whose parents never vaccinated her. In the early 1980s, she contracted preventable diseases:

> Twice during my time at Camelot, I caught an infectious disease. My parents, like CUT, didn't believe in immunizations, so when the measles and chickenpox went around, I caught them. Without anyone to attend me, I cared for myself and recovered slowly on my own. The epidemics forced CUT to reverse its policy on immunizations.[18]

If my cult had a formal vaccine policy, I never saw it enforced. By 1989 there were many unvaccinated kids running around our Montana ranch. A week before my second son Nathaniel's birth in June of that year, a pertussis epidemic started chewing its way through our school. Pertussis can be fatal to young children. Our doctors sprang into action and thankfully no one died, but my newborn son was at grave risk. It was a real scare—and I was furious.

We put Nathaniel on prophylactic antibiotics for a week. He was fine, but that's not exactly a warm welcome to the world. The pertussis outbreak was a wake-up call. Afterward, my mother required all children to be up-to-date on every vaccination or face exclusion from school. That's how it should be for everyone, everywhere—and largely was, until antivax propaganda began to erode public health mandates. It's a hard-earned lesson lost on too many 21st-century parents.

---

[1] Bragg, P. C., & Bragg, P. (1999). *The Miracle of Fasting: Proven Throughout History for Physical, Mental, & Spiritual Rejuvenation* (4th ed.). Health Science.

[2] The "Generally Recognized as Safe" (GRAS) designation is determined by the U.S. Food and Drug Administration (FDA) through scientific procedures or common use in food prior to 1958. This designation exempts substances from standard Federal Food, Drug, and Cosmetic Act (FFDCA) food additive tolerance requirements (U.S. Food and Drug Administration, n.d.). Retrieved from https://www.fda.gov/food/food-ingredients-packaging/generally-recognized-safe-gras

[3] Diapulse, developed by Diapulse Corporation of America in the 1960s, claims to use pulsed electromagnetic field (PEMF) therapy for wound healing and post-surgical recovery. Available studies show inconsistent results, with methodological limitations preventing definitive conclusions about its therapeutic value. Markovic, L., Wagner, B., & Crevenna, R. (2022). Effects of pulsed electromagnetic field therapy on outcomes associated with osteoarthritis: A systematic review of systematic reviews. *Wiener klinische Wochenschrift*, 134(9–10), 425–433. https://doi.org/10.1007/s00508-022-02020-3

[4] Muscle testing, or applied kinesiology, posits that muscle strength can diagnose health issues. Scientific studies demonstrate inconsistent results and lack of diagnostic reliability. The American Academy of Allergy, Asthma & Immunology advises against applied kinesiology for allergy diagnosis, citing a lack of scientific validity. Any perceived effects are attributed to the ideomotor response—a phenomenon where a person's expectations or beliefs unconsciously influence their subtle physical movements, creating an illusion of an external force or response. This same psychological mechanism explains the movement of Ouija board planchettes and dowsing rods. American Academy of Allergy, Asthma & Immunology. (n.d.). *Allergy testing*. Retrieved from https://www.aaaai.org/tools-for-the-public/conditions-library/allergies/allergy-testing

[5] Macrobiotics, from the Greek words macro (large/long) and bios (life), emerged from Sagen Ishizuka's late 19th-century dietary principles, later developed by George Ohsawa in the early 20th century. The philosophy emphasizes whole grains, vegetables, and legumes while avoiding processed foods, combining Eastern medicine with yin-yang principles. Michio Kushi subsequently popularized these practices globally through his educational initiatives and publications. Kushi, M., & Jack, A. (1983). *The book of macrobiotics: The universal way of health and happiness*. Japan Publications.

[6] Rejuvelac, popularized by Hippocrates Health Institute co-founder Ann Wigmore, is a fermented beverage made from sprouted grains. The slightly cloudy, tangy liquid is produced by soaking sprouted grains in water, allowing the mixture to ferment for one to two days, serving as a digestive aid and fermentation starter. Wigmore, A. (1986). *The sprouting book*. Avery Publishing Group.

[7] Kelley, W. D. (1969). *One answer to cancer*. Author.

[8] Armstrong, J. W. (1944). *The water of life: A treatise on urine therapy*. Health Science Press. The book advocates drinking urine as a health tonic, but this practice lacks scientific support and can be harmful. Urine is a waste product containing toxins and bacteria, which can lead to infections, kidney and liver strain, electrolyte imbalance, and dehydration. WebMD. (n.d.). *Urine Therapy*. Retrieved from https://www.webmd.com/diet/health-benefits-drinking-urine

[9] Orthorexia nervosa, while not formally recognized in DSM-5, was termed by Steven Bratman, M.D., in 1996. It describes an obsessive focus on dietary purity that can lead to malnutrition, social isolation, and decreased quality of life. Those affected often believe that common illnesses like colds or flu are direct results of "incorrect" or "impure" dietary choices. This belief represents a cognitive distortion, as viral infections occur independently of diet quality, though a balanced diet can support overall im-

mune function. Bratman, S., & Knight, D. (2000). *Health food junkies: Orthorexia nervosa: Overcoming the obsession with healthful eating.* Broadway Books.

[10] Prophet, E. C. (1993, July 10). Personal interview conducted by T. Prophet.

[11] Ayurveda, the traditional Indian system of medicine, classifies foods according to three doshas: vata (air/space elements governing movement and metabolism), pitta (fire/water elements controlling digestion and metabolism), and kapha (earth/water elements maintaining structure and immunity). Pole, S. (2013). *Ayurvedic medicine: The principles of traditional practice.* Singing Dragon.

[12] Scientific studies have found no significant evidence that dairy products increase mucus production. Pinnock and Graham (1986) investigated the effect of milk consumption on mucus production during respiratory infection and found no correlation. A more recent review by Balfour-Lynn (2019) confirms these findings, concluding that milk consumption does not exacerbate respiratory conditions. Both studies found no correlation between milk consumption and increased mucus production during cold virus exposure or exacerbation of respiratory conditions. Pinnock, C. B., & Graham, N. M. (1986). The effect of milk consumption on mucus production during respiratory infection. *American Review of Respiratory Disease*, 133(1), 57–60. Balfour-Lynn, I. M. (2019). Milk, mucus and myths. *Archives of Disease in Childhood*, 104(1), 91–93. https://adc.bmj.com/content/104/1/91

[13] Prophet, E. C. (1993, July 10). Personal interview conducted by T. Prophet.

[14] Scientific studies consistently demonstrate that homeopathy performs no better than placebo in controlled trials. Shang, A., Huwiler-Müntener, K., Nartey, L., Jüni, P., Dörig, S., Sterne, J. A., Pewsner, D., & Egger, M. (2005). Are the clinical effects of homoeopathy placebo effects? Comparative study of placebo-controlled trials of homoeopathy and allopathy. *The Lancet*, 366(9487), 726-732. Further systematic reviews confirm this conclusion: Ernst, E. (2010). Homeopathy: What does the "best" evidence tell us? *Medical Journal of Australia*, 192(8), 458-460. The British National Health Service also acknowledges there is no evidence that homeopathy is effective: National Health Service. (2023, October 15). Homeopathy. NHS Choices. https://www.nhs.uk/conditions/homeopathy/

[15] Tylor, E. B. (1871). *Primitive Culture: Researches Into the Development of Mythology, Philosophy, Religion, Art, and Custom.* John Murray. Animism, first extensively documented and analyzed by Tylor, posits that all objects, places, and creatures possess a distinct spiritual essence. This worldview forms the foundation of many indigenous societies, where it is believed that non-human entities—including animals, plants, rocks, rivers, and natural phenomena like thunder—have spirits or souls. A common thread across diverse animistic beliefs is the interconnectedness of all living and non-living things through a shared spiritual dimension.

[16] Vitalism is a doctrine that posits living organisms are fundamentally different from non-living entities because they are governed by a distinct vital force or life energy that cannot be explained solely by physical or chemical processes. This vital force was thought to imbue organisms with properties such as growth, reproduction, and self-healing. Vitalism's decline occurred through multiple scientific developments in the 19th century. While Wöhler's 1828 urea synthesis demonstrated that organic compounds could form from inorganic materials without a "vital force," subsequent discoveries in cell theory (Schleiden and Schwann, 1839), evolutionary biology (Darwin, 1859), and biochemistry contributed to its gradual replacement by mechanistic explanations of life processes.

[17] Members reconciled their spiritual beliefs with science by predicting that one day science would "catch up" and confirm the empirical reality of the Teachings of the Ascended Masters.

[18] Paolini, K., & Paolini, T. (2000). *400 years of imaginary friends: A journey into the world of adepts, masters, ascended masters, and their messengers.* Paolini International LLC. p. 46

CHAPTER NINE

Theosophy, Race, and Christian Nationalism

My cult gave me a front-row seat to observe the melding of our New Age fundamentalism with fascism. My father, Mark Prophet, was a conspiritualist to the core—before the term existed. Spiritually, he followed Theosophy, Rosicrucianism, and the Mighty I AM. Politically, he leaned far-right—shaped by the pre-civil-rights era of WWII and the early Cold War. He wasn't blazing any new trails. Mystics who came before him had already discovered that spiritual hierarchies translate into political ones. It's a tradition that runs from nineteenth-century Theosophy straight through to MAGA. As I've discussed, conspirituality forms a clear bridge to authoritarian politics.

Like many of my dad's peers, he was a staunch anti-communist, segregationist, McCarthyite, and member of the John Birch Society (JBS). Founded in 1958 by arch-conservative businessman Robert W. Welch, Jr., JBS espoused far-right, conspiratorial views, including the belief that communist infiltrators had taken over American institutions. For years, Dad subscribed to the JBS magazine, *American Opinion*, which was always lying around our house.

Twentieth-century roots of wealth and Christian Nationalism connect to Donald Trump's MAGA movement through eight main groups and their affiliates: The John Birch Society, the Fred C. Koch and Charles and David Koch organizations, The Family, founded in 1935 by Abraham Vereide, the Christian Broadcasting Network (CBN), established in 1960 by Pat Robertson, the National Association of Evangelicals (NAE), founded in 1942, the New Apostolic Reformation (NAR), founded in the late 1980s by C. Peter Wagner, The Heritage Foundation, established in 1973, and the Council for National Policy, co-founded by Paul Weyrich in 1981. To explore these connections, watch the 2024 documentary *Bad Faith: Christian Nationalism's Unholy War on Democracy* (Amazon Prime). These movements and their evolving alliances have shaped US history, forming the core of an anti-democratic insurgency dating back to our nation's founding.

I am referring to the 3/5 Compromise, written into the Constitution to placate slave states. This provision counted enslaved people as 3/5 of a person for Congressional apportionment while denying them political participation. This atrocity persisted for nearly a century, hollowing out the conceit of the Declaration of Independence that all men are created equal and endowed with unalienable rights to life, liberty, and the pursuit of happiness.

The same anti-democratic insurgency that led to the Civil War has never abandoned its goal of preserving an unequal, hierarchical society ruled by wealth and bolstered by the false claim that America was founded as a Christian nation. While some 19th-century Christians were abolitionists, others rationalized slavery as part of a God-ordained natural order that upheld the mythology of racial hierarchy. In the 20th century, Christian movements rooted in justice and equality worked to dismantle systemic oppression. The Civil Rights Movement, led by figures like Martin Luther King Jr., advanced racial equality in the United States, while liberation theology, championed by Gustavo Gutiérrez, Leonardo Boff, and Archbishop Óscar Romero, focused on uplifting the poor and oppressed in Latin America. In stark contrast, the core of modern Christian Nationalism lies within the US evangelical community, which has become increasingly anti-democratic, opposed to equality, and resistant to social justice.

Donald Trump is depicted by many evangelicals as a messianic figure—divinely overshadowed by Jesus. For many, MAGA ideology has now become religious practice. Some have taken up arms for what they see as an inevitable second civil war, embracing MAGA's violent rhetoric, lies, and dirty tricks. *That's not very Christlike.* They reject Jesus' teachings of love, acceptance, and forgiveness. They also dismiss America's founding ideals of equality under the law. They have never accepted the universality of voting rights—ramping up their attacks on suffrage since the Supreme Court nullified key parts of the Voting Rights Act in 2013.[1] Christian Nationalism clings to power—justified as a divine birthright—by any subversive means necessary.

Though fascism has often co-opted Christianity, its modern American variant is not driven solely by religion. It draws from a blend of influences rooted in earlier movements. These include the lost cause narrative of the Confederacy, Jim Crow laws, 1920s America First parades, the Ku Klux Klan, 1950s anti-communism and anti-desegregation efforts, and Christian anti-civil-rights activism in the 1960s. Phyllis Schlafly's Eagle Forum opposed the Equal Rights Amendment, and Jerry Falwell's Moral Majority mobilized evangelical voters in the 1980s.

In the 21st century, these ideological threads have evolved into a growing network. The Council for National Policy and the New Apostolic Reformation continue to wield significant influence, while the Tea Party galvanized anti-government sentiment beginning in 2009. The school-choice movement, initially framed as promoting educational freedom, has become a vehicle for defunding public schools and diverting public funds toward religious indoctrination. More recently, Turning Point USA has radicalized young conservatives, Moms for Liberty has championed book bans, and General Michael Flynn's MAGA3X played a central role in launching QAnon. Together, these forces represent the authoritarian core of modern Christian Nationalism.

While not always aligned, these movements share a common opposition to government regulations, secularism, democracy, science, diversity, social justice, and liberalism. Now, conspirituality has attracted former liberals into this orbit. Trump's re-election in 2024 represents a stunning victory for the century-old messianic project.

My father's journey exemplifies the intersection between Christian fundamentalism and New Age spirituality. His spiritual foundations lay in Theosophy and other esoteric traditions. He opposed most mainstream Christian churches, but shared their aim of preserving a hierarchical society, finding ways to blend his esoteric beliefs with conservative political activism. He gave a lecture series in late 1970 based on the 1955 Scientology book *Brain-washing: A synthesis of the Russian textbook on psychopolitics*.[2] And he had ideological and business reasons to curry favor with evangelicals. In February 1971, when I was six, he took me on a road trip to visit the world headquarters of the Christian Crusade in Tulsa. We met with segregationist, anti-communist Billy James Hargis for an hour before touring his publishing plant. I was fascinated by the huge commercial printing presses and factory-like folding, binding and trimming equipment. Dad was quite jealous of Hargis' ministry, which was much larger than ours.

It was a kind of one-upmanship. Dad saw himself as a peer of other Christian leaders and insisted our cult would one day reach even more people than Hargis. But my parents took live dictations from Jesus, so mainline Christians were never going to let us into their club. A few years later, they blackballed us as satanic. But evangelicals are perpetually mired in their own scandals, and Hargis was no exception. In 1974, he was ousted from the presidency of the religious college he founded after being credibly accused of seducing students—four male and one female. Some of those trysts reportedly occurred in the very office where my dad and I met with him.[3]

The connection between my cult and Christian Nationalism runs through Helena Petrovna Blavatsky, a charismatic Russian mystic whose influence extended to both far-right ideology and New Age spirituality. Born in 1831 in Yekaterinoslav, which is now Dnipro, Ukraine, she founded the Theosophical Society in 1875. Her writings, especially *The Secret Doctrine*,[4] blended Eastern religions with Western occultism, but they included troubling ideas.

One of Blavatsky's most controversial legacies is her concept of "root races"—a spiritual theory that would later be twisted to support racial hierarchies. Erin Prophet analyzes Blavatsky's theories in her 2024 paper "Racist or Liberating? The Difficult Transformations of Theosophical Root Race Theory."[5] She calls root race theory "one of two primary embarrassments around Theosophy." She notes that despite the electrifying nineteenth century discoveries of Darwin and Wallace, the understanding of race and evolution was in its infancy. This fostered speculation which led to several false theories that supported racial hierarchies, later hardening into so-called scientific racism and fueling the eugenics movement. Among these theories was "spiritual evolution," which tried to supplant natural selection:

Monogenism vs. Polygenism: Darwin espoused monogenism, the scientifically correct conclusion that all races of *Homo sapiens* are a single species. In contrast, nineteenth-century polygenism claimed races were biologically distinct and hierarchically ranked.

Civilized vs. Savage: Darwin wrote that "the civilized races of man will almost certainly exterminate and replace throughout the world the savage races," which led other scientists to harmonize evolutionary thought with false racial hierarchies.

Jaw Angle Theory: Promoted by T.H. Huxley, this theory placed Black people at the bottom of the evolutionary scale and Europeans at the top, supporting racial hierarchies and polygenism.

Racial Progression: Alfred Russel Wallace correctly concluded that "mankind was originally brown in color, and that white skin was a selective response to a cool, damp climate."[6] However, Robert Chambers falsely claimed an evolutionary progression of races from the Negro to the Malay, the American, the Mongolian, and the Caucasian.[7]

Spiritual Evolution: A core misunderstanding of natural selection led Blavatsky, Wallace, Massey, and others to adopt notions of mental or spiritual evolution. But natural selection means that existing organisms *do not evolve genetically*. Instead, changes occur over many generations as more adaptable members of a species dominate. Mental and spiritual changes through cultural adaptation are examples of *memetic* natural selection, a concept defined by evolutionary biologist Richard Dawkins in *The Selfish Gene*.[8] This means that more adaptable ideas spread through a population, while less useful ones die off.

Root Race Theory: Blavatsky proposed seven root races, each with seven sub-races. The first was the Demiurge, gigantic and ethereal. The second was Hermaphroditic, also gigantic and reproducing asexually. The third was Male and Female, appearing as a giant ape. The fourth was Sons of God, smaller beings who perfected language and used the human body as a vehicle for the soul. The fifth was Giants, corresponding to modern humans. The sixth is associated with the Buddhic soul, awakening dormant powers. The seventh is Godlike humans, who reproduce without sex and replace speech and intellect with spirit.

Erin notes that Blavatsky was conflicted, wanting to "own and disown Darwin," and observed that root race theory as presented in Theosophical sources is "inconsistent and confusing." Blavatsky telegraphed her lack of scientific seriousness about Darwin's *The Origin of Species* with ironic physical comedy: she kept a copy of the book in the hands of a stuffed baboon. Lacking the intellectual rigor to refute Darwin's science with better science, she tried to integrate it into her mish-mash of esoteric concepts. Erin quotes John Crow, who argues that bodily characteristics in Theosophical discourse were used to assign standing among root races and sub-races. This included "skin color and body features, particularly craniometrics," which reflected a racial hierarchy.[9]

Blavatsky's ideas about root races present a complex paradox that still echoes in today's spiritual and political movements. While she intended these as spiritual concepts, her framework created dangerous precedents. When she used terms like "Aryan"—then a common academic term for Indo-Persian-Europeans—she couldn't have anticipated how later movements would weaponize her terminology to support white supremacy.

The transformation from spiritual theory to racist ideology was predictable. Theosophy is incoherent—a jumbled collection of mystical concepts that made it particularly susceptible to manipulation—precisely the kind of syncretism Eco highlights in his treatise on Ur-Fascism. The eugenics movement of the early 20th century used this theological chaos to advance their agenda, exploiting the deliberate confusion between spiritual whiteness or lightness and racial purity. The seal of the Theosophical Society reflects the same scattershot approach—featuring symbols like the Egyptian ankh, the ouroboros, the Star of David, and the Aum symbol alongside the swastika. Originally a sacred Asian symbol, the swastika would later be corrupted by the Third Reich.

These appropriations were all plausibly deniable. Theosophical concepts of light and darkness, purity and contamination, evolution and hierarchy created a bridge between New Age spirituality and far-right ideology. By dividing humanity into civilized and savage races and linking darkness and blackness with contamination and evil, Theosophy paved the way for racist ideologies by offering spiritual doctrines that could be used to justify racial hierarchies, yet remained indifferent to their consequences. Though Blavatsky herself pro-

The seal of the Theosophical society

moted a globalist, universalist view of humanity and social justice, her ideas proved remarkably adaptable to exclusionary agendas.

This adaptability became explicit with Jörg Lanz von Liebenfels' 1905 publication *Theozoologie* and his founding of the Order of the New Templars that same year in Vienna, Austria—an organization dedicated to promoting a racialized reinterpretation of Theosophy. In 1915, Lanz formally introduced the term "Ariosophy" to describe this ideology, which cast non-Aryans as spiritually degenerate and justified racial purity as a divine mandate. Ariosophy abandoned Theosophy's universalism entirely, transforming its occult framework into an ideological foundation for völkisch nationalism and, later, Nazi racial theory.[10]

My father's spiritual lineage was shaped by another key movement that twisted Theosophical ideas: the Mighty I AM cult. Founded in 1930 by Guy and Edna Ballard, the cult merged esoteric philosophy with Christian Nationalism. The Ballards called it "Christian Democracy," a term introduced in a Saint Germain dictation. By the late 1930s and early 1940s, the Mighty I AM began attracting members from the Silver Shirts, a paramilitary, anti-Semitic cult founded in 1933 by William Dudley Pelley.[11] In the 1940 book *Psychic Dictatorship in America*,[12] Gerald B. Bryan claimed that the unnamed treasurer of the Silver Shirts later became the Ballard's treasurer and legal adviser.

Pelley was an open admirer of Nazi Germany and promoted racial essentialism along with nativist America-First propaganda. His 1929 article *My Seven Minutes in Eternity* detailed mystical experiences that positioned him as a charismatic spiritual leader.[13] Pelley's radical theocratic views coupled with his opposition to US involvement in World War II led to his conviction for sedition in 1942. This connection reveals how esotericism provided a vocabulary and framework for advancing nationalist and racist agendas.

Despite any lingering questions about the strength of its connection to the Silver Shirts, racial ideology was layered deeply into Mighty I AM imagery and practices. Their iconography depicted Jesus, Saint Germain, and other masters as Northern European—all blond-haired and blue-eyed. Though the I AM included a few brown-skinned Eastern masters from Theosophy, like the turbaned El Morya and Kuthumi, the Ballards' spiritual universe was fundamentally divided between light and dark. This dualism went beyond metaphor—they labeled their enemies "black magicians" and maintained segregated congregations well into the civil rights era. Exit counselor Joe Szimhart documents that the I AM sanctuary in Washington D.C. was segregated as late as 1998.[14]

Members of the Mighty I AM were purity fanatics, especially about sex. Bryan documents that the Ballards revealed an Ascended Master aptly named "The Goddess of Purity" who taught that "The sex urge was only to be used for procreation." He claimed this teaching broke up countless marriages. A sub-group within the cult, the "one-hundred-percenters," avoided sex even within marriage, because they believed it drained the life-force, causing premature aging. The Ballards taught that working toward the ascension was more important than having children. In addition to celibacy, the one-hundred-percenters avoided meat, alcohol, drugs, and even onions and garlic, which they believed led to demonic possession.

It's hard to overstate the impact of religious movements which connect godliness and purity to sexual abstinence, northern European features, and The Great White Brotherhood. Sure, this might have all been superficially in reference to spiritual whiteness and spiritual light. But Blavatsky's spiritual evolution *itself* is arguably about the sublimation of the lower human/animal nature and specifically sexuality. Remember, her seventh root race is supposed to reproduce without sex. Coincidence? What's the common slur against the so-called lower races? That they are more animalistic, less perfect, less pure, and more sexual.

My cult differed from the Mighty I AM in several important respects. Though both organizations hewed to Theosophical traditions and worshiped the same masters, our success led to a growing feud. By 1970 both my parents began to claim that the I AM cult was spiritually attacking us. In August 1976, my mother sent a memo to our teaching centers to "reverse the tide" against "I AM blasting decrees," which she blamed for *accidents* and *deaths* among our membership. "Reverse the tide" was a simple mantra designed to send "negative energy" back to its source. We called it the 7.05 decree, chanted at high speed and volume, in multiples of three: "Reverse the tide (3x), Roll them back (3x), Reverse the tide (3x) Take thy command! Roll them back (3x) Set all free (3x), Reverse the tide (3x)"[15]

Then she took the feud nuclear, giving a dictation from Saint Germain, in which he announced that he was *withdrawing his sponsorship* from the Mighty I AM entirely. To understand the severity of her pronouncement, recognize that Saint Germain was claimed by the I AM as their founding master—the spiritual equivalent to our founding master El Morya. It was nothing short of spiritually blackballing a rival cult. It was also a demonstration of how seriously she took the threat of hostile prayers. And that she deeply believed in the physical power of the spoken word to not only catalyze positive change—but also to cause deadly harm. A decade later, this would become a key point of contention at the Mull trial.

We also rejected the I AM cult's overt racism. From the date of our founding in Washington D.C., Black members were treated equally, and we welcomed interracial couples. By the early 1970s, my parents revealed the Black Ascended Master "Afra" as a member of The Great White Brotherhood. But that's another *Taijitu* paradox. My father was respectful to Black members in person, and I traveled with him in 1972 to visit our sizable congregation in Ghana. Yet he was a staunch supporter of Alabama's segregationist governor, George Wallace, and harbored a deep hatred of liberalism and US civil rights law. So it was in a segregationist context that his political and spiritual world views came into alignment.

An anecdote from my childhood provides additional perspective: Chief Justice Earl Warren presided over landmark Supreme Court rulings advancing the rights of Black Americans, including *Brown v. Board of Education* (1954), *Loving v. Virginia* (1967), and *Gideon v. Wainwright* (1963).

At age six or seven, I had no knowledge of that. I learned Earl Warren's name from a practical joke my dad played. He taped himself with a pocket recorder approaching a dog and saying, "Do you like Earl Warren?" The dog growled loudly. He played that tape at least a hundred times and laughed every time.

Dad was no friend to integrated schools. He often argued with the principal of Broadmoor Elementary over "sensitivity training," the 1960s term for what's now called wokeness or Diversity, Equity, and Inclusion (DEI). By fourth grade, he was fed up and pulled me out mid-year. That was the last time I attended public school. I was homeschooled at first, and later graduated from the private Montessori high school my parents founded.

My father embraced the popular right-wing conspiracy theories of his day, railing against "communists in the State Department," the Illuminati, the Bilderbergers, and the Rockefellers. He sold W. Cleon Skousen's *The Naked Capitalist*[16] and Gary Allen and Larry Abraham's *None Dare Call It Conspiracy*[17] in our bookstore. Both are poorly sourced books claiming that global elites and international banks controlled the world, threatening the American way of life—a longstanding anti-Semitic trope. If my dad were alive today, he'd probably be watching Fox News and following Steve Bannon and other MAGA stalwarts who rail against the deep state and one-world government. And he'd have likely voted for Trump all three times.

While dad dabbled in right-wing conspiracy theories, my mother developed them into an art form. By the mid-1970s, she had coined the paradoxical term "International Capitalist Communist Conspiracy," a topic she lectured on for the next 20 years. Building on earlier conspiracy books, she added original research done by our in-house politico, Murray Steinman. By the mid-1980s, she began promoting Antony Sutton's *The Order*, a book about the Skull and Bones society at Yale and its alleged secret control of the US government.[18]

She believed political conditions on Earth reflected an all-encompassing spiritual warfare that had raged in our galaxy for millions of years, involving aliens who interfered with human evolution. Was this a spiritual conflict on the astral plane or something she thought was physically happening? It was unclear. The lost civilizations of Atlantis and Lemuria were also ambiguous. Blavatsky claimed these continents sank due to technological abuse and sexual perversion. Were these myths, or history?

My mother espoused Zecharia Sitchin's 1976 sci-fi novel *The Twelfth Planet*—which the author claimed was non-fiction![19] It's a lurid account of interplanetary colonization of Earth by Annunaki from the planet Nibiru who used genetic engineering to create humans from apes, then interbred with them to produce offspring known as Nephilim. My mother melded this fictive anthropology with the International Capitalist Communist Conspiracy to conclude that powerbrokers controlling the world were either Nephilim, or simply "Mechanization Man," genetically engineered people who appear human but lack any connection to God. Believing this mythology, we dutifully read our prayer inserts, shouting against "…Atlantean science, UFOs, recombinant DNA, the Nephilim, Mechanization Man, the godless creation, and all perversions of the sacred fire.…" Beneath it all, I heard murmurings about satanic blood-drinking and pedophilia.[20] It was QAnon in all but name.

To call it syncretic would be to describe this grab-bag cosmology charitably. Mother threaded the needle between her International Capitalist Communist Conspiracy, her appearances at the Whole Life Expo discussing "The Lost Teachings of Jesus on Women's Rights," her rigid anti-abortion stance, and her support for Reagan's Republican Party. At our quarterly conferences, she found no conflict in hosting an anti-Soviet panel with a GRU defector one day and a session on Ayurvedic medicine the next. Looking back, she was quite the pioneer, blending alt-health, galactic conspiracies, and right-wing anti-communist politics long before conspirituality became fashionable.

I'll conclude with a coda of ironies.

A prayer from an Archangel Michael dictation my mother gave in 1984 ended up in the mouth of retired General Michael Flynn, the godfather of QAnon, in September 2021. Flynn, a 2020 election denier, has explicitly called for an American theocracy, demanding the United States adopt Christianity as its "one religion," blatantly violating the Establishment Clause. Hearing Flynn repeat my mother's prayer was chilling. I never imagined her words would be co-opted to serve the Trump/MAGA/Christian Nationalist agenda. But given her early foray into QAnon-adjacent content, it's fitting that it came full circle.

Shortly after the story broke, I spent 30 minutes on my podcast discussing the prayer, its spiritual significance, and why it's so dangerous.[21] Unlike Flynn, my mother was never anti-democracy—she believed in free and fair elections. But her political agenda was still far right. She wanted her religious principles to become law, including a strict federal abortion ban, and believed high political offices like the presidency were spiritual offices. I'm not sure she understood that theocracy and democracy are incompatible. Ironically, after Flynn used her prayer, he faced backlash from his Christian base for associating with what they deemed a satanic cult leader. If my mother were alive, she would have had a good laugh about *that*.

Despite nearly continuous alt-health treatments, my mother's time was cut short. Decades of untreated epilepsy may have contributed to her early-onset Alzheimer's. There's also speculation within our family that the hundreds of different elixirs and treatments she took may have contributed to her loss of cognitive function. Due to the wide variety of these remedies, it's unclear what she was taking or what harmful substances any of it might have contained. She took handfuls of pills. One thing is certain: none of that hokum improved her health or prolonged her life. Her cognition may also have been damaged by Depakote, an epilepsy medication linked to dementia. By the time she was 60, she no longer recognized me. She died at 70 in 2009.

---

[1] Shelby County v. Holder, 570 U.S. 529 (2013) The Supreme Court invalidated the Voting Rights Act's coverage formula, effectively ending the preclearance requirement.

[2] Church of Scientology. (1955). *Brain-Washing: A Synthesis of the Russian Textbook on Psychopolitics*. Church of Scientology.

[3] Religion: The Sins of Billy James. (1976, February 16). Time Magazine. https://web.archive.org/web/20090923033557/http://www.time.com/time/magazine/article/0,9171,918027-1,00.html

[4] Blavatsky, H. P. (1888). *The Secret Doctrine: The Synthesis of Science, Religion, and Philosophy*. Theosophical University Press.

[5] Stang, C. M., & Josephson Storm, J. A. (Eds.). (2024). *Theosophy and the Study of Religion*. Brill.

[6] Stepan, N. (1982). *The Idea of Race in Science: Great Britain 1800-1960*. Archon Books. p. 68

[7] Chambers, R. (1994). *Vestiges of the Natural History of Creation* (J. A. Secord, Ed.). University of Chicago Press.

[8] Dawkins, R. (1976). *The Selfish Gene*. Oxford University Press.

[9] Crow, J. (2017). *Occult Bodies: The Corporal Construction of the Theosophical Society, 1875-1935* [Doctoral dissertation]. Florida State University. p. 113

[10] Goodrick-Clarke, N. (1992). *The occult roots of Nazism: Secret Aryan cults and their influence on Nazi ideology*. New York University Press.

[11] William Dudley Pelley (1890–1965) was an American writer and political activist best known for founding the Silver Legion of America, or the Silver Shirts, a fascist and anti-Semitic organization inspired by Nazi Germany, in 1933. Gaining notoriety for his radical Christian nationalist and anti-Semitic views, Pelley's activities eventually led to his arrest. Convicted of sedition in 1942, he served eight years of a fifteen-year sentence for violating the Espionage Act during World War II. After his 1950 release, he remained politically active but marginalized until his death in 1965.

[12] Bryan, G. B. (1940). *Psychic Dictatorship in America*. New Age Publishing Company.

[13] Pelley, W. D. (1929, March). My Seven Minutes in Eternity. *The American Magazine*, 107(3), 17-19, 66-71. Pelley, W. D. (1929). *Seven Minutes in Eternity: With Their Aftermath, Together with a Biographical Sketch of the Author*. Robert Collier.

[14] Szimhart, J. (n.d.). Picasso Revisited and the Mighty I AM. https://www.jszimhart.com/essays/picasso-revisited-and-the-mighty-i-am

[15] Prophet, M., & Prophet, E. (1999). *Prayers, meditations, and dynamic decrees for personal and world transformation.* Summit University Press. p. 90-91

[16] Skousen, W. C. (1970). *The Naked Capitalist.* Self-published.

[17] Allen, G. E. (1971). *None Dare Call It Conspiracy.* Concord Press.

[18] Sutton, A. C. (1983). *The Order: What It Is and How It Began.* Veritas Publishing Company.

[19] Sitchin, Z. (1976). *The Twelfth Planet.* Stein and Day.

[20] When I was about 10 years old, I recall a specific phone call with my mother. She was on one of her tours, and she called me one day to "see if I was OK." On that call, she shared with me her worries about evil forces that did bad things to children. She mentioned one conspiracy involving the Satanic murder of children for their blood on the "feast of Purim," a classic trope of the anti-Semitic blood libel. There was another conspiracy she mentioned about dead children being hauled away in garbage trucks in New York City. Then she told me about men who kidnap young boys and "put their penises in their bottoms," which was the first time I understood the concept of child molestation.

[21] Black Sun Journal. (2021, October 11). *66: The world's most destructive organization* [Video]. *The Radical Secular.* YouTube. https://youtu.be/X3Pc3X_7Mto?si=KmTe9qXeuOfuUu8b&t=1847

CHAPTER TEN

My Family Business

Gregory Mull wasn't only seeking spiritual salvation. He had another motive for joining my cult that received significant attention at trial: His desire to be the architect of what Lawrence Levy called "The New Jerusalem," a name drawn from the millenarian trope of the Holy City. This referred to a proposed $33 million development at Camelot, including a 3,300-seat auditorium, classrooms, dormitories, and offices. But the plan was aspirational, since we lacked funding, had no permits, and faced obstacles like eminent domain and the California Coastal Commission. Despite this, Mull was eager to gain prestige as the lead architect. He testified, "I already was in the teachings and I felt elated and sought after. And I knew it was $33 million worth of building."[1] Despite his enthusiasm, Mull soon found himself struggling to reconcile his professional aspirations with my cult's lack of resources.

Ambition ran in both directions. My mother often cultivated strategic friendships with large donors, business owners, or members with professional talents. Mull described his relationship with her from 1975 to 1976 as being "always on her terms, but… very close."[2] When she visited San Francisco, Mull commonly took her out to dinner and to interior design shops. He testified that on one trip, my mother and her third husband, Randall King, visited his home and spotted a $10,000 antique armoire, which Mull called "the nicest thing I had in the house." He had wanted to show them its dimensions, but my mother told him El Morya would be very pleased to have it. The testimony conflicted with Mull's deposition in which he said he offered to donate the armoire on his own. Either way, he arranged to deliver the antique, which ended up in my mother's bedroom at our Los Angeles Ashram. He testified that he gave it away out of fear, saying, "How can you refuse God anything?"³

In late 1978, cult vice-president Monroe Shearer invited Mull to join staff. Mull sent letters discussing his expenses, but no formal agreement was reached before he started work in January 1979. His application had a question mark under "How do you plan to meet your expenses?" making the arrangement *ad hoc*, with Mull requesting monthly payments between $3,000 and $4,000. Payments were often late, leading to Mull to complain that his credit was being ruined.

Despite this, Mull wanted to donate his time, writing on February 11, 1979, "I am sorry to have to charge you anything, as I love serving…. the Ascended Masters." On February 22, he proposed reducing his expenses to $700 a month and offered to repay all money advanced, even promising, "I will give you 10 percent of all profit I make from the sale of my property." By March 9, he asked Shearer to formalize the arrangement, but Shearer replied, "Nobody receives money for doing anything here at Camelot. Why do you think you should?"—insisting that all future payments would be treated as loans.

Illustration of Gregory Mull working on architectural drawings at Camelot, Malibu, California c. 1979

Mull's struggle for compensation was emblematic of our dysfunction. Shearer's dismissive response reflected our two-tiered system. My mother would gladly pay going rates for high-powered professional talent. But if one of her followers had those skills, she would lean on them to provide their services *gratis*, with only a spiritual reward. Once someone became her chela, she no longer considered them worthy of compensation, and most chelas were satisfied with that arrangement: Belief compelled labor.

Cults operate like any other privately-held corporation. But belief is central to their algorithm, determining not only business practices but every facet of members' lives. At the top of our hierarchy was the Ascended Master El Morya, who served as our true CEO. My mother claimed he had personally wagered his "spiritual bank account" to found our cult. His authority extended beyond matters of faith to decisions about labor and finances. He's the master with whom she most closely identified. It wasn't clear where her personality ended and his began. If any question ever needed to be settled with finality, it was El Morya doing the talking. My mother was his public face to the world—bearing any consequences of his dictates.

Though structured as a non-profit entity, my cult was also my family business. For several years, our board of directors included only immediate family: myself, Erin, my mother, and her fourth husband Edward Francis, scion of a prosperous family from Dallas. He was our savvy vice-president and business manager, who joined staff shortly after graduating from Colorado College in the early 1970s. Even during early years when non-family members served on the board, they mostly rubber-stamped my parents' decisions. If the board ever balked, my parents would invoke El Morya's CEO authority. This changed in 1990, after the triple fiasco of the shelter project, illegal weapons purchases, and the fuel spill. The board was expanded to nine directors, and we granted them real power.

This highlighted the paradox of my mother's leadership, which depended on the board's faith in her spiritual authenticity. Our board expansion was effectively a demotion, signaling a loss of faith—not in El Morya, but in her capacity to interpret his will. If she truly had a divine connection, why had we faced disaster? Her messengership had been our spiritual north star, but it also financially sustained hundreds of staff. Since I left my cult, people have often asked me, "Did your mother sincerely believe in what she was doing, or was it all about the money?" I've struggled with this question for decades, and I'm still confounded by it. The only answer that makes any sense is "both." Where else do we find this tension? In the Supreme Court's 1944 *Ballard* decision, which blocked any inquiry into the truth of sincerely-held religious claims, even when large sums of money were involved.

While the law may shield sincerely-held beliefs from scrutiny, the question of my mother's sincerity continues to haunt me. I was close to her for thirty years, and her inner deliberations remain opaque. She spoke publicly about two different methods of channeling Ascended Masters. The first, in which she was fully aware, involved receiving visions or concepts and translating them into words. The second she called "ex cathedra," when her mind and body were taken over by the master. I asked if she lost consciousness, was aware of herself speaking, or saw the masters approaching before they took over her body. She demurred, saying it was "personal." In her book *Preparation for My Mission*, she described the experience:

> I learned that there were different kinds of dictations; some were like being a simultaneous translator at the United Nations.... During these dictations, I would listen to the mind of the master dictating his or her words to me, and focus on getting the concepts right.... In other dictations, I felt that I was allowing the master to use my vocal cords. These came to be called *ex cathedra* dictations, from the term used to describe the infallible revelations that are believed to come from the popes.... there is not even time for the brain of the messenger to interpret what is coming forth. It just flows out in a stream.[4]

I never got the impression that my mother was faking it. A change came over her during those sessions. It was an extraordinary performance that often left her exhausted. Still, I would be shocked if she didn't suffer self-doubt, being in a deep trance state in front of crowds and cameras. What if one day she couldn't pull it off? In her words, "I've always been the breadwinner of this whole organization. If I don't produce, if I don't lecture, if I don't get new members, if I don't write books, then the income doesn't come in. It's like the whole burden of being the provider for 700 people falls on me."[5]

Belief is central to identity formation. There's little difference between *belief* and *self*. I conclude that my mother *became* her beliefs and lost herself within them. At family events, even if she was being sweet, or silly, or playing a game, she never left her messenger role. Her astrological sign was Aries. That fit her Ram personality, which could flare up in a split second if she was displeased. As Erin observed, there were striking similarities between El Morya and her strict German father Hans Wulf. I never saw vulnerability or introspection until the late '90s, when her cognitive decline put her in a childlike state. During her prime years, she identified fully with her self-declared role as God's messenger, and she was always in command.

I understand curiosity about motives, which are pivotal not just to the legal defense of religious freedom but in determining responsibility. In a murder trial, the defendant's state of mind distinguishes manslaughter from first-degree murder. Courts rely on physical evidence and behavior to determine which. But no legal distinction can bring back the victim.

Sincerely-held beliefs are equally fraught. My mother was either channeling cosmic spirits, faking it, or she was self-deluded. During her lectures, she read—sometimes haltingly—from note cards. But her dictations were spontaneous, often rapid-fire monologues which could last an hour or more. As her AV man I can attest that there were no teleprompters or hidden earpieces. Scientifically, the only explanation is that these messages came from her brain, which moved her vocal cords. Were they sub-personalities? Expressions of subconscious ruminations? The laws of physics provide no mechanism for telepathy or spirit communication—and no reliable evidence has ever demonstrated their existence, making it inescapable that in some form it was always her speaking. In *Prophet's Daughter*, Erin said, "If there were masters, I had seen no evidence that we could communicate with them, and now believed that they could more safely be viewed as archetypes rather than guides."[6]

One clue may be her epilepsy. From the age of nine, my mother experienced petit mal (absence) seizures, causing brief loss of consciousness lasting seconds to a minute. These seizures blocked her from driving, riding a bicycle, or safely participating in most sports. Notably, she never had a seizure during a dictation. Later she suffered several tonic-clonic (grand mal) seizures, including one in 1989 that required her to be air-medevaced from Livingston, Montana to a hospital in Salt Lake City. Temporal-lobe epilepsy has been linked to vivid hallucinations, prophetic visions, and hypergraphia—an uncontrollable urge to write. Though she wasn't diagnosed with temporal-lobe epilepsy, many of her symptoms overlapped: an aura of white light, sleep disturbances, irritability, and grandiosity.

Any link between epilepsy and channeling remains speculative. Erin offered additional context: During her messenger training, she became our mother's seer in their altar work—a key part of my cult's decision-making process during and after the fraught years of shelter construction. Her assessment was blunt: "Mother and I were channeling the creative force for a deliberate purpose—to bolster her power, to deliberately manipulate people. It was for a good cause, one I believed in, but it was still manipulation."[7]

Those who embrace the haunted world of spirit-matter dualism remain undeterred by skepticism. They reject the idea that the brain is a self-contained neurological system, insisting instead that it functions as a receiver for unseen forces. To them, my mother's neurological condition wasn't a disorder—it was a divine conduit that "opened the channel" to spiritual beings. But no evidence has ever demonstrated that consciousness exists outside the brain. Spirit communication isn't merely unproven—it's indistinguishable from personal imagination. Yet thousands believed in her abilities, and that belief alone was enough to make her a cult leader.

The *Ballard* decision dealt with a more tangible assertion. The Ballards boasted that they had healed "hundreds" of people with incurable diseases. Because they sent their false claim through the mail, they were convicted of mail fraud in 1939 by the Southern District of California. But in 1944, the Supreme Court ruled that the jury should not have been asked to decide whether their religious claims were factually true. The First Amendment, they held, protects beliefs from judicial scrutiny. The Court didn't overturn their conviction outright, but it sent the case back for further proceedings, reinforcing the idea that sincerity—not truth—was the relevant legal standard in religious fraud cases.

The ruling described their claims:

> ...that Guy W. Ballard, during his lifetime, and Edna W. Ballard and Donald Ballard had, by reason of super-natural attainments, the power to heal persons of ailments and diseases ... and did falsely represent to persons intended to be defrauded that the three designated persons had the ability and power to cure persons of those diseases normally classified as curable and also of diseases which are ordinarily classified by the medical profession as being incurable.[8]

If the Ballards had healing powers, proving it should have been trivial: Demonstrate even one healing unexplainable by medical science. If they could have done that, they wouldn't have been convicted, and the case never would have reached the Supreme Court. But faith healing is peak charlatanry.[9] The real question is: Does it matter whether the Ballards *believed in it?* It's a tough call, and I'm not sure the Court got it right. Yet it's difficult to conceive of how to guard against sincerely held false beliefs while still maintaining freedom of conscience.

Justice Robert Jackson saw the problem: The price of religious freedom, he warned in his dissent, is that "we must put up with, and even pay for, a good deal of rubbish." And rubbish has consequences. False claims damage society. If cult leaders act *as if* their beliefs are true, so will their followers—and the money will flow. Financial success depends on doubling down in the face of doubt. A con man running a Ponzi scheme knows he's committing fraud. A cult leader selling spirits, miracles, or faith healings may not. Who could ever tell? To profess belief is to stay in business. To disavow it is to go out of business. As Upton Sinclair observed, "It is difficult to get a man to understand something, when his salary depends upon his not understanding it."[10] Every cult leader faces this conflict between truth and power. No matter how sincere, their goal is always to marshal other people's money and time.

My mother devoted all her time to our cult. She was a prolific writer and a dynamic public speaker. Whether she believed she was channeling masters, I can't say. But I know she sincerely believed her message was vital. It's not what she said, it's what she did. Her idea of a fun vacation was to retreat to a cabin or the beach and write for weeks at a time. At home, she was just as focused.

La Tourelle, now known as the "Broadmoor Estate Home," Colorado Springs, c. 2023

My cult house in Colorado Springs was a 17,000-square-foot mansion called *La Tourelle*, French for "The Little Tower." We lived there from 1966-1973. The red-brick palace, built in the late 1920s by Philadelphia pharmaceutical heir Thomas Harris Powers,[11] got its name from a three-story turret to the right of the front entrance that held a travertine spiral staircase leading to a twenty-foot-diameter office we called "the tower," where my mother spent her days and nights writing. When I was a child, she didn't usually tuck me into bed. Instead, I made the trek up that curved staircase where I would find her, fountain pen in hand, talking to her Dictaphone, or editing a manuscript with one of her staff. She worked as hard as anyone I've ever known.

Like many religions, my cult was a content-creator. From my father's first recorded meeting in 1957 to my mother's voice echoing on countless hours of audio recordings and TV programs, my parents harnessed the labor and money of thousands of people. Modern digital publishing is blindingly efficient, but in the mid-to-late 20th century, everything was analog and labor-intensive. Handwritten manuscripts were typed, Dictaphone tapes transcribed, newsletters typeset, mechanicals photographed, and printing plates burned. Mailing lists were curated, donations processed, and presses inked. Our mansion's basement hummed like a factory as printed matter was folded, stapled, and trimmed, envelopes were stuffed and addressed, and audiotapes were edited and duplicated. By the 1980s, we added video production to the mix, turning our operation into a full-fledged publishing machine.

A few years before I was born, my mother ran the small Davidson printing press she had set up in her 10th-floor apartment in Washington, D.C., churning out the early cult publications. In those years my parents rolled up their sleeves and worked like maniacs. But as my cult grew, low-paid or volunteer workers increasingly did all the grunt work while my parents focused on the big picture. In the 1960s, the staff stipend was $15-$30 per month. Only a few feet from the tower office where my mother penned her books were the doors to two large unheated attics that held rows of bunk beds where staff lived without plumbing. Our family occupied the luxurious second-floor residential quarters, and we enjoyed private bathrooms and a private dining room, while the attic-dwellers grabbed hasty showers in shared bathroom facilities.

Many of our members never set foot in any of our locations. They supported us financially, consuming our books and tapes from afar, without experiencing the intensity of residential cult membership. For those more deeply involved, membership was highly stratified. From casual supporters to the core leadership, there were nine levels of involvement, each representing a step up my cult's hierarchy. At the top were my parents, the Messengers, followed by the board of directors and church elders. Below them were the permanent staff, the Sons and Daughters of Dominion, probationary staff, and volunteer community members. At the base were Communicants, Keepers of the Flame, and subscribers to the Pearls of Wisdom newsletter.

Each level of membership came with its own commitments, both financial and spiritual. In the 1960s, Pearls of Wisdom subscriptions cost $40 per year, while Keepers of the Flame paid $10 monthly for a lesson booklet. With the founding of Church Universal and Triumphant in 1975, the Communicant tier introduced a 10-percent tithe pledge. Volunteer community members worked without pay and covered their own housing. Probationary staff received room and board, along with a small stipend, if they brought valuable skills. Sons and Daughters of Dominion, a spiritual tier, required initiates to take strict vows of renunciation.[12] Permanent staff pledged total financial commitment, while elders and board members had typically served for more than a decade.

To advance spiritually, members wanted to increase their involvement. Beyond the Communicant level, it wasn't easy. The prerequisite was to be accepted into Summit University and complete a three-month residential training program. There was no guarantee a person would gain volunteer status. To go from a volunteer to probationary staff, and from probationary to permanent staff, was even more rigorous. My mother approved or denied every application.

Unlike Gregory Mull, who demanded payment of his expenses, the majority of volunteers were people who *wanted* to donate their time and money, pay their own room and board, and commit their lives to my cult. And they might not be accepted? Maintaining an air of exclusivity was a key aspect of my cult's algorithm. Perhaps unknowingly, my mother employed behavioral science and rational choice theory to extract maximum labor and resources from her members. High barriers to entry and strict rules for membership screen out free riders and the less committed—while motivating those who are accepted to work harder and donate more. Every level of involvement demanded escalating commitments, reinforcing the devotion required to progress spiritually while maintaining organizational control.

This incentive is explored in a 1994 paper in the *American Journal of Sociology* called "Why Strict Churches Are Strong," by Laurence R. Iannaccone.[13] "Strict churches" follow Robert Jay Lifton's eight principles of thought reform, proclaiming "...an exclusive truth—a closed, comprehensive, and eternal doctrine. They demand adherence to a distinctive faith, morality, and lifestyle. They condemn deviance, shun dissenters, and repudiate the outside world. They frequently embrace 'eccentric traits,' such as distinctive diet, dress or speech, that invite ridicule, isolation, and persecution." Iannaccone notes that structures and rules that impose the highest costs on members produce the most successful cults. "Distinctive.... social customs constrain and often stigmatize members, making participation in alternative activities more costly. Potential members are forced to choose whether to participate fully, or not at all."

Iannaccone considers this a net positive, which it certainly is from the standpoint of the cult business. He disagrees that this is a problem for individuals, writing, "It follows that perfectly rational people can be drawn to decidedly unconventional groups. This conclusion sharply contrasts with the view, popular among psychiatrists, clinical psychologists, and the media, that conversion to deviant religious sects and cults is inherently pathological, the consequence of either psychological abnormality or coercive brainwashing."

I agree with Iannacone that rational people join cults. It's why I've stressed that no one is immune. Most people don't understand what they're getting into. And they're not prepared for the deep impact of thought reform tactics, which are geared to strengthen the cult at great personal cost to members. You should definitely heed the warnings from the clinical psychologists—and stay away from cults!

Cults are a lucrative business. But they're lumped in for tax purposes with 501(c)(3) non-profits. In the US, there are 1.48 million tax-exempt religious organizations. Most of them file IRS form 990, paying taxes on any non-charitable business income. Directors and shareholders of non-profits are prohibited from *inurement*—personally benefiting from the organization's funds or receiving excessive compensation.

Loopholes in these regulations are massive—large enough to fly a Gulfstream jet through, or in the case of preacher Joel Osteen, an Airbus A-319. Compliance relies on self-reporting and self-enforcement. The IRS audited only 0.52 percent of the 1.75 million tax-exempt returns in 2022.[14] Even when audits happen, the rules are so lax that non-profits almost never lose their exemptions. Likewise, applications for tax-exempt status are rarely denied, with only 59 out of more than 115,000 rejected in 2022.

Non-profits have leeway to make discretionary expenditures related to their charitable purpose without triggering inurement. But it's a fine line. My mother's expenses far exceeded her modest paychecks, which ranged from $500 to $2,500 per month. Her living costs were paid by the cult and sometimes directly by wealthy donors. She also authorized spending on personal projects, including extensive remodeling. While this can raise compliance issues, it's fairly standard practice for religious organizations, especially megachurches, where pastors often expense mansions, cars, and planes under the pretext of relevance to the ministry.

Compared to the large non-profits and megachurches, my cult was small potatoes. The Church of Jesus Christ of Latter-day Saints, commonly known as the Mormon Church, is worth well over $100 billion, possibly as much as $200 billion. Scientology holds assets of $2 billion and Liberty University $1.6 billion. At its peak in the late 1980s, my cult had a net worth of $50 million (about $125 million in today's money). While substantial, most of that value was tied up in the 33,000 acres of land we owned in Montana's Paradise Valley. We were staff-heavy and land-poor.

So how did we make ends meet?

Our daily operations relied on multiple revenue streams. The backbone was predictable income from tithes, weekly "love offerings" at services, and publication sales. Books, tapes, and seminars generated a few million dollars annually. We charged substantial admission fees to quarterly conferences, which in later years typically drew thousands of attendees. Summit University tuition also provided steady income. However, these regular channels weren't enough to fund major expansions or projects like the bomb shelters. Members were frequently called upon to support specific initiatives through targeted fundraising campaigns, such as the "Move Mother to Los Angeles" fund, the "Save Our Teachings" fund, and drives for large property acquisitions like our Camelot headquarters and "The Inner Retreat." These campaigns created a sense of urgency and personal investment in our growth.

Through at least the early 1990s, we didn't pay competitive salaries—or even minimum wage. Many of the 700 staff members were volunteers, some of whom even *paid us* for room and board. Those on payroll received small, fixed stipends, which by the early '90s rose to just $150 per month. During one cash crunch, even these payments were suspended, leaving staff to budget necessities like toothpaste, sanitary products, and clothing allowances on forms requiring approval.

We provided no health insurance. In later years, there were staff chiropractors, medical doctors, and a small clinic called "The Center for the Disciplines of Wholeness." However, hospital visits were out-of-pocket expenses, forcing staff to take outside jobs to pay off medical debt. This made me cringe, especially since many people worked 70 to 80 hours a week. During that period, we opted out of Social Security payroll taxes for any staff members who fell under the ministerial exemption, denying them participation in America's national retirement plan.

The extreme sacrifices demanded of staff weren't incidental—they were central to my cult's survival. By leveraging unpaid labor, my mother turned staff poverty into a financial strategy that sustained our growth.

The parasitic financial structure traced back to our founding. In 1958, when he was still located in the Washington, D.C. area, my dad took at least two pensioners into his home, giving them room and board in exchange for their Social Security checks. His five children also lived there, cramming into a single bedroom to make room for the boarders. Other than weekly collections, it was his first steady income as a cult leader. The move to our mansion in Colorado Springs in 1966 opened up even more space for expanding our staff.

Some members turned over their life savings and inheritances to finance our move to Colorado Springs—in exchange for the promise of room and board and future care. In spite of their donations and their advanced years, my parents expected them to work as hard as anyone else. One elderly woman named Phoebe washed dishes from morning to night. Another retired woman named Mary Spelzhaus taught me history and geography. She disappeared when I was six or seven. I found out later that my father excommunicated her after a disagreement. Based on her donations and years of service, she believed she had the right to room and board, and refused to leave. She had nowhere else to go. My father still ordered her to be physically dragged off the property.[15] Eventually, she reportedly found her way to a nursing home. The incident was typical of how my parents discarded people who were no longer of any use.

The early practice of total financial commitment that began with pensioners was later formalized for permanent staff. Anyone in this category had to fill out financial disclosure forms and sign over everything—bank accounts, real property, inheritances, trusts, pensions, even automobiles. The core group of permanent staff complying with this rule grew to about 200 people, and that number swelled further as the deadline for the bomb shelters loomed. In 1989, the board announced that a shelter space would cost $10,000 per person (about $25,000 in 2024 dollars) and extended the total-commitment requirement to anyone who wanted a guaranteed spot. A close friend handed over her $1 million trust fund—even after I begged her not to.

But even this can't explain how we piled up $50 million. Where did the rest come from? Real estate. Every brick-and-mortar cult needs two things: housing and a place to worship. Old mansions were perfect for both—bedrooms for residents and spacious living and dining rooms that could double as chapels. In the 1970s and 1980s, many such properties in distressed neighborhoods were going for pennies on the dollar.

We bought them at rock-bottom prices, rehabbed them with low-paid labor, used them as cult facilities for 10-15 years, and then sold them at a hefty profit—especially when the neighborhood gentrified. Mother sold a few of her remodeled residences, racking up gains. We owned motels and apartment buildings with names like *The Chateau Motor Hotel*, and *The Vassar Victoria*. We leased a youth wilderness facility with crude cabins known as *Camp Bloomfield*, to expand our housing in California.

But our crown jewels were our big-ticket properties. The 240-acre Gillette estate in the Malibu Hills, known as Camelot, cost $4.8 million in 1977—all raised from members. It became cult headquarters, and it's where I graduated from high school. We sold it in 1986 for $15.5 million. Another prime property, The Ashram, located at Country Club Drive and Arlington Avenue in Los Angeles, was bought in 1976 for $250,000 and sold less than a decade later for $2.5 million. Both have been used as locations for countless films and television shows.

We always centralized our assets. So, if members in a local chapter pooled their funds to buy a mansion or an apartment building to set up a teaching center, mother made sure we held title. The financial cycle was clear: members gave everything, allowing us to profit and expand. But when our properties sold, they got nothing back.

This worked out well for us in the buildup to the shelter project. Once she decided that nuclear attack was imminent, she put all our centers across the country up for sale. Everything had to go, even *La Tourelle*, my childhood home. That one stung. But there were bomb shelters to pay for. We bought it in 1966 for $125,000 and it sold for ten times that. It's now an $8,500-per-night luxury retreat called the *Estate Home*, part of the world-famous Broadmoor Hotel.

---

[1] CUT v. Mull, Superior Court of Los Angeles County C. 358191, (February 11, 1986) at 134:10-12
[2] CUT v. Mull, Superior Court of Los Angeles County C. 358191, (February 11, 1986) at 121:14-16
[3] CUT v. Mull, Superior Court of Los Angeles County C. 358191, (February 11, 1986) at 118:15-16
[4] Prophet, E. C. (2009). *Preparation for My Mission* (E. L. Prophet, Ed.). Summit University Press. p. 371

[5] Prophet, E. C. (1993, July 10). Interview by Tatiana Prophet [Interview transcript].

[6] Prophet, E. (2009). *Prophet's Daughter: My Life with Elizabeth Clare Prophet Inside the Church Universal and Triumphant* [Kindle version]. Lyons Press. (p. 252)

[7] Prophet, E. (2009). *Prophet's Daughter: My Life with Elizabeth Clare Prophet Inside the Church Universal and Triumphant* [Kindle version]. Lyons Press. (p. 177)

[8] United States v. Ballard, 322 U.S. 78 (1944), majority opinion author, William Douglas.

[9] Benson, H., Dusek, J. A., Sherwood, J. B., Lam, P., Bethea, C. F., Carpenter, W., ... & Hibberd, P. L. (2006). Study of the therapeutic effects of intercessory prayer (STEP) in cardiac bypass patients: a multicenter randomized trial of uncertainty and certainty of receiving intercessory prayer. *American Heart Journal*, 151(4), 934-942.

[10] Sinclair, U. (1935). *I, candidate for governor: And how I got licked*. Farrar & Rinehart.

[11] Gazette Staff. (2021, January 15). After 90 years, strange times, and sitting empty, Broadmoor Mansion is reborn in high style. *The Gazette*. https://gazette.com/life/after-90-years-strange-times-and-sitting-empty-broadmoor-mansion-is-reborn-in-high-style/article_fd4b1df9-fdfa-57aa-82a6-31107c3be4da.html

[12] The vows of renunciation for the Sons and Daughters of Dominion included the vows of poverty, chastity, and obedience typical to religious orders. There was also language about cutting ties to "worldly" relationships. And a section where initiates pledged lifetime personal loyalty to the Prophet family.

[13] Iannaccone, L. R. (1994). Why strict churches are strong. *American Journal of Sociology*, 99(5), 1180-1211. http://www.jstor.org/stable/2781147

[14] Smith, W. (2023, January 5). IRS data book reveals size, scope of nation's tax-exempt religious non-profits. *MinistryWatch*. https://ministrywatch.com/irs-data-book-reveals-size-scope-of-nations-tax-exempt-religious-nonprofits/

[15] Prophet-Lipinski, R. (personal communication).

CHAPTER ELEVEN

Past Lives

A core tenet of my mother's worldview was that all of us have lived past lives and will reincarnate again, unless we achieve our ascension. Her belief in reincarnation began at age four, when she felt transported from her sandbox to the banks of the Nile. Though her mother Frida was not especially religious, she validated the vision as a past life memory, introducing young Betty Clare to concepts of karma and divine justice. It was a key step in the construction of my mother's supernaturally-infused virtual world.

Later as they built their ministry, my parents drew on Theosophical teachings about souls evolving through repeated incarnations over vast cycles of cosmic time. They claimed they could read past lives through the *akashic* record—a concept introduced by Blavatsky proposing that events are spiritually imprinted on the universe. Their "revelation" of members' past lives delighted some and chagrined others. Most peddlers of reincarnation played it safer. Blavatsky focused on broad spiritual evolution of root-races across cosmic cycles, avoiding specific claims about who was who. Scientology let members "discover" their own grand histories through "auditing." Hindu and Buddhist traditions use reincarnation to explain karma and impermanence. But my parents maintained control over the revelation business. Only they could decode *akasha*, making them the sole authority over members' identities across time.

At La Tourelle, my father instituted knighting ceremonies for permanent staff which sometimes included big donors or particularly dedicated members. He would usually give each person a special title from the Camelot royal court like "Sir Gawain," or "Lady Elaine"—or some other historical figure—often telling them that they had actually *been* that character in a previous life.

Elizabeth and Mark Prophet conduct a knighting ceremony, using a stainless-steel sword at La Tourelle, during which past lives of members were revealed. Colorado Springs, c. 1969

The standard reincarnation cliché applied: Past lives tended to be illustrious or notorious figures. My family was full of royalty and renown. My mother told me I had been the Austro-Hungarian composer Franz Lehár (1870–1948), my sister Erin had been Gandhi (1869–1948), my sister Moira had been President John F. Kennedy (1917–1963), and my sister Tatiana had been Helena Roerich (1879–1955), co-founder of the Agni Yoga Society and early channeler of El Morya. Mother claimed her own past lives as the biblical Martha, Queen Nefertiti, Empress Elisabeth of Austria, Lady Guinevere of Camelot, and St. Catherine of Siena. Meanwhile, my father insisted he had been Sir Lancelot, the poet Henry Wadsworth Longfellow, King Louis XIV, the Sultan Saladin, and Pharaoh Akhenaten. His spiritual name "Lan-ello" is a portmanteau of Lancelot and Longfellow.

This wasn't merely a strange parlor game. My parents were serious. During my childhood, my mother spoke of Franz Lehár as if he were me, implying that I carried his personality traits and would therefore repeat both his mistakes and achievements. She bought me Lehár recordings and his biography and arranged frequent piano and violin lessons with staff musicians. She wanted me to be a musical prodigy. But there was a downside: she often told me I couldn't be trusted with money, convinced Lehár's financial blunders were mine to repeat.

When I was in my early twenties, I embraced my past life as Franz Lehár and let it go to my head. I read "my" biography with great interest and realized my mother was dead wrong about Lehár's finances. In truth, the composer was an international sensation, with his operettas, including *The Merry Widow* and *The Land of Smiles*, performed thousands of times worldwide in multiple languages. Lehár pioneered new ways for composers to control their work, founding Glocken Verlag in 1935 to secure the performance rights to his music and amass significant wealth. None of this, of course, has anything to do with me! But the story illustrates how deeply my parents immersed us all in their virtual world from birth—and how thoughtlessly they foisted their past-life expectations onto us, with little regard for accuracy or psychological impact.

Elizabeth Clare Prophet holds up pictures of Franz Lehár next to Sean Prophet, Santa Barbara, California c. 1974

This fantastical story begins even before my childhood. I had been in my mother's virtual visions for years—before I was born. She recalled,

"When I was pregnant with Sean, I remember that he started riding around in the car with us in the back seat. Mark and I could clearly see him there. But for a whole two or three years before that, he'd come and sit at the table wherever I was eating and start eating with me, as a little blond, blue-eyed boy."[1] Likewise, she claimed to have "met" my sisters—as their past-life avatars—before birth. And this held larger implications.

Her vision of what she believed were the souls of her children between lives shaped her strict natalist position on abortion. One of her bumper-sticker slogans was "Souls of great light are waiting to be born— HAVE ONE!" If souls could appear to my mother years before birth, it's clear why she believed God's plan justified every woman's obligation to carry their pregnancy to term. Never mind that by her own virtual rules, a soul denied incarnation through abortion could simply reincarnate elsewhere. None of it makes sense—but it doesn't need to—in order to accomplish its purpose. Like her claims about past lives, the framework of souls, reincarnation, and karma is an elaborate toolkit for real-world manipulation— easily molded into a pretext for relegating women to the status of broodmares, in dystopian *Handmaid's Tale*-style misogyny.[2]

An Illustration of King Arthur, Sir Lancelot, and Lady Guinevere.

Another gaping spiritual plot hole became apparent when I began critically examining my parents' past life claims. It stemmed from the Arthurian legends of Camelot, which were central to my cult's scripture. She dubbed our main chapel at Camelot "The Chapel of the Holy Grail," and later named our sanctuary at Ranch Headquarters in Montana "King Arthur's Court." These thousand-year-old Celtic myths concern fictional characters. Yet my mother incorporated them as foundational personalities of our theology. Her devotion to Camelot's pageantry created an ironic reincarnated love triangle: Our founding master El Morya was supposedly King Arthur, with my father and mother cast in the roles of Lancelot and Guinevere.

This confused me. My parents were supposed to be twin flames—so was their legendary romance justified? Or did Lancelot and Guinevere betray El Morya? Matters grew more tangled when, in the early 1990s, my mother revealed that El Morya's twin flame was alive—as a sex worker in New York City! She used the pejorative term "prostitute." Even if she was speaking metaphorically or weaving a spiritual parable, what purpose did these sentimental, tragic past life embellishments serve?

I can only conclude my mother believed her grandiose virtual tales were genuine. It's hard to imagine that someone of her intellect could fail to see the corrupting power of such stories. They cemented her leadership by dispensing existence even beyond people's current lives. Heightening the emotional intensity of my cult, and making her virtual world more spiritually and personally resonant—not only for her followers but for our family.

My parents' past-life virtual world-building was a confuse-and-conquer tactic. Psychologically, more choices can lead to paralysis.[3] People had to sort out several lifetimes of their personal history instead of one. And there was no objective reality to any of it—nor were there any checks or balances: Who was I? Sean Prophet, son of Mark and Elizabeth? Or Franz Lehár? King Solomon? Tycho Brahe? Samson? Or yet another figure—real or fictional—my parents assigned to me? Was my son Christopher the 15th-century polymath Paracelsus? Was my high school girlfriend the reincarnated Queen of Sheba?

Yikes.

It's fairly common to describe personality traits using historical or fictional archetypes, like a "Svengali," a "Cassandra," or a "Don Juan." But my mother wasn't speaking figuratively. These declarations not only created identity crises but reinforced her authority on a vast time scale, intertwining our spiritual mythology with both real and legendary history. This elevated her above being merely God's messenger: She positioned herself as a central figure in Western culture *and* mythology, making it even more difficult for anyone to challenge her.

There's a special irony in my mother's invocation of El Morya's twin flame. What are we to make of the psychology behind casting her own alter ego as a lovelorn master enduring the tragedy of separation from his fallen cosmic other half? Never mind that this twin flame was a Jezebel figure who rejected him for what my mother framed as the ultimate degradation: sex work. The lurid tale did little but portray El Morya as a cosmic cuckold while reinforcing spiritual sexual shame. It was a naked sympathy play—and it worked. This was right around the same time when El Morya was supposedly "benched" by his heavenly superiors, and restricted from helping us, because we hadn't been working or praying hard enough. *Poor El Morya!* People intensified their schedules and decrees even beyond their already superhuman levels.

The shocking dichotomy between our auspicious founding patron, "The Ascended Master El Morya," and a New York City sex worker provided the stark contrast my mother sought. It doesn't take a therapist to see that the more grandiose the story, the deeper the insecurity. My mother was famous, wealthy, and powerful—the picture of good fortune. Yet beneath her tales of past-life royalty and cosmic destiny lay the same inadequacy that had haunted her since childhood.

---

[1] Prophet, E. C. (1993, July 10). Interview by T. Prophet.

[2] Atwood, M. (1985). *The handmaid's tale*. McClelland and Stewart.

[3] Iyengar, S. S., & Lepper, M. R. (2000). When choice is demotivating: Can one desire too much of a good thing? *Journal of Personality and Social Psychology, 79*(6), 995–1006. https://doi.org/10.1037/0022-3514.79.6.995 While psychological theory suggests that more choice leads to greater motivation and satisfaction, findings from three experiments challenge this assumption. Participants were more likely to purchase products or complete tasks when offered fewer choices (6 options) rather than more (24–30 options). Additionally, they reported greater satisfaction and performed better when their choices were limited. Implications for future research are discussed.

CHAPTER TWELVE

Survivalism

My cult's forays into survivalism occurred in two phases. The first was related to a prophecy of war and cataclysm my father made on the evening of February 23, 1973—the last full day of his life. He told us to "declare independence from the Luciferian systems of the world," by converting all our funds into gold, silver, and survival supplies—christening the effort "Operation Christ Command." The plan was to move far away from

Tent city at the *Land of Lanello* conference in rural Colorado, c. July 1973. The Land of Lanello was the first "survival retreat" bought by The Summit Lighthouse, following Mark Prophet's apocalyptic 1973 prophecy of war and "world changes."

population centers—and especially from the NORAD nuclear command bunker which was tunneled into Cheyenne Mountain, just a few miles from our home.[1] When he died of a massive stroke the next morning, his deathbed warning became a divine decree. The air raid sirens that wailed at noon on the fourth Friday of each month in our neighborhood became a constant reminder that we lived at ground-zero.

Just two weeks before his death, we signed a contract to purchase a few hundred acres in rural Colorado that we called the "Land of Lanello" (using my dad's Ascended Master name). We bought loads of camping gear and clothing, and we later acquired several other small "survival retreats" in Idaho and Montana. That same year, select members pooled their resources to create a secretive business entity called the Rocky Mountain Sportsman and Survival Club (RMSSC), which acquired fifty AR-15-style rifles, a large cache of ammunition, and tactical gear.

In late 1973, we moved to Santa Barbara and founded a for-profit company called Lanello Reserves which sold dehydrated food, survival supplies, precious metals, and collectibles. Mom's third husband Randall King was put in charge. Since the company traded gold and silver, it also dealt in options and futures. But soon, with my mother's spiritual approval, King began the dangerous practice of buying futures on margin.[2] The market turned, and we were forced to cover margin calls with cult funds.[3] The losses grew too large, liquidating our positions and leaving us in debt. Erin wrote in *Prophet's Daughter* "Had the investment panned out, it could have subjected Randall and Mother to criminal prosecution."[4]

The Clayton brokerage firm sued Lanello Reserves and its parent company, The Summit Lighthouse, for $697,000—about $5 million in 2024 dollars. The case settled for an undisclosed amount. The IRS investigated The Summit Lighthouse for commingling tax-exempt funds with a for-profit enterprise—but stopped short of revoking our tax exemption. In 1975, to forestall any future IRS action, we incorporated a new tax-exempt entity called Church Universal and Triumphant. In 1976, we moved to Los Angeles. For the next decade we put survivalism on the back burner and grew our movement.

My cult's second survivalist phase kicked off when my mother predicted nuclear war in a dictation at the Penta Hotel in New York City in 1987. Her first deadline was October 2, 1989. When that date passed without incident, she updated her prediction. First to January 15, 1990, then February 8, then March and April. The previous two years had been a flurry of planning and shelter-building. It was monumental. The project cost $25 million 1990 dollars—in materials alone.

Our main shelter was located at Taylor Meadows near Mol Heron Creek, in the highlands above Gardiner, Montana. It had living space for 756 people, distributed among six pods with 126 bunks each. Each pod was composed of 13-foot galvanized steel culvert arranged into an H-shape. The pods were buried in two rows of three on either side of a massive 300-feet-long by 40-feet-wide twin-arch bunker called the Deep-Cor Shelter, which was stocked with seven years' worth of food and supplies.

The six pods each held a radiation decontamination facility, a radio/command center, twin diesel generators, a battery room, a water well, bathrooms and showers, a commercial kitchen, a medical facility, men's, women's and couples' dormitories, and a central assembly room known as the "hub." We also built a fully-buried livestock shelter out of twelve 40-foot cargo containers. The shelter complex was an underground "Noah's Ark" in every sense of that term.

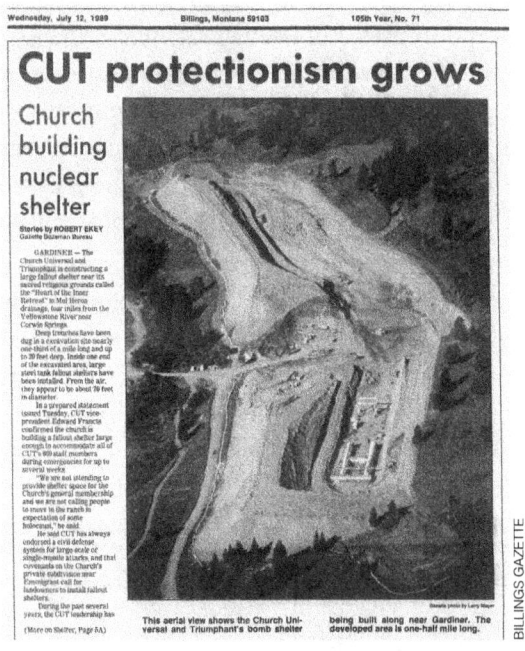

Billings Gazette, July 12, 1989—the nearly half-mile-long excavation for Church Universal and Triumphant's 756-person bomb shelter located at Taylor Meadows near Mol Heron Creek, Gardiner, Montana

Assembled shelter pod number one of six, prior to burial. Mol Heron Creek shelter complex, Gardiner, Montana c. 1989

The central twin-arch Deep-Cor Shelter was designed to hold food and long-term supplies for the 756 residents of the smaller shelter pods. Each arch is 300 feet long, 40 feet wide, and 20 feet high. It was eventually buried under 20 feet of fill. The air intake and exhaust shafts of shelter pods 1, 2, and 3 can be seen in the background of this photo. Mol Heron Creek shelter complex, Gardiner, Montana c. 1989

Radio towers, air intake/exhaust shafts, and shelter gun turrets made from heavily reinforced concrete, Mol Heron Creek shelter complex, Gardiner, Montana c. 1990

We focused on every detail required to sustain our lives and community after nuclear war. Yet we also knew that if the worst happened, desperate intruders might show up to demand our supplies. So we installed eight gun turrets made from "heavy concrete" reinforced with steel pellets and fibers. By the time we held the early 1990 drills, our underground installations throughout Paradise Valley were bristling with .223 and .308-caliber military-style weaponry.

Rumors about the cache of AR-15s from our first survivalist period circulated in the press for years, fueled by reports from ex-members like Don Trowbridge, who confirmed their existence on the Oprah Winfrey show.[5] Trowbridge recalled transporting a "truckload" of AR-15s and ammunition across state lines from Idaho into Montana in 1974. Our press spokesman Murray Steinman mocked him, claiming "no one's ever seen the guns, no one's ever used the guns," calling their existence "hypothetical." But Steinman was fully aware of the guns and may have been party to the original RMSSC purchase. Oprah asked directly, "Are you saying there are no guns?" Erin replied, "We've never seen them." I never saw them either until late 1989, when I worked all night with several permanent staff members to move them into a secret storage tank under the Deep-Cor shelter that also held our $5 million stash of gold. It was definitely a *truckload*—including tens of thousands of rounds of ammunition.

Also that year, under my mother's instructions, I helped a construction foreman named Robert hide a trove of documents related to the RMSSC. First we crammed several boxes of papers into a piece of 12-inch PVC pipe about 4 feet long and sealed it with water-tight end caps. Under cover of darkness Robert and I used a backhoe to bury the canister eight feet deep. The next day mother and Erin did altar work about our overnight caper and came back with the cryptic warning from El Morya, "You were seen." So the next night we dug up the canister and buried it a second time in a more secluded location near the shelters.

A few men within my cult's inner circle, including permanent staffer Vernon Hamilton and Edward Francis, made elaborate self-defense plans involving heavier armament. With my mother's spiritual approval, cosigned by Erin, they bought two armored personnel carriers and had plans to acquire a total of twenty .50-caliber Barrett anti-materiel rifles, along with a supply of armor-piercing ammunition. The APCs and Barretts were legal for private citizens to own. Francis and Hamilton's mistake was simple: they bought the firearms under a false name that they lifted from a dead attorney—ironically to avoid bad publicity.

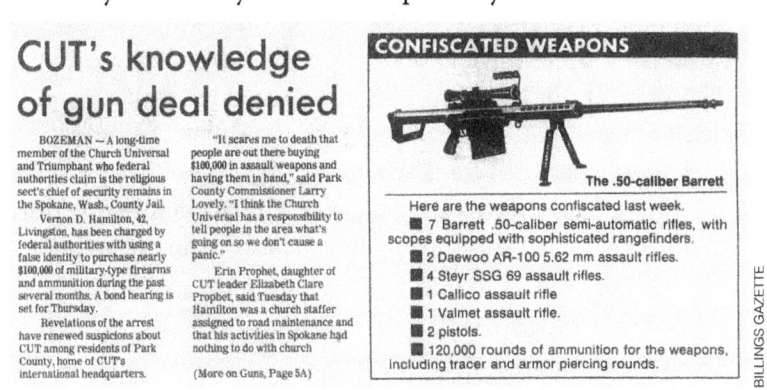

Billings Gazette, July 12, 1989

Back in 1989 at least, the Bureau of Alcohol, Tobacco, and Firearms (ATF) took its background checks seriously. After Hamilton's purchase of seven Barretts and other rifles, the feds flagged the false name and launched an investigation. In June of that year agents caught Hamilton at a traffic stop with a storage locker receipt in his car and a handwritten note from Francis detailing the plot. ATF searched the locker, finding the weapons and 120,000 rounds of ammunition, along with $100,000 in cash and gold coins. They arrested Hamilton and seized everything. The incident made worldwide headlines. Both my mother and Erin lied about their involvement in the weapons purchase. Erin only came clean when she published *Prophet's Daughter* in 2008, just before our mother died.

I knew about Edward and Vernon's weapons plan, and I knew my mother and Erin had spiritually approved it. I had given Vernon about $600 to buy me ammunition—which he bought but I never received. It was seized by ATF along with everything else. When the news of Hamilton's arrest broke, our family gathered at my mother's Mol Heron Canyon home to strategize.

She was convinced her house was bugged by the feds, so we walked about a hundred yards into the forest. Edward was stoic, speaking barely above a whisper. He told us our attorney, Milt Datsopoulos, was concerned that we could all be charged under the RICO act which carries 20-year prison sentences. Our corporation could also be subject to asset forfeiture, which could include our land. We had to eliminate any evidence linking my cult to previous weapons purchases that would establish a pattern of behavior.

Mother assigned me to drive to our warehouse at the Livingston Industrial Park to retrieve what Edward only half-jokingly called the "felony case." It was a tan leather suitcase stuffed with more RMSSC documents. I was terrified we were under surveillance and that I would be arrested on my way home. On the verge of tears, I demanded an explanation: "How could El Morya let this happen?" Mother glared at me with stony coldness and spat, "Stop your whining and *do your job!*" Despite being scared shitless, I borrowed a personal car that wasn't registered to the cult and drove to Livingston. I found the case where Edward had said it would be and brought it back to the ranch, burning the documents in my fireplace.

In the weeks and months that followed, my cult's survivalism and illicit arms purchases were discussed on almost every major talk show, including "Larry King Live," "Oprah," "Phil Donahue," "Nightline," and "48 Hours." The story was also frequently covered on network news. Both men pleaded guilty and received light prison sentences, four months for Hamilton, and one month for Francis. After their release, Hamilton was put on a lengthy probation. Though Francis was allowed to continue as our vice-president and business manager, he was sentenced to home detention during evenings and weekends. The men had used their own funds—and the private funds of other cult members—to buy the weapons, and proved that no cult funds were used. So we were in the clear from RICO. But that wasn't our only legal trouble.

Early in 1990, we had 500,000 gallons of diesel fuel, 120,000 gallons of gasoline, and 140,000 gallons of propane stored at the Mol Heron Creek shelter site. There were more than thirty 20,000-gallon tanks. In our mad rush to get everything ready by El Morya's deadline, we had hastily buried some of the tanks in frozen ground. During the spring thaw in April, several tanks ruptured. I was present at the shelter site with Edward and the work crew the day the leak was discovered. Our foreman Robert had been taking measurements and noticed that a few of the tanks were missing fuel. Edward was incredulous. We all walked up to one of the tanks in question, and Robert lowered a long wooden diprod into the fillpipe. Sure enough, the level was way down. But he didn't need to measure it. We could all smell gasoline.

As the awful reality dawned on us, Edward jumped into the air, whipped off his baseball cap, and hurled it to the ground. "Goddammit!!" he roared.

I had never heard him swear. We didn't know how much fuel was missing. But Edward knew that any spill would represent an environmental disaster. We would not only have to empty and dig up all the fuel tanks, we would face a firestorm of negative publicity and enforcement from multiple government agencies. He'd spent his entire adult life skillfully building and defending the financial and legal framework for our cult, through all the twists and turns of divine revelation. At that moment, everything he'd worked for came undone with a resounding finality.

Since they were intended only for emergency use, our shelters were constructed without building permits, which had already caused an uproar. We had been sued by the state of Montana. The National Park Service was already furious about the massive industrial project just a few miles from the border of Yellowstone Park. Our fuel spill came to be the last straw.

It was a predictable—and predicted—consequence. Our chief engineer, our construction supervisors, and Edward had been unanimous that burying

Billings Gazette, April 15, 1990

fuel tanks in frozen ground was unwise. Edward had tried to explain the dangers to my mother, but she gave no reprieve from El Morya's deadline, which had already slipped from October 2, 1989. So crews worked through the winter, trying to thaw frozen fill dirt with heating elements, using wackers and plate compactors to achieve the best density they could. But all that work was no match for Montana's subzero temperatures. It wasn't entirely our fault. There were serious welding defects in the tanks—which had split at their seams—and we collected damages from the tank manufacturer after a lawsuit. But the tanks we had installed during the previous summer were fine. The ones that leaked had all been bedded during the winter on frozen soil that was impossible to properly compact.

The spill was worse than suspected—32,000 gallons, mostly diesel fuel, but also gasoline. Some gasoline leaked into shelter #4, which was closest to one of the ruptured tanks, filling it with fumes and making it temporarily uninhabitable. Spilled fuel traveled through underground plumes and aquifers, fouling the pristine Mol Heron Creek. A measurable amount of fuel made it to the Yellowstone River. We faced environmental fines from multiple government agencies, including the *Coast Guard*—$10,000 for contaminating a "navigable waterway."

The cleanup took a year and cost $1 million. The remaining 590,000 gallons of fuel had to be removed from the site. The loss of that diesel made our brand-new $25 million shelter complex inoperable and worthless. Through his haste, El Morya had blundered into checkmate. The fuel leak marked the end of our shelter effort and exposed the dire price of elevating prophecy above the laws of the land—and the laws of physics. For the IRS it was just too many high-profile irregularities for a non-profit organization. So in 1991, probably under some public pressure, they finally revoked our tax-exemption, if only for that single year.

In the late '90s, one of the cult mechanics told me that they had converted the shelter generators to run on propane, which was unaffected by the spill. But the shelters are 35 years old. Generators and batteries don't last forever. Dehydrated food has a limited shelf life. Clothing and supplies deteriorate. Rats ate or contaminated nearly all of the bulk grain we had stored. As recently as 2008, cult leaders Lois Drake and Kate Gordon told the *Billings Gazette* that the shelters were operational and that stored food is rotated. I'm skeptical. Though it's possible the shelters might still function, and some of the food might still be edible, it's unlikely that anyone will ever make use of what amounts to my cult's biggest folly.

---

[1] Cheyenne Mountain Complex. (n.d.). *North American Aerospace Defense Command (NORAD)*. Retrieved from https://www.norad.mil/Newsroom/Fact-Sheets/Article-View/Article/578775/cheyenne-mountain-complex/

The North American Aerospace Defense Command (NORAD) facility, housed within Cheyenne Mountain near Colorado Springs, Colorado, is a critical site for monitoring and defending North American airspace. NORAD's responsibilities include detecting, validating, and issuing warnings of potential airborne threats, including attacks via aircraft, missiles, or space vehicles.

[2] Commodity Futures Trading Commission (CFTC). (n.d.). *Futures margin requirements*. Retrieved from https://www.sec.gov/investor/alerts/ib_marginaccounts.pdf

Trading commodity futures on margin involves borrowing from a broker to take larger market positions with a fraction of the total contract value, known as the margin. While this enables leveraged trading, it also amplifies both profits and losses. Even slight market fluctuations can result in gains or losses exceeding the initial margin, leading to financial exposure beyond the investor's initial stake.

[3] Securities and Exchange Commission (SEC). (n.d.). *Understanding margin calls*. Retrieved from https://www.sec.gov/about/reports-publications/investorpubsmarginhtm

A margin call occurs when an investor's margin account balance falls below the brokerage's minimum requirement due to adverse market movements. To meet this obligation, the investor must deposit additional funds or securities. Failure to do so allows the brokerage to liquidate assets to cover the shortfall, potentially leading to losses exceeding the investor's initial margin investment.

[4] Prophet, E. (2009). *Prophet's daughter: My life with Elizabeth Clare Prophet inside the Church Universal and Triumphant*. Lyons Press. p.98

[5] Winfrey, O. (Host). (1989, September 12). *The Oprah Winfrey Show* [TV broadcast]. Harpo Productions.

CHAPTER THIRTEEN

Levers of Control

Suffering demands justification. The more regimented the path, the greater the need to believe it fulfills some larger purpose. The prime directive for every cult boils down to one word: control. Our most fundamental lever of control was the demanding schedule. Members were required to attend 5 AM decree sessions, followed by noon decrees, and regular Wednesday, Friday, and Saturday night services. Sunday services began at 10 AM and often continued until late afternoon. Worship was layered on top of a grueling "9-9-6" work pattern—twelve-hour days, six days per week. If you weren't working, you were decreeing. Staff were supposed to get a half-day off on Saturday, but these breaks were frequently canceled due to important projects or spiritual crises. With barely any free time, members would scramble to complete basic life maintenance like laundry and errands on Sundays after services, if there was time at all.

Some of my cult's most disturbing controls were intimate violations—encroachments on personal autonomy that no one should accept. As previously mentioned, permanent staff surrendered their financial independence. But all categories of staff submitted to deep infringements on their identities: rules about sexuality, diet, marriage, music, books, grooming, clothing choices, childbearing decisions, with some even changing their names.

Misogyny was pervasive. My mother often ordered attractive women to crop their hair, while female ministers dress-coded women wearing form-fitting clothing. For several years in the '70s and '80s, most women and some men wore "Guru Ma" outfits designed to obscure body shapes—knee-length tent-like tunics over drawstring pants.

Strangely, through the process of thought reform, members agreed to this. Some even wanted these disciplines. But that's too easy an out. The Hindu-Buddhist concept of *chelaship* requires submission by the *chela* (disciple) to the *guru* (teacher). Ideally, this dynamic would resemble mentorship. In a cult, it becomes a master-slave relationship, with the guru wielding absolute power and the chela surrendering their "human self" in pursuit of enlightenment. The absence of checks on the guru's authority fosters abuse. In all such arrangements, the guru bears moral responsibility for the chela's well-being.

Our experts at the Mull trial framed his experience as a voluntary conversion, which is half true. While my cult employed Robert Jay Lifton's principles of thought reform, Mull was eager to embrace our disciplines. Thought reform, as I've stressed, is not transitive—it's *interactive*. This aligns with modern therapeutic methods that reject "perpetrator" vs. "victim" labels, focusing on mutual participation in dysfunctional systems.

Remember, cults are *algorithms* which reinforce member behaviors through complex feedback loops supporting the cult's *BOMP*—beliefs, outcomes, methods, and purpose. Expert testimony on coercive persuasion lacked scientific rigor, and it diverted attention from the question of why Mull surrendered his independence. Yet some of it remains relevant to religious trauma, the role of confession, the fear of losing salvation, and the struggle to leave a cult. Without naming it as such, Rabbi Robbins summed up the algorithm:

> Asserting that [a person's] unmet needs, both spiritual and emotional, sometimes even physical… are a consequence of [their lack of] enlightenment. And that the organization, its teachings… and theology will provide a panacea, a total answer and resolution to all of their spiritual and emotional difficulties. If the individual will make a total and complete surrender and commitment to the organization—turning over… the total spectrum of their life to the organization, they will then be saved.[1]

Dr. Margaret Singer testified that Mull's psychological changes began long before he started working at Camelot, calling it a "gradual accretion of powerlessness." She confirmed that "the thought reform program is a property of the organization,"[2] and that Mull exhibited symptoms of Post-Traumatic Stress Disorder (PTSD)—a diagnosis only officially recognized since 1980.[3] In her view, Mull suffered permanent psychological damage, including loss of self-confidence, loss of faith in humanity, and violation of his trust.

Singer defined seven elements of the cult algorithm:

1. A cult is led by a self-appointed person who claims to have discovered a

special mission.

2. A cult directs their veneration to the current living leader, more than to God or to abstract principles.

3. A cult's purpose tends to be primarily fund-raising and recruitment.

4. A cult tends to have a double-standard of ethics for insiders and outsiders.

5. A cult is elitist, claiming that members are superior and outsiders are inferior.

6. A cult tends to be totalitarian, with the leader having sole and ultimate power.

7. A cult has rules that cover almost every feature of life.[4]

Our algorithm was strengthened by teachings on karma and reincarnation that extended penalties beyond a single lifetime. This carried more weight than Christian threats of hell. Sins like leaving the path or denouncing the guru could incur great karma, requiring many future "embodiments" to resolve. Worse, members feared the second death. These fears led believers to relish their submission to the guru, viewing it as a way to pay off their karma in a single lifetime, escape from the "wheel of rebirth"—and punch their ticket to eternal life—the hottest commodity any religion or cult can offer.

My mother thus positioned herself as the broker of immortality, claiming not just a path to enlightenment but direct access to divinity—a control deeper than traditional religions could achieve. By focusing on coercion, both sides avoided a nuanced exploration of why people like Mull chose, time and again, to accept my mother as their guru.

As Iannaccone emphasized in "Why Strict Churches Are Strong," rigid control extracts a higher level of commitment and supports the cult's organizational success. Despite the pretext of a "guru-chela relationship," these abuses accomplished a cynical purpose, which came into particular focus through my cult's code of conduct for friendships, dating, and marriage. Staffers required my mother's written permission at every step—a process frustrated by delays—or even denials.

There were strict rules governing intimacy within marriage, including prescribed prayers before and after sex, which was limited to missionary position, twice per week, for no more than twenty minutes. Mutual masturbation, oral and anal sex were forbidden. Counseling couples on these rules was deeply uncomfortable. I was a baby-faced kid in my early 20s, forced to meddle in the marriages of people far more mature than I was, while admonishing them to follow rules I considered absurd. I hated every moment of it.

Same-sex relationships were not tolerated. My mother rooted this prohibition in our concept of *twin flames*, teaching that every soul has a male and female counterpart. As in Catholic doctrine, she felt that sex was for procreation. But she was conflicted. At times she understood the value of sex for its own sake. But she also adhered to the Ballard teaching that sex is a waste of spiritual energy. She taught that homosexuality is a perversion of God's will, a "misuse of the sacred fire" brought to Earth by extraterrestrial dark forces and passed down from hedonistic cults on the "lost continents" of Atlantis and Lemuria. My mother accused Gregory Mull of being a sort of grand galactic pooh-bah of gayness. It sounds crazy. But in the lead up to the *CUT v. Mull* trial she announced that he was the reincarnation of the original "fallen angel" responsible for bringing the "scourge" of homosexuality to Earth.

Such sordid bigotry didn't stop gay people from joining or remaining in my cult. Los Angeles-based journalist R. Daniel Foster was roped in at the age of 19, after his parents sent him to a gay-conversion therapist who was a member. He stayed for seven years, held in part by the ritual and pageantry. Foster remained celibate and participated dutifully in feverish prayer sessions to "Smash! Blast! Annihilate! Shatter! Dissolve! and Consume!" the gay-rights movement. After leaving at age 26, he wrote in *The Advocate*, "Was there ever a lower bottom to a man's self-hate? Or a greater height to the fear, paranoia, and foolishness of a religious movement?"[5]

Like Foster, a handful of gay people spent years on our staff, practicing celibacy or marrying opposite-sex partners. Those caught in gay liaisons were usually expelled. But there were exceptions. Two women confessed to a sexual relationship, and my mother let them stay, probably because she needed them. She compared their behavior to animals and sentenced them to sleep (separately) in the sheep barn for a month. Why anyone would remain in a group which stigmatized their fundamental nature is beyond my understanding.

We banned masturbation as a "waste of spiritual life force" and a "sin against God," citing Onan's death in Genesis. But let's be honest—masturbation is harmless, near-universal and unstoppable. A study during the Covid-19 pandemic reported that only 24.2% of men and 43.5% of women had abstained during the previous year.[6] Still, my mother was determined to make her followers squirm. In the early 1980s, she gave a dictation announcing that no one was allowed to attend worship services unless they had been masturbation-free for 30 days. The following week, the chapel was half-empty—and everyone knew why.

One awful incident of sexual humiliation still angers me. A dynamic woman in her late 30s was a firebrand in my cult and a skilled public speaker. She led much of our outreach in the late '70s and early '80s. (I'll keep her identity private.) A great organizer with a strong background in women's-rights activism, she rose quickly to become a minister and church elder. Despite her dedication and long hours, my mother dismissed her from staff. At a permanent-staff meeting, she aired the woman's "character flaws" and exposed the contents of her confession letters—which included lesbian fantasies and masturbation. This ethical breach shamed the woman in absentia, and served as a warning to staff: their confessions could be used against them.

My cult's control reached beyond intimate relationships into friendships. Members deemed "out of alignment" found themselves isolated as counselors directed others to avoid or abandon them. I saw friendships weaponized countless times, and I experienced it personally.

My best friend Will Adams and I were co-department heads for audio and video production. We had also been business partners. He confided a sexual infraction—technically a confession since I was an ordained minister. I had every right to hold it sacred under priest-penitent privilege, believing his remorse was sufficient. But Will decided to confess to my mother, who called us both into a meeting. She was furious that I withheld information and punished both of us—restricting his travel for a year and telling me I had lost the right to be his friend. I felt betrayed by both of them.

Why did she interfere in our friendship? Why did he accept her interference? It was a valuable lesson, which inched me closer to leaving my cult. I lost another chunk of my naiveté along with a friend. I watched many friendships and couples injured by cult disciplines. When married staff faced punishment, my mother required spouses to be present and cosign the penance. These callous incidents proved that when people abdicate their autonomy, relationships become a love-triangle with a living God. No human can compete.

We enforced a comprehensive cultural embargo—Lifton's *Milieu Control* in action—considering most popular culture "of the world" and "fallen." We were only allowed to watch "wholesome" and "uplifting" content, such as old musicals, classic films, or documentaries. Fiction and romance novels were generally banned.

Music was a particular battleground. Rock, jazz, blues, and popular music were off limits. Music at social events was limited to waltzes, polkas, and occasional western-themed square dances. Even roller and ice skating were restricted to times when our school could rent out the rink and play classical music. I was allowed to listen to folk artists like John Denver—but never top-40 radio. When I was a young boy, I sometimes snuck out with a battery-powered radio strapped to my bike. High school brought new temptations—1976-1980 was a fertile period for classic rock and disco, which were easily found on Los Angeles stations like KLOS, KMET and KIIS-FM. Kids at our school weren't shy about listening to the radio on headphones, taping songs, and trading albums.

Then in 1977, it all collapsed. My mother called a school assembly, gathering about 75 students in the "Little Theater," a 200-seat auditorium on our Pasadena campus. There were no teachers present, and my mother was visibly upset. She raged against rock music for what seemed like an hour. El Morya was furious. Our music was threatening the *spiritual survival* of the community. If it didn't stop, she would *close the school*. The kids were *personally responsible* for a drop in church donations. Then she told us where the teachers were—conducting a thorough sweep of lockers and dorm rooms. All our records, tapes, radios, TVs and stereo equipment were confiscated. I never got any of that stuff back, and I don't think anyone else did, either. They even took my John Denver records.

Control extended deeply into food and drink. My mother's antipathy for alcohol was legendary—understandable given her father's drinking and temper. But as with diet, she extended her personal preferences into a community-wide alcohol ban. Following the letter of the law, in 1991, after the "shelter cycle," I directed our general store to sell non-alcoholic beer and wine. People loved it. We could barely keep it in stock. Then El Morya—that old goat—decided to ruin our fun, declaring that even trace amounts of alcohol were spiritually unacceptable.

El Morya's near-beer ban echoed an earlier *root-beer* ban from the 1970s, delivered in a dictation from "The Ascended Lady Master Nada." At the time, I often hung around the audio-video department, run by a man named Alan Kozlowski, who became a mentor as he taught me how to operate sound equipment. I had discovered he kept a case of honey-sweetened Dr. Tima root beer in his office, and I always begged him for a bottle.

One day, I found him in the kitchen at our Santa Barbara center, pouring the root beer into the sink.

"What are you doing?" I exclaimed.

Alan replied, "The Master Nada said no more sodas. It was in a dictation."

"Please don't pour it out—give it to me!" I said.

He shook his head. "That would make me responsible for you disobeying the master."

I was crestfallen, watching him pour out every last bottle of that delicious brown elixir. Later, I asked him to play the dictation for me, and the words burned into my brain: "take care that you do not drink those carbonated drinks that are bottled." Always looking for loopholes, I silently wondered if *canned* soda was still OK?

El Morya struck again in the early 1990s, banning "desserts" for Ranch Headquarters staff. My mother had become increasingly vocal about sugar being the source of all ills. She was hypoglycemic, so perhaps it was true for her. Valid or not, many of our members began to regard sugar as a poison, or an addictive drug.

Recreational drugs were rare in my cult. My one teenage experiment with marijuana at a Malibu beach left me underwhelmed, and while some kids had past experience, drug use was minimal in our school. But we heard a lot about drugs in the dictations. In the early 1980s, pot was very illegal, and it was right around the time of Nancy Reagan's "Just Say No" campaign, with all the fevered rhetoric about marijuana as a "gateway drug." "The Ascended Master Saint Germain" called it the "death drug." And that convinced us kids that if we ever took one more toke, we would end up on the street, dead of a heroin overdose, with needles stuck in our arms.

Strict rules were an integral part of my cult's algorithm, which used all the typical world-rejecting tactics employed by authoritarian religions. There's no denying Iannaccone's social science that strict churches are strong churches. Without checks on their power there's nothing to stop cult leaders from tightening rules to solidify control. And those dots connect to the conservative moral foundations of authority, loyalty, and sanctity.

---

[1] CUT v. Mull, Superior Court of Los Angeles County C. 358191, (February 25, 1986) at 1120:8-18
[2] CUT v. Mull, Superior Court of Los Angeles County C. 358191, (February 26, 1986) at 1347:17-19

³ American Psychiatric Association. (1980). *Diagnostic and statistical manual of mental disorders* (3rd ed.). American Psychiatric Association. PTSD was officially recognized as a mental health disorder by the American Psychiatric Association in 1980, when it was included in the third edition of the *Diagnostic and Statistical Manual of Mental Disorders* (DSM-III). This recognition followed increased awareness of trauma-related conditions, particularly in veterans returning from the Vietnam War. Retrieved from https://psychiatry.org/patients-families/ptsd/what-is-ptsd

⁴ CUT v. Mull, Superior Court of Los Angeles County C. 358191, (February 26, 1986) at 1273:20-1274:27

⁵ Foster, R. D. (1999, June 8). From a galaxy far, far away. *The Advocate*. Retrieved from https://www.thefreelibrary.com/From+a+galaxy+far%2C+far+away.-a054796476

⁶ Herbenick, D., Fu, T. C., Wasata, R., & Coleman, E. (2023). Masturbation prevalence, frequency, reasons, and associations with partnered sex in the midst of the COVID-19 pandemic: Findings from a U.S. nationally representative survey. *Archives of Sexual Behavior*, 52(3), 1317–1331. https://doi.org/10.1007/s10508-022-02505-2

CHAPTER FOURTEEN

Sanctity

Sanctity serves a dual function in cults: it binds members through shared beliefs and rituals while blinding them to harm. Gregory Mull's testimony reveals both dynamics. He felt spiritually "controlled" by our teachings since attending Summit University in 1975, yet his fascination with them endured. When Ken Klein asked when he stopped being under my mother's control, Mull replied "I'm still working on it, but it is almost complete." This was in 1986—eleven years after his indoctrination.[1] Mull still referred to himself as a "slave," reflecting his chelaship.[2]

Lawrence Levy focused on surface levers of control like chanting, diet, colonics, and lack of sleep. But testimony from our kitchen secretary confirmed adequate nutrition[3] and practices like fasting and colonics were voluntary. Sleep may have been hard to come by in my cult, but that's a problem for 35-40% of Americans.[4] Yes, the decrees were annoying and a waste of time. And no, they didn't by themselves change anyone's minds. Believing they were effective was a form of sacred science, a component of thought reform.

At their core, these practices fostered group cohesion. Friendly expert witness Robert L. Moore testified that our decrees were "a very powerful ritual technique which is used by this group to create a sense of group solidarity and a sense of enhanced energy and commitment."[5] Engaging in shared rituals—whether decrees, fasting, or extreme diets—releases oxytocin, a hormone that promotes bonding and trust.[6] This biological mechanism helps explain how these activities bound members more tightly to the group, despite their lack of practical value—or even their harm.

Evidence confirms what the testimony revealed: Mull joined my cult because he wanted to be on the spiritual path, and our rituals helped influence him to stay. When pressed further by Klein, Mull confirmed that he was especially vulnerable because he "liked the teachings," and "believed in the teachings."[7]

Klein emphasized that Mull was free to "partake of the masters' teachings at the level of your own commitment." While Mull agreed that nothing prevented him from leaving, he testified that after attending Summit University he had come to fear the outside world—specifically "discarnate entities" he believed could jump from other people to him—stealing his light. He also feared "betrayers" who had left the cult. Mull signed the promissory notes, he explained, out of a fear of losing his ascension and facing "ten thousand years in outer darkness, or thousands of embodiments."[8]

Mull faced sky-high professional stakes. His architectural business had declined, leaving him broke and forced to borrow against his San Francisco home, renting out rooms to survive. He simply couldn't afford to donate his time, but working for us offered non-monetary compensation—he felt it was important to be "part of the elite" and "the hierarchy." He also testified that he "felt like Michelangelo," being commissioned for a prestigious project.[9] But he wanted a standard architectural fee as a percentage of building costs, something we weren't prepared to offer.

Instead of designing "The New Jerusalem," Mull was relegated to low-level remodeling tasks. This diminished his professional pride and deepened his growing disillusionment. He also discovered that his friendship with my mother wasn't as strong as he had imagined—a common issue with parasocial relationships, where one party feels a deep connection to someone who doesn't reciprocate—or sees the bond as transactional. After joining staff, Mull was disappointed that she was no longer available to talk to him. The lack of a "special relationship" left him feeling "inadequate and low."[10]

Mull's letters and testimony demonstrate a significant detachment from reality. He idolized my mother. His grandiose architectural ambitions ignored that our Camelot master plan was a fundraising tool for a hypothetical future expansion—not a project we were ready to build. Yet he gambled his future on it anyway. His spiritual thirst had led him to a fruitless search for external answers, short-circuiting his psychological progress, papering over his inadequacy and shame. He came to Camelot driven by ambition, yet he stayed even when it became servitude. He couldn't have it both ways. Lacking the self-worth to demand appropriate compensation—or failing that to walk away—he was trapped in a classic double bind.

But my cult was far from blameless. From January through August 1979, we ignored Mull's requests to clarify the business relationship. For eight months, we kicked him around like a football, neither committing to paying him a salary nor firing him. Paying his expenses each month without a formal agreement blurred the lines of his employment status. By the time he signed the first promissory note in September for $32,000—at seven percent interest—he testified, "I was already so involved with this cult that I would have signed or done or said anything. But I really didn't mean that I owed them or really wanted to owe or would pay them back.... My terms were simple: Pay my expenses."[11] He signed a second promissory note in October for $5,000 and received a final check, after which he worked without pay for seven more months.

So why didn't he quit?

The answer once again lies in Mull's internalized spiritual obligation. Even as his finances declined, his fears kept him bound, hoping his sacrifice would save him. But it was not to be. In May 1980 after missing a required payment, he repudiated the promissory notes, insisting that the $37,000 was compensation, not a loan, and offering to settle the matter for $10,000. The board terminated his employment and asked him to vacate his Camelot office within three days. Which he viewed as being "kicked out."

Mull's predicament exemplifies patterns of control that stretch back to the earliest human social organization. Far beyond my cult, deep ethical failures are reliable features of sacred and traditional moral systems that subvert personal autonomy and well-being in favor of service, sacrifice, and order. There's a constant tension between healthy autonomy and hierarchical, groupish moralities that require conformity and foster exploitation. Too many people seek the benefits of belonging—without considering its risks.

Cult morality diverges radically from common social norms. And reshaping the ethics of cult members is a key product of thought reform. Cult leaders appeal to a *higher law* that conforms to the mystical imperative. When you exit your cult, you'll need to reject this view, along with the moral confusion that made you susceptible to it. Your goal is to replace any vestige of sanctity with well-examined, internally-consistent, human-focused values.

Patterns of sanctified control emerged in our earliest social structures. The evolved anthropological foundations of cultic systems began with hunter-gatherers in the ancestral environment, where groups of 150 or fewer formed the basic social unit.[12] Protecting the tribe from hostile outsiders was a matter of survival. Group behavior was strictly regulated by tribal elders, and those violating tribal norms could be exiled, a potential death sentence.[13]

Agriculture enabled larger groupings and stricter hierarchies, with leaders of populations over a million inventing punitive gods as a form of social control—the origin of large-scale worship.[14] Until recently, Western anthropologists portrayed hierarchy as historically inevitable. However, David Graeber and David Wengrow's *The Dawn of Everything* revealed a more complex truth: egalitarian cultures have existed throughout history alongside hierarchical ones, including sophisticated North American indigenous societies whose principles later influenced modern democracy.[15]

This insight has particular relevance to understanding cults, which often justify their hierarchical structure through tradition. Yet while democracy offers an alternative, it represents a distinctly Western phenomenon. As Henrich, Heine, and Norenzayan demonstrated in their 2010 paper "The Weirdest People in the World?" WEIRD societies—meaning Western, Educated, Industrialized, Rich, and Democratic—comprise only 12 percent of the world's population—yet these characteristics are often mistakenly used as a baseline for the social sciences.

This tension between hierarchical and egalitarian organization reflects deeper patterns in moral psychology. Social psychologist Jonathan Haidt clarified this further by introducing Moral Foundations Theory in his 2012 book *The Righteous Mind: Why Good People Are Divided by Politics and Religion*.[16] He argues that liberal western morality is hamstrung and incomplete, because it includes only three of the six foundations of evolved human ethics: Care/Harm, Fairness/Cheating, and Liberty/Oppression. The other three foundations—Loyalty/Betrayal, Authority/Subversion, and Sanctity/Degradation—remain central to conservatism, order, and hierarchical systems. You'll recognize these three conservative moral foundations as the central organizing principles of cults, religions, and dictatorships.

Haidt argues that loyalty is essential for social cohesion and national unity, that respecting authority supports order, that tradition preserves wisdom, that sanctity protects the "moral capital" of a community, and that purity is a necessary antidote to broad dangers of contamination. Haidt even finds a way to wax poetic about the cultural relevance of servitude, the caste system, and multi-generational households, in the context of moral pluralism.[17] He's describing moral foundations *as they are*, not as any of us might like them to be. And he delivers excellent insights into the problem of cults. Especially his social experiments designed to create moral confusion, involving deliberate moral blinding. There's simply no denying that the moral foundations of loyalty, authority, and sanctity are the enabling factors for every cult abuse.

In hierarchical structures like cults, religions, dictatorships and militaries, the individual is subordinated to a shared purpose. Haidt calls it "flipping the hive switch." Our brains evolved to operate in both modes, which helps explain why people are susceptible to thought reform. As Dawson pointed out, soldiers are willing to sacrifice their lives for their unit. What flips their hive switch is shared meaning and purpose in defense of their nation—and more directly, their love for their fellow soldiers. Cult induction is similar, dangling a compelling mystical imperative that weaves together world transformation, individual salvation and group acceptance. Modern cults and religions mostly don't ask people to die for their cause but they do ask converts to embrace the shared mythology, subordinate their individuality, bond with each other and hand over the keys to their lives.

What does a cult recruit give up in return for that blissful feeling of acceptance into the hive? Well, everything. Cult members largely abandon fairness, harm reduction, and personal considerations in favor of collective well-being, submission to hierarchy, and dedication to group norms. But it's deeper than that. What kind of core values do groupish moral systems based on loyalty, authority, and sanctity produce? The short answer is: totalistic values resembling a miniature empire. Haidt makes a key point about the role of gods, "Groups create supernatural beings not to explain the universe, but to order their societies."[18] This recalls my discussion of *cosmos* vs. *nomos* in the social order. So, what kind of order do supernatural beings produce?

Linguist George Lakoff has an answer that rings true—at least for American Christian conservatives: The Conservative Moral Hierarchy.[19] God is at the top, the center of the "strict father" (authoritarian) model of morality, which justifies inequality in terms of a mythological "natural order" (see illustration below). A place for everyone, and everyone in their place.

George Lakoff
@GeorgeLakoff

The conservative moral hierarchy helps explain Republican attacks on affordable healthcare. Sound familiar?
georgelakoff.com/2017/07/01/two...

The Conservative Moral Hierarchy:
- God above Man
- Man above Nature
- The Disciplined (Strong) above the Undisciplined (Weak)
- The Rich above the Poor
- Employers above Employees
- Adults above Children
- Western culture above other cultures
- America above other countries
- Men above Women
- Whites above Nonwhites
- Christians above non-Christians
- Straights above Gays

Sound familiar?

GEORGE LAKOFF

2:19 PM · Jul 1, 2017

According to Lakoff's hierarchy, God looks most favorably upon rich, straight, white, male, Christian, American employers, who engage in colonialism and resource exploitation. The conservative moral hierarchy favors these mining, timber, manufacturing and fossil fuel CEOs, their transnational conglomerates and the politicians they bankroll. Extending that metaphor would make God a polluter and an exploiter. A purveyor of "manifest destiny," which represents ruin for most of humanity. It's not justifiable or sustainable. It's saying to one elite group, "Take dominion over the Earth."[20]

Yet throughout history, alternative religious models have emerged, worshiping nature, venerating goddesses, and supporting the nurturing-mother view: From Dianic Wicca and Paganism to the Greek and Roman goddesses Gaia, Demeter, and Ceres, the Hindu goddesses Durga, Kali, Lakshmi, and Sarasvati, the Egyptian goddess Isis, the Chinese bodhisattva of compassion Kuan Yin, and many more.

But modern religions are dominated by patriarchal cultures and the Abrahamic strict-father—who Jews and Christians call *Yahweh*, and Muslims call *Allah*. These 4.2 billion believers in Christianity, Islam, and Judaism make up more than half the world's population. Hinduism, Shaktism, Shinto, and some indigenous religions venerate feminine deities, though not exclusively. These have roughly 2 billion adherents. So the nurturing-mother religions don't wield the same political power. Nor have their cultures significantly reformed their strict, traditional hierarchies.

Such divinely sanctioned hierarchies create a template for dominance that extends far beyond American conservatism. When any system claims divine authority, similar patterns of exploitation emerge, each justified by its own sacred traditions. If we want a better structure based on justice and the nurturing-mother morality, which supports a democratic and inclusive social order, we can't just invert the conservative moral hierarchy. We must reduce hierarchy altogether in favor of a horizontal model. Humans in equilibrium with nature, mutual respect, strength through diversity, economic equity, collaborative workplaces,[21] empowered youth mentored by respected elders, cultural exchange, global cooperation and trade, racial, gender and LGBTQ+ equality, interfaith respect, and secularism.

Strict-father religions, patriarchal moralities, and hierarchical structures are deeply connected. Whereas members of nurturing, open groups aren't joiners—they participate because their boundaries are respected. Let's review the Kohlberg scale of moral development: Stage 1 is obedience and punishment, stage 2 is individualism and reciprocity, stage 3 is conforming to expectations, stage 4 is law and order, stage 5 is social contract and individual rights, and stage 6 is morality based on universal principles. People good at avoiding cults have usually reached Kohlberg stage 5—honoring social systems and their role within them. They are not asked—nor would they agree—to flip their hive switches and sacrifice their autonomy. They are likely to critically evaluate high-commitment groups, especially those at odds with widespread social norms, demanding blind allegiance, or harming the common good.

Open groups can be festive and entertaining, offering compassionate theology without threats of eternal damnation, reincarnation, or soul death. Members tend to dabble and move on, as both investment and exit costs are low. While this benefits members, it disadvantages cult leaders. Low-commitment groups are more benign than strict cults or churches but lack cohesion. Without a centralizing force, there's little money or power at stake. To authoritarian cult leaders, weakly committed members resemble free riders: they represent butts in pews but resist the intense thought reform required to extract maximum resources.[22]

High-commitment, hierarchical, exclusionary cults hold a game-theory advantage: market and evolutionary forces reward enforced order. The tension between nurturing and dominance is self-evident. Resolving it requires recognizing the consequences of strict-father morality, which fosters moral blinding through sanctity. As Haidt observes, "Sacredness binds people together, and then blinds them to the arbitrariness of the [sacred] practice."[23] This blinding effect is behind the most damaging traditions: slavery, human sacrifice, witch hunts, Sati (widow burning), and countless other atrocities. While secularism and human rights laws have reduced such practices, sanctity continues to shield systemic oppression, which sometimes hides within deeply entrenched cultural hierarchies.

In 2023, India became the world's most populous nation, with growing global influence. Its caste system is one of the oldest hierarchies, dividing people into four Varna: Brahmins, Kshatriyas, Vaishyas, and Shudras. Dalits, or "untouchables," fall outside caste. Thousands of Jati classifications tied to purity/pollution, occupation, and birth reinforce discrimination. Justified by religious notions of karma and dharma, the caste system governs occupations, food sharing, and intermarriage. Rooted in sanctity, it shares distant parallels with the American Conservative Moral Hierarchy, since both enforce rigid categories based on birth and perceived purity.

British colonial rule (1860–1920) intensified caste divisions for administrative control. India's 1950 Constitution sought to dismantle caste-based discrimination through Article 15, which banned discrimination by religion, race, caste, sex, or birthplace, and Article 17, which abolished untouchability. However, these deeply ingrained practices persist. Affirmative action to address historical injustices fueled competition among castes for quotas and political battles over voting blocs. Every effort to end the caste system has prolonged the system.

The enforcement of veiling laws in the Muslim world shows how sanctity-based control extends to women's bodies and behavior. While some Muslim women choose veiling as protection from the male gaze, the existence of morality police reveals the system's true nature. Iranian women who protest hijab laws face arrest, violence, and worse—their supposed "liberation" enforced through brutal oppression.[24]

Illustration of Islamic morality police confronting an improperly veiled woman

Female Genital Mutilation represents the most extreme violation. It permanently damages women's capacity for sexual pleasure, and it endangers their health and lives. The procedure, which has no medical purpose, has maimed more than 200 million women in 31 countries[25]—some of whom bleed to death.[26] It's a grievous form of intergenerational trauma as mothers and grandmothers participate in the mutilation of their daughters and granddaughters.

Many liberals suffer the same moral blinding as conservatives when confronting such harmful practices in marginalized cultures. They abandon the Harm/Care moral foundation in favor of protecting another culture's rules about Sanctity/Degradation, creating tension with the Liberty/Oppression foundation. In attempting to avoid discrimination or cultural imperialism, liberals often rationalize practices they would never accept in their own society. Aren't human rights always worth defending? Is a harmful practice by an oppressed minority any less harmful than if it were imposed by a dominant majority?

Many widespread sacred practices persist unchallenged, shielded by their prevalence and cultural sensitivity. These range from baptizing and circumcising infants, to Christian purity culture, to forced fasting at Ramadan and other dietary rules, to refusal of blood transfusions, to strict dress codes for women, to anti-LGBTQ+ discrimination. All of these violate one or more universal human rights. Modern institutions increasingly accommodate such practices under the banner of religious freedom. The 2023 Supreme Court ruling in *Groff v. DeJoy* requires employers to accommodate any "sincerely held religious belief," (the *Ballard test* again)—moving from secularism toward sanctity.

The deeply immoral examples I've cited violate any notion of well-being. These are exceedingly complex issues, and I can't begin to address their cultural nuances. But they demonstrate how sanctity binds communities through shared rituals, while blinding them to harm. The same dynamic that led Gregory Mull to seek belonging in my cult while ignoring his own well-being is evident on a global scale when any culture enforces sanctity-based rules.

Breaking free from sanctity requires recognizing its dual nature. We can acknowledge the need for meaning and belonging without succumbing to moral blinding. The path forward prioritizes human rights within communities that bind themselves together through shared values—rather than shared submission.

---

[1] CUT v. Mull, Superior Court of Los Angeles County C. 358191, (February 12, 1986) at 252:20-21

[2] CUT v. Mull, Superior Court of Los Angeles County C. 358191, (February 12, 1986) at 253:17-19

[3] CUT v. Mull, Superior Court of Los Angeles County C. 358191, (March 13, 1986) at pages 2349-2375

[4] Centers for Disease Control and Prevention. (n.d.). *Sleep and sleep disorders: Data and statistics.* Retrieved from https://www.cdc.gov/sleep/data-research/facts-stats/adults-sleep-facts-and-stats.html

[5] CUT v. Mull, Superior Court of Los Angeles County C. 358191, (March 6, 1986) at 1744:26-1745:1

[6] Beery, A. K. (2013). Life in groups: The roles of oxytocin in mammalian sociality. *Frontiers in Behavioral Neuroscience, 7*, Article 185. https://doi.org/10.3389/fnbeh.2013.00185

[7] CUT v. Mull, Superior Court of Los Angeles County C. 358191, (February 12, 1986) at 270-271: 25-4

[8] CUT v. Mull, Superior Court of Los Angeles County C. 358191, (February 12, 1986) at 231:23-25

[9] CUT v. Mull, Superior Court of Los Angeles County C. 358191, (February 12, 1986) at 358:21-24

[10] CUT v. Mull, Superior Court of Los Angeles County C. 358191, (February 12, 1986) at 364:9-11

[11] CUT v. Mull, Superior Court of Los Angeles County C. 358191, (February 12, 1986) at 388:17-21, 389:15

[12] Dunbar, R. (2021, August 28). Dunbar's number: Why the theory that humans can only maintain 150 friendships has withstood 30 years of scrutiny. Neuroscience News. Retrieved from https://neurosciencenews.com/dunbars-number-social-brain-19210/

Dunbar's Number, the theory that humans can maintain about 150 stable relationships, was proposed by Robin Dunbar approximately 30 years ago. This theory is based on the correlation between primate brain size and their social group sizes. Dunbar extrapolated this relationship to humans, leading to the well-known figure of 150. Despite various challenges, Dunbar's Number has remained a significant concept in understanding human social organization.

[13] Black, A. (2016). *A world history of ancient political thought.* Oxford University Press.

[14] Purzycki, B. G., Apicella, C., Atkinson, Q. D., Cohen, E., McNamara, R. A., Willard, A. K., Xygalatas,

D., Norenzayan, A., & Henrich, J. (2016). Moralistic gods, supernatural punishment and the expansion of human sociality. Nature, 530(7590), 327–330. https://doi.org/10.1038/nature16980

The study, *Moralistic Gods, Supernatural Punishment and the Expansion of Human Sociality*, explores how cognitive representations of gods as punitive and knowledgeable about human actions helped foster and sustain cooperation and trust in large, complex societies. This research supports the idea that belief in moralistic, punitive deities can increase impartial behavior toward distant co-religionists, contributing to the expansion of prosociality in large human groups.

[15] Graeber, D., & Wengrow, D. (2021). *The dawn of everything: A new history of humanity*. Farrar, Straus and Giroux.

[16] Haidt, J. (2012). *The righteous mind: Why good people are divided by politics and religion*. Pantheon Books.

[17] Haidt, J. (2012). *The righteous mind: Why good people are divided by politics and religion*. Pantheon Books, pp. 119–120.

"I could see beauty in a moral code that emphasizes duty, respect for one's elders, service to the group, and negation of the self's desires. I could still see its ugly side: I could see that power sometimes leads to pomposity and abuse. And I could see that subordinates—particularly women—were often blocked from doing what they wanted to do by the whims of their elders (male and female). But for the first time in my life, I was able to step outside of my home morality, the ethic of autonomy."

[18] Haidt, J. (2012). *The righteous mind: Why good people are divided by politics and religion*. Pantheon Books, p. 13.

[19] Lakoff, G. (1996). *Moral politics: How liberals and conservatives think*. University of Chicago Press.

[20] The Holy Bible, King James Version. (n.d.). *Genesis 1:28*. "And God blessed them, and God said unto them, Be fruitful, and multiply, and replenish the earth, and subdue it: and have dominion over the fish of the sea, and over the fowl of the air, and over every living thing that moveth upon the earth."

[21] Donaldson, R. M. (2022). *Collaborative power grab: A step-by-step guide for every leader on how to invite, attract, and cultivate collaborative power*. Collaborative Strategies Consulting Inc.

[22] In game theory, "free riders" are individuals who benefit from public goods without contributing to their creation or maintenance, leading to potential underinvestment in these goods. This concept also applies to cult organizations, where weakly committed members contribute less labor or money yet still benefit from the group's resources. This lack of investment from some members can challenge the cult's ability to maintain cohesion, grow, or achieve its objectives, leading to potential instability or dissolution if not addressed through internal mechanisms that encourage or enforce greater commitment and contribution from all members.

[23] Haidt, J. (2012). *The righteous mind: Why good people are divided by politics and religion*. Pantheon Books, p. 299.

[24] Human Rights Watch. (2024). *World report 2024: Country chapters - Iran*. Retrieved from https://www.hrw.org/world-report/2024/country-chapters/iran

[25] UNICEF. (n.d.). *Female genital mutilation*. Retrieved from https://data.unicef.org/topic/child-protection/female-genital-mutilation/

[26] CNN. (2021). *FGM in Sierra Leone: Breaking the silence*. Retrieved from https://www.cnn.com/interactive/asequals/turay-fgm-bondo-sierra-leone-as-equals-intl-cmd/

CHAPTER FIFTEEN

The Moral Landscape

> She: What makes you think that science will ever be able to say that forcing women to wear burqas is wrong? Me: Because I think that right and wrong are a matter of increasing or decreasing well-being—and it is obvious that forcing half the population to live in cloth bags, and beating or killing them if they refuse, is not a good strategy for maximizing human well-being. She: But that's only your opinion. Me: Okay.... Let's make it even simpler. What if we found a culture that ritually blinded every third child.... would you then agree that we had found a culture that was needlessly diminishing human well-being? She: It would depend on why they were doing it. Me: Let's say they were doing it on the basis of religious superstition. In their scripture, God says, "Every third must walk in darkness." She: Then you could never say that they were wrong.
>
> —Sam Harris, *The Moral Landscape*[1]

At an academic conference, neuroscientist Sam Harris sharply criticized one of his colleagues, using a thought experiment involving the ritual blinding of children. The power of his anecdote was to confirm that there is simply no greater ethical failure than moral relativism. His colleagues' depraved *diktat* exemplifies the collapse of academic liberalism as a moral force.

This stark example illuminates a crisis in moral philosophy: our inability to establish universal ethical principles in an increasingly complex world. To understand why *The Moral Landscape*[2] represents such a crucial breakthrough, we must examine the limitations of traditional moral systems, which fall short of providing the empirically grounded structure needed to address contemporary moral challenges.

We can connect Harris' ritual blinding thought experiment to every abuse justified by governments, religions and cult leaders, based on their sacred beliefs. To grasp Harris' approach, we'll need a brief refresher on traditional moral systems. I'll break them down into categories that correspond loosely with Jonathan Haidt's moral foundations.

Loyalty/Betrayal, Authority/Subversion, Sanctity/Degradation foundations:

Harris' colleague endorsed *divine-command ethics*, where actions are morally right if they align with divine will. Such practices are beyond question, with violations incurring social or spiritual consequences.

Virtue ethics prioritizes character over outcomes, suggesting actions from a virtuous character are inherently good—even when they cause harm. Honesty at the wrong time could endanger lives, while courage might veer into recklessness. Virtuous behavior doesn't guarantee virtuous results.

Deontology evaluates actions based on adherence to moral rules, irrespective of outcomes. Its strength lies in universal principles, yet it often dismisses consequences.

Social contract ethics concerns agreements among individuals to form a society. These contracts can align with Loyalty/Betrayal, Authority/Subversion and Sanctity/Degradation when emphasizing social cohesion

Illustration of Sam Harris' thought experiment involving the ritual blinding of every third child.

or with Harm/Care and Fairness/Cheating when upholding equity and minimizing harm.

Liberty/Oppression foundation:

Libertarianism champions individual autonomy, while minimizing state intervention. It defends the right to live freely while avoiding harm to others. Libertarians argue for voluntary exchange and strong property rights.

Harm/Care and Fairness/Cheating foundations:

Utilitarianism aims to achieve the greatest good for the greatest number, seeking to maximize happiness and well-being.

Natural law ethics derives moral principles from the natural world and human reason. But interpretations of natural law can differ due to cultural, religious, and personal perspectives.

Care ethics focuses on nurturing relationships and responding to the needs of others. It prioritizes the well-being of those directly involved in a situation through emphasizing interpersonal connections.

Ethical systems lacking foundations:

Moral relativism challenges the existence of universal moral truths, asserting that moral judgments depend on cultural or individual preferences. Based on anthropological observations, it lacks a fixed standard for evaluating well-being across cultures, hindering ethical critiques and global justice.

Moral nihilism denies the existence of moral facts—making right and wrong a matter of opinion.

Moral relativists and those who support divine commands would condone the brutal sacred practices I've discussed. Moral nihilists would struggle to condemn genocide, chemical attacks, or nuclear bombing, since there is no moral reality by which crimes against humanity could be judged.

Nietzsche famously rejected objective moral truths, largely as a critique of divine-command ethics. But his "will to power," "Ubermensch," and "master vs. slave morality" reveal sympathies for dominance. His ethics of flourishing emphasized creativity and self-overcoming but dismissed moral checks on power as slavish "resentment." This directly enables systemic abuse.

Some moral nihilists concede value in cultural perspectives on morality, and many cultures uphold sound moral principles. But just as many do not. Does crossing a border change the wrongness of rape? As of 2021, 20 countries allowed rapists to escape punishment by marrying their victims.[3] Some 2.6 billion women live in countries where spousal rape isn't punished.[4] Even in the West, rape enforcement can be ineffective.[5] The scourge of rape ties directly to male dominance and the conservative moral hierarchy.

No matter how severe, atrocities seem to find defenders who use tortured rationalizations rooted in their own arrested moral development. This can stem from postmodern rejection of universal truths or being raised in traumatic environments lacking healthy moral foundations, boundaries, or role models for justice and prosociality. We can understand why so many ancient cultures codified moral rules as divine commands—because who would challenge rules written by God? How else could rulers or citizens uphold moral precepts against their own poorly defined ethics?

Our challenge is to devise an empirical science of morality robust enough to remove the temptation to rely on divine commands. Harris does so, using three principles:

1. Morality concerns the well-being of conscious creatures.

2. The state of well-being is grounded in empirical facts.

3. Social science provides the data to establish best practices that support well-being.

These principles draw from utilitarianism, libertarianism, natural law, social contract, virtue, deontology, and care. But none of those systems demand verification of best outcomes.

Utilitarianism faces challenges in theory and practice. What of the "utility monster," a being that gained much more happiness than others? It would make no sense to squander all available resources on the utility monster. Real happiness follows resource distribution—people suffer when survival needs go unmet. That's why taxing the wealthy to support the poor at a subsistence level increases well-being far more than any loss of happiness among the wealthy. What of the famous trolley problem where we must choose one person to die in order to save five? The decision seems clear until you're the one on the tracks. Depending on how it's applied, utilitarianism can be good or bad.

Libertarianism minimizes government intervention with a seemingly clean principle: "let people do what they want, so long as they're not harming others." But this idea breaks down on a fundamental level—perceptions of harm vary widely. Right-libertarians rage against taxes and regulations while turning a blind eye to the harms of extreme wealth concentration, and some hypocritically seek to regulate reproductive health, gender transitions, and private sexual behavior. Left-libertarians claim to champion personal freedom while supporting bans on everything from plastic straws to flavored tobacco. No one stays consistently libertarian because everyone finds something they want to control.

Natural Law comes closest to what Harris is proposing. But it still falls short because of differing views about human nature, the weighing of competing priorities, and the applicability of reason to complex moral dilemmas. Interpreters of natural law can become self-appointed moral arbiters, and that role is fraught with the same pitfalls as divine commands.

Social contracts are expressed as constitutions, laws and norms. But these are a *product* of ethical principles, not a source. We must learn to empirically recognize which social contracts are better, and which are worse.

Virtue ethics and *deontology* fail because they focus inward. Questions like "How can I be more virtuous?" or "What are my duties?" cannot be answered without considering outcomes. Good character doesn't guarantee good results, and moral rules can default to traditions or majoritarian norms, ignoring consequences. Without an empirical foundation, these systems lack sufficient rigor to address real-world ethical challenges.

Only when virtues and rules are closely aligned with the public good can these systems support good ethics. And what is the public good? That can only be determined through accurate measurements of well-being through social science. Any sacred or non-empirical belief will produce less accurate results. Allowing less-accurate ethical systems to determine societal outcomes is negligence.

Recognizing that traditional moral systems fail without empirical grounding leads us to *The Moral Landscape*. Rather than deriving ethics from abstract principles, divine commands, or cultural traditions, Harris proposes a framework rooted in measurable reality: *the well-being of conscious creatures.* The shift from philosophical speculation to empirical investigation transforms ethics from a realm of endless debate into a field capable of evidence-based progress.

How can we develop an empirically grounded, internally consistent set of values? *The Moral Landscape* represents a three-dimensional surface of well-being, with peaks of flourishing and valleys of suffering. It's crucial to distinguish between the map and the

DALL·E / SEAN PROPHET

territory: the territory is measurable well-being, while the map comprises the evolving methods we use to achieve it. Like physical maps, moral maps are imperfect and must evolve through evidence to more accurately chart the terrain.

Recognizing the challenge of defining a universal standard, *The Moral Landscape* embraces moral pluralism. Rather than dictating solutions, it provides a way to navigate moral questions with evidence-based best practices. Many paths lead to happiness and flourishing, while others descend into suffering and despair. Defining the valleys of moral failure may be the simplest way to map the peaks of virtue.

The failures of sanctity I've discussed—brutal traditions and divine commands—sink into deep crevasses on the moral landscape. So do unprovoked wars, terrorism, mass shootings, ethnic cleansing, stonings, beheadings, torture, cruelty, and the silent violence of poverty. No empirical moral universe could place these on a moral peak, just as kindness, empathy, compassion, equality, fairness, reciprocity, love, and respect cannot occupy a moral valley.

Harris' thesis is known as *ethical realism*. It asserts the existence of objective moral facts, independent of belief. As he argues, such facts should be no more controversial than saying a long, healthy life is better than dying of cancer as a child. It doesn't matter how we define good health—it does not include chronic pain, broken bones, organ failure or death. Whatever problems there might be with utilitarianism, *we know we don't want its opposite*—the greatest misery for the greatest number.

What's clear in principle can be difficult in practice. The ruling classes have repeatedly imposed misery for power and profit, under the pretext of moral nihilism or sanctity. Complicating matters, moral premises are cobbled together from generalized survival instincts that evolved to keep social primates alive while living in groups of fewer than 150. We can't define perfect morality because our inherited evolutionary rules evolved to solve different—and often contradictory—survival problems.

"Perfect morality" is therefore an oxymoron. The peaks and valleys of The Moral Landscape *are* morality. They represent what exists. We need robust measurements on a global scale by social scientists to create functional models.

Moral leaders on the left sometimes misunderstand what works ethically at different scales. At the village level—groups of fewer than 150—principles like "be kind to your neighbor," "reward favors," or even "tolerate that asshole because he makes the tribe stronger" work fine. But in societies of millions, these rules collapse. People without social ties can act boorishly or brutishly toward one another, and no amount of love or kindness will stop them. That's why we need laws and cops.

Martin Luther King, Jr. demonstrated a deeper understanding of scale. While he consistently preached love and non-violence, he also recognized their limits. As he famously said, "It may be true that the law cannot make a man love me, but it can keep him from lynching me, and I think that's pretty important."[6] This insight reflects King's sky-high moral development, exemplifying Kohlberg stage 6—universal ethical principles combined with the courage to disobey unjust laws. King's grasp of scale and morality was essential to his transformative impact.

In defense of ethical realism, Harris quips, "Factual beliefs like 'water is two parts hydrogen and one part oxygen' and ethical beliefs like 'cruelty is wrong' are not expressions of mere preference."[7] He contrasts a "good life" and a "bad life." In the good life, an educated, prosperous career woman with a loving family ponders how to spend a billion-dollar grant. In the bad life, a widow in a war-torn nation flees after witnessing her daughter's dismemberment, with the killers gaining on her. For some, such moral distinctions are abstractions—a luxury afforded by living in societies protected by moral norms and laws. Anyone denying a moral distinction between the conditions that created these two lives should volunteer to trade places with the fleeing widow.

Real-world morality is filled with shades of gray and clashes between moral imperatives. Still, we can stake out territory on *The Moral Landscape*—if we get the big questions right, the rest follows. For years, I've enjoyed testing people's ethics with thought experiments like trolley problems or debates about cultural relativism. Recently, I developed a simpler, more effective moral yardstick: "the question."

Does society have a moral obligation to feed hungry children?

The answer is, of course, "yes." You wouldn't believe how controversial it can be. This seemingly obvious question reveals deeper moral failures and provides a perfect test case for Harris's empirical approach: It involves measurable outcomes, clear peaks and valleys of well-being, and competing moral claims about responsibility and intervention.

Why *are* there hungry children? The empirical reality is stark: In a world with an annual GDP exceeding $100 trillion, millions of children are not fed. Global hunger could be eradicated for $40 billion per year—less than 0.04% of GDP. In 2023, 2,640 billionaires held $12.2 trillion in combined wealth. A mere 0.33% annual tax on their fortunes could solve world hunger forever. These aren't matters of opinion—they are measurable statistics about human well-being.

They establish a *moral fact*, which follows directly from *The Moral Landscape*. **We must feed hungry children**. If morality concerns the well-being of conscious creatures grounded in empirical facts, then childhood hunger represents a deep valley on the moral landscape. The peer-reviewed scientific evidence is unequivocal: hunger in childhood harms physical and cognitive development, emotional well-being, and life outcomes. Harris asks, how can we reason with someone who denies the value of human well-being? If we care about collective well-being (the only *a priori* moral premise needed), feeding children is as morally essential as saving a drowning child or stopping a rape or murder.

This enrages moral nihilists and right-libertarians. Nietzscheans scoff at the "slave morality" of condemning the wealthy as evil, or resenting their power. Yet the wealthy don't feed the children—*and they could*—without noticing the cost. What else can we call such people? Right-libertarians express unbridled fury at the utilitarian idea that anyone would be coerced through taxation into feeding someone else's children. I've often been accused of wanting to build a "utopia." A utopia, where children are fed.

The *horror*.

Moral nihilism and right-libertarianism are far from neutral—they favor the wealthy and powerful. Non-morality and non-intervention leave the world to the metaphorical wolves, red in tooth and claw, who need no protection from morality or governance. The victims of such systems are always the most vulnerable. In this case, hungry children. As the Greek historian Thucydides observed, "The strong do what they can, and the weak suffer what they must."[8]

If they survive, a hungry child will become a damaged adult.[9] One with impaired cognitive skills and unlikely to achieve high moral development. This creates a vicious cycle: Failure to uphold the moral fact that **we must feed hungry children** undermines the moral capacity of future generations, making it less likely they will do the right thing. Imagine a leader who suffered malnutrition as a child saying, "Toughen up! I didn't have enough to eat, and I turned out fine."

There are many paths to the moral peak of feeding all children, whether through billionaire taxes, global food purchase levies, or mandated government relief. But failing to feed them—whatever the excuse—leaves us in a moral crevasse, perpetuating our depravity onto future generations. This isn't any more of a personal opinion than saying that cancer is bad. The empirical evidence makes clear that the impact of hunger on well-being is as grave as any physical disease.

In summation, if we want moral progress, sanctity in all of its permutations *must* be subordinated to best practices concerning the well-being of conscious creatures. It's fine to hold things sacred, so long as no one is being lied to or harmed. But if you hold divine commands or the hoarding of wealth above human well-being, you're in a deep ethical chasm. This is the all-important moral shift you'll have to make, to reach Kohlberg stage 5 or 6, and to rid yourself of cult sanctimony. It may take some effort to climb down from your sacred mountain, and back up to a peak of *The Moral Landscape*. But the journey is worth every labored step.

---

[1] Harris, S. (2010). *The moral landscape: How science can determine human values* (p. 44). Free Press.

[2] Harris, S. (2010). *The moral landscape: How science can determine human values*. Free Press.

[3] The Guardian. (2021, April 14). Marry-your-rapist laws in 20 countries still allow perpetrators to escape justice. *The Guardian*. Retrieved from https://www.theguardian.com/global-development/2021/apr/14/marry-your-rapist-laws-in-20-countries-still-allow-perpetrators-to-escape-justice

[4] Anderson, M. J. (2016). Marital rape laws globally: Rationales and snapshots around the world. In K. Yllö & M. G. Torres (Eds.), *Marital rape: Consent, marriage, and social change in global context* (pp. 177–186). Oxford University Press. https://doi.org/10.1093/acprof:oso/9780190238360.003.0012

[5] Avalos, L. (2016). Prosecuting rape victims while rapists run free: The consequences of police failure to investigate sex crimes in Britain and the United States. *Michigan Journal of Gender & Law*, 23(1), 1–76. https://doi.org/10.36641/mjgl.23.1.prosecuting

[6] Rosenberg, J. (2023, April 5). Martin Luther King Jr. Quotations. *ThoughtCo*. Retrieved from https://www.thoughtco.com/martin-luther-king-jr-quotes-p2-1779796

[7] Harris, S. (2010). *The moral landscape: How science can determine human values* (p. 14). Free Press.

[8] Thucydides. (2009). *History of the Peloponnesian War* (M. Hammond, Trans.). Oxford University Press. (Original work published c. 400 BCE)

[9] Batra, J., & Sood, A. (2005). Iron deficiency anaemia: Effect on cognitive development in children: A review. *Indian Journal of Clinical Biochemistry*, 20(2), 119–125. https://doi.org/10.1007/BF02867410
de Oliveira, K. H. D., de Almeida, G. M., Gubert, M. B., Moura, A. S., Spaniol, A. M., Hernandez, D. C., Pérez-Escamilla, R., & Buccini, G. (2020). Household food insecurity and early childhood development: Systematic review and meta-analysis. *Maternal & Child Nutrition*, 16(7), e12967. https://doi.org/10.1111/mcn.12967
Suryawan, A., Jalaludin, M. Y., Poh, B. K., Sanusi, R., Tan, V. M. H., Geurts, J. M., & Muhardi, L. (2022). Malnutrition in early life and its neurodevelopmental and cognitive consequences: A scoping review. *Nutrition Research Reviews*, 35(1), 136–149. https://doi.org/10.1017/S0954422421000159

CHAPTER SIXTEEN

Totalitarianism

> Nearly all western thought since the last war, certainly all 'progressive' thought, has assumed tacitly that human beings desire nothing beyond ease, security and avoidance of pain. In such a view of life there is no room, for instance, for patriotism and the military virtues.... Hitler knows that human beings don't only want comfort, safety, short working-hours, hygiene, birth-control and, in general, common sense; they also, at least intermittently, want struggle and self-sacrifice, not to mention drums, flags and loyalty-parades. However they may be as economic theories, Fascism and Nazism are psychologically far sounder than any hedonistic conception of life.... Whereas Socialism, and even capitalism in a more grudging way, have said to people 'I offer you a good time,' Hitler has said to them 'I offer you struggle, danger and death,' and as a result a whole nation flings itself at his feet.
> –George Orwell, Review of Adolf Hitler's *Mein Kampf*, in *The New English Weekly*, March 21, 1940

We've explored the dangerous moral blinding of sanctity through the lens of harm reduction and well-being. But what about the attraction of ideologies deliberately opposed to well-being? To understand this paradox, we must examine totalitarianism—a system that seeks to control not just the public sphere but individuals' inner lives and thoughts, subsuming both social order (*nomos*) and universal order (*cosmos*) to mold reality itself. It's a fount of quintessential dystopia, with a grim historical track record—never delivering well-being—and always devolving into madness, violence, ethnic cleansing, and genocide. As Hannah Arendt argued, totalitarianism moves beyond historical despotism. It's a distinctly modern phenomenon with five key features:

Ideology: A single, all-encompassing belief system claiming to explain every facet of human existence.

Terror: Fear and uncertainty as tools of population control.

Technology: Corruption of information, and monitoring of communication.

Dehumanization: The reduction of individuals to undifferentiated masses.

Inevitability: The presentation of the regime as the natural culmination of history.

It's a mystery why any democratic nation would choose totalitarianism. Yet history shows us nations repeatedly doing exactly that, tearing up their constitutions and surrendering their freedoms—after opening a Pandora's box of psychological and political deceptions. The mechanisms of totalitarian control closely parallel those of totalistic cults, revealing a crucial insight: the tactics of individual thought reform can scale to achieve national thought reform.

Dictators are cult leaders operating at a national level, with far greater resources and reach. They cultivate charismatic authority as messianic figures with divine mandates. They promote a mystical imperative. They establish personality cults and claim the power to define reality. They set rules they don't follow. And they dispense existence like monarchs, using purges, mass arrests, banishment, public ruination, and summary executions—horrors that would make lesser cult leaders blush. Most critically, dictators codify their ideology into state scriptures used to indoctrinate the population.[1]

Christopher Hitchens' metaphor of heaven as a "celestial dictatorship" provides a blueprint for earthly oppression.[2] Guns, guards, and attack dogs alone can't dominate millions. Even the most brutal regimes require some degree of compliance, achieved through propaganda and terror, often leveraging religious authority to stir despotic passions.[3] Voluntary submission to "divine will" is the most cost-effective form of control.

Absolute power masks vulnerability. "Godhood" is a highly political position that requires image management and vigorous quelling of dissent. As Erin Prophet reminds us, charismatic authority must be constantly refreshed—both in dictators and cult leaders. Both depend on complex networks, maintaining control through incentives and threats. Cult leaders rely on informers and their inner circle, dispensing spiritual rewards and punishments. Dictators must maintain their "keys to power," as explained in the illuminating video "The Rules for Rulers," by courting minions, empowering enforcers, and allocating resources.[4] It's a high-stakes game: a cult leader without followers is just another broke messianic fool, while deposed dictators can face gruesome public executions.

Cult scholar Willa Appel captures this paradox in her analysis of messianic leadership:

> The creation of a messianic society is a radical act. If the attempt succeeds, it brings tremendous power to the messiah—power that would be overwhelming even to the most well-adjusted individual. The messiah is hardly that. The adulation he receives confirms his belief in his superiority over everyone else, his true difference from the rest of society. His overweening belief in himself is the stick he wields for beating off his own insecurities. The excess of it reveals its other terrified side. So for the messiah, success is precarious, too. It is not based on a balanced view of the world and his place in it, but is instead like an enormous tottering cardhouse that grows more fragile as it expands.[5]

The inherent instability of autocratic power explains why the world has discarded monarchy, an archaic cousin of totalitarian dictatorship and cult leadership. Autocratic rule drives leaders to madness while devastating subjects.[6] The antidote began to emerge with the Magna Carta in 1215. This foundational document subordinated rulers to written laws and stripped the monarchy of its role as the final arbiter of justice.

The Australian Rule of Law Education Centre illustrates key principles. In strong democracies, *no one* can be above the law. Heads of state must not be immune from prosecution.[7] The rule of law is incompatible with monarchs, cult leaders, and dictators, since any autocrat would override it by decree. Budding autocrats in failing democracies consolidate their power by attacking the following ten foundations of legal accountability:

Presumption of innocence, requiring the state to prove charges of wrongdoing to a high standard of evidence.

Open, independent, and impartial judiciary, protected from ideological loyalties and financial conflicts.

Prohibition of retrospective laws, preventing punishment under laws enacted after conduct occurred.

Transparent lawmaking by the people through direct referendum or elected representatives.

Government agencies operating as *model litigants*, not unfairly disadvantaging citizens.

Fair and prompt trials, with rights to legal representation and protection from indefinite detention.

Separation of powers between executive, legislative, and judicial branches.

Punishment only in accordance with specific laws following *due process*.

Freedom to criticize the law and its administration without retribution.

Public accessibility of all laws, with no secret legislation.

These principles represent universal standards which predate and underpin democratic constitutions worldwide. Any erosion provides an early warning sign of totalitarian takeover. In the United States, separation of powers has weakened through the proliferation of executive orders, persistent congressional gridlock, and judicial overreach. Judicial independence has been compromised by the arch-conservative Federalist Society, which has a lock on judicial appointments under Republican administrations. Supreme Court Justice Clarence Thomas faces credible accusations of accepting political gifts, while Justice Samuel Alito has displayed Christian Nationalist symbols at his residence, including some associated with insurrectionist movements, while declining to recuse himself from cases related to January 6th. Chief Justice John Roberts implemented an ethics code in 2024, but its reliance on self-enforcement renders it ineffective.[8]

The Senate's handling of Supreme Court nominations illustrates further institutional decay. In 2016, the Senate refused to consider President Obama's nominee, Merrick Garland, for nearly ten months, citing the proximity to the presidential election. Yet in 2020, the Senate confirmed President Trump's nominee, Justice Amy Coney Barrett, just eight days before the election, after millions had already voted. Congressional oversight has deteriorated through ineffective lobbying regulations. Supreme court decisions like *Citizens United v. FEC* and *McCutcheon v. FEC* have led to a flood of dark money in politics. The increased use of omnibus bills and closed committee sessions has further reduced legislative transparency.

Each weakening of any principle of the rule of law undermines the others, making it harder to uphold the bedrock foundation that no one is above the law. Every totalitarian dictator drags their nation back nearly a thousand years, to a time before the Magna Carta, when monarchs could imprison, torture, or execute anyone at will and seize their property. Once that level of power is reached, what or who can stop them? The stakes could not be higher.

Totalitarian takeovers occur through military coups, civil wars, or the gradual undermining of democratic institutions. In the first phase of consolidation, aspiring dictators systematically restrict civil liberties, stifle dissent, and weaken institutional checks and balances. They pack courts with loyal judges, manipulate elections, and suppress opposition parties. The final phase arrives when the previous political system collapses—elections become empty performances, often producing lopsided margins exceeding 90 percent. Once freed from meaningful oversight by courts, regulators, or public opinion, the regime can escalate human rights abuses with impunity, including arbitrary arrests and extrajudicial killings.

The Russian and Chinese revolutions of 1917 and 1949 represent unique cases that transcend simple categorization.[9] These transformative events emerged from complex socio-political conditions rather than purely military conflicts. Modern totalitarianism has followed various paths: Adolf Hitler gained power through appointment as chancellor, while Benito Mussolini and Vladimir Putin were appointed as prime ministers. Military coups installed leaders like Francisco Franco, Augusto Pinochet, and Idi Amin, while figures such as Hugo Chavez, Recep Tayyip Erdogan, and

Viktor Orban achieved power through democratic elections.

Contemporary events demonstrate the robust appeal of dictatorship. In El Salvador, President Nayib Bukele's trajectory illustrates the fragility of democratic institutions. After changing his social media biography to "world's coolest dictator" in 2021, Bukele declared himself the winner of a second term in February 2024 before official results were announced.[10] His New Ideas party secured 58 out of 60 seats in the national assembly, following a period marked by extensive civil rights violations. Under Bukele's leadership, the government conducted extrajudicial killings and arrested 75,000 people without formal charges while dismantling judicial independence and filling state institutions with loyalists.[11]

Despite these violations of democratic principles, Bukele maintains an 87 percent approval rating among El Salvador's 6.3 million citizens. His popularity stems from tangible improvements in public safety—the murder rate dropped from 51 per 100,000 in 2018 to 2.4 per 100,000 by 2023—a twenty-fold reduction in just five years.[12] Totalitarian regimes can deliver concrete benefits, much as Mussolini was credited with making Italy's trains run on time. But these "improvements" come at enormous cost.

Bukele's rhetoric at the 2024 U.S. Conservative Political Action Conference (CPAC) revealed his hostility toward democratic institutions. He characterized them as "dark forces" that must be destroyed, advocating for the removal of "corrupt judges"—a term he applies to any judiciary that upholds the rule of law rather than executive authority.[13] He called for the next U.S. president to do "whatever it takes" to suppress opposition—an overt endorsement of authoritarian governance, which was met with cheers and thunderous applause from the American conservative audience.

Also at CPAC 2024, fascist firebrands Jack Posobiec and Steve Bannon minced no words:[14] "Welcome to the end of democracy!" Posobiec began, almost ironically. "We're here to overthrow it completely. We didn't get all the way there on January 6th." Bannon, chortling off-camera, replied, "Ho, ho, ho." Posobiec continued, "But we will endeavor to get rid of it and replace it with this right here," thrusting his fist high. "That's right," he proclaimed, "because all glory is not to government, all glory to God!" Bannon responded, "Amen!" and later led the crowd in a duplicitous, fist-pumping chant about the 2020 election, "Trump won! Trump won! Trump won!"

In Venezuela, similar patterns emerged as Nicolas Maduro orchestrated another fraudulent election in July 2024. Even after disqualifying opposition candidates and implementing restrictive anti-opposition laws, Maduro lost decisively to independent candidate Edmundo González Urrutia.[15] In response, Maduro simply declared victory, arrested 2,000 protesters, caused at least 22 deaths, and threatened to "pulverize" his opposition, whom he labeled "demonic forces."[16]

These contemporary examples return us to the profound insight from Orwell's 1940 review of *Mein Kampf*, illustrating how the seductive moral foundations of loyalty, authority, and sanctity are weaponized against democracy. Jonathan Haidt's research in *The Righteous Mind* confirms what history repeatedly demonstrates: humans are not universally satisfied by the moral foundations of care and fairness that underpin democratic societies—representing Orwell's "good time." Nor are they placated by stable, open societies operating under the rule of law.

Orwell's assertion that "Fascism and Nazism are psychologically far sounder than any hedonistic conception of life" must be viewed in the context of Germany's collective trauma following World War I and its aftermath: national humiliation, nearly two million war deaths, 287,000 deaths from the 1918 flu pandemic, and economic devastation from war reparations imposed by the Treaty of Versailles. The global Great Depression of 1929 delivered another crippling blow, pushing unemployment to 30 percent. After losing loved ones to war and disease, many families lost their jobs, businesses, and savings, creating widespread poverty. Any of those factors could have given the German population a collective case of PTSD. Taken together, they became the perfect storm—one that would usher in storm troopers.

To understand how trauma facilitates totalitarian takeover, we must explore PTSD. Trauma impacts the brain by triggering *fight* or *flight* responses, involving a surge of adrenaline. In PTSD, memories can provoke these reactions. Beyond the well-known *fight* and *flight* responses, trauma can induce *freeze* responses (manifesting as numbness and powerlessness) and *fawn* responses (where individuals submit to appease perceived threats). These form a self-reinforcing loop that prioritizes immediate survival over long-term reasoning. There's an evolutionary advantage to assuming a tiger is always lurking in the tall grass—better to falsely assume danger than falsely assume safety. This is why people with PTSD can feel most anxious when they're safe.

In Weimar Germany, widespread trauma primed the population for radical change. The collective cry became "Something must be done!" Just as individuals with PTSD may sabotage stable relationships to return to their abusers, traumatized populations can embrace authoritarian strongmen who promise to restore order through force.

The Weimar Republic might have stabilized given strong institutions and effective leadership. However, both were absent. The Weimar constitution contained critical weaknesses that undermined the rule of law: Article 48 permitted the president to override parliament by emergency decree, while Article 53 allowed presidential appointment of chancellors without parliamentary approval. Parliament itself was fragmented, with Hitler's NSDAP as the largest faction but lacking an outright majority. These institutional weaknesses, combined with the severity of the economic crisis, fueled political extremism that manifested in street battles between rival paramilitaries. Germany's elite class, desperate for stability, threw their support behind Hitler, critically underestimating his scapegoating, demagoguery, and willingness to abuse power.

On January 30, 1933, president Paul von Hindenburg's appointment of Hitler as chancellor presaged the end of German democracy. On February 27, the Reichstag (parliament) building was set ablaze in what historians consider a likely false flag operation, though it was officially attributed to Dutch communist Marinus van der Lubbe. Hindenburg issued the Reichstag Fire Decree the following day, suspending key civil rights and enabling the arrest of opposition politicians without trial. Under intense paramilitary intimidation by the Brownshirts and SS, the March 5 election delivered the Nazis a governing coalition. By March 23, the Nazi-controlled Reichstag had passed the Enabling Act, granting Hitler absolute power. He was now *above the law*, and totalitarianism was thus assured.

None of it had to happen. Despite its wounded state, Germany was secure and at peace with its neighbors. The greatest threat to Weimar Germany came from within. Remember, people with PTSD are most anxious when they are the safest. It's why war vets often struggle with quiet home life. They cry, "Something must be done!" So their limbic systems drive them to clamber aboard the noisiest demagogic caravans—just to keep moving while salving their wounds—without knowing their destination. Orwell summarized Hitler's totalitarian pitch in *Mein Kampf*, "Better an end with horror, than a horror without end." Dictators appeal to the loyalty, authority, and sanctity moral foundations, instinctively knowing they're the evolutionary carnival barkers that wait in the wings to drive mass populist movements. These thunder in with messianic fervor, sweeping away the rule of law in favor of a "new order."

History is repeating. Joe Biden's bland but stable presidency was confounded by leftover PTSD from Covid-induced inflation which led many traumatized Americans to vote for Trump. Following a multi-decade campaign by the right to undermine American institutions, Trump was able to seize a role that was prepared in advance. Early Trump adviser Steve Bannon knew the score. As he watched Trump descend the escalator in 2015 to announce his candidacy, he reportedly gushed, "That's Hitler."[17]

The MAGA phenomenon mirrors the scenario depicted in Sinclair Lewis' prescient 1935 novel *It Can't Happen Here*. The demagogic character Buzz Windrip employs familiar tropes that continue to resonate: appeals to racial superiority, attacks on journalism and intellectuals, promises of national greatness, and scapegoating of minorities. Lewis even captured Trump's mannerisms in his description of Windrip's oratory: "He would whirl arms, bang tables, glare from mad eyes, vomit Biblical wrath from a gaping mouth; but he would also coo like a nursing mother, beseech like an aching lover, and in between tricks would coldly and almost contemptuously jab his crowds with figures and facts—figures and facts that were inescapable even when, as often happened, they were entirely incorrect. Under the spell you thought Windrip was Plato, but that on the way home you could not remember anything he had said."[18]

As totalitarian movements gain momentum, citizens across the political spectrum can develop contempt for democratic institutions, focusing exclusively on their flaws and corruption. While progressive forces work to reform and strengthen these institutions, reactionary elements present a false choice between the failures of the "establishment" or "deep state" and the illusory strength of emerging autocracy. This deliberately ignores the possibility of institutional revival through measured reform. Anti-democratic forces employ a two-pronged strategy: undermining institutions through budget cuts and regulatory capture, then scapegoating the resulting dysfunction to justify authoritarian solutions.

The United States is in early 2025 just such a weakened democracy—not as institutionally flawed or economically beleaguered as Weimar Germany. But we still suffer from a degraded grip on reality, worsened by the daily trauma-porn blasting from Fox News and other fact-free propaganda outlets. These fear factories exploit weakened social cohesion, economic displacement from the eroded manufacturing base, cheap imports, immigration fears, and our increasingly conflicted national identity. And it's not just Fox viewers suffering from PTSD. Liberals reel from the stochastic terrorism of mass shootings, women are gutted over losing reproductive rights, LGBTQ+ people face persecution in half the states, and everyone fears rising prices and rents. Not to mention the slow-creeping subconscious dread of climate change that transcends political parties, whether partisans admit it or not.

Nations in such a debased condition are vulnerable to embracing single-party rule and a despot's iron grip. Through the lens of PTSD, even the relatively high levels of freedom and well-being in a weakening democracy can feel frighteningly bland. People feel that "Something must be done!" Methodical technocratic governance delivers prosperity, but it doesn't offer the red meat of boiling, performative rage displayed by reactionaries. The aspiring despot's appeal revolves around daily fulminations over dashed national expectations, glorifying their struggle to roll back human rights as the cure for historic wrongs—

aiming to restore the imagined glories of a nation that never existed.

Even when functioning as intended, democracy has fatal flaws. The worst is its reliance on *argumentum ad populum*—a logical fallacy.[19] Majorities can be mistaken, lacking the knowledge needed to make decisions that maximize well-being.[20] Majorities can be fickle, poorly informed, and may fail to grasp the fragility of self-rule. Many don't recognize would-be dictators—especially if they agree with them—and become frustrated with the slow pace of change. Decisions often hinge on party affiliation or charisma rather than policy, exacerbated by agitprop, disinformation, and conspiracy theories—all protected as free speech. Algorithms reward engagement with outrage, fostering polarized social media silos, while degraded political discourse incentivizes trolling and "owning" opponents. People can't make sound decisions when trapped in limbic-system reactions, leading them to embrace the lies of a demagogue.

The absence of strong campaign finance and advertising regulations allows wealthy interests to distort electoral outcomes. In counter-majoritarian systems like the United States, mechanisms such as the Electoral College, non-proportional Senate representation, and gerrymandering have enabled minority rule. The implications prove stark: less than 12 percent of the U.S. population, spread across the 21 least populous states, can elect 42 Senators[21] —sufficient to block legislation when combined with the filibuster—requiring 60 votes for cloture.[22] Those who insist that "The United States is a republic, not a democracy" seek to preserve these power imbalances, viewing majority rule as a threat.

In his 1941 book *Escape from Freedom*,[23] German social psychologist Erich Fromm identified another crucial vulnerability: oppressed populations dream of freedom, but upon achieving it, many experience anxiety that drives them to seek identity and purpose within hierarchical structures. As Fromm explained: "Modern man is free from the ties of the medieval world, where everyone had his appointed place, and where the future of each individual was largely determined by the social order into which he was born. But this freedom, which he possesses only in part, also creates new problems for him... He lacks a secure place in the world, and the burden of having to choose his own path fills him with anxiety."

This insight returns us to the role of trauma and PTSD in democratic decline. When feeling unsafe, trauma victims often think, "There must be dangers I'm not seeing," concluding that "Something must be done!"

Fromm's analysis helps explain the rising democratic malaise fueling American deaths of despair.[24] As he noted, "In the escape from freedom, the individual may choose self-destruction or the destruction of others.... He may become addicted to alcohol or drugs, or he may throw himself into wars or revolutions against established authority. He may also become cruel and sadistic, inflicting pain on others as a way of escaping from his own powerlessness."

Hannah Arendt's analysis fundamentally reshapes our understanding. She argues, "Totalitarianism differs essentially from other forms of political oppression known to us, such as despotism, tyranny, and dictatorship." Examining Hitler and Stalin's regimes, Arendt moves beyond left versus right, identifying totalitarianism as an apolitical and uniquely modern phenomenon that seeks to obliterate competing sources of meaning.

In analyzing Arendt's work,[25] philosopher Massimo Pigliucci describes Plato's classical hierarchy of government, ranked from most to least preferable: Aristocracy (rule by the best), Timocracy (rule by the brave), Oligarchy (rule by the rich), Democracy (rule by the people), and Tyranny (rule by one). Notably, Plato ranked democracy second to last, recognizing its vulnerability—a prescient observation that resonates with our current challenges.

To justify their authority, totalitarians must destroy truth. As Pigliucci notes, they differ fundamentally from traditional tyrants. Rather than seeking truth, wisdom or justice, they position themselves as executors of "natural" or "historical" imperatives, placing them not only above social contracts and constitutions but beyond moral reproach. The fusion of pseudo-natural law with moral certainty can justify any action whatsoever. The moral foundations of loyalty, authority, and sanctity only serve as bait for the masses. Once they consolidate power, their true totalitarian agenda emerges: raw force framed as the inevitable flow of nature and history, combined with a purifying moral nihilism. And by "purifying," I mean shooting "undesirables" into trenches.

The totalitarian elite maintains an unwavering belief that their leader will triumph over what others see as reality itself. The demolition of the boundary between truth and fiction has profound contemporary relevance. Avoidable excess deaths from COVID-19 misinformation and vaccine refusal in the US may exceed 300,000—a mass suicide that dwarfs even the deadliest cults.[26]

However, this modern tragedy pales in comparison to the consequences of Stalin's embrace of Trofim Lysenko's pseudo-scientific theories on plant genetics, which included Lamarckian concepts of inherited characteristics. In the early 1930s, Stalin implemented Lysenko's discredited ideas[27] across Soviet agriculture.[28] He imprisoned or executed more than 3,000 scientists who warned of catastrophe. This assault on scientific truth contributed directly to the Holodomor famine, which claimed at least 5 to 7 million lives in Ukraine alone, with many credible estimates reaching far higher.[29] When Lysenkoism spread to China, it increased the death toll by at least another 15 million.[30] The term "Lysenkoism" now serves as a warning about the lethal consequences of subordinating truth to autocratic power.

The totalitarian assault on truth exploits loneliness, a condition distinct from solitude. As Pigliucci explains, this distinction was first articulated by Cicero in *De Re Publica* and later elaborated by the Stoic philosopher Epictetus. While solitude enables independent thought, loneliness represents a state of isolation amid others, where meaningful connection becomes impossible. Loneliness leads to despair, while solitude fosters creativity and reflection. This presents a fundamental threat to totalitarian control.

Totalitarian regimes transform citizens into lonely individuals by severing their political and social bonds, reducing them to masses of interchangeable components. This enforced conformity has become increasingly feasible in modern societies, where traditional community ties have eroded. The same loneliness that drives individuals into cults makes populations vulnerable to totalitarian movements. Both require suppression of thought and surrender to authority.

The United States has now succumbed to fascism, entering a pre-totalitarian period fraught with danger. If MAGA consolidates power and succeeds in destroying democratic institutions, we face a marriage of twentieth-century totalitarian methods with twenty-first century surveillance and social control. The combination of ubiquitous digital monitoring, artificial intelligence, and sophisticated propaganda techniques exceeds even Orwell's darkest imaginings. When these capabilities merge with loneliness, a desperate hunger for meaning, PTSD, and ideological manipulation—they create the potential for a dystopia more terrifying than anything yet seen.

---

[1] Mao Zedong. (1964). *Quotations from Chairman Mao Tse-tung*. People's Liberation Army. Compiled by the People's Liberation Army, this collection of Mao Zedong's quotes became a key tool for indoctri-

nation and political mobilization during the Cultural Revolution. While no longer actively promoted, it remains a historical document and object of curiosity.

Hitler, A. (1925). *Mein Kampf*. Eher Verlag. Adolf Hitler's manifesto outlining his Nazi ideology, including anti-Semitism, Lebensraum, and Aryan supremacy. It served as a cornerstone of Nazi propaganda and indoctrination.

Gaddafi, M. (1976). *The Green Book*. The World Center for the Study and Research of the Green Book. Muammar Gaddafi's presentation of his "Third Universal Theory" for direct democracy and pan-Arabism. Mandatory reading for Libyan students and officials, its legacy is contested due to its contradictions and authoritarian views.

Kim Il-sung. (1972). *On the Juche Idea*. Foreign Languages Publishing House. Kim Il-sung's foundational text for North Korea's Juche philosophy of self-reliance and national independence. It remains a mandatory guide for citizens, but interpretations differ on its legitimacy and practical application.

Kim Il-sung, & Kim Jong-il. (n.d.). *Little Red Book of Kim Il-sung and Little Red Book of Kim Jong-il*. North Korean Government Publications. North Korean collections of quotes and excerpts similar to Mao's, promoting the Juche ideology and consolidating the Kim family's rule.

Xi Jinping. (2014–2022). *The Governance of China* (Vols. 1–4). Foreign Languages Press. A collection of speeches and writings by China's current leader, Xi Jinping, presented as a guide for governance but viewed by some as a tool for strengthening his cult of personality. Its potential use to justify authoritarian policies raises concerns.

[2] Hitchens, C. (2007). *God is Not Great: How Religion Poisons Everything*. Twelve.

[3] Catholic Church in South America: Pinochet, A. (Chile) leveraged the Church for legitimacy and repression despite being an atheist. Trujillo, R. L. (Dominican Republic), dubbed "Defender of the Faith," used religious authority to suppress dissent. Videla, J. R. (Argentina) collaborated with the Church during the "Dirty War," where silence enabled human rights abuses.

Russian Orthodox Church: Stalin, J. (Soviet Union) formed a pragmatic alliance with the Church, using religious rhetoric for patriotism during World War II. Putin, V. (Russia) established a close relationship with the Church, promoting shared values for traditionalism and social control.

Other Notable Examples: Hirohito (Japan) was presented as a living god; Shinto ideology was used for obedience and expansionism. Henry VIII (England) established the Church of England to control religion and politics. Hussein, S. (Iraq), dubbed "Defender of Islam," manipulated religious narratives for image-building and Sunni support. Khomeini, R. (Iran) established a theocratic state, using Shi'a Islam for social control and legitimacy.

[4] CGP Grey. (2016). *The Rules for Rulers* [Video]. YouTube. https://youtu.be/rStL7niR7gs

[5] Appel, W. (1983). *Cults in America: Programmed for Paradise*. Columbia University Press.

[6] Keltner, D. (2017, July/August). Power causes brain damage. The Atlantic. https://www.theatlantic.com/magazine/archive/2017/07/power-causes-brain-damage/528711/

[7] Olmert, E. (Israel) was convicted of bribery and obstruction of justice. Lula da Silva, L. I. (Brazil) was convicted of corruption and money laundering. Chirac, J. (France) was convicted of diverting public funds and abuse of trust. Park Geun-hye (South Korea) was convicted of abuse of power, bribery, and coercion. Fujimori, A. (Peru) was convicted of human rights abuses and corruption. Berlusconi, S. (Italy) was convicted of tax fraud. Katsav, M. (Israel) was convicted of rape and sexual harassment. Lee Myung-bak (South Korea) was convicted of bribery and embezzlement. Perez Molina, O. (Guatemala) was convicted of corruption. Roh Tae-woo (South Korea) was convicted of mutiny, treason, and corruption. Sarkozy, N. (France) was convicted of corruption and influence peddling.

[8] UPI, & Politico. (2024). Chief Justice John Roberts introduced the first formal ethics code for the U.S. Supreme Court in 2024, featuring five canons focused on judicial integrity and avoiding impropriety. However, the code has been criticized for lacking enforcement mechanisms, relying instead on self-regulation by the justices. This move followed several ethics controversies involving justices and

was seen as an attempt to restore public confidence amid pressure from Congress for a more robust framework.

[9] The Russian and Chinese revolutions, despite their dramatic and violent moments, differed significantly from classic military coups or civil wars. While both involved power shifts, they weren't driven solely by elite factions within the existing regimes.
The Russian Revolution (1917) emerged from widespread social and political discontent, leading to the rise of socialist movements like the Bolsheviks. The Chinese Revolution (1949) involved decades of civil war, Japanese invasion, and peasant uprisings, deeply rooted in the grievances of the rural masses. Both revolutions were complex socio-political upheavals fueled by popular discontent and diverse ideological currents, not merely sudden power grabs by military forces.

[10] Yahoo Finance. (2023). El Salvador President Bukele's policies have been met with mixed reactions. *Yahoo Finance*. https://finance.yahoo.com/news/1-el-salvador-president-bukele-145801785.html

[11] WOLA. (2023). Amid rising violence, El Salvador fails to address reports of extrajudicial killings. WOLA. https://www.wola.org/analysis/amid-rising-violence-el-salvador-fails-address-reports-extrajudicial-killings/

[12] ITV News. (2023). El Salvador's murder rate has fallen dramatically, but at what cost? *ITV News*. https://www.itv.com/news/2023-06-26/el-salvadors-murder-rate-has-fallen-dramatically-but-at-what-cost

[13] AP News. (2024). CPAC: Nayib Bukele and Trump discussed at conservative conference. *AP News*. https://apnews.com/article/cpac-nayib-bukele-trump-conservative-dc454b92a57fad8907b376b6eacf-5b7e

[14] Mediaite. (2024). "Welcome to the end of democracy": Trump booster Jack Posobiec vows to finish what began on Jan 6, as Steve Bannon cheers on. *Mediaite*. Retrieved from https://www.mediaite.com/trump/welcome-to-the-end-of-democracy-trump-booster-jack-posobiec-vows-to-finish-what-began-on-jan-6-as-steve-bannon-cheers-on/

[15] New York Times. (2024). Venezuela's Maduro faces new election results. *The New York Times*. Retrieved from https://www.nytimes.com/2024/07/31/world/americas/venezuela-maduro-election-results.html

[16] The Guardian. (2024). Nicolas Maduro's crackdown intensifies following election. *The Guardian*. Retrieved from https://www.theguardian.com/world/article/2024/aug/05/nicolas-maduro-venezuela-election-crackdown

[17] The Guardian. (2022, December 11). 'That's Hitler, Bannon thought': 2022 in books about Trump and US politics. *The Guardian*. Retrieved from https://www.theguardian.com/books/2022/dec/11/trump-books-2022-politics-bestsellers-haberman-woodward

[18] Lewis, S. (2005). *It Can't Happen Here*. Signet Classics.

[19] Argumentum ad populum, or "appeal to the people," fallaciously assumes something is true or good simply because many people believe it. Popularity doesn't equate to accuracy, and this tactic exploits our desire to conform to the majority.

[20] Tax policy provides an example of argumentum ad populum in action. While some voters may support tax increases, most will favor tax cuts. However, neither group necessarily understands how to calculate an optimal tax structure that balances public service funding with economic growth. Furthermore, many voters support tax policies based on their personal financial interests rather than the broader economic implications, often misunderstanding how changes will affect different income groups.

[21] Identifying the 21 lowest population states (2020 Census): Wyoming (576,851), Vermont (643,077), Alaska (733,391), North Dakota (779,094), South Dakota (886,667), Delaware (989,948), Rhode Island (1,097,379), Montana (1,084,225), Maine (1,362,359), New Hampshire (1,377,529), Hawaii (1,455,271), West Virginia (1,793,716), Idaho (1,839,106), Nebraska (1,961,504), New Mexico (2,117,522), Mississippi (2,961,279), Kansas (2,937,880), Arkansas (3,011,524), Nevada (3,104,614), Iowa (3,190,369), and

Utah (3,271,616).

Total population of these 21 states: 37,174,921

Total population of the U.S. (2020 Census): 330,759,736

Although these states represent only 11.2% of the U.S. population, they elect 42 senators, who have the power to block legislation favored by the remaining 88.8% of the population. While these states do not always vote as a block, this imbalance demonstrates the counter-majoritarian structure of the U.S. Constitution, which is further exacerbated by the Senate filibuster rule.

[22] The U.S. Senate filibuster allows extended debate that can block a vote on legislation unless 60 senators vote for cloture (ending debate). This rule effectively grants significant power to the minority party, enabling them to prevent the passage of laws that may have majority support.

[23] Fromm, E. (1941). *Escape from Freedom*. Holt, Rinehart and Winston.

[24] Case, A., & Deaton, A. (2022). Deaths of despair in comparative perspective. *Annual Review of Sociology, 48*, 299–317. https://doi.org/10.1146/annurev-soc-030320-031757

[25] Figs in Winter. (n.d.). *Totalitarianism as a novel form of government*. Retrieved from https://figsinwinter.substack.com/p/totalitarianism-as-a-novel-form-of

[26] Stoto, M. A., Schlageter, S., & Kraemer, J. D. (2022). COVID-19 mortality in the United States: It's been two Americas from the start. *PLOS ONE, 17*(4), e0265053. https://doi.org/10.1371/journal.pone.0265053

[27] Lysenkoism. (n.d.). In *Wikipedia*. Retrieved from https://en.wikipedia.org/wiki/Lysenkoism

[28] Lamarckism: Jean-Baptiste Lamarck (1744–1829) proposed a theory of evolution known as Lamarckism, suggesting that organisms could pass on to their offspring characteristics acquired during their lifetime.

[29] Rosefielde, S. (2009). *Red Holocaust: Communism and the Ukrainian Famine of 1932-1933*. Routledge.

[30] MacKinnon, F. (2009). *China's Great Leap Forward: The Revolution Derailed*. Oxford University Press.

CHAPTER SEVENTEEN

MAGA

Author's note: The second Trump administration represents a rapidly escalating crisis for American democracy that began to unfold just as this book was going to press. This chapter is frozen in place as of February 1, 2025

The difference between a totalitarian dictatorship and a cult is a matter of size, power, and degree. The more powerful and less accountable a cult leader becomes, the more totalistic their rule. Take any totalistic cult, give it state power—military, secret police, media control—and you get the Third Reich, Donald Trump's intended post-2025 America, or Stalin's Soviet Union. Cults use the same psychological chains, but when small, they are less dangerous, held in check by functioning governments. But when cults escape these guardrails, all bets are off.

The MAGA cult demonstrates this progression perfectly, having already reformed the thoughts of about one-third of the American electorate. In the November 2024 election, this gave Trump an electoral college win of 312-226 over Kamala Harris, with 49.8% of the popular vote. The slogan "Make America Great Again"—borrowed from Ronald Reagan's 1980 campaign—carries a much darker tone under Trump precisely because it represents the transformation from political movement to national cult. Reagan projected optimism and unity, addressing inflation, unemployment, an energy crisis, and the decline of American power after the Iranian hostage crisis and the Soviet invasion of Afghanistan. Trump's version is all confrontation—fueling resentment, dividing Americans, and weaponizing his followers against immigrants, experts, human rights, democratic culture, and most critically America's system of Constitutional checks and balances.

MAGA disdains democratic values, norms, and institutions, and has already weakened American sovereignty, undermined national security, and tarnished the country's global standing. Russia and China are entrenched autocracies, while India's democracy erodes under Modi's Hindu nationalism.[1] If the world's remaining superpower can't sustain a robust democracy, where will it survive?

Now that Trump has won a second term, it might be tempting to view him as a mainstream figure. But let's dig deeper. In 2016, he won with just 27 percent of eligible voters,[2] improving to 31 percent in 2024.[3] This falls far short of a mandate, though it demonstrates MAGA's growing strength as a population-scaled cult. The result reflects voter apathy and suppression. Democratic turnout dropped by over 9 percent from 2020, with big losses among young men—especially Black and Latino men—while Trump expanded his margins with white women. Bias against Kamala Harris as a woman of color likely played a decisive role.

Democratic voters who stayed home failed to grasp the stakes. They should have heeded the lessons of Erdogan, Orbán, and Bolsonaro—leaders who rose by rallying loyal minorities amid low turnout in disillusioned democracies.

The Trump administration is now implementing a deeper assault on democratic institutions, following the blueprint laid out in *Project 2025*. This Viktor Orban-linked Heritage Foundation document, along with Steve Bannon's long-running plan to "deconstruct the administrative state," serves as an authoritarian playbook to dismantle federal bureaucracy.[4] By purging civil servants and military brass while staffing agencies with loyalists, the MAGA agenda is threatening citizen health and safety, fair elections, and the separation of powers. This maximalist version of the unitary executive theory theoretically grants future presidents the same authority, but the institutional damage inflicted by these policies—not to mention ongoing brain drain—makes future course corrections exceedingly difficult.

Following its first pillar, the administration is dismantling the independence of federal agencies, putting them under direct White House control. Elon Musk wasted no time—locking agency officials out of their computer systems, and installing his own updates. Under the second pillar, Trump's team is installing loyalists in government positions, using a database of MAGA-approved personnel to block anyone ideologically uncompliant. The third pillar's "academy" aims to indoctrinate remaining government workers, erasing all traces of support for civil liberties, social justice, secular education, climate action, diversity, equity, and inclusion—creating a MAGA Ministry of Truth. The fourth pillar provided the exact playbook the administration is using to execute these changes at breakneck speed.

The administration's policy goals mirror Project 2025's authoritarian wish list:[5] federal bans on abortion and pornography, censorship and book banning, rolling back LGBTQ+ rights, targeting diversity, equity, and inclusion (DEI), gutting the Federal Reserve's independence, cutting taxes for the wealthy and corporations, establishing a supermajority requirement to raise taxes, and killing clean energy mandates while promoting fossil fuels.

Trump is now consolidating the power to turn the US military against US citizens. During his first term, he threatened to invoke martial law, ordered federal forces to clear peaceful protesters in Lafayette Square, and repeatedly suggested using the military to "restore domestic order." His first administration already flirted with undermining the Posse Comitatus Act of 1878, which bans domestic use of the military. Project 2025 explicitly calls for repealing it—and the administration is working to do so—seeking direct presidential control over National Guard units, while embedding loyalists throughout the military command structure.

The real threat is to the rule of law itself. Transforming the federal bureaucracy from a merit-based system to one of patronage will undo protections dating to the Pendleton Act of 1883.[6] Stripping the independence of the Department of Justice and FBI is set to turn these storied agencies into totalitarian enforcers. Donald B. Ayer was the deputy attorney general under George H. W. Bush. He warned: "Project 2025 seems designed to let Donald Trump function as a dictator, completely eviscerating restraints built into our system. He wants to destroy any notion of rule of law.... If Trump implements these ideas, no one in this country would be safe."[7]

Project 2025 becomes even more alarming in light of Trump's demonstrated contempt for legal accountability. His pattern of evading justice through delay, intimidation, and political pressure has already proved terribly effective. As his criminal cases illustrate, being above the law isn't just Trump's goal—it's increasingly his reality.

In 2023, Trump faced four indictments across New York, Florida, Washington, D.C., and Georgia—covering the January 6 insurrection, mishandled classified documents, and falsified business records related to Stormy Daniels.[8] By early 2024, a jury awarded $83.3 million in damages to E. Jean Carroll, who was sexually abused by Trump, followed by a $450 million civil fraud judgment against the Trump Organization. His May 2024 conviction on 34 felony counts went nowhere when Judge Juan Merchan sentenced him to "unconditional discharge." The other criminal cases have been dropped or rendered irrelevant.

The Georgia RICO case charging Trump and 18 others with 2020 election interference faced immediate MAGA attacks. His co-defendants successfully disqualified Fulton County DA Fani Willis on December 19, 2024 over her personal relationship with a colleague. Special Counsel Jack Smith hit wall after wall prosecuting him for January 6, the fake-electors scheme, and theft of classified documents. The cases were buried in motions claiming presidential immunity while witnesses like Brad Raffensperger faced intimidation. Trump and his allies continually framed the investigations as "witch hunts" designed to sabotage his 2024 presidential campaign. After Trump's victory, Smith wound down his work and resigned.

On July 1, 2024, the U.S. Supreme Court ruled that presidents have absolute immunity from prosecution for official acts during their tenure. This led Judge Aileen Cannon to gut the classified documents case, claiming Trump's handling of materials fell within presidential duties. She had already dismissed the original indictment citing prosecutorial misconduct, forcing delays through refiling. These hurdles derailed Smith's prosecution—an effort rendered moot by Trump's return to power.

SCOTUS unanimously denied an appeal of a Colorado case which brought a 14th Amendment challenge to Trump's eligibility for the presidency, based on his seditious conduct during the 2021 insurrection. Despite any temporary victories, Trump's legal troubles would have sunk him, had he remained a private citizen. What's instructive here is that regardless of any empirical facts of any charge or lawsuit he's ever faced, Trump attacked every judge, the court system, and the rule of law. It's all *"UNFAIR!!"* But what he really thought was unfair is that he was not above the law. As president, he may now very well *be* above the law.

Trump began turning MAGA against democracy before he ever ran for office. He claimed seven US elections were rigged: 2012 general election, 2016 primary and general elections, 2018 midterms, 2020 primary and general elections, and 2022 midterms. He pre-declared the 2024 election rigged—but quickly accepted the "mandate" after winning. His 2020 "Stop the Steal" campaign was a full-blown attack on democracy, aimed at overturning an election he lost. After 61 of his 62 baseless court challenges were thrown out, he encouraged the infamous January 6, 2021 violent insurrection at the Capitol.[9]

As heard at the 2024 CPAC, MAGA has only grown bolder. They're still set on finishing their 2021 coup attempt. Eight Senators and 139 Representatives became post-facto collaborators by voting against certifying Biden's 2020 victory in Arizona or Pennsylvania.[10] Over 100 MAGA members of Congress who tried to disenfranchise millions of voters won re-election—reflecting how deeply Trump's cult has rooted itself in America's political landscape—whether through gerrymandering or pervasive thought reform. For them, laws are for suckers, and lost elections are mere obstacles. On his second Inauguration Day, Trump pardoned or commuted the sentences of every January 6 rioter—even the ones who committed violent assault of police officers—even though they'd all been convicted under due process of law. Further, he purged all Justice department employees who'd ever been involved in their prosecutions.

Trump's orgy of retribution won't stop there. We don't need to "wait and see." It's baked in. To get a sense of what's on tap, it's useful to revisit McSweeney's[11] comprehensive list of over 1,000 atrocities from his first term. But now, there are fewer checks on his power: he enjoys a much friendlier 6-3 conservative Supreme Court and a much tighter grip on the Republican Party. He's now in a position to punish his enemies through legal persecution, imprisonment, or worse.[12] His agenda seems straightforward, as Heather Cox Richardson predicted on December 13, 2024: Personal revenge, destruction of institutions, and graft.[13]

To grasp MAGA's danger, consider the sheer volume of respected institutions and people Trump intends to punish with his newly acquired powers. A partial list includes: The FBI, CIA, US Postal Service, NFL, UN, WHO, CDC, NOAA, NATO, EU, National Weather Service, major media outlets, California, New York, EPA, IRS, Justice Department, multiple cities, the Pentagon, Defense Department, Gold Star Families, Navy SEALs, and former military leaders like James Mattis and Mark Milley (whom he implied should be executed for treason).

Trump has attacked a long list of politicians, especially Democrats, calling them "criminals" or "traitors" or "the enemy within"—Hillary Clinton, Joe Biden, Elizabeth Warren, Alexandria Ocasio-Cortez, Adam Schiff, and Nancy Pelosi among them, along with Biden's family, Barack and Michelle Obama, and on and on and on. He demands absolute loyalty from Republicans and attacks any who defy him as "Republicans in name only" (RINOs) with the same ferocity he normally reserves for Democrats. Most of these Republicans were simply loyal to American laws and political norms—above Trump himself.

It's clear that MAGA remains a growing force that has by no means peaked. Don't expect it to fizzle out in 2028 or thereafter. It's a robust, illiberal neo-Confederate cult—well-funded, with a sprawling media infrastructure and a legion of acolytes nurturing its metastasizing anti-democratic ideology. While Trump is its current figurehead, there's no chance MAGA dies with him. Hundreds of prominent MAGA quislings stand ready to carry on his assault on the United States. This cult will never stop trying to bury the rule of law—and the Constitution—unless we, the people, stop them.

It comes down to this: for Trump to be right and his cult vindicated, every person, institution, agency, scientist, armed forces general, health official, state, prosecutor, judge, election worker, and media outlet he's ever attacked would have to be conspiring against him. Reality itself would have to be wrong. This is why he's a totalitarian, not merely a dictator. He didn't just run for president four times—he's always been running for Emperor of Reality, and Dispenser of Existence. In the eyes of MAGA, Trump is always right, even when he's wrong. And if you're not MAGA, you're vermin—to be exterminated.

Trump projects a messianic self-image suffused with martyrdom: a savior, wronged by the world, fighting impossible odds. He will remain a sacred figure to his followers for generations. No one since Andrew Johnson, Jefferson Davis, or Robert E. Lee has divided the United States on such a profound and national scale. Not even during the Civil War was the Capitol breached. And never has a president so despised the government he was elected to lead.

This should be a warning to his cult members that he will burn down anything or anyone who gets in his way. Nothing this man has ever said or done has been to help his cultists, or the nation. He's taken their money and their loyalty and squandered it for his own venal purposes, like every other cult leader. As he destroys the rule of law, they won't be any safer than the people they perceive as their enemies. History shows that authoritarian leaders from Stalin to Pol Pot had no qualms about turning on their most loyal supporters when those supporters were no longer useful.

To his cultists I say simply, if he can go after them—he can go after you.

I still believe even the most ardent MAGA members value their personal freedoms and civil liberties. Which makes it hard to stomach the open totalitarian rhetoric at CPAC 2024—or Trump voters on TV declaring "We want our dictator!"

Vice President J.D. Vance might be an even worse threat. An ultra-reactionary in the vanguard of the New Right, Vance openly embraces "regime change"—to tear up the US Constitution and impose a non-democratic, post-liberal style of governance.[14] He wrote the foreword to *Dawn's Early Light: Taking Back Washington to Save America*, by Kevin Roberts, President of the Heritage Foundation and architect of Project 2025. Its original subtitle was *Burning Down Washington to Save America*, complete with a wooden match over the word "Washington."

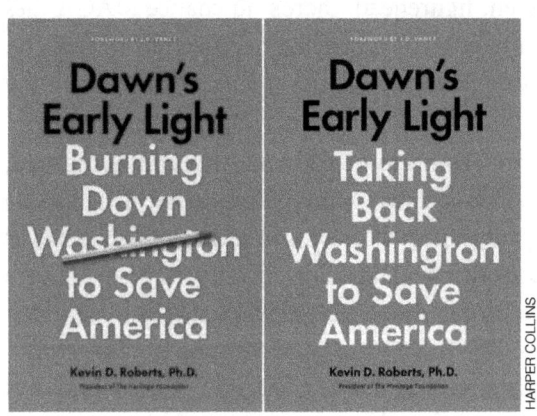

Two covers, two titles—one virulently anti-democratic book.

Regardless of the revised title, the incendiary message remains. I can only point out that the German elites who clamored for Hitler's appointment as chancellor didn't fully understand what they were signing up for. Neither do American reactionaries today. They believe they can subvert the rule of law for their own gain without plunging the nation into totalitarian madness.

History says they're wrong.

Many who supported Trump did so because they believed he would fight for their values. But the erosion of freedoms, safety, and justice under his leadership leaves us all vulnerable—including those who believed in him most. We're now all strapped onto the MAGA cult bus, wherever it may take us. Our near-term reality is now defined by Trump and his minions, including power-mad authoritarians like Steve Bannon, Vivek Ramaswamy, Russ Vought, Kash Patel, Michael Flynn, Stephen Miller, and Jack Posobiec, to name just a few. Consider the dark portent of Elon Musk's Inauguration Day Nazi salute. Like other citizens throughout history who have found themselves in the throes of a totalitarian takeover, we may be forced to watch our institutions crumble under sustained assault. The authoritarian breakthrough may already have occurred. If our checks and balances fail, we'll have no choice but to adapt to whatever atrocities may be in store, until we can unify in overwhelming numbers to throw the bastards out—provided the US ever holds another free and fair election.

There's a reason Jim Jones moved his cult to the jungle of Guyana, beyond the reach of the rule of law, before murdering nearly 1,000 people. And there's a much shorter distance between Jonestown, the Holocaust, and the carnage Donald Trump and his lackeys intend to inflict on the United States of America than most would care to admit.

---

[1] Freedom House. (2024). *Freedom in the world*: India. Retrieved from https://freedomhouse.org/country/india/freedom-world/2024

[2] In the 2016 U.S. presidential election, Donald Trump received approximately 62,984,828 votes out of an estimated 231,556,622 eligible voters, equating to about 27.2% of the eligible voting population.

[3] As of the final certified results of the 2024 U.S. presidential election, Donald Trump secured approximately 74.65 million votes, representing 49.8% of the total votes cast. The total number of eligible voters in the United States was estimated to be around 239 million, making Trump's share approximately 31.2% of the eligible voting population.

[4] The Heritage Foundation has received funding from the Orbán-backed Danube Institute and Hungarian oligarchs with state ties. In 2021, it hosted a Danube Institute fellow and has accepted donations from Orbán allies, including advisor Zoltán Balog and businessman Gábor Széles, whose company has won major government contracts. Leaked emails show Heritage staff coordinating pro-Orbán messaging with his advisors before his 2019 U.S. visit. Orbán's government has cited Heritage research to justify crackdowns on immigration, LGBTQ rights, and independent media, fueling criticism that Heritage is compromised and advancing Orbán's illiberal agenda in the U.S.
New Republic. (2023). Heritage Foundation's ties to Orbán's regime. *The New Republic*. Retrieved from https://newrepublic.com/article/179776/heritage-foundation-viktor-orban-trump

[5] Project 2025: Project 2025. (n.d.). In *Wikipedia*. Retrieved from https://en.wikipedia.org/wiki/Project_2025#cite_note-Stone_2023-9

[6] Pendleton Civil Service Reform Act: Pendleton Civil Service Reform Act. (n.d.). In *Wikipedia*. Retrieved from https://en.wikipedia.org/wiki/Pendleton_Civil_Service_Reform_Act

[7] Guardian. (2023). Trump's revenge game plan alarms experts. *The Guardian*. Retrieved from https://www.theguardian.com/us-news/2023/nov/22/trump-revenge-game-plan-alarm

[8] Indictments against Donald Trump: Indictments against Donald Trump. (n.d.). In *Wikipedia*. Retrieved from https://en.wikipedia.org/wiki/Indictments_against_Donald_Trump

[9] USA Today. (2021). Trump's failed efforts to overturn election numbers. *USA Today*. Retrieved from https://www.usatoday.com/in-depth/news/politics/elections/2021/01/06/trumps-failed-efforts-overturn-election-numbers/4130307001/

[10] New York Times. (2021). Electoral College objectors in Biden's victory. *The New York Times*. Retrieved from https://www.nytimes.com/interactive/2021/01/07/us/elections/electoral-college-biden-objectors.html

[11] McSweeney's. (n.d.). The complete listing of atrocities. *McSweeney's*. Retrieved from https://www.mcsweeneys.net/articles/the-complete-listing-atrocities-1-1-056

[12] Washington Post. (2023). Trump's revenge game plan raises alarm. *The Washington Post*. Retrieved from https://www.washingtonpost.com/opinions/2023/11/13/trump-threaten-punish-enemies-president/

[13] Richardson, H. C. (2024, December 13). December 13, 2024. *Heather Cox Richardson's Letters from an American*. Retrieved from https://heathercoxrichardson.substack.com/p/december-13-2024

[14] Politico. (2024). Is there something more radical than MAGA? J.D. Vance is dreaming it. *Politico*. Retrieved from https://www.politico.com/news/magazine/2024/03/15/mr-maga-goes-to-washington-00147054

CHAPTER EIGHTEEN

Apophenia

The human brain functions on what futurist Ray Kurzweil calls the Pattern Recognition Theory of Mind. Finding patterns and making order out of chaos is its primary function, and it's very good at it—sometimes too good.[1] The essential need for meaning, combined with hyperactive pattern recognition, pulls people into conspiratorial thinking and cults.

The rise of AI in the early 2020s offers a new lens for understanding our minds. Machines analyze data quickly and reveal hidden patterns we miss—better diagnoses, material discoveries, and sharper weather forecasts. But machines are limited by their training data, struggling with patterns outside what they've learned. When faced with ambiguous input, AI typically signals uncertainty or fails to generate an answer.

Humans are different. We excel at recognizing novel patterns and reasoning from limited examples, but we also compulsively create meaning from randomness. We see faces in inanimate objects (pareidolia) and connect unrelated phenomena (apophenia)—cognitive byproducts that once provided survival advantages by favoring false positives over false negatives. Pareidolia is a subset of apophenia, which encompasses all perceptions of patterns in random data.[2] While these traits were adaptive in ancestral environments, they are now frequently maladaptive, fostering widespread superstitions and erroneous beliefs. Evolution favors *satisficing* over precision, rewarding traits that function well enough to ensure survival and reproduction, even at the cost of significant cognitive distortions.

Our brains crave internal order. Unlike AI, humans don't process data quickly or objectively, especially when removed from familiar surroundings. Sensory deprivation experiments show that isolation breeds delusions, hallucinations, and heightened suggestibility. In *Cults in America*, Willa Appel compares this to social upheaval: "When the environment becomes unstable, people lose the informational anchors that help them interpret experience... they become more susceptible to persuasion."[3] In this vacuum of meaning, conspiracy theories flourish.

With its hyper-focus on connections, apophenia fuels conspiracy theories and statistical misinterpretations, especially during crises when trust in institutions erodes. Remember that Dr. Lorne Dawson noted that people crave meaning more than life itself, particularly in uncertain times. Appel illustrates this through a superstitious tribe's response to tragedy: when a house collapses and kills a family member, they reject technical causes, blaming witchcraft instead. This apophenic thinking provides order, control, and a scapegoat—though it doesn't lead to stronger houses.

The same compulsive meaning-making drives the just-world fallacy. When random misfortunes happen to good people, they "must have had it coming" for past karma, or it's "part of God's plan." It's much more comforting to blame victims or divine will than to accept that calamity can strike anyone without reason. These apophenic beliefs maintain a simple, ordered sense of the world—but run roughshod over objective reality.

Cult psychology exploits the same evolutionary drive to avoid uncertainty. Humans, like other great apes, dolphins, some birds and other animals, can think about our thoughts.[4] This metacognition often leads to anxiety and reduced functionality. Focusing on survival—building boats or weapons—was more adaptive than overthinking existence. Apophenia offered a simple escape from overwhelming complexity. Even minor crop failures in our ancestral past could trigger beliefs that "nature gods" were angry—an early form of trying to make sense of a capricious universe.

During the 1960s and 1970s, many joined cults to make sense of their lives. The era was marked by upheaval, shattering America's post-WWII calm. Conflict over civil rights, new cultural norms, new music, free love, the Vietnam War, and the breakdown of nuclear families put the nation on edge. Many sought refuge in residential cults and communes that offered a "village" for those burned by traditional families—a place to find purpose and escape the treadmill of wages and rent.

Catering to this existential hunger, my parents crafted a new-age narrative based on Theosophy and the Mighty I AM cult. These movements had attracted millions in the 19th and 20th centuries with their vivid tales of spiritual forces behind world events.

Our members believed:

"We know who our friends are. We know who the forces of darkness are. The Ascended Masters have our back. There's a divine plan. And we can save the world, and make our ascension."

Like villagers attributing misfortune to witchcraft, apophenia brought quick resolution to our new recruits. Positive events proved divine protection, while misfortunes were blamed on dark forces—requiring more prayers and spiritual commitment. They drifted from real-world explanations into magical thinking, since too much curiosity could break the illusion and force a return to the chaos they had just fled. Each new anecdotal "proof" gained through confirmation bias led them deeper into my cult's apophenic worldview.

The forces driving cults and conspiracies in the 2020s dwarf previous movements, with MAGA and its sub-cults QAnon and Christian Nationalism leading the charge.[5] Twentieth-century seekers fled conventional society to join residential communes. Today's digital cults offer a more insidious form of escape. The 1960s and 1970s were tame compared to recent upheavals: climate chaos, the crumbling post-WWII order, Obama's election followed by Trump's norm-shattering presidencies, Covid-19, information warfare, Black Lives Matter and MeToo, abortion rights rollbacks, immigration battles, rising inequality, and the global fascist surge which has led to 18 straight years of declining freedom.[6]

While yesterday's seekers had to change their lives to enter their alternative reality, modern cults reach recruits through their phones. My cult's Ascended Masters delivered prophecies through dictations in crowded auditoriums—QAnon spreads its dogma through cryptic posts that reach millions instantly. We tracked "fallen angels" through complex spiritual revelations, they track the "cabal" through byzantine "drops." Methods evolve, but apophenia remains.

The harbinger of 21st-century reality distortion was 9/11, which spurred a renewal of American conspiracy fever that echoed some reactions to the Kennedy assassination. Seeds of this were planted earlier through 1980s and 1990s talk radio, with figures like Art Bell and Alex Jones—who later started InfoWars. Fox News emerged in 1996, and the late 1990s internet turbocharged muckraking right-wing sites like The

Drudge Report, Newsmax, and WorldNetDaily. By the 2020s, thousands of unreliable commentators and influencers broadcast globally, aided and abetted by slick government propaganda channels like Russia Today, TRT World, PressTV, and CCTV/Xinhua.

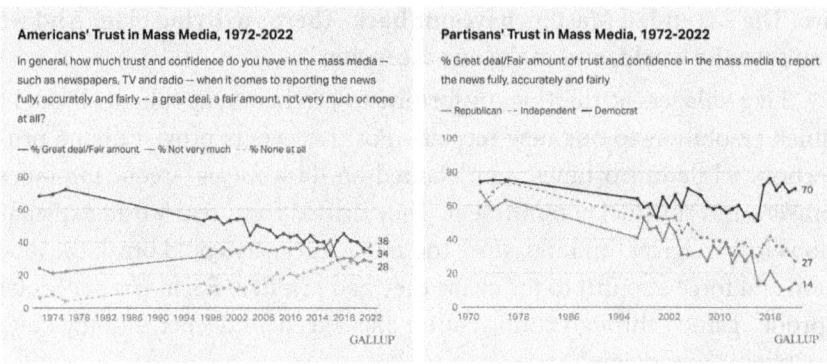

Americans are increasingly misinformed under this flood of low-quality content, with Democrats being a notable exception as their trust in mainstream media rebounded to near-1970 levels. Despite falling trust, journalistic standards at network TV and newspapers of record mostly remain consistent, with retractions when errors occur—something notably absent from propaganda outlets like Fox News.[7] Trust in reliable sources has plummeted as bogus news surged, especially among groups favoring lower-quality outlets. By 2022, 38 percent of Americans had no trust in mass media, surpassing the 34 percent with at least some trust.

This information vacuum, combined with mounting chaos, pushes many into Appel's predicted sensory deprivation zone—making them delusional, suggestible, and desperate for answers. Here's the trap: once people start finding patterns in randomness, their capacity for reality-testing weakens. Each socially "confirmed" conspiracy validates their apophenia, whetting their appetite for even more outlandish connections. The brain delivers a dopamine hit, rewarding each new discovery, creating an addictive loop of revelation and certainty.

Demagogues and cult leaders exploit this addiction like drug pushers, peddling apophenic nonsense like "Jewish Space Lasers," "They're eating the pets!" "Childless Cat Ladies," "Pizzagate," and "Great Replacement Theory." Even Taylor Swift became a target, labeled a "Pentagon psyop" by Jesse Watters of Fox News, alongside smears linking her to the Church of Satan. It wouldn't be surprising if the MAGA cult blamed their clogged toilets on illegal immigration. The more outlandish the claim, the more it affirms insider knowledge—and loyalty to hidden truths missed by outsiders. Reality becomes whatever confirms existing beliefs and reinforces in-group solidarity. Contradictory evidence is dismissed as "fake news," while insiders who acknowledge it are vilified as impure or disloyal.

Thirty-nine percent of Americans, including 72 percent of Republicans, deny the 2020 election results despite the statistical impossibility of 7 million fraudulent votes and no credible evidence at the state level of significant fraud.[8] The MAGA cult rejects empirical reality beyond elections—denying climate change while feeling its effects, raging against vaccines and public health, and claiming crime is at an all-time high in 2024 when rates are historically low. They baselessly assert illegal immigrants are voting *en masse*, and they attacked the Biden economy despite its record-breaking performance.

"Faith leaders" within Trump's cult pray over him at "Turning Point Action," Duluth, GA, October 23, 2024

Widespread detachment from reality is a recipe for disaster, and it's boom time for cults—but these aren't your granddad's cults. While cults aren't new, today's forms are unprecedented. QAnon has grown into a massive national and global movement, trapping ordinary people in a state of paralyzed, apophenic panic. The Republican Party has subsumed QAnon dogma.

Stories of recovering ex-members like Ramona highlight the trauma involved—so much that she wouldn't reveal her last name.[9] During Covid, she and her boyfriend stockpiled food, bought guns, and ran late-night bug-out drills to practice fleeing their home. She spent hours doomscrolling until anxiety overwhelmed her. Her exit from QAnon began when she announced plans to return to school—triggering violent arguments that ended her relationship. As I've repeatedly stressed, all cults are anti-intellectual. Knowledge is their Kryptonite. Special knowledge can't survive rigorous inquiry.

QAnon employs Lifton's eight principles of thought reform without physical contact—a significant innovation. *Milieu control* occurs as members dive into siloed forums where only approved narratives survive. "Q-drops" and prophecy updates provide *mystical manipulation*. Rejecting outside sources maintains *purity*. Members *confess* their awakening stories. Solving puzzles and decoding predictions becomes *sacred science*. Insider *jargon* like "where we go one, we go all" and "the storm" binds believers. *Doctrine* reframes personal experiences. The cult *dispenses existence* through identifying who belongs to the evil cabal. These methods have successfully duped your friends and neighbors, who've been red-pilled into cult insanity—without ever leaving their homes.

Game designer and anti-fascist researcher Jim Stewartson compares QAnon to alternate reality games (ARGs). On my podcast in 2021 he explained: "These are big, viral experiences that people would go through online, crossing into the real world. They'd go on scavenger hunts, trying to find a phone buried in a cake somewhere. If you didn't give people proper guidelines and boundaries, they'd drive themselves crazy trying to find a puzzle that didn't exist or that didn't have a solution. In game design, those are terrible things, right? We saw that behavior and said, let's put a guardrail here."[10]

Stewartson's colleague sent him Reed Berkowitz's *Washington Post* article, which describes QAnon as the "gamification of propaganda."[11] Berkowitz wrote of an ARG where a mistake led players to a false clue, leaving them stuck: "They experienced an apophany. They hadn't seen a clue—they'd created one in their minds. QAnon is a mirror reflection of this dynamic: Apophenia is the point."

Stewartson added, "There is no Q. And it's really important to be clear about that. It's a LARP—a live action role play. Mike Flynn was always behind it. MAGA3X started QAnon, in terms of writing the first drops. James Brower and a troll named Microchip worked for MAGA3X, and MAGA3X was run by Mike Flynn—the group that, frankly, swung the election to Donald Trump in 2016. They ran a whole bunch of those ops, the Huma stuff, the Wiener emails, Pizzagate."

QAnon drops breadcrumbs in the form of clues from various sources, using hashtags and media links. As messages are reposted, they accumulate false details. It might start with something innocuous, like shapes resembling horns in an image, suggesting devil worship. As members "do their own research," they embellish, finding unrelated horned images. Eventually, they feel they've solved a mystery, when they've actually been caught in a cult-directed loop. Reed Berkowitz notes, "When you figure it out yourself, you own it," describing how the sense of discovery activates their brain's reward system.

DALL-E / SEAN PROPHET

Stewartson compares QAnon to the *Poltergeist* trope of TV snow—static that causes viewers to see false patterns. He explained: "If you sit somebody in front of snow long enough, they will see shit. All people, literally everybody—community is very important. You get people in a community together trying to solve something, it almost doesn't matter what the puzzle is, because it's fun. It's interesting."

It's uncanny that something as simple as an *unsolvable puzzle* can have such a profound impact when magnified by community enthusiasm. Thus QAnon emerges as a fully-formed skeleton of a new religion, stripped of religious content to appeal to new age conspiritualists and non-believers alike. It's ingenious—a physical devil: You don't need a God to hate pedophiles.

For Christians it concretizes the enemy by painting secular elites as contemptible devil-worshipers who also happen to rape children. This motivates Christians toward even more extremist forms of the politics and religion they already espouse, merging totalitarianism with end-times evangelicalism. This vision strengthens established churches by providing tighter community, greater member investment, and a keener sense of order. It confirms their intuitions of persecution, while making apophenic sense of the world. It's nothing short of a 21st century update to the Book of Revelation,[12] another story written by Christians under persecution long ago.[13]

Let's review my cult's narrative:

"We know who our friends are. We know who the forces of darkness are. The Ascended Masters have our back. There's a divine plan. And we can save the world, and make our ascension."

The QAnon story:

"Where we go one, we go all. We know who is in the evil cabal. Donald Trump has our back. The Storm is the plan. We can defeat the blood-drinking pedophiles, and advance our collective power."

The Storm is classic millenarian eschatology—the study of death, judgment, and final destiny. Millenarian theology often predicts a return to Edenic innocence or a leap forward into a golden age. QAnon's Storm is exactly this: a dramatic apocalyptic event where the global cabal will be exposed and brought to justice, triggering mass arrests, military tribunals, and a Great Awakening to hidden truths.[14] This will purge society of its deepest corruptions, kicking off a utopian era, with Donald Trump as the key messianic figure.

The structure of this story mirrors my cult's narrative, with Trump substituting for the Ascended Masters. Once someone is drawn into QAnon, every unfolding event becomes proof that the plan is in play. Every setback for Trump is further evidence that the cabal is out to get him. Every MAGA win brings them closer to The Storm. Trump generates a continuous scatter of chaos, which forms the white noise the cult interprets through their apophenic lens. Each new development reinforces their righteousness. The cult stays hyper-engaged with Trump's daily battles. In their view, he cannot fail, because win or lose, he's the Messiah, and the will of God is always on plan.

Appel's 1983 analysis in *Cults in America* could have been written today. While millenarianism comes in diverse forms, its central trope remains characteristic of Ur-Fascism: the *deus ex machina* transformation of the human condition leading to a cessation of struggle and the Golden Age. This hasn't changed since Revelation. Appel pulls no punches in her critique:

> In many ways, the millenarian vision plays a role for adults similar to that of fairy tales for children… a kind of symbolic language that gives external form to inner experience…. Children live in a world governed by giants, all-powerful, all-knowing giants whose rules are often hard to ascertain and whose good will is so critical…. The millenarian vision is surprisingly similar. It depicts a dangerous, evil world, which like that of the fairy tales is peopled with 'creatures' of superhuman proportions…. The millenarian fantasy appeals to people whose world has suddenly overturned, who find themselves in familiar surroundings that no longer make sense. Cult followers are people whose expectations have been thwarted. They feel cheated and resentful but either too disoriented to cope with the situation or are excluded from the legitimate avenues of redress.[15]

Secularization in the United States accelerated after *Engel v. Vitale*, 1962,[16] and *Abington School District v. Schempp*, 1963,[17] which banned mandatory prayer and Bible readings in schools. The "nones," who are people unaffiliated with any religion,[18] have now become America's largest religious demographic.[19] Though most Americans still believe in God and the power of prayer, fewer than half pray daily. Christians have become a mere majority and are now forced to share the nation with other faiths and the growing ranks of nonbelievers. They haven't taken these changes well. Even while enjoying strong legal protection for their own religious freedom, they tend to view others' exercise of their freedom *not to believe* as immoral, satanic, and a form of persecution.

QAnon, like earlier satanic panics,[20] is narrowly focused on child sexual abuse,[21] suggesting deeper anxiety over shifting family dynamics, divorce rates, single-parent families, evolving gender roles and the perceived vulnerability of children. This reflects Appel's emphasis on "thwarted expectations" and being "excluded from avenues of redress." Absent totalitarianism, there's no way to reimpose "traditional values" on a democratic society which has largely rejected them.

> The value of the fairy tale is that it allows for the expression of anger and resentment in a permissible way. Anonymity protects both the child and the objects of his anger. The followers of a messianic cult, however, need not refrain from naming their enemies. Unlike the child, they are not intimately bound up with or dependent on the objects of their wrath, so the targeting of their anger is cathartic. Thus, in the millenarian vision, Satan often has a distinct name and identity.[22]

The core of this fantasy is that Satan, along with Babylon, Mammon, worshipers of Moloch, the Cain civilization, and Sodom and Gomorrah, will be brought down in a single cataclysmic event. "Behold, I make all things new." (Revelation 21:5, KJV)

> In the millenarian kingdom, the Saved live in a paradise on Earth where 'there shall be no more death, neither sorrow nor crying, neither shall there be any more pain: for the former things are passed away.' How they live, how they rule and what ruling entails is completely absent in these tales. All we are told is that the previously existing power relations have been reversed.... The messianic vision also serves to legitimize antisocial feelings, and like the fairy tale it absolves its followers of responsibility... at the end of the fairy tale, the hero becomes an individual, a successful adult who happily rules his kingdom.... In the messianic vision, he doesn't, and instead returns to the childhood fold where adulthood, like some hideous burden, is thankfully abdicated for ever after.[23]

Appel makes clear that childhood fairy tales carry a superior moral message to petulant millenarian fantasies. The reversal of power relations forms the messianic goal, but QAnon prophecies don't extend beyond military tribunals and executions of the cabal. Their vague ideal of a new society maps onto the Holy City myth, but they don't discuss the details of governance, except that God will rule. This is chilling. God, in this context, is a metaphor for unchecked power, conforming to totalitarian systems: Arendt's natural order and Trump's MAGAfied dispensing of existence. It also recalls Fromm's freedom from the burden of choosing one's own path, keeping followers frozen in an arrested stage of moral development. When citizens withdraw from adult responsibility, it clears the field for political leaders to commit atrocities. Instead of happily ever after, millenarians are courting genocide.

While QAnon followers explore digital rabbit holes, my cult was old school. We dug *actual* holes we planned to occupy. Different era, same delusion. We weren't chasing pizza pedophiles or Jewish space lasers. We had our own flavor of conspirituality and our own world-rejecting rationales. We managed to prep for doomsday twice, because one apocalypse just wasn't enough.

Here's the paradox: people in my cult weren't crazy. And they weren't social outcasts. They were bright, young, idealistic people seeking community—along with answers to life's big questions. Yet somehow they—we—ended up stockpiling food and ammunition while giving up on civilization. Wacky as it sounds, it gave us an unparalleled sense of clarity and purpose. Jump in a time machine and trade your internet doom-scrolling for some good old-fashioned bunker-digging, and you've got yourself my cult's 1980s version of QAnon. Technology evolves, but millenarianism is evergreen.

Let's hear from ex-members in their own words, taken from interviews I conducted from 2007-2012. Most of them went through the full bomb-shelter experience. But in spite of the struggles they faced, they all valued the experience. Some met spouses, had children, and made friendships that survived their cult exit. I asked what convinced them to join:

> *Donald Trowbridge:* You know, it's serious, but also exciting. Talking about the possibility of what we could do in the future to help the world, save the world, improve ourselves. So I couldn't wait at that point to get out of the Air Force and move on and join 'em. I'm ready to go, this is my life's purpose. Mark Prophet comes out to the gate "Hi Don, how are you?" [I said,] "Yeah, I feel like I'm home."

> *Mark Filipas:* I was always interested in metaphysics and spirituality; the Summit Lighthouse books were all over the new-age bookstores in Los Angeles at the time. It was just a pretty intelligent blend of Eastern and Western ideas and religions. 'Cause ultimately I decided that I wanted to be a part of kind of this world-changing organization. But it was definitely—it evolved into a lot of camaraderie—you made a lot of friends. Everybody that I met there were just truly nice people.

> *Rick Barney:* The community was what I really loved; I loved the people. I was looking for answers. When I first found the teachings back in '76, I really felt that I had found someone who—who knew the answers.

> *Will Gilchrist:* I was at the Philadelphia library and found the *Intermediate [Studies] of the Human Aura* and there was pictures of chakras and the chakra man and the violet flame and the colors and things like that.[24] So that was quite captivating at first. And I read the book and I saw a picture of Elizabeth Clare Prophet, and as soon as I saw the picture of her, I felt some attraction. I didn't know what it was, I was only 17 at the time, but that's how it started. Her influence was a major impact. I listened to her like a parent. There was this "aha," this is what I was looking for.

> *John Waid:* I got out of the Air Force in 1967—wanted to find something to explain the unanswered questions that kept coming into my mind. So I started to study the Eastern religions. The corporate and business world was not for me, I wanted to be independent. I just seemed to find a lot of kindred thought and kindred spirits, a lot of good fellowship. I was a young single person at the time, lonely in my 20s, and I got a lot of comfort, a lot of fulfilment there. It fit what I wanted to do.

> *Stan Holt:* In particular the idea of reincarnation was really appealing to me; it made a lot of sense. I remember when I first set eyes on Elizabeth Clare Prophet, you know I immediately had this impression of somebody who was larger than life. You know it was really a peak experience I would say. There seemed to be inner confirmation. You know a feeling of—that this is right for me, this is true, this is what I want to do. You can't really articulate or intellectualize it. It was just really kind of a deep feeling.

> ***John Eastwood:*** At the end of 1977, I contacted a meditation group and there was a lady in there who had some literature on quote the Ascended Masters which I'd never heard of before and there was a pamphlet in there with a picture of Elizabeth Clare Prophet on the cover. Her face, her smile fell into my heart and there it stayed. They did not have any groups at all here in Australia.
>
> ***Anna Maletta:*** I was interested in bettering myself through doing devotions, different diets and different ways of living. And I did have to extricate myself entirely from my old life in New Mexico. My family was upset, the man that I'd been living with for the past six years was upset. It didn't matter to me. I just wanted to pursue this and I felt like it had a purpose. I liked being a part of a working community. I mean it was just really great to just be a part of something and just do what you're told. I was like a perfect little 'chela' is what they called 'em, just a perfect little slave. I mean I gave up every bad habit and vice you could ever imagine, I just learned to control everything about the passions and different things inside of me, and I looked at it as a form of self-improvement.

In *Prophet's Daughter*, Erin notes that more than half of new members were repeat-seekers of alternatives to traditional religion. But they weren't growing more cautious from their experiences in other cults. Some were cult-hopping, repeating patterns and cycles, having no idea they were about to board a millenarian juggernaut.

> The alternative beliefs of most church members predated their orbit of Elizabeth Clare Prophet. More than half of those surveyed had left the religion of their birth well before joining Church Universal and Triumphant, and had belonged either to another New Age group or a Hindu or Buddhist sect… They would say, 'Mother takes me places spiritually that other gurus can't.' Some believed their contact with my mother was preordained, having dreamed of her before ever seeing one of her books or posters. Some simply wandered into one of her public lectures with no particular goal in mind and stayed because they liked the people. Not a few had been looking for stability after an excess of drugs or rootless living, wandering through the Summer of Love in Berkeley, or living in a VW bus.[25]

On the surface, it all sounds so hopeful and innocent—idealistic hippies and world-changers rejecting traditional religion and society. Coming together to find answers to life's questions, make new friends, and walk a spiritual path. Some people seeking strict discipline. But when we hear people say they want to change the world, we don't give enough thought to what that means and how difficult it is. As previously discussed, trauma can freeze cognitive and moral development. This includes those stuck in earlier Kohlberg stages who may focus on rigid, simplistic frameworks of right and wrong. Holding a goal of world change can reflect the naiveté of Piaget's pre-operational stage, where a child confuses their small, controllable world with the vast, uncontrollable world beyond.

Positive world change means credibly challenging the deep roots and vast power structures of the status quo. It requires overcoming the desires and interests of billions of people, many of whom are perfectly fine with the way things are—or want very different changes. When someone says, "I want to change the world," what we should hear is, "I want to move Mount Everest." A few hundred or even tens of thousands of people aren't any more likely to move Mount Everest than a single person. World change requires influencing millions or billions of people, and even then, only incremental, gradual changes are possible: chipping away at Mount Everest with rock chisels. That small progress won't satisfy the messianic impulse.

Building a foundation for world change requires reaching Kohlberg's Stage 6 of moral development—full adult morality, which recognizes universal ethical principles and a broader moral landscape. Perhaps only one percent of people reach this stage. Most are stuck in Stage 4 (law and order) or Stage 5 (social contract). Moreover, the influence of most people is limited to their immediate village—no more than 150 individuals. To quote the Serenity Prayer, relating to a world of 8 billion people with self-honesty requires a lot of accepting "the things I cannot change."

My cult stockpiled guns and food, and built bunkers. Similar crack-ups can be expected for any millenarian system based on world-rejection and world-purification. Cult leaders and their followers start out wanting to make the world a better place, but they underestimate the difficulty of the task—and their own reaction to failure. It's not a huge leap from "I want to fix the world" to the sulky, spurned attitude of a child: "If the world won't listen to me, then the world must be destroyed."[26]

Ex-members spoke of their inner conflict as my cult shifted its emphasis in the 1980s from the spiritual path to Montana doomsday preparations. Committed to my mother's divine revelations, most chose to obey and prepare. Walking away seemed too risky—what if the prophecies were true? A few remained faithful but ignored the apocalyptic warnings, keeping their jobs and avoiding extreme survivalism. This selective belief made no sense to me. Why follow a prophet yet cherry-pick which of their prophecies to believe? The contradiction highlights the complexity, cognitive dissonance, and inconsistencies of cult membership.

---

[1] Kurzweil, R. (2013). *How to create a mind: The secret of human thought revealed*. Viking.
This book outlines Kurzweil's Pattern Recognition Theory of Mind, which argues that cognition is fun-

damentally about detecting and processing patterns. He presents this theory as essential to replicating human intelligence in AI, aligning with his broader vision for merging human and machine cognition.

[2] Wikipedia contributors. (n.d.). Apophenia. In *Wikipedia*. Retrieved from https://en.wikipedia.org/wiki/Apophenia

[3] Appel, W. (1983). *Cults in America: Programmed for paradise*. Columbia University Press. p. 24

[4] Research suggests that several animal species exhibit metacognition, including primates, dolphins, elephants, corvids, rats, dogs, and some fish. Studies indicate that great apes and rhesus macaques can monitor their own uncertainty, dolphins opt out of difficult tasks when unsure, elephants recognize themselves in mirrors, and corvids adjust their behavior based on memory recall. Rats have demonstrated uncertainty monitoring, dogs seek information when they lack knowledge, and manta rays have passed the mirror test, suggesting a degree of self-awareness. While human metacognition is more advanced, these findings indicate that reflective cognition is not uniquely human Smith, Beran, Couchman, and Coutinho 2008 *Psychonomic Bulletin & Review* 15(4) 679–691 https://doi.org/10.3758/PBR.15.4.679

[5] Wikipedia contributors. (2024, August 14). QAnon. In *Wikipedia*. Retrieved August 14, 2024, from https://en.wikipedia.org/wiki/QAnon

LaFrance, A. (2020). The prophecies of Q. *The Atlantic*. Retrieved from https://www.theatlantic.com/magazine/archive/2020/06/qanon-nothing-can-stop-what-is-coming/610567/

[6] Freedom House. (2024). Freedom in the World 2024: Mounting damage: Flawed elections and armed conflict. Retrieved from https://freedomhouse.org/report/freedom-world/2024/mounting-damage-flawed-elections-and-armed-conflict

[7] Retractions and corrections are part of ethical journalism standards advocated by organizations like the Society of Professional Journalists (SPJ) and the American Press Institute (API). These standards emphasize the importance of striving for accuracy and correcting errors promptly.

Society of Professional Journalists. (2014). SPJ Code of Ethics. Retrieved from https://www.spj.org/ethicscode.asp

[8] Washington Post. (2023, September 8). Public opinion and the 2020 election. Retrieved from https://www.washingtonpost.com/politics/2023/09/08/public-opinion-2020-election/

[9] Klepper, D. (2024, January 31). Days of darkness: How one woman escaped the conspiracy theory trap that has ensnared millions. Associated Press. https://apnews.com/article/covid19-trump-conspiracy-theories-qanon-facebook-f79a3af0e04487890e3976fea6f03867

[10] Prophet, S., & Occhipinti, J. (Hosts). (2021, November 22). A Theocracy of Disinfo (No. 72) [Video podcast episode]. In The Radical Secular. YouTube channel Black Sun Journal. Retrieved from https://youtu.be/6bGffrT6smQ?si=urVVrOC50XYaZVXZ

[11] Berkowitz, R. (2021, May 11). QAnon resembles the games I design. But for believers, there is no winning. *The Washington Post*. Retrieved from https://wapo.st/42yUUQ4

[12] The Holy Bible, King James Version. (1769/2017). Revelation. Cambridge University Press.

[13] John of Patmos, traditionally identified as the author of the Book of Revelation, was a Christian prophet and exile who lived in the late 1st century CE. His work, Revelation, is believed to have been written around 95 CE during the reign of Emperor Domitian—a time of significant persecution for the early Christian community. His vivid and symbolic visions offer a powerful message of hope and perseverance, and his influence on Christian eschatology and theology has endured for centuries, making Revelation one of the most studied, debated, and revered books in the New Testament.

Bauckham, R. (1993). *The Theology of the Book of Revelation*. Cambridge University Press.

[14] "The Storm" in QAnon lore: QAnon adherents believe that mass arrests of alleged cabal members—triggered by sealed indictments in U.S. federal courts—will occur; that the accused will be tried in military tribunals rather than civilian courts; that former U.S. President Donald Trump plays a pivotal role as a secret-war hero against the cabal; that a "Great Awakening" will reveal the cabal's crimes; that

suppressed secrets (including advanced technologies and cures) will be revealed; and that a utopian aftermath of peace, prosperity, and justice will follow the cabal's defeat.

Rothschild, M. (2021). *The Storm Is Upon Us: How QAnon Became a Movement, Cult, and Conspiracy Theory of Everything*. Melville House.

[15] Appel, W. (1983). *Cults in America: Programmed for Paradise*. Columbia University Press. p. 25

[16] *Engel v. Vitale*, 370 U.S. 421 (1962): The United States Supreme Court ruled that it is unconstitutional for state officials to compose an official school prayer and encourage its recitation in public schools. This decision was based on the First Amendment's Establishment Clause, which prohibits the government from making any law "respecting an establishment of religion."

[17] *Abington School District v. Schempp*, 374 U.S. 203 (1963): The Supreme Court ruled that mandatory Bible reading or the recitation of the Lord's Prayer in public schools is unconstitutional, grounding the decision in the Establishment Clause of the First Amendment.

[18] Pew Research Center. (2021, December 14). About three-in-ten U.S. adults are now religiously unaffiliated. Retrieved from https://www.pewresearch.org/religion/2021/12/14/about-three-in-ten-u-s-adults-are-now-religiously-unaffiliated/

[19] DeRose, J. (2024, January 24). Religious "nones" are now the largest single group in the U.S. National Public Radio. Retrieved from https://www.npr.org/2024/01/24/1226371734/religious-nones-are-now-the-largest-single-group-in-the-u-s

[20] The 1980s and 1990s Satanic Panic was a widespread moral panic characterized by fears of Satanic ritual abuse by secretive cults. Fueled by sensational media reports, dubious psychotherapy practices, and law enforcement accepting such claims at face value, the panic led to false accusations and prosecutions of numerous individuals and day care centers. Extensive investigations debunked most claims, revealing a cultural phenomenon influenced by paranoia and a misunderstanding of alternative religious practices.

Victor, J. S. (1993). *Satanic Panic: The creation of a contemporary legend*. Open Court.

[21] It's an odd dynamic that among many QAnon members, child sexual abuse refers only to pre-pubescent children. Post-pubescent children in at least 40 U.S. states are allowed to marry with parental or court permission at ages ranging from 15 to 17, with some states like Oklahoma having no minimum age and others allowing girls to marry if pregnant.

Wikipedia contributors. (2024, August 14). Child marriage in the United States. In Wikipedia. Retrieved August 14, 2024, from https://en.wikipedia.org/wiki/Child_marriage_in_the_United_States

[22] Appel, W. (1983). *Cults in America: Programmed for Paradise*. Columbia University Press. p. 30

[23] Appel, W. (1983). *Cults in America: Programmed for Paradise*. Columbia University Press. pp. 31–35

[24] Prophet, E. C. (1977). *Intermediate Studies of the Human Aura*. Summit University Press.

[25] Prophet, E. (2009). *Prophet's daughter: My life with Elizabeth Clare Prophet inside the Church Universal and Triumphant* (pp. 49–52). Lyons Press.

[26] The "Need for Chaos" encapsulates a subset of the population's tendency toward actions that could destabilize societal norms and institutions. This inclination—rooted in world-rejecting beliefs and a millenarian outlook—reflects deep alienation from social, economic, and political systems perceived as irredeemably corrupt. These individuals desire not just change but a radical, even apocalyptic, transformation of society. According to a 2019 study by Michael Bang Petersen et al., such attitudes may be held by an estimated 20–30% of the U.S. population, indicating a significant minority that sees upheaval as a path to renewal.

Petersen, M. B., Osmundsen, M., & Arceneaux, K. (2019). The "Need for Chaos" and Motivations to Share Hostile Political Rumors. PsyArXiv. Retrieved from https://mediawell.ssrc.org/news-items/a-need-for-chaos-and-the-sharing-of-hostile-political-rumors-in-advanced-democracies-psyarxiv-preprints/

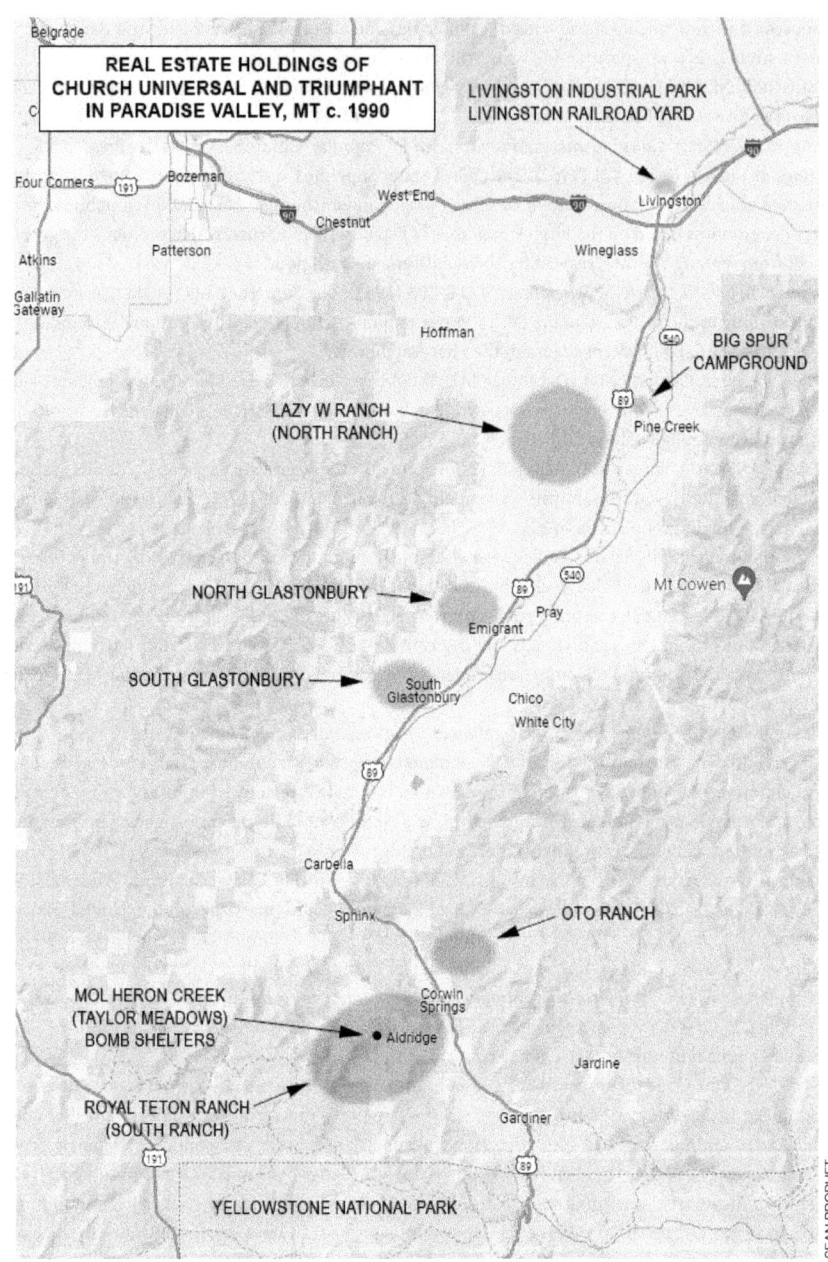

Montana's Paradise Valley, showing approximate location and scale of Church Universal and Triumphant's major land holdings c. 1990. A substantial percentage of this land has been sold outright, or placed under conservation easement during the past 35 years. Glastonbury North and South remain residential subdivisions, with many bomb shelters still present. The cult headquarters is now at Corwin Springs.

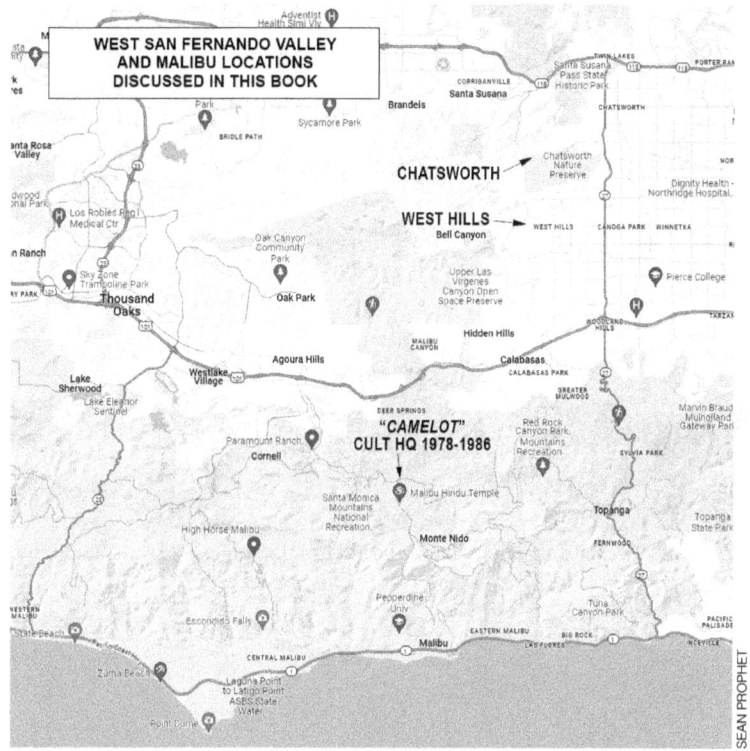

The Camelot property is the former King Gillette Ranch, a 240-acre parcel located at the intersection of Mulholland Highway and Las Virgenes Road. It is now part of the Santa Monica Mountains National Recreation Area.

Elizabeth Clare Wulf c. 1961

Church Universal and Triumphant/The Summit Lighthouse/Royal Teton Ranch Headquarters, Gardiner, Montana, 2012

Mol Heron Canyon, Gardiner, Montana, 2012. Shelter site visible upper middle, shelter construction facility, (also known as "Food Barn 2"), lower left.

Sean Prophet's baptism 1964. The "Chart of Your Divine Self" is visible in the background. During the early years of the cult, there was an intense focus on nationalistic symbols, following the Mighty I AM influence. Note the US flag, the US Eagle dominating the globe, and the "Freedom Forge" anvil wrapped in gold foil. In later years, the US flag remained but the other nationalistic symbols were retired.

Elizabeth Clare Prophet with father Capt. Hans W. Wulf, Red Bank, New Jersey c. 1965

Sean Prophet's first birthday, Virginia 1965. Left to right, Beth Prophet, Becky Prophet, Sean Prophet, Elizabeth Clare Prophet, Dan Prophet, Marcia Prophet, and Mark Prophet's first wife Phyllis Prophet

Elizabeth Clare Prophet, La Tourelle, Colorado Springs, Colorado, c. 1968

Sean Prophet and Erin Prophet, front door of La Tourelle c. 1969

Sean Prophet 6th birthday party, with Elizabeth and Mark Prophet, La Tourelle, Colorado Springs, Colorado, May 1970

Sean Prophet 6th birthday party, La Tourelle, Colorado Springs, Colorado, May 1970

The Summit Lighthouse India Tour, at the Taj Mahal, Agra, Uttar Pradesh, India 1970.
Mark Prophet and children in first row, left to right Moira Prophet, Sean Prophet, Erin Prophet.

Mark and Elizabeth Prophet with Mother Teresa, Calcutta, West Bengal, India 1970

Mark and Elizabeth Prophet and The Summit Lighthouse tour group meet with Indian Prime Minister Indira Gandhi 1970

Mark Prophet and Sean Prophet with Indira Gandhi 1970

Sean Prophet leads a decree session at the Santa Barbara "Motherhouse," with Mark and Elizabeth Prophet, c. 1971

The Summit Lighthouse congregation in Accra, Ghana. Elizabeth Clare Prophet, Sean Prophet, Mark Prophet (center), with Bishop Herbert Krakue (center right), 1972

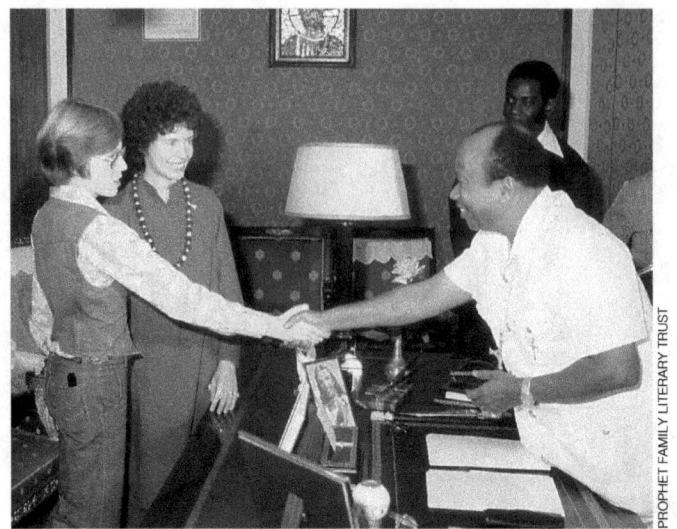
Sean Prophet, and Elizabeth Clare Prophet meet President William R. Tolbert, Jr. of Liberia, Monrovia, Liberia, 1978

Elizabeth Clare Prophet and Sean Prophet, Mol Heron Creek, Gardiner, Montana, 1981

Elizabeth Clare Prophet delivers a dictation in the "Heart of the Inner Retreat," Gardiner, Montana, July 1988

Elizabeth Clare Prophet delivers her July 4th address in the "Heart of the Inner Retreat," Gardiner, Montana, 1988

CHAPTER NINETEEN

Seeding Mull's Vendetta

On June 6, 1980, my mother, Edward Francis, and Monroe Shearer held a two-and-a-half-hour meeting with Gregory Mull at Camelot to discuss his financial obligations. The mood was tense. Throughout the meeting, my mother repeatedly threatened Mull's spiritual salvation, browbeat him, and challenged his devotion to the teachings. The conversation was tape-recorded and later played at trial, offering an unfiltered view of the psychological power she wielded over followers like Mull.[1]

She began the meeting with an invocation, casting an air of divine authority over the proceedings. As Mull tried to speak, my mother seized control, interrupting him sharply: "You're meeting here on my terms, not on your terms. Now I'm asking you a question and I want an answer to it!" She accused Mull of being ungrateful, insubordinate, throwing tantrums, expressing hatred, and "betraying me to the core." She condemned his "shallow consciousness," labeling it abominable, and warned he would be judged.

Mull wavered, saying, "I don't mistrust you Mother. I mistrust members of your board. I don't know how much direction you have received from them or whether they act on their own." It was his last attempt to shift blame away from her, but she seemed to relish the confrontation.

"Don't give me those mamby-pamby excuses, those mealymouthed excuses," she raged. "That's an absolute abomination!… It's a disgrace and I charge you before almighty God!" Though in full control, she still grew defensive: "I want you to know that I am not on trial. Your mistrust of my board is your mistrust of me!"

Then she turned to the financial dispute. "You have no reason to expect, given the tenor and wavelength of this entire community, that you would be paid in kind at the level of professional rates which you now claim you should be paid in retrospect for all the work you've done."

Illustration of Elizabeth Clare Prophet in Saint Germain's Office at Camelot, meeting with Gregory Mull, Edward Francis, and Monroe Shearer, Malibu, California, June 6, 1980

Mull pushed back, "I was never told that when I came down here that I would have to support myself or that I would lose my property." His frustration was clear, as though he still believed this was a misunderstanding.

But my mother dismantled any notion that he had been wronged. "You didn't support yourself. We gave you room and board. A lot of staff members don't even get room and board.... It was $37,000, that comes out to $3,700 a month. That is more than the entire board's salary. And we gave this to you as a loan because each time you asked for it, you said 'The minute I sell my house, I will pay it back.' Why did you say you would pay them back if you thought these monies were due you for professional services? Why didn't you say, 'This is not a loan. This is what I require for services rendered.' And we could have then said to you, 'Well, Gregory, you know we cannot hire you on that basis. We cannot afford that.'...It would have been very simple.... Why did you sign a promissory note for these funds if you thought you were due this payment?"

Mull explained, "Because I thought my home would sell quicker than it did, and I didn't mind being out like $20,000. But I should have spoke up at the point when it was getting over that amount, but I thought it was obedience to remain silent and just let the masters work it out.... I never lied to you, I never deceived you, and I never did it intentionally." Mull then outlined his difficulties selling his home, due to sky-high mortgage interest rates of around 18 percent. His tone was almost apologetic, as though he hoped that by providing these details, my mother would see reason. "My home was first listed for $260,000, then reduced to $240,000, then to $199,500. I felt I would get $240,000 for it and it was on this basis that I felt I could pay you back...."

She mocked him, "So now you sold your house for less. And I'm supposed to bear the burden of that? What folly!" Then she steered the conversation back to spiritual consequences: "You are ready to throw your whole life and your whole chelaship down the tubes by treating The Great White Brotherhood this way?"

Her words landed like a grim sentence. She invoked the parable of the "Rich Young Ruler" from the Book of Matthew, in which Jesus tells a young man that to inherit eternal life, he must sell all he has and give to the poor. She told Mull, "Never in the history of this organization has anyone.... weaseled out of the church $37,000." She then referenced the story of Ananias and Sapphira from the Book of Acts, in which a couple who withheld proceeds from a land sale were struck dead for "tempting the spirit of the Lord."

It was a spiritual threat. Shaken but trying to maintain his composure, Mull asked, "Are you saying that I will die if I do not fulfill your commitment?"

She answered, "Absolutely not."

He pressed, "Then why are you reading it to me?"

She turned icy, "Because it's the law, because it's sacred scripture, and because it happened. And you should have the fear of the Lord in your heart for doing what you are doing. I am not your judge and I refuse to judge you."

But she had already convicted him. Mull tried to regain some ground, "I don't have that much fear, except I want to make my ascension."

"You want it on your terms, Gregory. You're not willing to pass this initiation. Your taking exception to what I'm saying effectively concludes our relationship." She added, "The teaching of Pallas Athena, which is clear, says that you come to a certain place on the path and money becomes the initiation."[2]

Though money was the central focus of the meeting, my mother minimized it. "I couldn't care less whether you pay this debt, because God does not let me down. But you have let God down and you will suffer. You will suffer greatly for this." The words fell like a curse. Yet she still maintained a veneer of benevolence, "I'm very concerned about your path. I am not concerned about the money."

Desperate for a reprieve, Mull begged, "Then show me by just forgiving the entire amount."

Neither my mother nor Mull broached the subject of the donated $10,000 armoire. It would have been trivial for my mother to have said, "I can't forgive the entire amount, but in recognition of your financial difficulties and your kindness in donating your armoire, I'll deduct $10,000 from the promissory notes."

But she remained steadfast. "I do not lawfully have the right as a representative of the Darjeeling Council, as a representative of your soul, to forgive that debt.... You are showing that the teaching and the path and your ascension is not worth going, selling all that you have, and buying the one pearl of great price."

Mull asked, "You mean I will not make my ascension if I do not pay it?"

She dodged his question. "I am not making any threats, Gregory. I am not threatening you. I am not judging you. I am giving you a teaching.... Before any court in this world, I want you to know, I would be awarded that money. And I'm not going to go to court with you—because money is not the issue. Your soul, your salvation, and your chelaship is the issue."

Mull tried to negotiate, "I'm not asking for the ultimate. I only ask for my bills. I've asked for understanding.... I gave you services for that [money]. It wasn't that I took it from you."

Mother laid out her spiritual *quid pro quo*: "It wasn't for that. If your service was for money, then you lost the entire benefit of reward for chelaship. The whole thing is torn up."

She then softened her approach. "I want to witness to you that.... my attitude toward you is one of love." The shift in tone felt rehearsed—because it was. I had observed my mother using this tactic many times before. Then she renewed her assault, "As long as you live, you will be burdened by the fact that you did not accept the correction when your entire soul hung upon that teaching."

It was a masterful stroke. Mull was trapped between her "love," and her threats of spiritual consequences. Then she concluded, "Now I want to tell you how this is going to be resolved. I do not have in my power to forgive you your debt. But I will sign a paper today stating that I will not sue you, and that is tantamount to forgiving you because I can never get it from you. You will never hear from me again. You will not be harassed. No one is going to decree against you. You can go, and you're free. But I am suspending you from this activity if you are going to stand in this way, because of your attitude and not because of the money."

Mull admitted, "I have [already] resigned as a communicant of Church Universal and Triumphant and as a Keeper of the Flame in the fraternity. At the time I offered you the $10,000, I had the $10,000 in the bank."

Mother asked if Mull was now withdrawing his offer of $10,000, "And you can walk away from all this for the coin of the realm?" Making reference to the betrayal of Christ by Judas.[3]

Mull explained that he only had $5,500 left, and he took out his checkbook. She accepted the last of his savings on the spot. Shifting to sympathy she said, "Gregory, I'm very concerned as to what you are going to do for your livelihood. Do you know?"

Mull, struggling under the burden of his financial ruin, answered meekly, "Continue to be an architect."

"Do you think you have the clientele in this area that you have in San Francisco?" she asked, hinting that she knew he had no viable professional prospects outside the cult.

"I don't have it at all," he admitted tersely, "I have zero money." He put on a brave face, "But I have—you know—it always comes in. I am very good at breaking even, so it will be alright."

Mother commiserated, "I want you to know that I understand the burden that was upon you that prompted you to renege on this debt, and even on the $10,000. I know the feeling of financial burden."

Mull echoed her sentiment, "I've had it for years, it's horrible."

Then she withdrew her compassion and drilled into Mull's vulnerabilities. "You've had it for years because of your 10 o'clock substance," she said, referencing the "10-4 axis" on my cult's "cosmic clock," implying selfishness and disobedience. "You've squandered the light of God in various activities in this and previous lives," she continued, alluding to Mull's earlier confession of homosexuality, suggesting that his financial troubles were not just his own doing—but karmic retribution. "You've squandered that very life-energy that now is becoming so elusive to you and is such a problem. And it is returning karma."

Using "supply"—our cult's jargon for money—she offered a lifeline with a stern caveat: "I trust that if you go out of here in harmony and love, you will have a magnet to attract the necessary supply. But to go out of here in mistrust of me or disapproval of my board, it's a wedge in your consciousness… that will compromise your supply." As usual, my mother's magical thinking dominated. If "negative energy" could cause health problems, why not money problems too?

As the meeting drew to a close, in a bizarre full-circle moment, she said, "We are your friends, Gregory. I think you've been a very dear friend…. I'm grateful we could at least reach a chord of love. One chord has been struck on the piano. Now you can go in peace."

Mull actually thanked her. Then she handed him a tape of the meeting.

Her approach was formulaic—just another day in the life of a cult leader. I witnessed many such chastisements and pivots and saw far too many people crumble under her rebukes. Gregory Mull's case was no different—except this time, the encounter was recorded, and the world would finally hear it.

At trial, Levy asked, "Did the church help him in any way at that point?" My mother replied, "The church was fully prepared to help him in any way he would like to have been helped," claiming Mull didn't want her assistance. Levy objected, calling her answer "non-responsive and self-serving." The objection was sustained.[4]

The meeting occurred about a week before my high school graduation, and at the time, I knew nothing of it. But my mother was preoccupied—as usual—with her busy schedule. Once Mull left Camelot, she had no intention of helping him or even thinking about him. She likely moved on to her next meeting or went up the stairs opposite Saint Germain's office to her private dining room in the Gillette mansion, where her personal chefs would typically serve her a gourmet meal. Those perks shielded her from the struggles of her staff and followers.

With foresight, she would never have given Mull the recording of the meeting. But she saw nothing shameful in it, believing Mull would want to relive the badgering for the good of his soul. Rather than understanding she had just seeded a vendetta from the most formidable enemy she would ever have, she thought she had done a good deed. Such was her spiritual hubris—her blindness to how her words would be perceived outside her orbit, let alone by a jury. It was the same hubris that would culminate in her prayer for world judgment a decade later.

In *Coercion or Conversion*, Erin quotes jury foreman Carole Snow, who described the tape-recorded mauling Mull received as a "tough business meeting." I've sat through plenty of tough meetings, and never once—outside my cult—have I heard Bible stories or spiritual metaphors used to threaten someone's immortal soul over any amount of money. Nor have I seen someone's financial woes blamed on their sexual past or their karma. No, this wasn't a "tough business meeting."

It was the anatomy of cultic abuse.

My mother's sway over Mull hinged on his belief in her mantle as God's messenger. During the meeting, she quipped, "Don't you realize the Brotherhood has trusted me with the salvation of this planet?"[5] Any non-believing associate would have backed away—or laughed outright. But Mull remained under her spell. It was the kind of raw power play that had become second nature for her, reinforced by years of domineering interactions. Each act of deference from her chelas had deepened her belief that she could use her divine authority to deflate any opponent.

Then the "savior of the planet" took a haughty tone she could never have used in a business context:

"I would have tossed you long ago. It's not been easy having you around, Gregory. You've been a very difficult person. I've been glad to carry your cross and carry you with me because God sent you here for whatever reason he sent you here. If he sent you here ultimately to betray me, that is between you and him or whoever you're serving. I will never stop loving you, but I'm not going to let you be in the circle of this community doing the things you've done."[6]

This is how she chose to represent the "love" of the creator of the universe—to a desperate man.

But she was fully in character. The regal algorithm she deployed against her followers also acted on her—forcing her to live up to her guru reputation. Even more than spiritual teachings, it was her chronic abuse that became the defining hallmark of her messengership. In *Coercion or Conversion*, Erin noted that the Mull meeting was "mild compared to other 'discipline' sessions I'd seen my mother conduct."[7]

My youngest sister, Tatiana, witnessed similar incidents with depressing regularity. As the baby of the family, she endured more of my mother's abuse than the rest of us. And she saw even more of my mother's special cruelty toward her personal staff.

> Even some on the permanent staff did not see the real hard-core 'Mother' who showed cruelty to her followers. Then you had an even closer inner circle of people who saw her almost on a daily basis. So these were the people who did audio-visual, these were the people who did the publishing and editorial, and these were the people who prepared her food, and worked in her house. These people saw the violent persona that was Elizabeth Clare Prophet, and it was all under the pretense of a very intense spiritual training that was completely 'needed' and 'necessary' for their 'spiritual growth.' It was called 'chelaship.'

The dynamics of this spiritual training took different forms for different followers. One group lived the outer experience, while another faced a much darker reality.

> We had an outer chelaship, too. But outer chelaship was just listening to her lectures and saying that you were a chela and reading the lessons. Inner chelaship of the inner circle was basically being willing to have your entire personality chopped up into little bits and scattered into the wind. You'd go home feeling like you're about this high because you can't do anything right, including heat up a bowl of soup. And then being OK with it and coming back the next day, after decreeing most of the night and maybe having like four hours' sleep. And I guess there are many ways people justified it. I did not like it.

Despite our mother's looming presence and overwhelming authority, Tatiana instinctively recognized her conduct as abusive. At twelve years old, with no frame of reference beyond cult life, she found the courage to confront her.

> I said to my mom when I was like twelve, "Mommy, why do you have to yell at Catherine? Why do you have to yell at Mary?" "Well, sweetheart, there's a very specific reason why I do that. Do you think I like it? No. The masters want me to train them."

My mother later relayed the exchange to her congregation as a heartwarming anecdote, spinning Tatiana's concern into a parable about how "necessary" it was for staff to endure her chelaship. Tatiana recalled the reaction.

> Everybody in the audience was like, "Ohhhh, that's so cute! Awww, she was concerned about what was going on there." But even though they were told that these inner people got chelaship, they never witnessed it.

Years later, during her graduate studies, Tatiana gained perspective about our mother's personality and the cult dynamics she witnessed. The trauma she observed through a child's eyes could now be understood through the lens of psychology.

> I started to see everything through that paradigm. Hmm, let's see, what is this about? Is this about her? Yes. Is this about everybody else's spiritual ego? Yes. Is that what they're feeling when they're whipped up into this fervor? Yes. They're feeling important. And later on, with my experiences in graduate school in psychology, it all just kept reinforcing that theory. It was a cautious theory that I was testing. And it was perfect, it was just so true. She was an egomaniac.

What began as a child's protective instinct evolved into a deep understanding of our cult's levers of control. Tatiana's dual perspective—as both insider and trained observer—revealed the stark truth about our mother that she denied through spiritual rationalization: Her power derived from her capacity to break people down to almost nothing, and rebuild them in service of her "divine" mission.

---

[1] CUT v. Mull, Superior Court of Los Angeles County C. 358191, (February 18-19, 1986) at pages 569-704

[2] My mother often wielded such mythologies to magnify her chastisements. Her reference to Pallas Athena shows how our syncretic Theosophical tradition appropriated earlier myths. Athena, one of the most prominent Greek deities, is known for her birth—fully formed from Zeus's mind—and in my cult she was also known as the "Goddess of Truth," with "Pallas" referring to her common depiction brandishing a spear.

[3] Matthew 26:14-16 (KJV) "Then one of the twelve, called Judas Iscariot, went unto the chief priests, And said unto them, What will ye give me, and I will deliver him unto you? And they covenanted with him for thirty pieces of silver."

[4] CUT v. Mull, Superior Court of Los Angeles County C. 358191, (February 18-19, 1986) at pages 730:22-25

[5] CUT v. Mull, Superior Court of Los Angeles County C. 358191, (February 19, 1986) at 664:6-8

[6] CUT v. Mull, Superior Court of Los Angeles County C. 358191, (February 19, 1986) at 665:1-12

[7] Prophet, E. (2018). *Coercion or conversion? A case study in religion and the law: CUT v. Mull v. Prophet.* Linden Books. p. 67

CHAPTER TWENTY

Mother Under Oath

It was the biggest mistake of her life.

It took six years, but my mother finally faced accountability in Department 50 of the Los Angeles Superior Court. On February 18-19, 1986, she sat beneath fluorescent lights as her own sadistic words boomed from a cassette player before judge, jury, and reporters. Then she found herself in the dock, being grilled and mocked by Mull's attorney Lawrence Levy. A rare occasion on which she was in an environment she did not control. What began as a dispute over unpaid loans would expose our cult's true nature—and cost a man his life.

So how had she come to face this unwelcome reckoning?

Mull's finances crumbled after the June 1980 meeting, forcing him to reassess years of submission to my mother's "chelaship." His new reality transformed him from devotee to critic. In a November 7, 1980 letter, he declared independence: "I thank God I am free from your domination and gross and cunning manipulations. I see through you now for what you are: a tormented child by both parents." He branded Edward Francis and Monroe Shearer "your dishonest, vulgar swearing board."

Mull shredded my mother's spiritual facade: "You have covered yourself on all bases, Mother of the Universe, Vicar of Christ, Guru, Messenger for the Great White Brotherhood, God incarnate. How can anyone doubt you, question you—if they do, they are kicked out and belittled.... Those really close to you get out, or stay because the end justifies the means, fattening their egos with personal authority over others."

Years later, in *Coercion or Conversion*, Erin acknowledged these power dynamics[1] and wrote of her "new understanding and empathy for the experiences of Gregory Mull, my former stepfather Randall King, and everyone who testified against the church at trial."[2]

This forces a fundamental question: Was our mother truly a messenger of God—a legitimate guru fit to shepherd souls? If so, her cruelty carried divine sanction, and in that hypothetical universe, anyone who betrayed our cult—Mull, King, Tatiana, and myself included—would face the second death. But in this universe? My mother systematically justified pointless cruelty.

If there were masters behind my mother's chronic abuse, they would be more correctly called monsters. To borrow Christopher Hitchens' phrase once again, any God sponsoring such monsters would be running the universe as a fascist "celestial dictatorship." That's no universe I would want to inhabit. Not for eternity, not even for a moment. If God were such an unmerciful tyrant, I would proudly sprint to my second death at the "court of the sacred fire."

Illustration of Elizabeth Clare Prophet on the witness stand in Los Angeles Superior Court, Department 50, February 1986

By November 1980, Mull had reached the same conclusion. He cursed my mother: "You stand next to the Great Whore as the False Prophet deceiving the very elect of God. May your day be done quickly in the name of God for the sake of the innocent you have deceived."

He demanded the return of his $5,000 and warned my mother and the board to stop maligning him to members: "Either I hear from you by December 8, 1980 or you will be hearing from me indirectly.... You either resolve this, or you will have one of the biggest enemies you have yet had out to expose you."

Misjudging Mull's determination, my mother escalated. She had our attorney Marvin Gross draft a letter dripping with the same imperious, wounded tone she had taken in the June meeting: "It is incredible to me that an adult member of a respected profession could write such a vicious and vindictive letter.... I have never seen such an abusive and threatening letter directed either to a woman or to a minister, and such a complete lack of willingness for a grown man to take responsibility for his own circumstances."[3]

Erin later described it as a letter that "threatened to sue Gregory for libel, slander, and collection of the remaining money. If Gregory would quit speaking out against the church, [we] would drop the whole matter." This act of intimidation, couched in legalese, formed the basis for Mull's extortion claim, later dismissed before trial. But it backfired, galvanizing Mull's campaign to expose us. He contacted reporters, filed complaints with the county building department, and organized public meetings—stirring up enough trouble to force building inspections, structural modifications, and the closure of one of our classroom buildings.

My mother treated Mull's campaign like an act of war. In March 1981, she directed our board to sue Mull to collect on the $37,000 in promissory notes—even though she had repeatedly promised not to. Her rationale? Mull had broken his promise to "go in peace." It was a terrible miscalculation.

Gregory Mull's attorney Lawrence Levy, video interview, Sherman Oaks, California, February 21, 2009

In response, Mull retained Los Angeles attorney Lawrence Levy, who countersued for $253 million, alleging intentional infliction of emotional distress, involuntary servitude, fraud, quantum meruit (reasonable pay for services) and assault. He then took his vendetta national—interviewing ex-members, hosting public meetings, and generating bad publicity in several states. He even visited my grandparents Hans and Frida Wulf in Red Bank, New Jersey under false pretenses, claiming to be my mother's "friend." He had cast himself as our enemy, and my mother reciprocated, labeling him the "Beast of Blasphemy" and encouraging members to pray against him.

Both Gregory Mull and his daughter Linda Witt testified that he feared for his life, worried that an unhinged cult member might try to kill him. Former friends from the cult were already shunning them in public.[4] Thankfully, our cult was relatively obscure and its members peaceful. Larger, more prominent cults like MAGA pose a greater risk of stochastic violence when leaders condemn an outcast—we've seen mere accusations of "betrayal" provoke death threats and even assassination attempts.[5]

In a 2011 interview, Erin reflected on the escalating conflict:
> I think that the Mull situation could have been defused if my mother had been a little older and wiser.... He wrote a letter saying that she was the next thing to the 'Great Whore.' He was very angry, using a lot of biblical imagery. And then she responded and took a dictation that didn't use his name, but talked about the fact that the mouthpiece of the 'Beast of Blasphemy' was attacking the church.[6]

Ananias and Saphira. The Great Whore. The Beast of Blasphemy. Deceiving the elect of God. It was clear that two could play at spiritual name-calling. But my mother failed to grasp her vulnerability. She showed no compassion for Mull, ignored her legal exposure, and underestimated his resolve. Her callous dismissal of his financial struggles and imperious reaction to his cross-complaint catalyzed our eventual loss. Worse, she seemed blind to how a working-class jury would perceive her perks, entitled behavior, and reliance on unpaid labor. Instead of negotiating, she escalated to DEFCON 1, treating the case as spiritual warfare.

With hindsight, she squandered several hundred thousand dollars in legal fees alone—more than ten times her loss on Mull's promissory note. She dragged our cult through a self-created crisis, causing immense emotional distress. Grueling prayer vigils by our worldwide membership lasted for years, and our loss led to great financial hardship as members paid off the $1.56 million judgment.

Where was the shrewd businesswoman who built our miniature empire against all odds? Lost in her own self-importance. This was especially true as Mull's health deteriorated. At trial, his multiple sclerosis left him frail, his tongue involuntarily flicking in and out of his mouth. He could barely hold himself together in court, while my mother and her legal team appeared young, healthy, and prosperous. Despite her Biblical knowledge, she missed the optics: in that courtroom, *she* was Goliath, and *Mull* was David.

Lawrence Levy was stunned we chose to try the case. "When I sued for $253 million, it was done almost tongue-in-cheek. I wanted them to get off their high horse and talk realistically. Gregory was so fearful of your mother, if she had just said, 'OK, forget the $35,000 and I'll give you $10,000 to go away and shut up,' he'd have taken it, and done it.... At any time before trial, they could have walked away for peanuts. I didn't want him to go through a trial because of his deteriorating physical condition."[7]

But my mother refused all settlement efforts. Erin later reflected:
> When my mother heard about his multiple sclerosis diagnosis, she felt that it was his karma for all the attacks he'd made on her. When you have an opponent who gets MS, you settle. Most normal people would settle. Here's a guy with big medical expenses who's going to look pathetic to a jury. It was her sense of righteousness and that God was on her side. Nobody put the brakes on to say, 'well wait a minute, no matter what he did in a past life, why do we need to go to court?'[8]

After we refused settlement, Levy shifted his focus to securing maximum damages. He was no Boy Scout and never claimed to be—so expecting him to fight "fair" by limiting the case to financial disputes was naïve. Despite his casual courtroom demeanor, Levy was a practiced and charismatic litigator. His moppish hair and disarming appearance gave him the charm of a champion of the common man. With snide remarks and knowing looks, he built a substantial rapport with the jury.

My mother had cast her battle with Mull as a personal Armageddon. But in Levy, she met her match. Going after my mother for her bravado and hypocrisy, and pushing the boundaries of *US v. Ballard* to expose the jury to our religious beliefs was brilliant strategy. It was Levy's best approach to puncture our pretense of spiritual aggrievement. He used the levers of emotion effectively, swaying the jury toward compassion for Mull and ultimately prevailing in a battle he had never intended to fight.

Sadly, it was a battle that claimed Mull's life. He died of his infirmities in July 1986, three months after the trial concluded. Levy reflected,
> There was medical testimony at the time of the trial that the stress he went through—it's a miracle he survived the trial.... Almost up until the time of his demise, he still believed Elizabeth had this enormous power. He still believed when he was in the hospital if she would relent, he'd get well. But when he passed away, he was at peace. And he was at peace for one reason, that the truth came out about what Elizabeth was doing to people and had done to him.... I would give my contingency fee back, and I'm sure Greg's daughter would do also if even with MS, Gregory would still be around.[9]

Throughout the trial, Mull had to endure our defense attorney Ken Klein's systematic misrepresentation of cult life. To be clear, my cult had put Klein up to this, and he was only doing his job. Our carefully orchestrated strategy directed him to paint a picture of level-headed followers who neither idolized my parents nor faced consequences for leaving. This meta-lie, woven through leading questions, portrayed our cult as a benign spiritual community. Even when cross-examining expert witness Dr. Margaret Singer, we maintained this fiction, falsely claiming our code of conduct applied only to Summit University students.[10] In truth, the code governed all staff and Montessori International students, who faced expulsion for breaking it.

As Klein presented witness after witness, a clear pattern emerged in their testimony. As a representative example, former cult treasurer and board member James McCaffery described his time at Camelot as "very good" and denied any teachings that encouraged fear of outsiders, isolation from nonmembers, or the belief that only church members could make their ascension. When asked whether members were taught that Elizabeth Clare Prophet was "God incarnate," McCaffery stated, "I think that using that particular phrase would probably be easily misconstrued," instead framing her as "a representative of God.... a possibility for each of us individually also." He also recalled public statements from both her and Mark Prophet saying, "We do not claim, and have never claimed to be perfect."

McCaffery further testified that he experienced no fear of retaliation upon leaving the church and had never heard teachings suggesting that ex-members would face consequences such as losing their ascension or enduring "10,000 years of re-embodiments."[11]

I knew James McCaffery well. A former aerospace engineer, he was a friendly and loyal man who efficiently managed our cult finances from my childhood until the early '80s. Yet, his kind-heartedness may have made it difficult for him to reconcile the harmful system he helped administer. McCaffery's experience was far removed from the rank-and-file. As a board member, he earned a higher salary, dined in our private board dining room, and enjoyed more control over his time. He was less subject to the strict disciplines that governed most staff members' lives. McCaffery's answers whitewashed the reality of cult life, denying things he would have known—or should have known.

Crucially, McCaffery left on good terms. He never challenged my mother's authority nor spoke out against the cult, so he had no reason to fear shunning or retaliation. Yet, as someone who attended hundreds of dictations from my parents, he would have heard repeated claims that their teachings were 99 percent accurate and that ours was the best path to the ascension. Dictations often warned of "straying from the path" and being "cast into outer darkness, where there shall be weeping and gnashing of teeth." This is standard biblical fare, from the Book of Matthew, which was paired with the idea that our teachings were a "special dispensation" for our time that might not be available again for tens of thousands of years. It was all common knowledge among our members, which created a climate of fear.

McCaffery would have also known of the frequent disciplines and expulsions justified by the supposed infallibility of the masters. While my parents occasionally admitted petty or inconsequential mistakes, they never disavowed their divine edicts. There were indeed "updates" to the teachings, but they were shoehorned into place within our canon and did not involve admissions of prior error. McCaffery would also have been aware of the strong insider-vs.-outsider dynamic in my cult, along with the rules discouraging contact with critical outsiders or non-believing family members. Yet his testimony glossed over these realities.

McCaffery's careful evasions paled in comparison to my mother's lies under oath. When asked about Mary Spelzhaus, an elderly worker who had been physically dragged to the curb at La Tourelle in the early 1970s, my mother claimed no knowledge of the incident.[12] She denied that staff needed her permission to marry, though this was an ironclad rule.[13] She characterized her "suggestions" to followers as mere advice they were free to ignore—a laughable claim given that her words were treated as divine directives carrying serious consequences if disobeyed.[14]

Her deceptions grew more brazen. She insisted that teachings about marital sexuality were not rules and denied any karmic consequences for failing to follow them, though cult ministers consistently taught couples that acts like mutual masturbation and oral or anal sex would prevent their ascension.[15] She reframed her authorization of Mull's marriage as "spiritual advice" rather than the required permission it actually was.[16] When questioned about Mull's removal from Camelot, she distanced herself by saying she was merely "informed" of the board's independent action[17]—though she had received a call in Hawaii about Mull's fate, and the board would never have acted without her explicit consent.[18] She claimed ignorance about using a straw buyer for the Forbes Ranch purchase in 1981, despite her iron grip on all major transactions.[19] Former staffer Rick Barney confirmed in a 2010 interview that he was indeed that straw buyer, acting under the board's direction.[20] She denied knowing the contents of Mull's clearance letter,[21] though she had discussed his confession of homosexuality openly in family settings and shared it with the board and permanent staff.

Perhaps most telling was her response when asked about communication with the Ascended Masters. "I think everyone in our church talks to the Ascended Masters," she testified—a statement that misrepresented her claimed role as the sole messenger of God.[22] If everyone could speak directly with the masters, her unique authority would have been meaningless.

The cold truth is that once on the witness stand, my mother became a cornered animal fighting to preserve herself and her cult. Looking back, I'm not entirely surprised she lied in court, but reading the transcript still pained me. Her elisions raise a crucial question: If she was so confident in her messengership, the validity of her teachings, and the righteousness of her behavior toward Mull, then why change her story to sway a jury? Why not proudly acknowledge our harsh rules and disciplines, and her absolute authority over her chelas? If she truly believed herself a divine messenger, she would have stood on those principles, trusting God to protect her. Her caginess suggests that—despite her bravado—she was well aware that her behavior toward Mull and her chelas was deeply problematic.

---

[1] Prophet, E. (2018). *Coercion or conversion? A case study in religion and the law: CUT v. Mull v. Prophet.* Linden Books. p. 14

[2] Prophet, E. (2018). *Coercion or conversion? A case study in religion and the law: CUT v. Mull v. Prophet.* Linden Books. p. 7

[3] Prophet, E. (2018). *Coercion or conversion? A case study in religion and the law: CUT v. Mull v. Prophet.* Linden Books. p. 19

[4] CUT v. Mull, Superior Court of Los Angeles County C. 358191, (February 24, 1986) at 982:5-9

[5] The January 6 Capitol attack, the Gretchen Whitmer kidnapping plot, the death threats against election officials like Brad Raffensperger, and the pipe bombs sent by Cesar Sayoc are all stark reminders of how incendiary rhetoric from leaders causes radicalized followers take matters into their own hands—without direct orders.

[6] Prophet, E. (2011, September 6). Personal interview.

[7] Levy, L. (2009, February 21). Personal interview.

[8] Prophet, E. (2011, September 6). Personal interview.

[9] Levy, L. (2009, February 21). Personal interview.

[10] CUT v. Mull, Superior Court of Los Angeles County C. 358191, (February 26, 1986) at 1316:23-26

[11] CUT v. Mull, Superior Court of Los Angeles County C. 358191, (March 4, 1986) at 1374-1378

[12] CUT v. Mull, Superior Court of Los Angeles County C. 358191, (February 18, 1986) at 499:20-25

[13] CUT v. Mull, Superior Court of Los Angeles County C. 358191, (February 18, 1986) at 514:2-4

[14] CUT v. Mull, Superior Court of Los Angeles County C. 358191, (February 18, 1986) at 514:24-515:3
[15] CUT v. Mull, Superior Court of Los Angeles County C. 358191, (February 18, 1986) at 515:9-19
[16] CUT v. Mull, Superior Court of Los Angeles County C. 358191, (February 18, 1986) at 517:10-12
[17] CUT v. Mull, Superior Court of Los Angeles County C. 358191, (February 18, 1986) at 558:23-563:5
[18] Prophet, E. (2018). *Coercion or conversion? A case study in religion and the law: CUT v. Mull v. Prophet*. Linden Books. p. 16
[19] CUT v. Mull, Superior Court of Los Angeles County C. 358191, (February 19, 1986) at 712:22-713:2
[20] Barney, R. (2010, June 1). Personal interview.
[21] CUT v. Mull, Superior Court of Los Angeles County C. 358191, (February 19, 1986) at 739:27-740:7
[22] CUT v. Mull, Superior Court of Los Angeles County C. 358191, (February 19, 1986) at 741:26-742:1

CHAPTER TWENTY ONE

Apologia

During the Mull trial, nearly two dozen friendly witnesses painted a portrait of cult life that bore no resemblance to reality. They testified they were well-adjusted, happy, and healthy, willingly embracing their spiritual disciplines without fear of karma or divine judgment. They described unpaid labor as a joy, denied any abusive "chelaship," and claimed no one experienced shunning or isolation. According to our witnesses, my mother was not seen as "God incarnate" but merely someone "setting an example." This orchestrated parade of denials revealed how thoroughly my cult had mastered the art of self-justification.

Like all cults, we built our defenses on familiar ground. Our doctrines appropriated mythology from the Mighty I AM cult, Theosophy, and fragments of older traditions like Hinduism, Buddhism, the Kabbalah, and Judeo-Christian scripture. Just as mainstream religions, particularly Christian theology, develop elaborate apologetics to defend their unsupported claims about such topics as theodicy and scriptural inerrancy, my cult created an arsenal of justifications to explain away its contradictions and abuses. The most fundamental was a simple deflection:

1. "Other religions do it too." The argument goes, "Other religions ask for donations, require sacrifices, volunteer labor, or have strict rules, so why are we being criticized?" This apologia leans heavily on whataboutism, deflecting criticism by pointing to conversion practices or invoking religious freedom. It's the *tu quoque fallacy*,[1] meaning "you, too," which avoids scrutiny by pointing to others' flaws rather than addressing our own. Religious freedom never absolves abuse.

Dr. Robert L. Moore testified:
> Every religious group is interested in influencing the behavior of its members. That's part of what all religions do. In other words, what some would call "thought reform," other people call "Christian education." Other people call a Synagogue educational program "learning how to live the Jewish life." There is no such thing as a religion, a religious group of any kind, whether it is Methodist or Baptist or Catholic or Jewish or Islamic that does not have an investment in influencing the ideas, the behaviors, the attitudes, the values of its members. That is part of every religion. And so when I get asked, "does a particular group have an investment in controlling the behavior and values and thinking of its members?" They all do.[2]

Moore didn't believe our members lost their autonomy through conversion because when people became disillusioned, they left—comparing it to divorce or leaving the military.[3] But his testimony missed the point. Yes, all religions influence behavior, and people did leave my cult, just as they leave every cult. But the focus shouldn't be on those who manage to escape—it should be on those who remain. The aim of conversion isn't just to keep someone in place. It's to manipulate them into believing their choice to stay is freely made.

My definition encapsulates this: *"The word 'cult' describes how humans without sufficient knowledge and coping skills adapt to abusive systems and grow to defend them, even at the cost of their lives."* This applies to most religious conversions. But in cults, the algorithm design compels a higher level of entrapment.

2. "The leader's personal life is separate from their spiritual leadership." Apologists often argue that sexual misconduct or other scandals have no bearing on the leader's spiritual authority. They'll claim, "The leader is flawed, but the teachings are still valid." This is classic *special pleading*[4] where exceptions are made which would never be tolerated in others. It relies on *cognitive dissonance*[5] enabling *authoritarian hypocrisy*.[6]

In 1971, my 32-year-old mother became enamored of a handsome 22-year-old cook named Randy Kosp. As their relationship deepened, El Morya urged him to drop his anglicized Greek surname and use his full given name, so he legally changed it to Randall King. Their affair began with intimate massages well before my father's February 24, 1973 death.

Shortly after my father's passing, their relationship escalated to sex in my mother's circular tower office, where she penned the books that became my cult's scriptures. Randall was "living" in the tower just ten days after my father died. Together, they knelt before a gold statue of Mother

Mary while she took a dictation granting them permission to be married.[7] Soon after, she promoted him from cook to president.

Mother hid the affair for months, during which a pregnancy scare turned out to be a miscarriage. I remember vividly the day she left the hospital in a wheelchair, looking dejected. On October 16, 1973, the pair eloped to Idaho for a mountaintop wedding. When they returned, they sat my sisters and me down in our Santa Barbara home, announcing that we had a "new daddy." We jumped for joy, yelling "Randy and mommy got married!"

A week later at a conference in San Francisco, I watched my mother, channeling Archangel Gabriel, summon Randall before the congregation, thundering, "Randall Charles King..." The master anointed him as her husband and protector and the father of her next child, a special cosmic "avatar" meant to be born under the 1973-1974 appearance of the comet Kohoutek. But the child never came.

I don't judge my mother or Randall for their affair. Sex between consenting adults is hardly a crime. But still—she policed everyone's sex life but her own, causing untold heartbreak for cult members. So the exposure of her hypocrisy in court was a fitting consequence.

The marriage clouded her judgment. At age 24, Randall was far too young and inexperienced to be my cult's president. Both wanted independent income to support our family's lavish lifestyle. In 1974 they formed the "Prophet-King Investment Club," persuading staff members to sign documents they hadn't read, which they didn't know authorized Randall to invest cult funds on their behalf. Soon, under the umbrella of our for-profit arm, Lanello Reserves, Randall was trading silver futures on margin, with my mother's full knowledge and consent.

As the scheme unfolded, they were already making plans to spend their paper profits. We toured expensive homes in Santa Barbara, literally measuring for drapes. Then the market plummeted, and Randall faced astronomical margin calls he couldn't cover. This was the origin of the Clayton Brokerage scandal mentioned earlier. As the crisis deepened, there were heated late-night board meetings. I would often awake to the sound of arguing, sometimes accompanied by the crash of heavy objects and breaking glass. Randall was demoted from the role of president, and he spent the balance of his time in my cult supervising photography and advertising. Their marriage ended the same way it began, when Randall had his own affair with his secretary and my mother filed for divorce in 1978.

Most members remained unaware of these events until Levy exposed them during the Mull trial. In his closing argument, Levy pointed his finger at my mother, declaring, "Where is El Morya? Who in this courtroom talks to El Morya? Sitting right over there on that side is El Morya," suggesting that the master El Morya was my mother's alter ego. The revelation of her affair and subsequent financial misdeeds stripped away her carefully constructed image of infallibility.

My mother tried to spiritualize her humiliation, turning to Revelation 11:3-13, claiming that her martyrdom was the fulfillment of the prophecy of the Two Witnesses, slain by the "beast from the bottomless pit," their corpses lying "in the streets of the great city" until their resurrection. She later claimed that being mocked for her master was one of her proudest moments. But no one had ever so thoroughly pierced her pretenses.

3. "The leader got bad advice." Apologists often claim the leader was misled by their inner circle, suggesting they "got bad advice." This tactic shifts responsibility onto lower-ranking members. But authoritarian leaders maintain tight control over their advisers, hand-picking them for loyalty. Although dissent is possible, the inner circle most often functions as an extension of the leader's will. Blaming them preserves the leader's image of infallibility while dodging accountability. And if a leader does take bad advice, it reflects their own lack of vision.

This apologetic surfaced during Mull's June 1980 meeting, when he attempted to deflect blame onto the board rather than challenging my mother directly. At trial, she repeatedly shifted blame for questionable tactics onto her subordinates. But Levy cornered her, baiting her into admitting she made every significant final decision.

It's like a car salesman saying, "I need to run that by my manager." The salesman already knows the bottom line and is just trying to extract more money. El Morya was my mother's invisible manager, just as she became the invisible manager for department heads. They knew most staff rarely saw her in person, so her directives—filtered through intermediaries—went unquestioned. Deflecting to a higher or lower authority was a core operating principle at every level of my cult.

4. "Some people managed to negotiate." Cults highlight cases where members negotiated better treatment, suggesting the system isn't truly authoritarian. This relies on *survivorship bias*[8] where success stories overshadow those who were punished or expelled. Most members lacked the means to negotiate. Those who succeeded were typically insiders, and their rare exceptions cannot justify a system designed to marginalize dissenters.

All negotiations are governed by need-power dynamics: The party with the most power has less need to negotiate, while the one with greater need has less power. Success requires the weaker party to offer something valuable. But in cults, the leader holds all the cards. This leaves followers without leverage—unless they possess rare skills or make themselves indispensable.

The cult leader is a spiritual billionaire. Just as a CEO might grant a raise to secure loyalty, a cult leader may grant exceptions to favored followers—but as a calculated move to deepen control. Unlike a CEO, who controls only material conditions, a cult leader wields spiritual authority. An employee can find another job, but a cult member often believes leaving means existential ruin.

In the Mull trial, sociologist Dr. James Richardson testified that many seekers negotiate with groups they intend to join: "What we quite often ran into were people overtly negotiating with groups as to 'what do I have to do to be a member? Do I have to give up this or that? What can I get out of it?'"[9] This sounds a lot more like investigation and selection. The seeker isn't expecting concessions but simply choosing which group aligns with their needs and values. True negotiation requires concessions from both parties.

Richardson cited Mull's attempts to negotiate. In a 1975 letter to Randall King, Mull threatened to quit unless a photo he bought was replaced, adding "I do hope this can be resolved." The photo was replaced, but this was mere customer service, not true negotiation. Richardson pointed to Mull's later letters requesting expense payments and offering to settle promissory notes for $10,000 as evidence he was "rational" and "looking out for his own future."[10] But if Mull had successfully negotiated his compensation, there would have been no lawsuit.

5. "Volunteers are giving their lives to God." Joining staff meant taking a vow of poverty. Historically, such vows originate in Christian monasticism, where leaders *and* followers *both* renounced wealth for spiritual growth and collective sacrifice. St. Benedict insisted abbots live simply alongside monks, while St. Francis set an example through absolute poverty. British theologian Derwas Chitty echoes this in his 1966 book, *The Desert a City*[11] where early monastic leaders like Saint Antony and Pachomius renounced personal possessions, embodying the ideal of shared poverty and humility. This ideal of shared deprivation becomes corrupted into *spiritual elitism*[12] when cult leaders justify luxury by claiming their wealth reflects spiritual attainment or is required to support their divine mission.

Randall King testified that our family's personal expenses and benefits in the late 1970s would have required an annual pre-tax salary of $200,000[13]— roughly $1 million in 2024 dollars. Yet, in her June 6, 1980 meeting with Gregory Mull, my mother falsely claimed she supported our family on her cult paycheck, which was $670 per month, about $8,000 per year.[14]

She knew exactly what she spent. Homes in Westlake Village and Malibu. The Gillette Mansion. Private schooling. World travel. Elaborate stage costumes. Specialty foods. Multiple cars with drivers. Personal staff, cooks, and security guards. Then there was the "Gold Bus," a converted Continental Trailways passenger model with blue and purple stripes. A chronic insomniac, my mother frequently had drivers cruise Los Angeles freeways all night or drive a few hundred miles up the California coast and back, because the motion lulled her to sleep. The wasted diesel fuel, labor, and maintenance costs were incalculable.

Even my cult's savior, jury foreman Carole Snow, was queasy about my mother's extravagance, questioning whether my mother really needed to live in her beach house in Malibu in order to write effectively.[15] The contrast between leadership luxury and follower deprivation was justified through an even more insidious claim—that suffering itself was spiritually beneficial:

6. Touting the Virtues of Harsh Discipline: "It made people stronger." Many cults romanticize the deprivation they impose, claiming hardships are necessary "tests." This *false virtue fallacy*[16] equates the willingness to suffer deprivation with moral goodness. But coerced suffering doesn't foster personal development—it's a tool to erode autonomy. This was nowhere clearer than in our approach to housing and food.

While my mother enjoyed her beach house and mansion, staff members faced appalling conditions. The lucky ones lived in our San Fernando Valley apartment buildings. Others had dormitory space at Camelot, though many rooms were repurposed as offices. Staff members with offices often slept in them, as Gregory Mull did. The less fortunate made do with foam pads in classrooms, storage rooms, basements—wherever they could find space. Our tape archivist Jeffrey reclaimed a semblance of privacy by moving his mattress into the archives, sleeping among thousands of audio and video tapes.

More disturbing was Camp Bloomfield,[17] which we renamed "Camp Victory." This rented facility, owned by the Foundation for the Junior Blind, housed Summit University students, high school students, and staff from fall through spring. Located in the Malibu Hills near Leo Carillo State Beach, it was a 45-minute bus ride from Camelot. We got it cheap because it was actually a summer camp for kids, with cabins offering scant protection from the elements—no heat, no reliable hot showers. Winter temperatures in the Malibu Hills drop to near-freezing. I heard constant complaints about the cold from my high school classmates.

The cabins at Camp Bloomfield aka Camp Victory. c. Early 1980s.

Michael, a high-school student, lived in a pump room at Camelot next to "Swan Lake." Open to the elements, it flooded during rains. The room housed live electrical equipment for the pond's pumps and sluice gate. Unbelievably, he shared this cramped, dangerous alcove with our high school math teacher.[18]

But the worst was what I discovered at age 15 while riding my dirt bike in the hills. I found an ancient water tank from the 1920s King Gillette Ranch. Someone had cut a crude door into the rusted metal. Inside were four cots neatly arranged, with cheap dressers and plastic containers for belongings. They'd rigged a car battery for lighting. It was just shy of a homeless encampment. Could people really live like this? Did my mother know?

Of course, she knew about the housing shortage, if not the specifics. We cut those corners to save money. My mother and the board deemed such conditions acceptable for "Maitreya's Mystery School."[19] What could I do? I was too embarrassed to mention the water tank. Living at Camelot under any conditions was considered the ultimate spiritual privilege. While others froze and suffered in decrepit housing through my family's neglect, I had no power to change anything. So I would simply return to my comfortable room in the Gillette mansion or hop in the car with my mother and her driver, off to sleep on high-thread-count sheets at her Malibu beach house.

While our food was generally adequate, my mother used dietary rules to enforce spiritual authority. In the late 1970s, she introduced a numerical system in order of decreasing purity. The "number 1 diet" consisted of raw vegetables, soaked seeds, and nuts, while "number 5" allowed cooked vegetables, grains, bread, dairy, and meat—closer to a standard American diet. The message was clear: heavier diets limited spiritual progress.

Dietary control peaked in July 1982 after our "John, the Beloved" seminar, when my mother introduced "Clare's Lunch" every Wednesday. She enforced the number 1 diet as a practice she compared to Holy Communion—an act of love for the community. When elderly members with dental issues struggled with raw food and requested alternatives, my mother, channeling El Morya as Camelot's hostess, dismissed their concerns as spiritual weakness. She told them to chew thoroughly and accept what was offered, comparing it to proper etiquette when visiting someone's home.[20]

In his closing argument at trial, Levy highlighted the "Clare's lunch" incident as an example of cultish control: "We heard about food right up until the time we had heard about Mother's Clare's Lunch. And what did dear old Elizabeth tell us then? 'You got teeth and you got saliva. I don't want to hear any more complaints. Chew.'"[21] If this had been an isolated incident, I might accuse Levy of grandstanding. But it wasn't. My mother's obsession with "right eating" only intensified through the 1980s and 1990s. Until the end of her ministry, she continued blaming staff diets for their ailments, even though most could only afford to eat the commissary food she tightly controlled.

By constraining basic needs while preaching the virtue of sacrifice, my cult created an environment where submission became a mark of spiritual progress. Control over members' physical existence was intertwined with manipulation of divine authority to justify prayers with harmful intent.

7. **"God wouldn't let it happen."** *Imprecatory prayers*—wishing harm or death upon others—were rationalized by claiming no harm could occur unless God allowed it, absolving the supplicant of responsibility. This *moral abdication*[22] dismissed harmful intent under the guise of divine will. Some claimed these prayers merely reversed "negative energy," *victim-blaming*[23] the target for any harm. Others insisted the prayers couldn't hurt anyone because they were offered with "love."

In *Coercion or Conversion*, Erin describes the role of decrees during the Mull trial. In our Camelot chapel, we projected images of Gregory Mull, Randall King, and their lawyers onto a screen. Hundreds of members shouted decrees laden with "military metaphors," as she describes them, calling for Archangel Michael to drop "blue-lightning bombs" and "smash, blast, annihilate, shatter, dissolve, and consume" our enemies, or "reverse the tide" of their negative energy.

Levy exposed these practices in court. He questioned witnesses about their decreeing habits, played recordings, and had my mother perform the 10.14 "Astrea" decree at high speed to highlight its emotional intensity.[24] He even had Randall King recite the "smash, blast, annihilate" mantra.[25] Ken Klein's First Amendment objections were overruled.

We left blank spaces in our decrees to insert names of people or conditions needing divine intervention. During the trial, this included Mull, opposing counsel, hostile witnesses, the judge, and jurors. When Levy asked my mother if she had written the "Insert on Personal and Impersonal Hatred" decree, she testified that it was "composed by staff"—a half-truth, since she edited and approved every publication. Asked if Mull's name was used, she insisted, "I have no idea what was filled in this empty space," another shameless, almost Trumpian lie. She then launched into a lengthy justification of imprecatory prayer, denying harmful intent. Levy objected, labeling her response nonresponsive and self-serving, and the judge sustained it, directing the jury to disregard her explanation.[26]

I knew these rituals from childhood. By age five, I had mastered the "smash, blast" mantra with its finger jabs forming an asterisk. "Smash" was vertical, "blast" horizontal, "annihilate" diagonal, "shatter" the opposite diagonal, "dissolve and consume" two jabs to the center. As kids, we turned it into a game, laughing as we "blasted" each other when adults weren't watching. But now I recognize that thousands of people chanting violent metaphors in unison is no joke.

Here's the paradox: My cult claimed decrees could change physical reality but denied they could harm. If our "sacred science" worked at all, then it could certainly be weaponized. My mother knew this on a visceral level. A decade earlier in 1976 she had blamed the I AM "blasting decrees" for literally *killing* our members, then revoked Saint Germain's sponsorship in retaliation. Her position was clear—and on record. When Levy asked, "Do you teach that the spoken word can affect someone?" she finally told the truth: "Yes I do teach that."[27]

8. Selective Experience / Positive Testimonials, "The cult did some good things" / "The leader was kind to me personally." As with our trial strategy, apologists cherry-pick positive examples to downplay systemic harm. "Not all members experienced abuse," they argue, or cite warm testimonials. This *moral licensing*[28] uses a few good deeds to excuse broader wrongdoing. The tactic relies on *hasty generalization*[29] and *anecdotal fallacies*.[30]

The few genuinely happy members of my cult acted as social seeds, promoting favorable narratives and silencing criticism. These selective stories created a *public relations buffer*,[31] and the *illusion of choice*,[32] implying that suffering members must have chosen their plight. Or that it was something other than a predictable outcome of my cult's algorithm. Which helped members avoid coming to terms with their complicity.

What I recall is the community underclass living in poverty without healthcare, ruled by an authoritarian leader, while our family lived in privilege. Holidays were ruined by all-day church services. Parents worked themselves to exhaustion, sacrificing time with their children. Our school plays were religious-themed command performances that monopolized our time for weeks or months—undermining our education. Even my wedding day was shared with nine other couples.

Then there was my near-blanket impunity. For example, as a teenager I rode my loud Yamaha dirt bike all over Camelot, sometimes disrupting classes. It was great fun, but my behavior reflected a bratty double standard. Cult members worked tirelessly while I flaunted my privilege.

I have good memories with my sisters and our Montessori high-school classmates. Kids are adaptable, and we created moments of joy despite the draconian rules—exactly the kind of selective experiences that apologists would later cite to minimize systemic harm. We held traditional proms each year that were spectacular, even if strictly chaperoned. Sometimes they were at Camelot, or at one of our stately mansions in Los Angeles or Santa Barbara. And we went on elaborate field trips, once to Washington, D.C., and then a senior trip to the U.K. Those trips were enriching and transformative. But none of it compensated for the exploitation that we all knew existed, yet no one dared speak aloud.

Sean Prophet rides a Yamaha dirt bike while wearing a Summit University t-shirt at Camelot c. 1978

Every memory is thus tainted by the recognition that it was all built atop a lie. Especially the oft-repeated canard that the cult's children and teenagers were responsible for spiritually "holding the balance" for the world's wayward youth. Any coming-of-age transgressions therefore carried a global karmic burden. We simply weren't allowed to be kids. Behind every Kodachrome smile, whether in our childhood photographs or in the cult's promotional materials, was a shadow of deeper pain that was intrinsic to my cult. Camelot was many things, but above all it was an illusion: It was never remotely as happy or free as apologists might suggest.

9. Selective Free-Will Defense This defense rests on a contradiction: the cult's teachings of spiritual exclusivity must be simultaneously true (keeping members in fear of damnation) and false (allowing ex-members to avoid consequences). It's a logical impossibility that reveals the underlying manipulation. Leaders downplay this inherent *psychological coercion*,[33] portraying the group as a voluntary path even as implicit fear controls followers.

This mirrors other forms of entrapment. Just as people remain in abusive relationships or toxic jobs through fear and loyalty, cult members become bound by their compromised will. Like a high-pressure sales environment where casual shoppers browse freely while committed customers face relentless manipulation, the cult maintains different standards.

Less-committed members may drift at the margins, but the truly faithful face escalating demands for conformity.

David Passeger's testimony revealed both subtle and overt control methods. Even non-resident "Keepers of the Flame" underwent invasive interviews about their "sins," recorded on computerized forms every six months.[34] Though not physically restrained, Passeger testified he was held captive by the belief that my mother was "in direct contact with God, that the Holy Spirit was there physically, and that if I left I would be letting down God and myself and it would take me another 10,000 years to get back to that point." When Levy asked who told him that, Passeger replied, "Mrs. Prophet in the videotapes." His department head reinforced this fear, labeling critics as "betrayers" and reincarnations of the Pharisees who condemned Jesus.[35]

Despite such blatant control tactics, apologists argued at trial that such beliefs shouldn't affect anyone's choice to stay or leave. All while continually downplaying the stark truth that my cult *explicitly* taught members that wrong choices would destroy their souls. The Selective Free-Will Defense represents the ultimate apologetic distortion, using less intense experiences of fringe members to mask the indoctrinated dependence of the faithful, maintaining an illusion of free choice that—for many—was anything but.

---

[1] The tu quoque fallacy (Latin for "you too") occurs when someone responds to criticism by accusing their opponent of similar behavior, rather than addressing the argument. It's an attempt to divert attention by claiming the other party is hypocritical, without engaging with the original point.

[2] *CUT v. Mull*, Superior Court of Los Angeles County, C. 358191 (March 6, 1986), at 1761:3-20.

[3] "When a person gets tired, disillusioned, fed up, they get up and leave. Just like when a person gets tired and fed up in a marriage, they leave. When they get tired and fed up about being in the military, what do they do? They go A.W.O.L." *CUT v. Mull*, Superior Court of Los Angeles County, C. 358191 (March 6, 1986), at 1763:8-13.

[4] Special pleading occurs when someone applies a standard or rule to others but makes an exception for themselves or their argument without providing a valid justification. It often involves asking for leniency or special consideration for one's case while denying the same to others, creating a double standard. This fallacy undermines fairness by allowing inconsistent reasoning.

[5] Cognitive dissonance occurs when an individual experiences psychological discomfort from holding two or more conflicting beliefs, values, or attitudes simultaneously. To reduce this tension, people often change one of the beliefs, justify the conflict, or minimize its importance. It is a key concept in understanding how individuals reconcile contradictions between their actions and beliefs, often leading to rationalizations or behavior changes to resolve the inconsistency.

[6] Authoritarian hypocrisy occurs when leaders impose strict rules on others but exempt themselves, creating a double standard. This maintains power by allowing leaders to benefit from privileges while demanding obedience and sacrifice from followers, undermining fairness and moral authority.

[7] *CUT v. Mull*, Superior Court of Los Angeles County, C. 358191 (February 20, 1986), at 785:10-16.

[8] Survivorship bias occurs when conclusions are drawn based only on those who have succeeded or survived, ignoring those who did not. This leads to skewed perspectives, as it focuses on visible successes while overlooking the failures, which often provide crucial context. In groups or systems, survivorship bias can result in an overly optimistic view, as the challenges or harm faced by those who failed or left are disregarded.

[9] *CUT v. Mull*, Superior Court of Los Angeles County, C. 358191 (March 13, 1986), at 2389:26-2390:2.

[10] *CUT v. Mull*, Superior Court of Los Angeles County, C. 358191 (March 13, 1986), at 2396:9-10.

[11] Chitty, D. (1966). *The desert a city: An introduction to the study of Egyptian and Palestinian monasticism under the Christian empire*. Basil Blackwell.

[12] Spiritual elitism occurs when spiritual leaders justify extreme wealth, power, or status by claiming superior spiritual knowledge or enlightenment. They assert exclusive access to divine truth or special insights, framing their material excess as a sign of spiritual attainment. This mindset reinforces inequality, elevating the leaders above their followers, who are often expected to live humbly or sacrifice in contrast to the leaders' elevated status.

[13] *CUT v. Mull*, Superior Court of Los Angeles County, C. 358191 (February 20, 1986), at 841:9-25.

[14] *CUT v. Mull*, Superior Court of Los Angeles County, C. 358191 (February 18, 1986), at 597:26-28.

[15] Prophet, E. (2018). *Coercion or conversion? A case study in religion and the law: CUT v. Mull v. Prophet* (p. 135). Linden Books.

[16] The false virtue fallacy occurs when someone attempts to justify harmful or questionable actions by framing them as virtuous or beneficial. This fallacy falsely equates suffering or hardship with moral goodness, suggesting that actions like forced deprivation or strict control are justified because they build strength or character. It masks exploitation or abuse by portraying it as necessary for personal or spiritual growth, overlooking the negative consequences.

[17] Camp Bloomfield burned to the ground in the Woolsey Fire in 2018. Retrieved from https://en.wikipedia.org/wiki/Camp_Bloomfield

[18] Personal communication with "Michael" (individual chose not to reveal last name), 2024.

[19] The term "Maitreya's Mystery School" draws from esoteric and New Age traditions central to the Church Universal and Triumphant (CUT). Maitreya, seen as an Ascended Master in CUT, is modeled after the future Buddha in Buddhist esotericism. The use of "mystery school" refers to ancient secret schools where spiritual initiates were taught hidden knowledge. By combining Maitreya's figure with the mystery school concept, CUT positioned itself as a place of advanced spiritual instruction and initiation under the guidance of Ascended Masters, promising enlightenment and ascension to its members.

Prophet, E. C. (1986). *The lost teachings of Jesus*. Summit University Press.

Melton, J. G. (1994). *Encyclopedic handbook of cults in America*. Routledge.

[20] *CUT v. Mull*, Superior Court of Los Angeles County, C. 358191 (March 13, 1986), at 2366:11-2369:16.

[21] *CUT v. Mull*, Superior Court of Los Angeles County, C. 358191 (March 19, 1986), at 2708:16-19.

[22] Moral abdication refers to the act of relinquishing responsibility for one's actions or decisions, often by deferring it to an external authority or force, such as divine will, fate, or societal norms. In this process, individuals or groups avoid accountability by claiming that the consequences of their actions are beyond their control. This abdication shifts the blame or moral weight away from the person and onto something else, creating a moral loophole that justifies harmful behaviors without accepting responsibility.

[23] Victim blaming occurs when responsibility for harm is shifted onto the victim, implying their actions or characteristics contributed to their suffering. This deflects accountability from the perpetrator. For example, in fraud cases, victims might be blamed for being naive, or in cyberbullying, they might be faulted for their online presence, suggesting that their misfortune was avoidable had they acted differently. This minimizes the wrongdoer's responsibility and shifts focus away from the actual harm

caused.

[24] *CUT v. Mull*, Superior Court of Los Angeles County, C. 358191 (February 19, 1986), at 763:13-764:19.

[25] *CUT v. Mull*, Superior Court of Los Angeles County, C. 358191 (February 19, 1986), at 811:5-8.

[26] *CUT v. Mull*, Superior Court of Los Angeles County, C. 358191 (February 19, 1986), at 1094-1098.

[27] *CUT v. Mull*, Superior Court of Los Angeles County, C. 358191 (February 19, 1986), at 1103:1-3.

[28] Moral licensing occurs when individuals or groups justify unethical or harmful behavior based on prior good deeds or virtuous actions. By performing a positive act, they feel entitled or morally "licensed" to engage in actions that would otherwise be considered wrong, believing the earlier good balances out or excuses the negative behavior. This psychological effect can create a false sense of moral immunity, allowing harmful actions to be rationalized or minimized.

[29] The hasty generalization fallacy occurs when someone makes a broad conclusion based on insufficient or unrepresentative evidence. This leap to a generalized conclusion without adequate data leads to faulty reasoning, as it relies on too small or biased a sample to accurately reflect the broader reality.

[30] The anecdotal fallacy occurs when someone uses a personal experience or isolated example as evidence to support a broad conclusion, ignoring more reliable or comprehensive data. This fallacy overlooks larger patterns, leading to faulty reasoning based on limited, non-representative anecdotes.

[31] A public relations buffer is a strategy used by organizations or individuals to present a positive image that deflects or minimizes criticism. By highlighting favorable stories, testimonials, or selective information, this buffer creates a shield that distracts from or softens the impact of negative issues, controversies, or misconduct. This tactic helps manage public perception and maintains a veneer of legitimacy or respectability while avoiding direct engagement with the core criticisms.

[32] The illusion of choice refers to a situation where individuals believe they are making free decisions, but their options are actually limited or manipulated in such a way that their "choice" is largely predetermined. This technique is often used in marketing, politics, or manipulative systems like cults to give people the perception of autonomy while subtly steering them toward a specific outcome. The appearance of freedom masks the underlying control, making individuals feel empowered even when their decisions are heavily constrained or influenced.

[33] Psychological coercion is the use of emotional or mental manipulation to pressure someone into compliance, often against their will. Techniques like fear, guilt, or intimidation are used to control behavior, leaving the individual feeling they have no real choice.

[34] *CUT v. Mull*, Superior Court of Los Angeles County, C. 358191 (February 24, 1986), at 999-1000.

[35] *CUT v. Mull*, Superior Court of Los Angeles County, C. 358191 (February 24, 1986), at 1018:5-6.

CHAPTER TWENTY TWO

Rumspringa

My foray into the outside world at 20 wasn't a deliberate cult exit. It was a Los Angeles version of *Rumspringa*,[1] the Amish rite of passage where teenagers explore life outside the group, only to return home. As a child, I didn't know what it meant to be outside my cult, or to be a seeker. I only knew life from inside, watching others join our flock. By my teens, I found our rituals, rules, and obsession with world change stifling. I couldn't wait to be normal. In ninth grade, I became disgruntled and made a laminated wall calendar to count down the days until high school graduation, after which I planned to leave. The older I got, the more our constant condemnation of "fallen" ordinary people made me think we were the weird ones. I longed to understand and participate in the outside world—not to change it. But realizing that dream of independence wouldn't come easily. In the meantime, I tried my best to lead a normal life.

My teenage attempts at romance revealed how difficult that was. My mother's jealous interference began with my first love in my senior year of high school. When my girlfriend bought me gifts, she made me return them. Clothes? She banned me from wearing them. College bound, I took a road trip from Los Angeles to Northwestern University in Evanston, Illinois. My girlfriend came with me. Mother had approved the trip, but she later exploded—screaming and calling me "sick"—when she discovered we had been intimate. She made my girlfriend crop her beautiful hair, banned her from speaking to me, and treated her like an adulteress. I watched helplessly as my mother waged total war against this young woman. It was my first real heartbreak. But far worse, it was traumatic and grossly abusive to my girlfriend, whose only crime had been loving me.

A year later I took time off from college and returned to Los Angeles. Mother again interfered with a relationship I pursued with a Summit University student. Spies reported I had stayed the night at her off-campus apartment. Mother expelled her without hesitation—"You knew and agreed to the rules," she told her, then tried to set me up with a "proper" woman on staff I had no interest in. Was this just typical controlling-parent behavior? Maybe. But mother's power to exact revenge on everyone I dated went far beyond a normal household.

By the time I turned 18, I learned to be more cautious, and follow the rules. I was working at Excalibur Video Systems, my cult's downtown Los Angeles TV production company on Wilshire Boulevard. There I met Amanda, a vivacious woman with a great sense of humor. We worked together for about a year, and there seemed to be plenty of chemistry. Excalibur eventually closed due to financial difficulties, and most workers transferred back to Camelot. Amanda was working in the audio-video department as my assistant. I wanted to ask her out, but protocol required I get my mother's permission. She granted it, but whatever she said to Amanda ruined everything. We had one awkward dinner date, and when I asked her out again, she said she wanted a "celibate marriage."

"Marriage?" I gasped. "I'm not ready for that. I'm just trying to get to know you better."

She said, "Sean, I'm really not here to date anyone at all, I came here to be on the spiritual path."

I transferred Amanda out of my department to avoid her—an immature and spiteful abuse of my authority. Years later, my mother admitted she had read her confession letters and decided she wasn't right for me. No one wanted to mess with the guru's son after being warned. Mother could discipline or expel any woman interested in me, making me radioactive.

My first chance at real love finally came at age 20 when I met Kathleen Mattson, who also worked in our audio-video department. Kathleen was from Edmonton, Alberta and six years my senior. She joined my cult in 1982 after graduating from the Dalcroze School of Music in New York City. She had been through two quarters of Summit University and was assigned to work in our tape duplication facility at Camelot.

We talked and joked and bonded in the spring of 1984 during the production of a youth-recruitment film called The Marine Tribute. It featured cult middle- and high-school students marching in formation in white uniforms around our 240-acre Malibu campus. After several days together on set, I knew Kathleen was special, and I wasn't about to screw it up.

Production of *The Marine Tribute* at Camelot, Malibu CA, spring 1984

Kathleen Mattson (behind camera lens) on set of *The Marine Tribute*, Malibu, CA, spring 1984

I decided not to seek my mother's permission to date Kathleen. With all that romantic wreckage in my past, I declared my intentions up front. I warned her about my mother's meddling, but she was undeterred. Years later, she reflected, "I had been through this with mothers of boyfriends who just did not like me. I knew no one was going to be good enough for her first and only son. It was something she was going to have to go through eventually."

Word got back to my mother that we were an item. She agreed to let us go on one supervised date to that year's high school prom. But she did her best to keep us apart, making us travel in separate vehicles to the 1984 July conference in Montana. When the conference ended, no one was paying attention. I drove back with Kathleen in my car, and sealed the deal. We took a magical route through Yellowstone and Grand Teton National Park. As we rolled into Los Angeles, we stopped at Zuma Beach and kissed for the first time under the moonlight. I told her, "I was afraid I would never find anyone like you." We became inseparable.

The Gillette Mansion at Camelot, Malibu, CA

By fall, everyone suspected we were having sex. Kathleen had been spotted leaving my room in the Gillette mansion. Mother called me to a meeting that November and said, "It's pretty obvious you and Kathleen have been breaking the code of conduct for months. I have no choice but to dismiss her from staff. I can't have a double-standard going on here."

I snapped back, "If you kick her out, you're kicking me out, too." Mother didn't back down, so I submitted my resignation. I had no idea what I was in for. I had no money, and my mom certainly wasn't going to help. We drove off in my car with a few belongings—crashing for weeks in Kathleen's tiny trailer off campus. Eventually, we scraped together enough to get a dingy $550/month apartment in Encino. Kathleen kept her part-time retail job selling crystal jewelry, and I looked for steady work.

Then I learned what happens when everyone turns their back at once. Kathleen had been renting a 10-year-old blue Subaru from a staff member who she thought was a friend, with the intention of buying it. Her "friend" demanded she return it immediately. That same day, her boss—one of the cult's big donors—fired her. My best friend and former business partner, Will Adams, informed me I was off all future projects. My mother orchestrated it all. She wanted to bring Kathleen and me to our knees, and she nearly succeeded. Those were rough months.

Mother told the staff that Kathleen was a cat-woman from another planet. In her vivid hallucination, on the astral plane Kathleen had black fur, glowing green eyes, and was sent by the forces of "death and hell" to derail me from my spiritual path. The slander outraged me. It strengthened my resolve to make my own way.

I found work as an assistant editor at Varitel Video, a TV post-production facility. Kathleen became a receptionist at a film production company. We got our shit together and paid our rent. But my cult wasn't done with us yet.

Kathleen Mattson in the kitchen of our first apartment, Encino, CA 1985

On my 21st birthday in May 1985, I came home expecting to go out with Kathleen for my first legal drink. As I opened the door, about 40 people yelled, "SURPRISE!!!" It was the entire crew from the audio-video department, crammed into our tiny flat. Mother was playing the long game. I was genuinely happy to see my former colleagues. But there's no way they came to the apartment of the prodigal son and his "cat woman" on their own.

The whole episode was tough on Kathleen, who was torn between her love for the "path" and the "teachings," and her love for me. She said, "I knew in your mother's eyes we were doing something wrong. I was very devoted. I loved the practices. It had become my cosmology. But for me it wasn't a question if I was going to leave the relationship. There was just no way I could do that. But the inner conflict was intense. I was not sleeping, and it was just eroding my work and my life."

By September 1985, we moved to a nicer apartment in Studio City and conceived our first child. We hadn't been careful, but I still wasn't ready. We weren't going to abort. We still believed my mother's draconian teaching that abortion was murder. When mother heard about the pregnancy, she sent Will to deliver a message: "You don't have to have this child or be with Kathleen. There's always a place for you at Camelot if you make the right choice." I told him to get lost. But mother wasn't done. She called Kathleen directly and *suggested she have an abortion*—of her own grandchild, contradicting her ironclad—and very public—anti-abortion stance. I only learned about that duplicitous call nearly 40 years later while interviewing Kathleen for this book.

A week later, my mother invited me to her Malibu beach house for dinner. Will was there. After dinner, they worked on me all night. By 5 am, they had convinced me to break up with Kathleen, send her to our Vancouver teaching center, and move in with Will in North Hollywood. And I did it. I was 21, without good role models, being pressured by my mother and my best friend to retreat back into the small, childlike world of my cult, avoiding the adult responsibility of fatherhood.

For Kathleen, it was a brutal betrayal. I have no idea how she ever forgave me. She said, "That was very dark. But I had this weird sense that it was a test. I believed it would eventually come out alright. No matter what, it was your baby and her grandson. It was hard being around the people in the teaching center—there was a shunning. People were sickly sweet, but underneath I could tell I was being persecuted by your mom and the Ascended Masters. But I believed in you. I knew you were scared, and that Will and your mother had turned you away from *you*."

In the weeks that followed, I was depressed and lonely. I couldn't face Kathleen or her grief—and refused to speak to her by phone. Will rewarded me for following the "guru"—hiring me for side jobs again. Mother poured poison in my ear: "It's not your *karma* or your *dharma* to raise this child." But I knew it was all wrong. I endured a month or two of such deep emotional pain that I woke up every day tasting metal. One day, crying in the bathroom at work, I had a moment of clarity: "Why the *fuck* would the Ascended Masters tell me to abandon my own child? No God would want that. I'm going to love and raise my child."

I came home and told Will my decision. My mother called, furious. "I'm cutting you off. If you marry Kathleen and have this child, we're done." I ignored her threat and called Kathleen, admitting my terrible mistake. I begged her to come back. She didn't hesitate: "I love you. Of course, yes." I put her plane ticket on my credit card, and she was home the next day. Will moved out immediately, having failed as my saboteur. Later, Kathleen said, "I never considered not coming back."

Mother eventually climbed down from her high horse and resigned herself to a grandchild, and the "cat woman" as her daughter-in-law. Kathleen and I got married in a group ceremony at Camelot, with nine other cult couples, on Christmas Eve, 1985. But it wasn't a warm homecoming or real acceptance. A slot in a group wedding was her grudging consolation prize, and we both knew it. The wedding was a ponderous, turgid affair with a lengthy dictation from "Mother Mary." It dragged on until 2 am, leaving us nothing but an exhausted drive home to North Hollywood on our wedding night. But we didn't care. Christmas morning, we awoke together as husband and wife, with our unborn child. And that was the greatest gift of all.

We found a new roommate to replace Will and share the rent. I found a better job at Composite Image Systems (CIS), a film transfer facility that was a technology pioneer in the budding visual effects industry. We were both blossoming. She was in maternity clothes, and we bought a crib and a stroller. My work buddies at CIS even threw me a baby shower. I was shocked at their kindness. I hadn't realized I could find a welcoming community or real friendships outside my cult. In early May, just in advance of my 22nd birthday, Christopher was born. He was—and is—simply amazing. Summer of 1986 was a fantastic time. We had a newborn son who rocked our worlds, and we were financially stable. It felt like the worst was behind us.

But mother had other plans. If it was my best summer, it was her Waterloo. That was the year of the *CUT v. Mull* trial. Even though I was temporarily on my own—and out of my cult's inner circle—I had been well aware of her difficulties. In spite of my rage at her hostile treatment, I was concerned. And this was still on some level my family business. So I had taken vacation time from my job to attend several days of the trial because I wanted to support her.

In July 1986, a few months after the adverse Mull verdict, we got an offer from Soka Gakkai International to buy the Camelot property for $15.5 million. They wanted us out by December 1986. Mother accepted and performed another biblical ritual: Shaking the dust of California off her feet,[2] and making plans to relocate to Montana.

At the same time, the masters issued dire prophecies of judgments and earthquakes for the Los Angeles area. It was eerily similar to the millenarian behavior of the Mighty I AM cult in the 1940s, after it also lost a major legal battle in Los Angeles. The I AM headquarters wound up far inland—in Santa Fe, New Mexico. Likewise, Mother wasn't just moving our headquarters. She was telling everyone to leave coastal cities. When people asked where they should move, she told them that the only safe cities were away from the coasts: Minneapolis, Denver, Atlanta, Dallas, and Chicago. She suggested moving to Bozeman, Livingston, or the Paradise Valley in Montana to be close to our new headquarters. As fall approached, I feared being left behind. Though living separately with my own family, I was mentally *still in my cult*. And I became increasingly obsessed with my mother's deadly prophecies. But we couldn't afford to move.

Sean Prophet, with Christopher Prophet, June 1986

Kathleen was more level-headed. She reflected, "I was on this adventure with this man I loved, and this woman who had this wild imagination. I almost tried to believe because everyone was smitten with her ideas. But there was no logic to it. I was not afraid of Los Angeles falling into the ocean."

I wish I had been as skilled as Kathleen at distancing myself from my mother's fears. But I was young and naïve, and I was a living example of the power cult leaders exercise. In November I called my mother and asked what I should do. She said, "Let's get together and talk about it." Kathleen and I and little baby Christopher drove to Malibu to meet her at Zuma Beach. We walked onto the sand, and she made her pitch. "What if you go back to

Northwestern and finish college?" I asked, "How could I afford that?" She said, "Well, you can be ordained as a minister, and the church can pay you a salary. You would have to lead services and have responsibilities to our congregation there." It was the last thing I wanted to do. But according to her prophecies, my life depended on it. I told her I would think about it.

Driving home, I was in the Twilight Zone. I watched the sun sink over the calm Pacific and imagined tsunamis of divine retribution washing over the Malibu Hills. I looked over at Kathleen and down at my tiny son. I treasured the fledgling life we had started to build. Contemplating our move, I already missed Los Angeles. But the cult part of my brain was winning this battle.

Was it real fear of cataclysm? Or just social pressure as my former community pulled out of the city? I can't really say. There might have been a certain attraction to returning to the fold to be a cult VIP again. Not having to worry about traffic or paying rent. Having people look up to me and defer to my position. I wasn't mature enough to understand the fool's bargain I was about to make. But what sealed my fate was the twenty years of indoctrination: I was the son of God's representative on Earth. So long as I believed in her authenticity, mother was like the Sun in my Solar System. I had drifted toward the outer planets, but I could not escape her gravity.

A few days later, I accepted her offer.

She was overjoyed. I made arrangements to re-enroll at Northwestern and put in my notice at CIS. My last day would be the Friday before Christmas. All employees got Christmas to New Year's Day off, with three additional unpaid days. I took the unpaid days and used the time to pack.

Mother called me at home, asking, "Isn't it a workday?"

I said, "Yes, we're packing."

She asked, "Are you on paid holiday?"

I replied, "That's not until next week."

She argued, "Why don't you pack next week? You can't be taking time off from work."

We had already covered our December bills. I explained, "Mother, we have a lot to do, we need that time."

Then she ground my dignity to powder: "Well if you expect this church to support you and pay your way through college, you'd better learn to be more responsible!"

It's the moment my cell door clanged shut for another seven-year sentence. And I heard it like a thunderclap. My mother was once again in control of my smallest decisions, and I knew her dominance over me could only grow more complete as I left my budding career and became financially dependent on her. I should have called CIS right then and begged for my job back. But I didn't. Because even though I had lived and worked for two years outside the cult, the cult was still very much inside me.

Reflecting on that consequential fork in the road nearly forty years later, I have profound regrets. My job at CIS was assisting Price Pethel, a top-notch Hollywood colorist and compositor. I had lucked into working with a crack team of innovators. They all went on to become major players in feature-film color-grading and visual effects in the 1990s, at shops like Digital Domain, Company 3, EFILM Digital Laboratories, and Disney. Starting in early 1987, I would have been working on *Star Trek: The Next Generation*. I would have worked on several of the top-grossing films of all time. It was an epic lost opportunity. I also walked away from one of the best mentors in the business, who I still count as a dear friend.

If you didn't grow up in a cult, you may struggle to understand how I could have failed to recognize the terrible life choice I was making. Why wasn't I more rational like Kathleen? Why couldn't she talk me out of it? Like most Amish youth who return after Rumspringa, my mind was nothing close to my own at age 22. My cult was all I had known and its hooks were buried deep. I still fully believed in the pantheon of Ascended Masters, and I didn't want to let them down by making the wrong choice. My mother's prophecies were like a flashing red neon sign I couldn't ignore, because I still considered her cosmology more concrete than any physical reality.

But I also have compassion for my former self. I simply lacked the confidence to step away from the sad little child's world where everything was under my mother's control, into the adult world of risk and reward. Like so many who seek false spiritual certitudes, I didn't yet comprehend that her millenarian prophecies were merely world-rejecting speculation—representing her futile attempt to move Mount Everest. So I made the only choice I was capable of making: Interrupting my fragile new life to put the fate of my little family back in her hands once again.

---

[1] Wikipedia contributors. (2024, August 14). *Rumspringa*. In Wikipedia. Retrieved August 14, 2024, from https://en.wikipedia.org/wiki/Rumspringa

[2] The Holy Bible, King James Version. (1769/2017). *Matthew 10:14*. Cambridge University Press.

CHAPTER TWENTY THREE

Doubts and Dissent

Think of it as backing out of a con: Someone sold you an investment scam. You put your savings into it, bought into the promises of life-changing returns. In your fantasy, you had already quit your job, bought the bigger house, the boat, and were jetting off to that tropical paradise. Spiritually, that's what being in a cult is like. You've "made it." Except there's no tangible evidence for any of it, just your socially constructed cult experiences and whatever else the leader convinced you to believe. Once you fall for a con, you have a choice: cling to the fantasy of your life of leisure, or face the fact that you've been scammed, and you're worse off than before.

As should be clear from the sad tale of my rumspringa, cult membership is a state of mind. I was physically and financially independent from my cult for two years, but I still couldn't break free because I wasn't mentally independent. No one can talk anyone else out of a cult until that person is ready to leave, which is why interventions by family members so often fail. The pain of staying must be greater than the fear of leaving. And once you're in a cult, there's pain either way. The cult ideology and its charismatic leader set the trap, but the seeker complies, buying into every stage of thought reform. To leave a cult means reversing this process. It must be deliberate, step-by-step, and it's going to hurt.

In scams and cults alike, loss aversion takes center stage. Cult leaders know they can keep members chasing the sunk costs of their time, money, and emotional investment. Like a con artist's promises of untold riches, cult membership traps you with illusions of your unrealized gain of salvation and purpose. You'll resist accepting the loss of your time, money, and dreams with every fiber of your being. The truth will feel unbearable.

It's possible to be aware of cult dynamics—while believing your own cult is different. That's disconfirmation bias: dismissing all evidence that applies to you. Recall the woman with the $50,000 shoebox. No one is immune. No one wants to admit they made a mistake. So the first step is acknowledging that you joined a cult. Like any bad relationship, you have to recognize you've fallen into a life-hole, and getting out will take effort. It's about taking stock: "What are my options now?" Regardless of what you do next, you're not getting that time or money back.

The metaphor of the elephant and the rider can help you forgive yourself for past mistakes. Popularized by social psychologist Jonathan Haidt in *The Happiness Hypothesis*[1] the elephant represents your emotional side—powerful, instinctive, and largely unconscious. This maps onto your limbic system. The rider symbolizes the rational part of your mind—your prefrontal cortex. Haidt says, "The elephant is far more powerful than the rider, but it is not an absolute dictator." You rode your elephant into your cult; to get out, you'll need to tame it or, failing that, change the path you're riding on. Being "of two minds" is a time-worn, even biblical trope, seen in everything from addiction to persuasion, and all forms of human behavior. "For the good that I would, I do not: but the evil which I would not, that I do."—Romans 7:19 KJV.

The cliché "love is blind" is another classic elephant-rider dilemma. Doubting your cult resembles falling out of love. One morning you wake up and realize, "This relationship is no longer serving me. I don't feel seen or valued." But that means leaving the safety of the familiar—loneliness, upheaval, logistics. So the temptation is to deny what you *know*, favoring what you *feel*, hoping things improve. Sometimes that works in relationships. But a cult is zero-sum. The leader takes everything: your time, effort, and money vanish into a black hole. The community? The relationships? None of it comes from the leader. Those bonds are just the bait for other seekers. It's a cold but accurate assessment of cult social dynamics.

Cults are traps, and that's true even if they don't trap everyone. Compare the danger to substance or process addictions. Some people drink or use drugs in moderation while others fall quickly into addiction. Some people navigate the fringes of cults without becoming enmeshed. Cult defenders often use these less-committed individuals as proof that members can scale commitment up or down at will. But that doesn't mean cults are safe, it only means that some people have stronger resistance. Others lack the emotional regulation skills to avoid getting trapped, especially those who are vulnerable due to heartbreak, misfortune, or existential hunger. Freedom of religion doesn't eliminate danger—just as the legality of alcohol or gambling doesn't prevent addiction.

Caveat emptor.

The potential for enmeshment in cults is particularly dangerous for those frozen in Kohlberg's stage 1 morality (age 4-10) or Piaget's preoperational cognitive stage (age 2-7)—where "mommy and daddy are always right." Such people can distrust the outside world but view those in their immediate circle as safe. Authoritarian cult leaders can become parental figures, giving members the illusion of returning to a simpler, trusting childhood. But this regression means that to find adult freedom, you'll have to grow up and leave home again. A mature perspective accepts that relationships are complex and prone to betrayal—especially in a cult environment.

When I first began doubting my cult, I often thought, "I have some great friends here. Wouldn't it be amazing if I could just stay with this group of people, without the cult?" But that was naïve. Cult friendships are built on mutual thought reform and trauma bonding—they're like being stranded on an island without a ferry to the mainland. To sustain a cult friendship, both people have to swim ashore, strip away the cult's influence, and find each other again. And it's a love triangle, involving loyalty not just to each other but to the leader, the dogma, and the group's purpose. Without that foundational third wheel, the bond can fall apart.

My complex friendship with Will Adams confirms this principle. I met him at age 17 while working as the resident Chyron operator at Excalibur Video Systems (EVS).[2] Will was a part-time support engineer, nine years my senior, who had been a rock drummer in the early '70s, touring with Robin Trower. He became like an older brother to me—almost as influential as my mother. I now see he was always her surrogate.

EVS was loosely tied to my cult. It was a commercial video production and post-production company, founded in 1978 by two permanent staff members to help offset the cost of the expensive equipment needed for our television ministry. We worked with many non-cult clients—Chiat-Day, Telepictures, Robert Abel and Associates, Merle Norman Cosmetics, and the Crenshaw Christian Center, to name a few. We edited some early MTV videos like Steve Miller's "Heart Like a Wheel" and Diana Ross' "Muscles." Compared to Camelot, EVS was a permissive environment.

I kept my growing album collection in the Chyron room. Since rock music was part of our projects, no one minded if I played records. Will noticed my music and struck up a conversation, asking if I had heard Jethro Tull, Yes, or Emerson Lake and Palmer. I hadn't. My tastes were mainstream rock and disco. We bonded over music—and started hanging out. Over the next year, Will introduced me to the prog-rock catalog, taught me air drumming, and immersed me in everything he knew about studio sound recording—mic technique, mixing, critical listening. I learned to identify every instrument and production method in complex tracks. Will was cool—not like the uptight culties on staff.

Our friendship deepened. I felt I could talk to Will about anything, and he shared everything with me—his past life as a touring musician, psychedelic drugs, women, sex, and his regrets. Will and his girlfriend had been living a carefree life in Santa Barbara—they loved the beaches, smoking pot, playing live music, and taking long bike rides. One day in the late 1970s, they wandered into our teaching center, a stately Spanish-style mansion on the corner of Santa Barbara and Padre Street that had once been a B'nai B'rith synagogue. There they met Paul, a permanent staff member in his late 30s, and confirmed celibate bachelor, who explained the cult's teachings and gave them some literature.

Paul asked if they were married.

"No, but we are really in love," Will answered.

"Are you living together?" Paul asked.

"Yes, we are."

"Well, you know that's against Ascended Master law. There's no sex allowed before marriage," Paul said.

Will objected, "We share a room, and we only have one bed, it's a foam pad…"

Paul suggested, "You could always cut your mattress in half, that way you wouldn't be tempted to have sex."

And so, Will cut his bed in half. He started bringing his girlfriend to services and then to a conference in Los Angeles. She wasn't pleased with his new obsession and soon left him. I wondered, was Paul proud of himself for wrecking Will's relationship? He was technically right about the cult's teachings on sex, but I can't help but think that Paul's celibacy—and perhaps envy of Will's happiness—prompted his "advice." Whatever Paul's motives might have been, I never understood Will's self-sabotage. His devotion to my cult cost him everything—his carefree life, his love, and his happiness. Despite his pain, he clung to our teachings, convinced they were his true path.

Will tolerated my criticisms of my mother and even agreed with me sometimes. But looking back, his early openness was part of a longer con. In the parlance of Orwell's *1984*, Will was the O'Brien to my Winston Smith. By letting me color outside cult lines, he built a trust with me that my mother never could. Given her history of meddling in my relationships, it's clear she and Will had an understanding—she would turn a blind eye to our transgressions, so long as Will remained her spy. Though our friendship was real, it was also a setup.

After EVS closed in 1983 due to financial troubles, Will and I bought cameras and launched Aquastar, a video production business. We shot commercial projects during the week and recorded cult services on weekends. But when I left on my rumspringa in late 1984, Will excluded me from the business we had founded together, ending our partnership without payment or apology. Will's betrayal over Aquastar was just one of many ups and downs in our friendship. Like most cult relationships, ours was a complex dance between genuine connection and divided loyalties. Despite several estrangements over many years, neither of us could fully let go.

Years after I left the cult, we resumed a casual friendship. By the late 1990s, Will had a corporate training job that frequently brought him to Los Angeles, and he stayed at a hotel next to the airport. We would meet for sushi and late-night conversation, and I would crash at his hotel. One of those nights was September 10, 2001. The next day, an early morning call from his wife alerted us to 9/11. We watched the towers fall on TV, then looked out the window at the endless rows of planes grounded at LAX.

A few years later in a different hotel room, I confronted Will about his cult beliefs, blurting out, "Will, come on now. You're way too smart to believe in Ascended Masters. What are you still doing in the cult?"

He replied, "No, no, I've had spiritual experiences that I can't explain any other way."

I asked, "What do you mean, explain? You had an experience, but what does that mean? How can any experience confirm this elaborate theology?"

Will said, "I've known about this my whole life—experiences I've had going back to when I was a child. When I found the teachings, it was like coming home."

"OK," I pressed, "but why *these* teachings? How do your spiritual experiences confirm the existence of Ascended Masters, or that they spoke through my mother?"

He answered, "I had the same masters speak to me before I even found these teachings. I've seen violet flame around your mother during dictations. It's all as real as you sitting here."

I choked, "Voices in your head? Violet flame?? I'm her son, and I've never seen *anything* like that. I've never heard any voices that didn't come from my own mind. Have you considered that your experiences might be a figment of your imagination? That your brain might be broken?"

I watched the color drain from his face. I knew I had crossed a line. By challenging him, I reversed our roles—I was no longer the 17-year-old kid but the older brother calling him out. Will couldn't handle difficult conversations. It was the last time I saw him. He stopped taking my calls or responding to my emails. At the end of our friendship, just as in the beginning, my cult was always the priority. His devotion doomed any chance of reconciliation.

In 2011, a mutual friend called to inform me of Will's death. I was stunned. He was only 55, taken by aggressive lung cancer despite never smoking tobacco. He'd been sick for 18 months but told our mutual cult friends not to tell me. They knew how close we had been, but residual cult loyalties kept me in the dark.

I wish I could have said goodbye. While I don't regret challenging Will's beliefs, I would have apologized for being so harsh about it. I would have forgiven him for spying on me all those years. But I had come to personify a central challenge to his identity—the last thing he wanted to confront while he was dying. It's all sad. The singular truth of his life is that he was a brilliant man who invested the lion's share of his identity into his guru. And that's a tragic choice.

Cult friendships are always strained. Let me reiterate: For relationships to thrive, the cult leader must be removed from the equation. Otherwise, honest dialogue is impossible. There can be no shared doubts, no safety in the bond, no planning to leave together, and no mutual support through the transition. Cult friends often turn into "O'Briens"—loyal not to you, but to your "higher self"—beholden to the leader and dogma. That means they'll betray you to "the Party," "for your own good," if they sense you're slipping away.

Sinclair Lewis describes the dilemma in *It Can't Happen Here*:
> Under a tyranny, most friends are a liability. One quarter of them turn "reasonable" and become your enemies, one quarter are afraid to stop and speak, and one quarter are killed and you die with them. But the blessed final quarter keep you alive.[3]

Even if a cult friend shares your doubts, they may not be as far along as you. They could be white-knuckling or—like Will—they may be cult lifers. If you get ahead of them and reveal too much, they might feel threatened. Because now you're including them in your pain and loss. So they might dismiss your doubts, end the friendship, or rat you out.

On the opposite end of the spectrum, over-the-top displays of spiritual fervor can serve as a cult's social currency. When I was still a rebellious teenager, Will and I coined a nasty epithet for the most obsequious devotees: "Uglets." My cruel, childish disdain and Will's covert cynicism cut through a thick layer of sanctimonious bullshit. The uglets strutted across campus, noses up, shouting devotional aphorisms and flaunting holier-than-thou spiritual pride. With faux serenity and a forced smile, they were the early birds for the 5 am decree sessions, and they lingered after services, assuming a meditative pose. They didn't wait to be told to chop off their hair or wear ridiculous clothing—they flaunted their submission. It was no less of a peacocking display than a bodybuilder flexing on the beach. "Look at me! No ego here. No remaining human self. Just the purest expression of spiritual advancement on the planet!" The competitive piety seen in cults is no different from any social scene, but operating under radically different norms.

One of those norms is the drive to purge oneself of ego and desire, shedding identification with the *self*. This drive runs deep in New Age thought and permeates the Western Esoteric Tradition.[4] The second noble truth in Buddhism is that suffering is caused by desire. The authentic teaching isn't that desire is bad, but rather that suffering arises from the ignorant pursuit of grandiose desire.[5] What some Western New Age Buddhists might overlook is that desire extends beyond material wants—it includes existential hunger and spiritual longings for meaning and purpose.

You desired to join your cult because it gave you purpose and fulfilled emotional needs, and getting out requires an even stronger desire for freedom and self-ownership. Desirelessness, egolessness, and selflessness won't help. It's a boomerang—wanting to rid yourself of ego and self *requires* an ego and a self. If you ever succeeded, you'd cease to exist. You want a self strong enough to uphold boundaries, but not so inflated that it alienates others.

Unwinding thought reform means restoring self-confidence and a healthy ego without tipping into hubris. To escape a cult, you *must* break faith with the leader and the dogma. Idolizing your cult leader or clinging to spiritual experiences will trap you, just as it trapped Will. You need to understand how thought reform works—and how it worked on you. But you also need to restore your own healthier methods of belief formation, based on critical thinking, evaluation of evidence, and finding less biased information sources.

Justified true beliefs must come from a reflective process where you're free to explore varied perspectives, seek out independent information, and make reasoned decisions aligned with your core values. Unless you seek help from a therapist or exit counselor, it's a journey you'll have to make alone. Revealing your doubts to a fellow member could get you expelled before you're ready. The cult's power structure and social scene are designed to punish thoughtcrime.

I recall an incident of dissent that took place at our Santa Barbara center in 1971. There was a retired gentleman named Robert Zimmerman who did all the fine carpentry work on the property and was a skilled plasterer and painter. He lived and worked at the center, setting up shop in our basement. At seven, I felt like his grandson as he taught me woodworking. He built a custom lectern for my parents and railings for the altar. He textured the walls and ceilings in the chapel with fine filigree patterns of gold and white that looked like swirling flames. He added flecks of mica that sparkled in the sun to our white exterior stucco walls. There was hardly a room in the building untouched by his artistic hands.

Robert clashed with my parents over a project. They pulled rank: "The decision's final. El Morya wants it that way." Robert replied, "Well, maybe the Masters can make mistakes. Maybe they're not perfect." Rather than working through the disagreement, my dad called a staff meeting and kicked him out on the spot. I was horrified because Robert was practically family. But my parents only cared about preserving their authority: *"Robert said the masters can make mistakes!"* Absolute loyalty was worth more to them than the loss of a valued community member.

But that's how cults operate. To maintain the eight principles of thought reform, they had to let Robert go. He had violated at least four of the principles: the mystical imperative, purity of the masters, doctrine over person, and dispensing of existence. Unchallenged, he might have inspired others to question, risking the cult's stability. Zero-tolerance for dissent was a brittle but necessary aspect of cult life.

Robert's willingness to confront my parents showed he wasn't yet a true believer. He retained some mental independence. Over the years, I observed that banishment of such people was the rule, not the exception. This undercuts the "negotiation" apologia I previously discussed—through which cult defenders insist that dissent was possible, because some "got away with it."

My parents' rule was capricious, not absolute. Provided they showed contrition, some who were expelled from staff remained members in good standing. Others were declared *persona non grata* and barred for life. Our system was a spiritual *monarchy* in every sense of the word. And when members believed they could be cut off from God or lose their immortal soul, the trauma of summary excommunication could be severe indeed.

---

[1] Haidt, J. (2006). *The happiness hypothesis: Finding modern truth in ancient wisdom*. Basic Books.
[2] The system I used was called the Telemation Compositor, which was later replaced by the Chyron. The term "Chyron" has now become generic for onscreen TV titles.

³ Lewis, S. (2005). *It can't happen here* (M. A. Schorer, Ed., p. 202). Penguin Classics. (Original work published 1935)

⁴ The Western Esoteric Tradition is a broad term encompassing a range of mystical, spiritual, and occult practices and philosophies in the Western world. Dating back to antiquity, it includes elements from Gnosticism, Hermeticism, Alchemy, Astrology, Kabbalah, and the Christian mystic tradition, among others. This tradition emphasizes the pursuit of hidden knowledge or wisdom (esoteric means "inner" or "hidden"), personal spiritual development, and the exploration of the relationship between the divine and the natural world. Influential throughout history, it has shaped various aspects of Western culture, philosophy, and religion, blending with other traditions and continually evolving. The Western Esoteric Tradition is characterized by its diverse and syncretic nature, appealing to those seeking alternative spiritual paths outside of mainstream religious practices.

Hanegraaff, W. J. (2013). *Western esotericism: A guide for the perplexed*. Bloomsbury.

⁵ Truth of Suffering (Dukkha): Life inherently involves suffering, stress, and dissatisfaction. Truth of the Cause of Suffering: Suffering is caused by desire, attachment, and craving. Truth of the Cessation of Suffering: Cessation of suffering is attainable through relinquishment of desire. Truth of the Path to the Cessation of Suffering: The Eightfold Path leads to the cessation of suffering.

Gethin, R. (1998). *The foundations of Buddhism*. Oxford University Press.

CHAPTER TWENTY FOUR

Reclaiming Your Power

It's nearly impossible for a cult leader to control someone who owns their orgasm. This is why cults and religions tend to be almost universally sex-negative. And it's why I've spent considerable time in this book exploring my cult's quirky sexual taboos. Powerful biological urges that are near-universal present a golden opportunity for cult leaders to use sexual guilt to set their followers at war with themselves. Any spiritual explanations for sexual repression are beside the point—which, as I've stressed—is always control. Some cults like the Osho movement, NXIVM, the Children of God, the 19th century Oneida Community, and others have taken the extreme opposite approach, encouraging open sexuality among members. This is equally manipulative, since members wouldn't generally be able to find such diverse sexual options outside their cult, binding them ever more tightly to the group. Extreme denial and indulgence are the flip sides of the same coin of control, representing yet another *Taijitu* paradox.

Sociologist and cult expert Janja Lalich describes the strategy:
> Cult leaders seem to realize rather quickly... that a great source of power can be found in the sexual control of their followers. Most people come into cults with certain personal values, including having a sense of their own sexual preferences, behaviors, norms, and expectations... Enforcing sexual submission may be considered the final step in the objectification of the individual as cult member... Once sexual control is in place, no part of life is left untouched by the cult leader's influence.[1]

It may be difficult to understand how the true-believer mentality keeps people in bondage—sexual or otherwise. It's natural to think, "Cult leaders are such obvious frauds. Why would anyone agree to any of that? Why don't people just walk away?" But that reflects a lack of empathy, much like what I blurted out to my friend Will in that hotel room. It would be like telling a devout Muslim to just "stop believing" in Allah, or saying to a Christian, "It's obvious you weren't 'saved' by someone dying on a cross 2,000 years ago," or telling an abuse victim to "just leave" their abuser, or a depressed person to "smile, go outside, and be happy." None of that works. People are prisoners of their identities, beliefs, and their cult leaders.

Only self-critical thinking can help anyone start peeling away the layers of thought reform. That's why I covered the existential questions early in this book. I don't expect true believers to accept my answers right away, if ever. They're great tools for those ready to use them, but most people in cults aren't ready. It's aspirational, "This is what I had to figure out. Maybe you can too." It took me many years to get there. But if I had those insights back then, it would have made my journey easier. If you've come this far, you're well on your way.

Beware of peer pressure. Doubting is lonely, but necessary. Remember, we are social animals with a deep evolutionary drive to conform because, for much of our history, being cast out of the tribe meant death.[2] Cults exploit this primal fear. But in modern society, leaving a group isn't a death sentence. It might feel like it, but healthier social groups await once you leave an unhealthy one.

Despite strict rule enforcement, cults rely on internal compliance. If you are feeling doubts, try experimenting with private, internal non-compliance. For instance, if your cult has a ritual for silent prayer or mantras at certain times, sit quietly and think of something else instead. Note your act of dissent and savor reclaiming your power.

Try breaking a food or beverage rule and see how that feels. Skip a required meeting, saying you don't feel well. It's not a lie—your discomfort is genuine. If you're uneasy about a spontaneous activity, excuse yourself to the restroom. If others close their eyes in prayer, keep yours open. Each of these small rebellions does more than just challenge rules—it rewires neural pathways that were conditioned to obey, striking the root of thought reform. The key is to *start making independent choices*, no matter how small, to condition yourself toward autonomy.[3] No one has to know about your dissent until you're ready to share it.

During group sessions or lectures, mentally talk back. If something feels wrong, acknowledge it to yourself: "That's wrong!" If swearing is taboo, amplify it mentally: "Fuck you!" or "That's fucking bullshit!" If you're being verbally abused and don't feel safe to confront the person, confront them with your inner voice. Say everything you wish you could say, unleashing a private torrent of defiance. Cuss like a drunken sailor if that helps you feel empowered—but do it silently. Recognize that no matter how intimidating they may seem, *no one owns you.*

If your cult has sexual taboos—like reading erotic fiction, indulging fantasies, or masturbation—break them as a revolutionary act. Taking full control over your body and its pleasures is foundational to self-ownership. Think of all the ways you use your body to serve someone else's agenda. Why not serve yourself sometimes? Don't be fooled into believing abstaining is character-building. Self-discipline is avoiding *self-harm*. Masturbation is healthy, can help you sleep, reduces stress, and releases endorphins.[4] For men, it improves prostate health; for women, it can alleviate menstrual cramps; and for both it creates feelings of mental and physical well-being. Guilt about self-pleasure is rooted in ancient myths and purity culture. As I've noted, it's one of the most pointless forms of self-denial ever devised.

If you have a safe place to keep a journal, do so. During my last few years in the cult, I wrote coded notes in my day planner. These notes captured disagreements with dogma or observations that countered cult gaslighting. If I saw something unjust, I would jot it down, registering my objection with myself. I sometimes cryptically documented my acts of non-compliance in writing. It helps more than you realize. Remember, I was part of my cult's monarchy, and yet I still had to conceal my own rebellion. And it helped me.

This isn't obstinacy for its own sake. It's testing the waters for reclaiming your identity—you have to crawl before you can walk. As you go deeper, especially with journaling, your thoughts may start pouring out like a dam bursting. Rage or frustration might come in LARGE CAPITAL LETTERS!!!! Let it flow, but keep it safe from prying eyes. Cults are not above searching your personal belongings, especially if someone notices a change in your behavior.

The watchful eye of other cult members is a significant concern. You won't be able to hide your inner dissent forever. Complex post-traumatic stress disorder (CPTSD) is common after long-term cult trauma, and it often involves hyper-vigilance to others' emotional cues. If you're exploring doubts, someone may detect those subtle shifts and question you. Be prepared with a reasonable, spiritually acceptable explanation to protect your privacy.

Recall my discussion of QAnon, one of the most dangerous online cults. Many other cults are "extremely online." In the near future, these may well become the dominant type. If you're in one, you have physical privacy—a major advantage. You won't need to hide your dissent as carefully. But don't underestimate the risks lurking in your own mind. Thought reform trains you to be your own jailer. That's how online cults function: without physical isolation, they must burrow deep into your psyche. Millions of people have been "red-pilled" from the comfort of their own homes. Online cult membership parallels addiction in how it conditions behavior and rewards engagement. Emotional bonding during interactions can stimulate oxytocin, while anticipation of shared revelations or mystical manipulation can trigger dopamine. If you're in one of these groups, the only way out is to disengage gradually and replace unhealthy patterns with positive relationships and activities. The same techniques of non-compliance and journaling apply here, except your dissent remains mental rather than physical.

Many remain under the spell of celebrity from a lifetime of watching films and TV. Seeing someone on a glowing screen, knowing others are watching too, gives the speaker undue credibility. Even if it's a Zoom call or streaming video, the effect can be similar to binging a Netflix series. Cult content uses hooks and cliffhangers as effectively as episodic television. Whatever their shortcomings, cult leaders know how to retain an audience through charisma and storytelling. Their goal is to maintain their hold on your attention and to get you to donate your time or your funds.

If you're in an online cult, reduce your consumption of their content. Cut back time spent on forums, chats, and video calls. If you're in QAnon or a similar group, stop chasing pointless "solutions" to unsolvable puzzles.

Make fewer commitments to group activities and events. Seek disconfirming information, even if it makes you uncomfortable. Read critical articles. Resist dismissing them as "haters" or "the media." Could the "haters" have a point? Does "the media" mean multiple credible sources? Consider that the broader perspective might be valid. Learn to vet information objectively.[5] Speak with ex-members or lurk in their forums—you don't have to post. Any form of non-compliance helps break the pattern of online cult routines.

When you start retreating from your online cult, expect a barrage of messages trying to pull you back in. If you're still in doubt-and-dissent mode, keep it all at arm's length. Pursue alternative hobbies. Focus on family activities and non-cult friendships. If you're unsure, don't burn bridges. Let people know you're OK but just "have some personal shit going on." If they keep prying, master the art of non-response—use the *gray rocking* technique by staying neutral, unemotional, and uninteresting, like a dull gray rock that blends into the background. This discourages further attempts to manipulate or control you. It's all part of the process of reaching the tipping point when you're ready to make that final decision to exit your cult.

There's no single foolproof path. It all begins with doubt and the all-important small acts of non-compliance. Each time you don't comply, you notch a little victory. Each time you absorb disconfirming information without recoiling, you're that much closer to thinking for yourself. Each time you act to serve your own mental, physical and emotional needs, and flout the rules of your cult, you take back another small slice of control. These private victories build the inner strength you'll need for bigger decisions ahead—and with each small act of rebellion, the iron grip of thought reform weakens.

---

[1] Lalich, J. (2010). Dominance and submission: The psychosexual exploitation of women in cults. *Women & Therapy, 19*(4), 89–100. https://doi.org/10.1300/J015v19n04_06

[2] Baumeister, R. F., & Leary, M. R. (1995). The need to belong: Desire for interpersonal attachments as a fundamental human motivation. *Psychological Bulletin,* 117(3), 497–529. https://doi.org/10.1037/0033-2909.117.3.497

[3] Self-conditioning is a method where individuals apply behavioral psychology principles to alter their own thoughts and behaviors. By rewarding positive actions or applying consequences to negative ones, it aids in overcoming undesired mental states and habits, facilitating personal improvement.
Skinner, B. F. (1953). *Science and human behavior.* Macmillan.

[4] Coleman, E. J., & Bockting, W. O. (2013). *Masturbation as a means of achieving sexual health.* Routledge.

[5] Ad Fontes Media. (n.d.). *The interactive media bias chart.* Retrieved from https://adfontesmedia.com/interactive-media-bias-chart/

CHAPTER TWENTY FIVE

The Dweller on the Threshold

There is no single way to flee a cult, but "flight" is no exaggeration. The challenge is: How do you flee from yourself? At some point, the cult penetrated your inner world, and you agreed to its terms. Each day that you remain, you re-commit to your predicament. So how do you begin to un-agree? Systematically doubting your belief system is a necessary first step. Journaling, secret dissent, mental non-compliance—these are all solitary acts. But the next step is social. The deeper your entrenchment in the cult, and the more exalted your position in its hierarchy, the fiercer the peer pressure will be.

In a close-knit commune, your relationships are rooted in cult identity. As I've stressed, marriages, friendships, and even parenting depend on mutual adherence to the leader and dogma, creating relationships with divided loyalties. Your spouse and friends may not have fallen in love with you—they fell in love with *you+beliefs+leader*. In some cases, marriages were arranged by the leader. These unions might rest on personas both parties adopted for their cult roles. Strip away those overlays, and the relationship may lack shared values. If one spouse leaves the cult and the other stays, it's almost always splitsville. Even when both leave together, the marriage often suffers. A cult exit can be as traumatic as the loss of a child or parent.

My marriage was affected—even within the cult. After we left Los Angeles in January 1987, Kathleen and I moved to an apartment in Evanston, Illinois, where I began attending Northwestern University. And that's when we began to have our first marital troubles. Kathleen said, "I was pretty stressed as a new mother and pretty isolated. I really longed for my personal family, especially my brothers." This created a growing emotional rift, as I was consumed with school and ministerial duties. Kathleen spent her time caring for our infant son, Christopher. Complicating matters was the presence of my intellectually precocious sister, Tatiana, who began attending Northwestern at the age of fifteen. She often joined us for meals and witnessed some of our arguments. While they were ordinary spats, they disturbed Tatiana, and she reported them to our mother. And that's when things got weird.

Successful relationships require mutual self-awareness and honesty. Cult relationships struggle under the weight of the leader's interference and the oppressive dogma. The purity aspect of thought reform buries much of the human personality beneath a layer of shame. In my cult, prayers like "They Shall Not Pass"[1] and "I Cast Out the Dweller on the Threshold"[2] became a daily reaffirmation of our culture of affliction—paranoia of both external dark forces and the inner dark side. We feared that black magicians and sinister entities on the astral plane were always attacking us. These ideas borrowed heavily from the Mighty I AM cult. Members were also taught to fear their own humanity as the "dark side," equating natural emotions with the "Dweller on the Threshold"—similar to the Christian devil.

These prayers were acts of self-abdication. Repeated as many as 144 times in sequence, they built to a fever pitch, railing against "black arts," "nefarious deeds," and the "synthetic self." In the theology of my cult, the Dweller on the Threshold symbolized the accumulation of a person's negative thoughts, actions, and unresolved traumas from past and present lives. The Dweller, for all its mystical trappings, represented our natural humanity—the darker impulses, unresolved pain, and authentic emotions that cult ideology forbade. Phrases like "transmutation with the Violet Flame"[3] demanded we eradicate these parts of ourselves. Such decrees became a relentless assault on our identity. Overcoming this "Dweller" is seen as a necessary step to cross the threshold and unite with the "Higher Self" or "I AM Presence." This struggle leaves no room for self-expression or authentic relationships.

Instead of treating us like adults who needed to work through our marital difficulties, my mother spiritualized our arguments and took sides. She told Kathleen that her Dweller on the Threshold was on the rampage—as a wolf attacking her jugular. She held Kathleen responsible for our discord. I resented the interference. My little sister didn't know any better and was just trying to help. But I knew things weren't that simple and that I bore some of the blame.

As soon as my mother took sides, it made me want to defend Kathleen. As she often did when it suited her, my mother treated me as if I could do no wrong. There was that third wheel of the living God in my marriage again. Then it dawned on me how easy it was for spiritual pronouncements to become a tool of manipulation. How can anyone disprove a spiritual claim asserted without evidence? It drove a wedge in my marriage and made sorting things out harder than it needed to be.

Through her theology of the Dweller, my mother believed that through verbal repetition, cult members could defeat imaginary forces of darkness and reverse millions of years of human evolution to become something we're not: half-humans, over-identified with "upper chakra"[4] characteristics of divinity, love, and light, while suppressing "lower chakra" sexuality and desire, along with necessary protective emotions like anger. Those decrees psychologically pounded away every day at parts of ourselves with a metaphorical sledgehammer. None of it worked. Nor would anyone want it to.

A great illustration of the futility of simplistic notions of good and evil is the *Star Trek* original series episode, "The Enemy Within."[5] The plot is straightforward: a transporter accident splits Captain Kirk into his good and evil halves. The evil half is deceptive, violent, and rapey. The good half is feckless, unstable, and weak. Hijinks ensue as the two halves of Kirk battle it out. The episode ends with the good Kirk persuading the evil Kirk that they can't survive without each other, whereupon they are reunited by the transporter.

As an allegory for psychological wholeness, that episode shines. It illustrates the Jungian notion that our darker impulses are integral to who we are. Your decision to leave your cult is also a decision to embrace your dark side and become fully whole again. After years of sledgehammering yourself with denial, this might be the hardest transition. Because to other split-off people, your humanity represents everything they're still running away from.

Important caveat: in Jungian psychology, "evil" and the "dark side" are metaphors representing the unconscious "shadow-self." But these metaphors also describe fundamental aspects of evolved behavior. Along with cooperation, traits like violence and self-preservation helped humans become Earth's apex predator. The shadow also contains repressed positive traits, such as creativity, sexuality, or spontaneity. These traits are typically repressed by individuals and society to promote conformity and form stable communities. But they haven't disappeared. The more they're denied, the more unpredictable they become. Jung suggested that unacknowledged elements of the shadow can manifest in harmful ways, such as through projection, neuroses, or aggression, leading to destructive behavior when they are not integrated into conscious awareness.[6]

Have you ever wondered why highly religious and spiritual people are hypersensitive to "negative energy?" Why they are perturbed about any symbolism they consider dark or satanic? Why even mild displays of anger send some people into a tizzy? Why others can't manage to keep their minds out of other people's bedrooms? Why concerned parents are ready to burn children's books that discuss history and sexuality in honest terms? These are unwelcome reminders that resonate with the dark, angry, or sexual aspects of themselves they've been trying to sledgehammer out of existence. Their pain is self-inflicted. Like the good half of Captain Kirk, they've rendered themselves unfit for command.

So be prepared. When you take back your power and embrace your whole self, you'll trigger those who are still repressing theirs. You're not just challenging cult doctrine, you're challenging the repressed shadow-selves of everyone around you. When they attack you, recognize they're not at war with you—they're at war with themselves. You're just a messenger, reminding them of their own non-resolution. And messengers get shot.

I came across a Darth Vader meme around 2012 that read, "The Dark Side Is With You Always."[7] I wasn't drawn to it for the imperial propaganda or the allure of a villain who massacred Jedi children and destroyed Alderaan. Instead, it's an important reminder that like Anakin Skywalker, we all retain the capacity for evil. I made it into a poster—and I keep it hanging on my wall so I can't forget.

Shadow repression isn't a problem confined to extremist cults. Most people are trapped by simplistic notions of good and evil and the harmful just-world fallacy. They accept that evil lurks in the world and recognize complex TV characters like Tony Soprano, Walter White, Dexter Morgan, or Don Draper. But they fail to see it within themselves. Instead, they project their repressed darkness onto outsiders, different cultures, or imaginary demons. This delusion perpetuates fear, division, and scapegoating. If the idea of having a dark side disturbs you, ask yourself what valuable qualities you might be suppressing. What parts of yourself could you embrace to become more complete, powerful and authentic?

If you're splitting off parts of yourself, how can you be a fully realized adult? How can you avoid hiding behind a cult leader who promises to save you from yourself? Repressing your dark side fosters dependence on external authority to manage the parts of yourself you refuse to integrate—while shadow integration gives you tools to develop autonomy. Achieving Kohlberg's stage 6 of moral development isn't just about ethical framing—it requires recognizing that, as Alexander Solzhenitsyn said, "The line dividing good and evil cuts through the heart of every human being. And who is willing to destroy a piece of his own heart?"[8]

Embracing your dark side isn't psychobabble, nor is it about justifying crimes or evil acts. It's about developing a relationship with parts of yourself you've denied. Like the whole Captain Kirk, you want to harness your killer instinct to make yourself more responsible, effective, and decisive. You want that dark side *on your side*.

Shadow repression explains why so many American Christians joined the MAGA cult led by the non-believing, amoral Donald Trump. It's not just about banning abortion, shutting down immigration, or enhancing Christian privilege. While they want those things, there's a deeper issue: Christian doctrine is based on the false duality of human good and evil. Archetypes like God vs. devil, heaven vs. hell, sin vs. salvation make it hard for Christians—MAGA or otherwise—to integrate their shadow selves. Many remain locked in a constant struggle, forever looking outward for enemies to fight instead of reconciling with their own darker nature.

Traditional American Christian values encourage love, forgiveness, generosity, piety, restraint, honesty, and selflessness. Yet Christians often split off their hatred, greed, envy, pride, violence, lust, and deceit, projecting these traits onto the devil through the concept of "sin," much as my cult externalized evil through figures like the Dweller. This projection enables widespread denial that good Christians are capable of evil acts. Hannah Arendt's concept of "the banality of evil" is relevant here. In describing Adolf Eichmann, Arendt pointed out that he was not a sociopath or Nazi fanatic, but an ordinary person who followed orders without critical thought. Similarly, Christian repression of darker traits fosters moral disengagement and a refusal to acknowledge capacity for harm.

As Arendt observed:
> The trouble with Eichmann was precisely that so many were like him, and that the many were neither perverted nor sadistic, that they were, and still are, terribly and terrifyingly normal. From the viewpoint of our legal institutions and of our moral standards of judgment, this normality was much more terrifying than all the atrocities put together.[9]

Arendt's insight into the banality of evil reveals how moral nihilism and spiritual pride, rooted in Christianity's good-vs.-evil dichotomy, have paved the way for American Christianity's devolution into hateful Christian Nationalism.[10] Enter Donald Trump, a modern messianic figure who invites people's split-off dark sides to come out and play. The vulgar, pugnacious Trump, much like the darker Kirk, thrives on raw power and unleashed impulses—traits that resonate far more deeply with split-off Christians than their professed Jesus. That is, unless you count the straight, white, gun-toting MAGA-Jesus, who bears more of a resemblance to Darth Vader than any humble Son of God.

MAGA-Jesus says, "I came not to bring peace, but a sword." —Matthew 10:34-36 KJV

This is why Trump-thumping nationalist denominations are growing[11] while liberal Christian traditions are secularizing.[12] Compassionate Christians are appalled[13] by the decline in values but miss the deeper problem: the false good-vs.-evil dichotomy at the core of their doctrine. America's religious landscape is imploding as long-simmering tensions erupt, driven by a widespread dearth of psychological wholeness.

Were Christian values ever reliably decent? Consider the party realignment following the Civil Rights Act of 1964. Southern Democrats, known as Dixiecrats, were remnants of the pro-slavery Confederacy, staunch supporters of segregation and Jim Crow laws. After Lyndon Johnson signed the Civil Rights Act, most Dixiecrats fled to the Republican Party, aligning with a conservative base that included many evangelical Christians. Historically, both Dixiecrats and later establishment Republicans preached family values while engaging in behavior that starkly contradicted them.

In the pre-Civil War period, many Christians were abolitionists, driven by their faith to fight slavery. At the same time, many Southern Christians actively participated in and defended slavery, citing Biblical justification.[14] This dual legacy underscores the lack of moral unity within Christianity on questions of human rights. Long before Trump, right-wing religious leaders were embroiled in scandals involving systemic sexual misconduct, financial corruption, and hypocrisy. Preaching piety and restraint, they were often guilty of abuses that contradicted their own teachings. Widespread patterns of abuse and institutional cover-ups have further exposed the disconnect between doctrine and practices.[15] This raises grave questions about the efficacy of Christian values, especially when their champions fail to uphold the principles they claim to represent.

Trump disdains such hypocrisy, saying the quiet parts out loud. He engages in open corruption, adultery, and authoritarianism, destroys the rule of law, and tried to overturn a democratic election in 2020. Shadow-repressed people loved him for it. Unlike hypocritical Christian leaders, Trump flaunts his dark side, enabling his supporters' deceit, misogyny, racism, and hatred. It's the key to his ugly charisma. The day after he was sworn in for his second term, Episcopal Bishop Mariann Edgar Budde urged him to show "mercy" to immigrants and LGBTQ+ people. Instead of engaging in self-reflection, he lashed out—calling her a "Radical Left hard line Trump hater."[16] Trump's embrace of his shadow is pathological, exploiting his followers' repression rather than encouraging self-honesty. True shadow-acceptance is not about indulging harmful impulses—but rather recognizing them as part of human nature while redirecting them in service of better values.

More generally, Trump divides Americans into "killers" and "losers." That is to say, predators vs. prey, which is Hitleresque. In a basic, reductive way, he is correct. Like all human beings, Americans have always been killers. The dark side of our nation has always been with us, and we could never have fixed what we refused to see. Trump's behavior serves as a stark warning: when our savagery takes over completely—instead of integrating with our better natures—it can only lead to catastrophe.

Instead of keeping a lid on the split-off dark side of our national psyche with the kinder, gentler pretenses of yesteryear, we're now seeing the volcanic venting of long-repressed hatreds. The denial of human nature—enforced by Christian denominations including my cult—was bound to fail. Without integration, the repressed shadow will always reassert itself. If it hadn't been triggered by Trump, there would have been some other catalyst. Integration of America's collective shadow requires national introspection and cultural honesty. Reckoning with our history of violence, racism, and exploitation—rather than denying it—creates the space for wholeness. Absent that, the villain behind the villain that may end American democracy is the long-term force of shadow-repression that led so many people to flock to MAGA Christian Nationalism—as an avenue of toxic liberation for their dark sides.

---

[1] My Ascended Masters. (2024). Decree 20.07: *The Judgment Call: They shall not pass by Jesus Christ*. Retrieved from https://www.myascendedmasters.org/2024/decree-20-07-the-judgment-call-they-shall-not-pass-by-jesus-christ/

[2] Summit Lighthouse. (2024). Decree 20.09: *I cast out the dweller on the threshold by Jesus Christ*. Retrieved from https://summitlighthouse.nl/20-09-i-cast-out-the-dweller-on-the-threshold-by-jesus-christ/

[3] The concept of transmuting darkness with the Violet Flame is a spiritual practice associated with the teachings of the Ascended Masters, particularly in the I AM Movement and the Church Universal and Triumphant. The Violet Flame is believed to be a high-frequency spiritual energy that can transmute negative energies and karma into positive, harmonious conditions. This practice is often associated with the Ascended Master Saint Germain.
Prophet, E. C. (1998). *The creative power of sound: Affirmations to create, heal and transform*. Summit University Press.
Prophet, M. L., & Prophet, E. C. (2004). *The science of the spoken word*. Summit University Press.
Booth, A. (2003). *The masters and their retreats*. Summit University Press.

[4] In Western New Age spirituality, the seven chakras are viewed as energy centers that span from the base of the spine to the crown of the head, encompassing the Root (Muladhara), Sacral (Svadhishthana), Solar Plexus (Manipura), Heart (Anahata), Throat (Vishuddha), Third Eye (Ajna), and Crown (Sahasrara) chakras. This system reflects a dichotomy between the "upper" chakras, associated with higher consciousness, and the "lower" chakras, linked to basic human instincts and emotions. The Heart Chakra serves as a bridge between these two realms. This perspective can sometimes lead to an imbalanced focus on spiritual transcendence at the expense of addressing physical and emotional needs.
Judith, A. (2004). *Eastern body, western mind: Psychology and the chakra system as a path to the self*. Celestial Arts.

[5] *The enemy within*. (1966). *Star Trek: The Original Series* (Season 1, Episode 5). NBC.

[6] Jung discusses the shadow and how repressing it can lead to unpredictable consequences. Specifically,

see his discussion of the shadow and its integration in Chapter 2, "Ego and the Shadow."
Jung, C. G. (1959). *Aion: Researches into the phenomenology of the self* (R. F. C. Hull, Trans.). In *The collected works of C. G. Jung* (Vol. 9, Part 2). Princeton University Press. (Original work published 1951)
[7] Oskoui & Oskoui. (n.d.). Designs. Retrieved from https://society6.com/oskouioskoui/designs
[8] Solzhenitsyn, A. (1973). *The Gulag Archipelago*. Harper & Row.
[9] Arendt, H. (1963). *Eichmann in Jerusalem: A report on the banality of evil* (p. 276). Viking Press.
[10] Wikipedia contributors. (n.d.). *Christian nationalism*. In Wikipedia. Retrieved from https://en.wikipedia.org/wiki/Christian_nationalism
[11] Gallup data shows a growing divide between Americans identifying with conservative religious traditions and those associated with liberal Protestant denominations. Membership in conservative religious traditions has increased moderately, rising from 38.9% in 2016 to 41.3% currently, while membership in liberal traditions has dropped more sharply from 16.9% to 13.8%. Gallup. (2022). Religion. Retrieved from https://news.gallup.com/poll/1690/religion.aspx
[12] "Liberal Protestants have seen a much steeper decline in their ranks, with many shifting to no religious affiliation, a trend that has doubled over the past few decades." Burge, R. (2021). *The nones: Where they came from, who they are, and where they are going*. Fortress Press.
[13] Several religious leaders have criticized the alignment of Christianity with nationalism and right-wing politics.
Pavlovitz, J. (2020). *Stuff that needs to be said: Boldly saying what's right in a world gone wrong*. Chalice Press.
Schenck, R. (2018). *Once militantly anti-abortion, evangelical minister now lives 'with regret'*. Retrieved from https://www.npr.org/transcripts/628000131
Westfall, S. (2020, February 25). *Religious right defector Frank Schaeffer takes on pro-Trump evangelicals and abortion alike*. Newsweek. Retrieved from https://www.newsweek.com/religious-right-defector-frank-schaeffer-takes-pro-trump-evangelicals-abortion-alike-1488650
Kratzer, C. (2021, January 19). *Essentials for dealing with Christian Trump supporters*. Chris Kratzer. Retrieved from https://chriskratzer.com/essentials-dealing-christian-trump-supporters/
[14] Genesis 9:25–27: Often cited to argue that the descendants of Ham (interpreted as Africans) were cursed to servitude.
Ephesians 6:5: "Slaves, obey your earthly masters with respect and fear, and with sincerity of heart, just as you would obey Christ."
Colossians 3:22: "Slaves, obey your earthly masters in everything; and do it, not only when their eye is on you and to curry their favor, but with sincerity of heart and reverence for the Lord."
1 Timothy 6:1: "Let all who are under a yoke as slaves regard their own masters as worthy of all honor, so that the name of God and the teaching may not be reviled."
[15] *The Houston Chronicle's* 2019 investigation revealed "hundreds of sexual abuse cases involving Southern Baptist ministers and volunteers" spanning over two decades (Tedesco, Downen, & Mellnick, 2019). A *Fort Worth Star-Telegram* editorial in 2022 highlighted a disturbing pattern of abuse, cover-up, and denial within Southern Baptist churches, documenting over 700 victims of sexual misconduct since 1998 (Fort Worth Star-Telegram Editorial Board, 2022). Additionally, a 2022 report by Guidepost Solutions found that leaders of the Southern Baptist Convention mishandled allegations of sexual abuse and mistreated survivors (Guidepost Solutions, 2022). High-profile cases involving figures like Jerry Falwell Jr. and Ravi Zacharias have brought further attention to the issue, and blogs like *Joe My God* regularly highlight new allegations and scandals involving anti-LGBTQ rhetoric coupled with sexual misconduct (Jervis, n.d.).
Tedesco, J., Downen, R., & Mellnick, T. (2019, February 10). *Abuse of faith: Southern Baptist sexual abuse spreads as leaders resist reforms*. Houston Chronicle. Retrieved from https://www.houstonchronicle.com/news/investigations/article/Southern-Baptist-sexual-abuse-spreads-as-leaders-13588038.php

Fort Worth Star-Telegram Editorial Board. (2022, May 25). *Southern Baptists fell into same-old awful pattern on sex crimes: Abuse, cover-up, denial. Fort Worth Star-Telegram.* Retrieved from https://www.star-telegram.com/opinion/editorials/article261745562.html

Guidepost Solutions. (2022). *Southern Baptist Convention sexual abuse report.* Retrieved from https://static1.squarespace.com/static/6108172d83d55d3c9db4dd67/t/628a9326312a4216a3c0679d/1653248810253/Guidepost+Solutions+Independent+Investigation+Report.pdf

Jervis, J. (n.d.). Joe My God. Retrieved August 14, 2024, from https://www.joemygod.com/

[16] Bennett, B. (2025, January 22). *'I am not going to apologize': The bishop who confronted Trump speaks out.* TIME. https://time.com/7209222/bishop-mariann-budde-trump/

CHAPTER TWENTY SIX

War!

The anticipation leading up to my cult's shelter drills in March, 1990 was excruciating—like waiting on pins and needles for the end of everything. We had put ourselves on a war footing. El Morya set an interim deadline of January 15, which then slipped to February 8, heightening our dread. But by February 9, major portions of our shelter complex remained unfinished, so Taylor Meadows blazed with construction lights, and it was crawling with vehicles and equipment through heavy snowstorms, 24/7.

Construction was grueling even under ideal conditions. Our blast-resistant design required culverts and tanks to be buried at least as deep as their diameter. Earth arching would ensure overpressure from a nuclear explosion transferred through surrounding soil rather than crushing the structures. The living pods and fuel tanks needed a minimum 13 feet of earth cover, the Deep-Cor shelter more than 20 feet. Backfilling had to be done in six-inch lifts compacted to specific density. But subzero temperatures and snow forced us to clear surfaces and heat the fill dirt to thaw ice—a procedure that violated best practices. With El Morya's hard deadlines, we believed we had no choice. War felt inevitable.

My mother's 1987 prophecy was more nuanced. She warned the US needed missile defenses and described our shelters as an insurance policy. Many in my cult embraced this interpretation: obedience to the prophecies might avert nuclear holocaust, since the "fallen ones" would have less reason to attack us. But by early 1990 Mother told a select few people in our inner circle that nuclear war could no longer be held back. She also claimed the Soviets were directly targeting our ranch. We hoped they would miss our shelters by at least half a mile, the minimum survivable distance according to our design criteria.

In *Prophet's Daughter*, Erin recalls the vague outlines of this "inner" war prophecy from her "altar work" with our mother a year earlier:

> This question was the outcome of a chain of logic Mother had been pursuing since the end of 1988 when she decided that it was America's karma to be punished. She had me write a lecture in which she quoted Matthew 25, where Jesus speaks of dividing the compassionate sheep from the selfish goats. The lecture went on to say that America had abdicated her destiny, specifically by hurting her own people through pollution, abortion, the Tuskegee syphilis experiments, etc., and by abandoning other peoples such as the Hungarians, Czechoslovakians, Tibetans, and pre-Holocaust Jewish refugees. It seemed clear to Mother that the "karmic cycle" had arrived when the goats in America should be punished for these sins. The members of our church were sheep and naturally did not deserve the same punishment. Therefore, now was the best time for war to occur since the maximum number of sheep would be saved.[1]

While I follow her logic, I struggle to accept that my mother's shift toward embracing the judgment of the United States was driven solely by metaphorical "sheep" or "goats" or the complex political sins she referenced in her lectures. These weren't strictly *America's* sins. Most were the sins of America's *power elite*—the same elite we often decreed against—involving secret government betrayals committed without popular approval.

My mother's millenarian persecution complex provides a more focused explanation: She was still furious at America's legal system for rejecting her as God's messenger during the Mull trial, exacerbated by her repeated losses on appeal.[2] She also chafed at ongoing negative press coverage, and the reliable opposition from neighbors that had plagued us in all our locations since the 1970s. Her anger extended to modern civilization itself: abortion, homosexuality, rock music, pornography, and more. She had failed to move Mount Everest in her preferred direction, and now it was judgment day.

I can't fathom her rationale. Either way, the idea reeks of *collective punishment*—a classic totalitarian trope. As God's messenger she apparently believed she had not only the divine authority, but the *moral and spiritual right* to make that decision—even if it meant condemning billions to death.[3]

Our first drill took place at midnight on the "Ides of March"—March 15, 1990. Though much work remained, the shelters were functional. The Deep-Cor shelter was packed with seven years' of food and supplies, along with our print, audio, and video archives. We stored a dozen Isuzu pickup trucks on a car transporter for post-reemergence use, plus two armored personnel carriers and even our 40-foot multimedia production truck inside the cavernous structure. Our life-support systems had passed their tests and were running on generator power.

Mol Heron Creek shelter site at approximately 2 a.m., February 9, 1990, as work proceeds during heavy snow. Taylor Meadows, Gardiner, Montana

That evening, buses brought staff to the site. Women, children, and the elderly saw the project for the first time, arriving on wheeled carts through futuristic four-foot tunnels to their living pods. Many were awestruck. The shelters were far more luxurious than most staff housing. My mother invited a radio host from New England to participate in our drill, and he later quipped, "It was high-tech—they took me into Star Wars." The only unfinished business was our septic drainfield: Sewer lines were stubbed out into a pit, functional if war occurred. But health codes forbade us from using our toilets and showers without permits. We weren't going to risk fines and a lawsuit. So hundreds of people used 5-gallon buckets to relieve themselves in close quarters, creating a nasty, stinking mess.

At ten minutes to midnight, we made final preparations, including disconnecting the batteries on our vehicles. Mother called me on my walkie-talkie and told me to order everyone inside. I barked her warning through a bullhorn, "Attention, all personnel! Get in the shelters now.

Whatever you're doing—it doesn't matter. Save yourselves!" After confirming everyone was inside, I climbed into shelter #3 and closed the hatch.

A glaring irony undermined the premise of our drill: My mother's husband Edward Francis was stuck in their home a mile away, immobilized by an ankle bracelet. It was a test of his faith, and he chose reason. He didn't take my mother's prophecy seriously enough to risk violating his probation. Our press spokesman Murray Steinman stayed with him "to be near the telephone," and for moral support. They played Monopoly while the rest of us cowered.[4]

Underground, we prayed all night, presumably to prevent the war. Obviously, no bombs fell. We proved we could get everyone in and out of the shelters without incident, but my mother seemed ill at ease. She insisted war was still coming. She and Erin formulated a new prophecy, declaring the need for a second drill. Her mood was so intense, I thought she might crack—which made me believe next time would be the real thing. We were scheduled to be in the shelters again with everything "buttoned up" by noon on March 26.

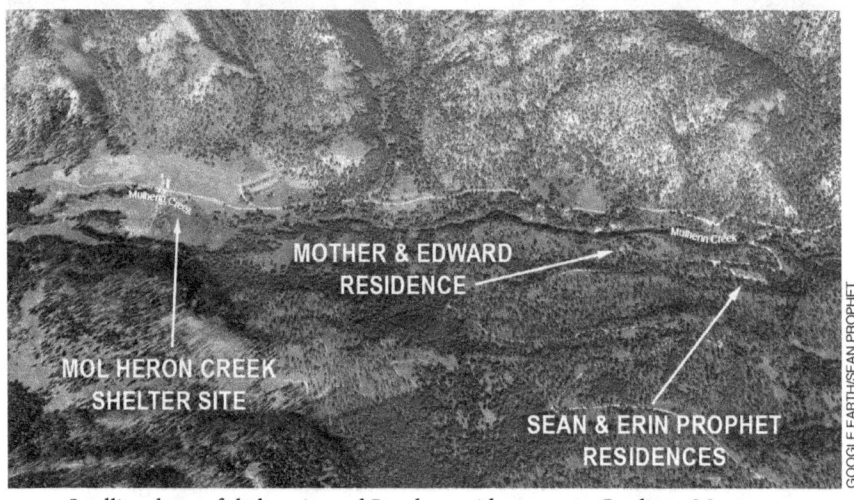

Satellite photo of shelter site and Prophet residences near Gardiner, Montana.

All our preparations were complete: stored food, deep wells that brought fresh water directly into the shelters, over half a million gallons of fuel, weapons, ham radios, and $5 million in gold. Edward had even secured $25,000 of freshly minted US coins in our vault, which he planned to use as an *ad hoc* currency after the war. Beyond our Mol Heron site, there were scores of operational shelters throughout the Paradise Valley which participated in our drills. These scattered bunkers held thousands of members who had spent the past two-and-a-half years preparing. Many of them had arrived from all over the world in recent weeks to hunker down during what mother had called a "danger period." This was the day she had been waiting for. The maximum number of "light bearers" were safe. She could now pull the trigger.

Early that morning, my mother, Erin, and I took a walk down the long gravel driveway outside her double-wide manufactured home, which was nestled on a forested terrace of Mol Heron Canyon about a mile from the shelter site. She got straight to the point: she needed our spiritual mantles to call for God's judgment on the United States. Erin described the scene in *Prophet's Daughter*:

> Mother asked Sean to join us in calling down the judgment. Believing in the power of our prayers, my brother took time to argue with her: Was this really God's will? Weren't there a lot of good people in the world? He could be stubborn but so could she. In the end, he agreed, and the three of us gave that prayer just hours before we descended into the shelters.[5]

I betrayed myself and all humanity. Standing in that serene forest on a crisp Montana morning, I prayed to God for a judgment that we suspected could lead to billions of deaths. The awful reality is this: At the time, I truly believed we held the power to launch nuclear war. I'm glad I protested, but "following orders" is no defense. It was a double-bind. I believed that to disobey my mother was to disobey God.

As Erin wrote, "We who believed we had unique influence with God accepted her suggestion that we use it for destruction. It was now convenient to our purposes for the whole world (or at least our civilization) to die."[6]

There's no doubt that if my mother had access to a nuclear launch button, she would have pushed it that day. That's how committed she was to the cold necessity of judgment. Not because she wanted to *personally* murder billions. Even then, I knew the scale of death she envisioned in her prophecies was an abstraction she just couldn't comprehend. Calling down judgment was clinical and detached. But the true horror of nuclear fire raining down on American, European and Russian cities—and the subsequent mass starvation of billions of helpless people—was a whole different matter. Despite her often fiery "guru" persona, I had seen her compassion for collective human suffering. She held a keen awareness of history and its implications. More than any other part of my cult story, this was a level of sheer madness that defies explanation.

With a political science degree from Boston University focused on Soviet foreign policy, along with her early work at the United Nations, my mother embodied a lifelong commitment to peace, justice, and diplomacy. She was horrified by unprovoked wars like the Soviet invasions of Hungary in 1956 and Afghanistan in 1979, and she was ambivalent about the US war in Vietnam, particularly our covert bombing campaigns in Laos and Cambodia. As a girl of seven, she visited London in 1946 and witnessed the aftermath of The Blitz, later reflecting, "I resolved I had to live my life and serve my nation and all the nations so that something as dreadful as this war could never happen again."[7]

But this deeply-rooted empathy clashed with her self-declared role as God's messenger. By 1990, this paradox forced a choice, and her empathy lost. As the instrument of *God's will*, she believed she had no choice but to act, regardless of consequence. That was the immense, blinding scale of her messianic ego.

In moral terms, if she believed she held the power to command God to destroy the world, there was no distinction between fervently praying to launch nuclear weapons and actually launching them. Perhaps a sliver: usually she prayed for her calls to be "adjusted according to the will of God." But that day, there was no request for mercy. Because she was confident she already knew God's will—which she confused with her own. The world had persecuted God's messenger, and for justice to be done, the world had to be destroyed. *I know this* because over my repeated objections, she demanded I pray to help her destroy it.

Absolute power corrupts absolutely, and it corrupted my family into an act of absolute inhumanity. This was our spiritual Jonestown moment, our fantasized Tokyo Subway Sarin attack—on a far grander scale. It underscores the mortal danger posed by cults lacking external accountability. What keeps messianic leaders from committing mass murder is mostly that they lack the power to do so. Given enough power at such time when they feel sufficiently persecuted, all messianic leaders will eventually push that button.

After our wicked prayer, my mother, Erin, and I made last-minute preparations. This time, our noon deadline allowed Edward and Murray to join us in the shelters—at least temporarily. Cars, trucks and buses streamed up Mol Heron Canyon as the logistics of shepherding 756 men, women, and children underground got into full swing once again.

Kathleen and our two boys got into our truck, and I loaded our bags. Nathaniel, less than a year old, was oblivious, while Christopher, nearly four, thought it was a grand adventure. He was excited and laughing as we rode the wheeled carts through the tunnel to shelter #3. Each of the six shelters, designed to comfortably house 126 occupants, had spacious bunks with private storage cabinets, but the central "hub"—a ten-by-twenty-five-foot assembly room—felt like a submarine. As more people arrived, they squeezed in to the crowded venue, some spilling into adjoining corridors.

Elizabeth Clare Prophet's driveway and former residence in Mol Heron Canyon, near Gardiner, Montana c. 2007. The foreground represents the approximate location where Sean, Erin, and Elizabeth Clare Prophet said their prayer for world judgment, on March 26, 1990.

My mother called the assembly to order and gave the same directive, which was broadcast via text message to the other five shelters: it was time to call for the judgment of the United States. People in shelter #3 were stoic and focused, some nodding in agreement, and no one objected. My mother explained that this war had been predicted by the "third secret" of the Fatima prophecy.[8] Though the Vatican had not disclosed the full contents, she speculated it foretold a "great war," aligning it with millenarian beliefs. She said the time had come to anchor that prophecy with intensive prayer. She also instructed people to wield ceremonial stainless-steel swords, which we believed could cut through negative energy and amplify our efforts. Despite the cramped quarters, some attempted to follow this ritual—their blades whooshing uncomfortably close.

A Shelter "hub" central assembly area, under construction c. 1989

Mother hand-wrote her interpretation of an appropriate Fatima prayer and had me type it up in the command center. I printed copies for our shelter and relayed it to the others. It began, "Beloved Mother Mary, Let the right arm of your Son Jesus Christ descend in vengeance for the evils continuing in the Earth!"

As the session intensified, my mother's voice grew louder, projecting into a deafening *kihap*: "BOLTS of blue lightning. BLAZE through. BIND the fallen ones." She used this vocal technique as a release of *fohat* (Theosophy's "concentrated fire"). Soon she was shouting, "ARCHANGEL MICHAEL, LET THE BOMBS DESCEND, LET THE BOMBS DESCEND, LET THE BOMBS DESCEND!" I had been taught since childhood that Archangel Michael was a protector, not an angel of death. But I also knew him as the cosmic "dispenser of existence," pouring out the vials of the seven last plagues from Revelation. I had reluctantly co-signed the earlier prayer, but this felt horrifying. Remaining mostly silent and unenthusiastic, I wondered how others justified it? Weren't they thinking of their families out in the world, or the billions of other innocent people? Erin later wrote about a truck driver, David Svoboda, who refused to participate, and left the shelter that day. I had always respected the man, and his courage haunts me. If only more of us had followed his lead.

As day wore into night in our windowless enclave, there was no felt sense of time. The prayer session dragged on endlessly. Edward left by 6 pm, to comply with his home detention. Eventually, Erin's disgust became clear as she retreated to her bunk. My mother's intensity waned, and the crowd in the hub thinned. By 9 or 10 pm, I went to the command center for a radio check. The chatter was ordinary. I reported back to my mother: "All quiet. No bombs." She retired to her cabin, and I did the same. Kathleen and the boys were fast asleep. The eerie subterranean silence was broken only by the soft hum of the HVAC system.

The next morning, we climbed out of the shelter and saw the sun shining on the snow-capped Sportsman's Peak. The sky had never looked bluer, and the air crackled with normalcy. I was ecstatic—and relieved—that our prophecy and prayers had failed. It felt like a rebirth. Kathleen took the boys home. She hadn't believed the prophecy, later reflecting, "It really wasn't that much of a far cry from what your mother had been doing all along, calling for the judgment of humanity. I was used to it. I believed in the serious nature of our preparations. I saw that it gave you purpose. But this idea that there would be a war and then everything would be good afterward and we'd start over was inconceivable to me."

Book Cover: *The Vials of the Seven Last Plagues* showing an artist's rendering of Archangel Michael pouring out his vials.[9]

I walked to the food trailer and grabbed a quick breakfast of coffee and buttered toast. People were chatting as if it was any other day. But I felt a gathering, simmering rage at my mother, stronger than anything I had felt during our many confrontations. Because her world betrayal was worse than anything I had seen her commit before. What had I just been a part of? We bet everything on the end of civilization—and then tried to make it happen. We were all-in on a nuclear war we had first feared, and then somehow decided we *wanted*? My mother left herself no escape from her prophecies, and she dragged all of us down with her.

I was wracked with guilt. As I write these words 35 years later, I'm still in shock over the depravity. It weighs on my conscience as the most outrageous betrayal of human values I've ever committed. Thank the stars and the galaxies that our delusions had no power, and that we were merely another link in the long chain of the world's messianic lunatics.

Illustration of Elizabeth Clare Prophet and her devotees in our shelter calling for the judgment of the United States of America.

There's still a lot of denial around our momentous ethical breach. On the surface, the drills were meant to test our shelter systems, but it was our humanity that was on trial. Erin wrote, "After the drill, few people spoke about what we had done: praying for the destruction of our country. Some tried to say that it never happened, but others could not forget." To this day, my cult maintains that the shelters were nothing more than a prudent insurance policy. They'll never admit that we prayed for global genocide. But everyone who was there knows damn well what we did.

If I had to pick a moment that sealed my determination to leave my cult, that was it. How dare she? I wish I had driven home and started packing. But it took years for my little seed of rage to finally grow large enough to break through my cult programming. Just a few weeks after that final shelter drill, the fuel spill rendered our shelters useless. I suspect my mother wouldn't have been so eager for the bombs to fall in May rather than March. It's a stark demonstration of the shadow-side of survival prepping, which breaks the social contract. It's too easy to say "let the world burn" when you're sitting in a state-of-the-art bunker, on a pile of food and fuel. On April 8, my mother's 51st birthday, El Morya gave a self-serving dictation saying, "Your very preparedness itself has forestalled certain events." It was the ultimate in bogus framing, and I knew it. And everyone who was in those prayer sessions in the shelters should have known it.

Every experience in my young life of 25 years now funneled down to this single, inexplicable moment. Everything I had worked for and thought I stood for hung in the balance. How was I to reconcile my mother's divine authority with her ethical collapse or her stupefying lack of foresight? The failure of her prophecy wasn't merely the impotence of our call for world judgment, or the positively shocking absence of nuclear war. My mother—as the messenger of God—hadn't been able to foresee the preventable and wholly incompetent follies of our ill-fated gun deal, nor the devastating fuel spill. Some "prophet" she was! Her hubris persisted despite repeated warnings from Edward, engineers, and staff about rushing the fuel-tank installation. Those were the bleakest of days. The scale of our moral, legal, and logistical fuckup was beyond conception. We hadn't just prepared for an apocalypse—we had willed it into being.

---

[1] Prophet, E. (2009). *Prophet's daughter: My life with Elizabeth Clare Prophet inside the Church Universal and Triumphant* (p. 228). The Lyons Press.

[2] The California Court of Appeal affirmed the Mull verdict in April 1989. The U.S. Supreme Court declined to review the case in January 1990.

[3] A study published in *Physics Today* in 2008 modeled the potential environmental and human consequences of a large-scale nuclear war. The study explored scenarios involving the use of thousands of nuclear warheads and concluded that such a conflict could result in the deaths of up to 2 billion people globally. The catastrophic outcomes would stem from the combined effects of blast, fires, radiation, and particularly the long-term impact of nuclear winter, which would severely disrupt global agriculture and lead to mass starvation.
Toon, O. B., Robock, A., & Turco, R. P. (2008). Environmental consequences of nuclear war. *Physics Today*, 61(12), 37-42. https://doi.org/10.1063/1.3047679

[4] Prophet, E. (2009). *Prophet's daughter: My life with Elizabeth Clare Prophet inside the Church Universal and Triumphant* (p. 222). The Lyons Press.

[5] Prophet, E. (2009). *Prophet's daughter: My life with Elizabeth Clare Prophet inside the Church Universal and Triumphant* (p. 229). The Lyons Press.

[6] Prophet, E. (2009). *Prophet's daughter: My life with Elizabeth Clare Prophet inside the Church Universal and Triumphant*. The Lyons Press.

[7] Prophet, E. C. (2009). *Preparation for my mission* (T. Prophet & E. L. Prophet, Eds.). Summit University Press. p. 56.

[8] The Fatima Prophecy refers to a series of apparitions and messages that three shepherd children—Lúcia Santos and her cousins, Francisco and Jacinta Marto—reported receiving from the Virgin Mary in Fatima, Portugal, in 1917. The prophecy is divided into three parts, or "secrets," with the third secret being the most controversial and often linked to predictions of nuclear war. The Third Secret of Fatima was written down by Sister Lúcia in 1944 and sealed in an envelope, which was later sent to the Vatican. It remained undisclosed until 2000 when the Vatican released its official interpretation. The secret is described as a vision of an angel with a flaming sword, the suffering of various religious figures, and

a city in ruins. Some interpretations of the Third Secret suggest that it predicts a global catastrophe, potentially a nuclear war. These interpretations often focus on the "city in ruins" and the "flaming sword" as symbols of nuclear destruction. Some also believe that the secret warns of the consequences of humanity's sins and the need for repentance and conversion to avoid a catastrophic event.

Vatican. (2000). *The message of Fatima*. Retrieved from https://www.vatican.va/roman_curia/congregations/cfaith/documents/rc_con_cfaith_doc_20000626_message-fatima_en.html

[9] Prophet, E. C. (2009). *Vials of the seven last plagues*. Summit University Press.

CHAPTER TWENTY SEVEN

Exit, Stage Left

The shelter project left my cult in shambles, and members financially ruined. Throughout construction, I had asked myself tough questions about how we would survive if there was no nuclear war. The organization and its members bought millions of dollars in supplies and equipment on credit. Bills for shelter contract labor were coming due. Our vast expenditures had committed us to world destruction just as deeply as my mother's prayer. Even selling the $5 million in gold didn't cover our obligations. Many long-time staff became disillusioned, and some left.

During the shelter project, I had co-managed the Engineering and Planning department. With the shelters *kaput* except for the fuel cleanup, there was nothing left for me to do. So I transferred back to the audio-video department. We returned to our former schedule of TV and audio production, as mother resumed lecturing and planning new conferences and tours. She held an intensive seminar that summer on time management, handing out Franklin Day Planners to staff.

The self-help guru Napoleon Hill, author of the 1937 book *Think and Grow Rich*,[1] became a cornerstone of my mother's recovery plan. Hill's principles of positive thinking and "Master Mind" language aligned closely with our cult theology, which was rooted in New Thought and the Law of Attraction. To that end, our print shop cloned what later became the Franklin-Covey Day Planner system, and we mass-duplicated cassette tapes of Hyrum Smith's training program—pirating the time-management products instead of buying them. The only reason printing the planners was cheaper was that we didn't pay competitive wages. It was a vicious cycle, emblemat-

Audio Video department staff painting our building at Ranch Headquarters, 1991

ic of my cult's algorithm which devalued staff labor.

Nevertheless, the program inspired new projects, including religious music and choir recordings. Kathleen spearheaded a push to develop early-childhood educational products, called "bit kits," introducing advanced topics like chemistry and history. Our theater troupe, the Paradise Players, performed regular shows at the Ranch Kitchen restaurant and recorded two cowboy-themed folk albums that Will Adams and I enjoyed producing. In board meetings, we discussed repurposing shelter shop facilities for commercial furniture production—a project that never came to fruition. We spruced up Ranch Headquarters, hosted a July conference, and revisited long-term development plans for better facilities and staff housing. There was new optimism in the summer and fall of 1990. My cult might get back on its feet, after all.

I began to consider staying. Mother asked our department to research satellite distribution for our public-access cable shows, and I envisioned building a world-class TV and sound studio. I proposed producing multimedia educational programming for the home-school market. I was planning a future where we became more sensible and commercial, and less of a cult. By 1991, we were more focused on outreach and community improvements. People relaxed and had summer fun: fishing, rafting, hiking, playing volleyball. We repainted the audio-video building, held barbecues, and took family road trips. I thought we might finally have a shot at normalcy.

But it was a pipe dream. My cult was entrenched in its dysfunction. One point I kept stressing in board meetings was that our structure was hurting us. Staff salaries were still $150 per month, and no one had any tangible incentive to invest in our community. Without fundamental change, our hard work and ideas would go to waste. No one on staff would ever achieve financial stability, be able to afford a home, take real vacations, or send their kids to college. And we still didn't have health insurance.

It was communism without benefits, "from each according to their abilities—screw their needs." Staff often gave their life savings to the community

Will Adams and Sean Prophet grill for the AV department crew, 1991

but left with nothing. I suggested attracting new money and talent by offering refundable shares, starting profitable businesses under our corporate umbrella, and building staff equity. That was heresy. My cult was never going to decentralize power or share its wealth. We were used to treating staff as fodder. All my attempts at reform fell on the board's deaf ears. Because I was challenging all the corrupt principles that had kept us in business for 30 years, along with the social theory of "Why Strict Churches Are Strong."

In 1991, a post-shelter IRS audit forced one change: profit-making departments like the restaurant and general store were spun off into a for-profit entity. We revived Lanello Reserves, Inc., the company that went bust in the '70s over trading silver futures, and I became president of its three-member board. My cult salary in the early '90s was $500 per month, with an extra $100 per month for my role at Lanello Reserves. Kathleen earned $150 per month. Housing, food, and utilities were provided, along with our vehicles. But with three kids and all their expenses, we still couldn't save.

I read *Wealth Without Risk* by Charles Givens,[2] which emphasized that household risk of bankruptcy from healthcare expenses was greater than any other potential casualty. Kathleen and I paid cash for our children's births and pediatric care, but we had been lucky to avoid hospital bills. When I asked my mother for a $100 per month raise to buy health insurance, she invoked selective scruples, insisting it would be wrong to make an exception for her family—despite routinely bending rules in our favor when it suited her. "Don't worry," she said, "if anything happens, I'll make sure you're taken care of." Her dismissiveness stung—was I supposed to beg her for money despite my executive roles? I asked, "Are we ever going to address staff health insurance?" I already knew the answer. We didn't produce enough value.

Doctrinal tensions were also brewing. Kathleen began to explore Carl Jung's shadow integration concepts, particularly through *Women Who Run with the Wolves* by Clarissa Pinkola Estés.[3] That's when Kathleen and I first began to realize that my cult's fixation on casting out The Dweller on the Threshold was a form of damaging shadow-repression. We learned that anger and the dark side can be valuable tools, so we never said the Dweller decree again. I recalled my mom's "cat woman" hallucination and something clicked: Our spiritual path was about splitting-off valuable animal instincts, particularly regarding anger and sexuality.

A confrontation brought this to a head. Kathleen's co-workers betrayed her in a meeting with my mother. "These were people who I thought were my closest friends." Kathleen said. Now they wanted her fired.

She leaped to her feet, shouting, "You're lying! *You* said I was a 'master teacher'!"

She pointed at another, "*You* told me I was a great person to work with," and then told my mother, "I will not apologize. I embrace my anger. These are violations and lies!"

And then she stormed out of the room.

My mother was unprepared for Kathleen's outburst, because no one was allowed to express anger in front of the guru. No one was allowed to express anger—except the guru. But strangely, instead of yelling, Mother asked Kathleen meekly, "Do you really believe it's okay to embrace your rage?" Then she requested a copy of *Women Who Run with the Wolves*. I thought it was promising that she was curious, but her narcissism ran too deep for real change. Her theology revolved around denying the shadow side, sledgehammering it with "Dweller" calls and transmuting it with the "Violet Flame." Her sociopathic prayer during the shelter drill revealed just how much of her own dark side she had split off.

I was proud of Kathleen for not taking anyone's shit. Years later she reflected, "In the beginning when I first met your mom, I used to shake when I saw her. I couldn't even talk to her. By the end, there I was, challenging her in front of her staff."

I was about to have a different sort of doctrinal revelation. Recall El

Morya's near-beer ban, which became pivotal to my cult exit. I learned of it from Erin's husband Michael Reed while we were building redwood decks on our neighboring houses in Mol Heron Canyon. It was exhausting work in the summer heat, so we always had a six-pack of cold near-beer in the fridge.

One day the two of us were taking a break and he said to me, "You know, Erin told me that some people are complaining about the near-beer. I think she's going to take it to the altar." Meaning, Erin and my mother would ask El Morya what to do.

I thought, "Oh, come on. There's less alcohol in near-beer than in orange juice. What's there to decide?"

I joked to Michael, "If El Morya gets that petty, I'm not sure this is the right place for me." We both laughed.

In *Prophet's Daughter*, Erin wrote about several conservative mothers who had complained that the "vibration" of beer bottles in community trash cans made them uneasy. It wasn't the environment they wanted for their kids. As a result of their letter, El Morya gave a fiery denouncement of near-beer in a dictation and banned it from our community. I was sitting in the front row. The moment he broached the subject, I flashed on my conversation with Michael Reed. El Morya's words felt like daggers. This was pure politics! She and Erin had actually gone and done it!

Sean Prophet visits his former home in Mol Heron Canyon near Gardiner, Montana and the deck where Michael Reed revealed the existence of the near-beer complaint letter, 2007

Afterward, I burst into my mother's sacristy and demanded, "How could you?"

Without hesitation, she said, "Sean, I had to. There were empty beer bottles piling up in trash cans all over the place. It's just not appropriate for a spiritual community."

Holy fuck! Did she realize what she was admitting? She had used El Morya's authority to take sides in a petty community dispute. She tried to soften the blow but made things much worse by adding, "I don't mind if *you* want to drink near-beer."

The near-beer dictation and her response clarified several things: She was subordinate to meddlesome busybodies—the "Karens" of our community. She breezily embraced a double standard for me. She cracked down on yet another harmless pastime. Banning near-beer branded us as religious extremists, prioritizing appearance over substance. Once an edict from El Morya is released in a dictation, it becomes official cult scripture—irrevocable for all time.

I didn't care about the near-beer. Sure, I liked drinking it, but what shook me was the sheer cynicism of my mother's abuse of divine authority. When Lawrence Levy pointed at her in that Los Angeles courtroom and said, "Sitting right over there on that side is El Morya!" he nailed it. My mother *was* El Morya. More recently, Erin and my mother together were El Morya. They had learned nothing from the disastrous failure of their prophecies. I struggled to adjust to this fresh confirmation: there could be no further doubt my mother was a spiritual fraud, or that I was her pawn. My roles as cult vice-president and president of Lanello Reserves were empty titles. My mother and sister were corrupt.

Illustration of El Morya destroying a case of near-beer

Soon after, my mother, Kathleen, Erin and I were on an official visit to the cult's pre-primary school, located about five miles away from headquarters at the OTO Ranch. It was a children's performance and catered lunch just before a board meeting, where we planned to discuss educational priorities. My son Christopher and Erin's son Mark were both at the school. After the kids' presentation, we all sat down to eat lunch as a family. Shortly after we began, mother looked at her watch and said, "I should probably get going, I don't want to be late for the board meeting. You and Erin come along when you're finished." So about twenty minutes later, we finished eating, said goodbye to our kids, and drove to the meeting.

Erin and I walked into mother's office, where the board was assembled, and she growled at us. "Why are you two always late to meetings?" We both stared. I finally said, "You knew where we were, and you gave us permission to finish our lunch." She refused to see reason, insisting, "That's no excuse, you knew the time, and you just dawdled there with your kids. I'm sick of your lackadaisical attitudes!" Erin and I locked eyes in stunned silence as we sat down. Mother continued her diatribe, "I'm fining each of you five hundred dollars! And that goes for any board member who's ever late to a meeting again!" Had mother completely lost it? Erin and I bit our lips in feigned contrition, but I struggled not to burst out laughing. Was she *trying* to drive us both to quit? Neither of us ever paid our fines.

I was losing my relationship with my only living parent. And I still didn't have health insurance. So I did the only thing I could to protect my family: Without her approval, I convinced the other two members of the Lanello Reserves board to grant me the $100 per month raise I needed. It was early 1993, and I finally secured a health plan for Kathleen, the boys, and me.

Several months later, my mother found out and canceled my raise. I was livid. She ducked my calls for days. I knew I could always find her in our chapel. So I waited until she was leading a decree session. When she dismissed the service, I saw her surrounded by members clamoring for her attention. I had to wait my turn. She saw me and looked away, seeming to take extra time on purpose.

Finally I could wait no longer and pushed my way toward her. "We need to *talk*!" I said, "Do you want to do this *here*?"

She broke away from the crowd and headed to her sacristy. As soon as the door shut, I said firmly, "I hope you understand that by cutting off my health insurance, you're endangering my family."

"This is non-negotiable," she raged. "I won't have you making unilateral decisions."

I was seething, "You're making it impossible for me to work for you. You're leaving me with no options."

She put her hands on her hips and said I was "out of alignment" and needed to "change my vibration." In other words, submit. I had heard it all before. Then she launched into a litany of spiritual and actual punishments she had in store for me. My face burned as my vision narrowed, and I began to tune her out. It was like a film scene where the sound drops, a high-pitched whine takes over, and all I could see was her mouth moving in slow motion…

I bolted out of the sacristy, slamming the door on her mid-sentence, adrenaline surging. I jumped in my cult Suburban and tore up Mol Heron Canyon. At home, I threw on a jacket and stormed up the steep dirt road behind my house. This was our final showdown. I chanted affirmations in rhythm with my steps: "I will *not* give up. I will *not* submit to her. I *will* stand up for myself. I *will* take care of my family." The words became part of my breathing. Gradually I slowed my pace. My rage was replaced by calm. "*I can do this!*" I hiked two or three miles up the forested switchbacks, lost in thought.

I finally made it to the ridgeline, where I could see the wide vista of the southern Paradise Valley—breathtaking in every season. I stood and stared for a long moment, recognizing that my time in Montana would soon end. I would have to resign, pack, return to Los Angeles, find a job and a home, and rebuild my life. At age 29, with a family of five and a seven-year hole in my resume, it wouldn't be easy. But staying in my cult was mercifully no longer an option. With a new sense of purpose, I started back down the mountain.

MEMORANDUM

TO: Staff and Community members
FROM: Sean and Kathleen Prophet
DATE: September 23, 1993
RE: **Our Future Plans**

It is with ambivalence that we must tell you that we have reached a decision to leave our positions on staff. This decision has come after much soul searching and many sleepless nights.

We have a number of reasons for this decision, but it is chiefly a matter of doing what we believe to be best for ourselves and for our children. Each of us would like to pursue opportunities that are not available to us at the Ranch. For Sean, these have to do with career goals in sound and television, and for Kathleen in education. We would also like to see our children gain exposure to a wider range of American culture.

We both feel deeply sorry that we will not be able to directly participate in the realization of the worthy goals of the community. We continue to share these goals and hope that we will be able to make some contribution in the future.

Because of our positions of responsibility, this change will not be effective until the end of 1993. We had discussed our plans with a few close friends, and unfortunately the information began to spread. We are writing this memo at this early date so that you will hear the story "from the horse's mouth," and not from the rumor mill.

Both of us have much to accomplish in the next few months. For this reason, we would not like to comment further or discuss the circumstances surrounding our departure. We would appreciate it if you would allow us to complete our assignments without being compelled to do so.

We are appealing for your understanding of our hearts and our decision. We have both experienced a great deal of professional, personal, and spiritual growth during our time at the Ranch and we will certainly miss everyone a lot.

SCP/KAP:scp

I told Kathleen about defying my mother and said we should start planning to leave. I was nervous about her reaction, but Kathleen was way ahead of me. "You're a board member. These are her grandchildren. We should have health insurance. It's ridiculous." She had seen how my mother's behavior affected me. "This isn't working, it's obvious," she said. "Before, you had hope, thinking you might change things. She used to sort of listen to you. You gave it your all. Now, she's shut down. Plus, I don't want my kids going through elementary and high school here. Let's get out. It's time."

On September 23, 1993, Kathleen and I posted a memo in the commissary announcing our resignation, effective at year's end. We used the mildest language, avoiding mention of health insurance or our real reasons for leaving.

My mother accused us of sowing "division and criticism." It reminded me of Soviet tactics, where dissenters were labeled "hooligans" or "counter-revolutionaries" for expressing the smallest discontents. She had our memo removed.

Over the next three months, I wrapped up my remaining cult projects. One was an album of *kirtan*, or Bhajans to the Hindu deity Shiva. We recorded instrumental tracks at cult member Cole Braunley's home studio in Bozeman. He graciously hosted our percussionist Kerry and me for a week and contributed his skillful sympitar playing. We shared meals and a lot of friendly conversation.

Then he asked, "I hear that you're leaving the church. What brought that on?"

I replied, "Too many things to count. I really need to take care of my family and develop my career. I feel like I've done all I can do, and I don't really see a future for us here."

His face froze. He curled his lip disgustedly and said, "Well, so much for being the Buddha, then!"

And there it was, that classic dispensing of existence: You're either with us, or against us. You're either on The Path, or you're headed for the second death. Cole didn't see my humanity. He only saw my symbolic role as the "Buddha" and whatever that meant to him. I was embracing full integration of my light and dark side, entering the adult world of independence and risk. I was making my prison break, while he remained trapped in the cult's thought reform and shadow repression. I don't say this condescendingly. I knew Cole was a kind and decent man, but at the time, he was caught up in idolatry of my spiritual titles and roles. I feel compassion for anyone in that mentality, because of how difficult it was for me to escape.

Cult inmates often react badly to anyone leaving, especially someone from the inner circle. It forces the question of why someone would reject what they've made their central focus. They almost never take the lesson—choosing character assassination instead. The next three months felt like Klingon discommendation, as members turned their backs and folded their arms, one by one.[4] I was Jonathan Livingston Seagull, branded an *outcast*.[5] None of it had anything to do with me. I had become a symbol of betrayal, which catalyzed a flare-up of members' psychological war with themselves.

By December, Kathleen and I were still wracked with internal conflict. She was facing a crisis of faith and purpose, grappling with the sunk costs of her 12 years in the cult and the sudden death of her father, Gust Mattson. "I was questioning everything, life, death, the Ascended Masters, and I was really fucking lost," she said. "I no longer had a center point of any organizing principle. You needed to go back to Los Angeles for your career, but I suddenly wanted to be closer to my family, and I was drawn to more wild places like Vancouver Island. For you, that was out of the question, so I was already struggling."

I was waffling, too. I asked Kathleen, "What if we don't have to leave? What if I can get my mother to agree to health insurance?"

"Do what you have to, but I can't stay," she said.

It was the first time in our nearly ten years of marriage she had given me an ultimatum—would she leave me? She later reflected, "I couldn't stay there with you hating life. More than anything else I was trying to shock you into making the decision that you were on the edge of making. For me, all the good things about the community were already gone. It was nothing like the great adventure with cool people that I thought it would be. Many of my friends had left."

Kathleen's clarity is precisely what I needed. I negotiated a severance deal with the cult board and Lanello Reserves. My mother stayed out of it. They gave us about $6,000 and a 10-year-old rust-colored Subaru sedan from the motor pool worth about $2,500. And *that* was the cult-VIP treatment. Most people walked away with nothing.

I still had to face my mother one last time. She invited us to stop by her house at Ranch Headquarters for sandwiches and coffee on our way out.

After a week of packing our house into a 26-foot U-Haul, it was time to roll. Kathleen and the boys were in the car, and I drove the truck down Mol Heron Creek Road for the last time. Despite everything, I realized I would miss the Ranch. It was the kind of blustery socked-in January day that only Montana's mountain valleys can deliver. But it was spectacular—the most unique and isolated place I've ever lived.

My mother was warm, playing with the kids and wishing us the best as we ate our sandwiches. It was bittersweet. Then she pulled me aside into the kitchen and became the Ram once again.

She accused me of treating her badly, making karma, and ignoring the looming threat of nuclear war. Then, narrowing her eyes, she said, "If you want a place in our shelters, you'll need to bend the knee in chelaship and change your vibration!" It was the most direct dispensing of existence I had ever heard: *comply or die*.

I called her bluff, saying "I would rather die than spend another minute in a bomb shelter with you." It was the declaration of independence I hadn't been able to make seven years earlier. For the first time, I understood: no one can foretell the future.

I saw the crippling weight of her pain—and the personal cost of her obsession with doom. In another universe, she might have said, "Sean, I'm deeply hurt that you're leaving. I wish I knew how to make things right." In this universe, her fate was to be the unflinching guru, holding the line for El Morya, at any price. The messenger of God couldn't indulge her maternal feelings—which she buried under the scars caused by decades of her totalitarian rule. Perhaps her imperial pique was intensified by her early-onset Alzheimer's, a progression Erin documented in *Prophet's Daughter*.

If I had known about her illness—and had more maturity—I might have reversed roles and cautioned her, "Mother, please stop. I know it's not easy for you to see me go. But don't threaten me. I want a relationship with my *mother*, not the messenger of God. I want to forgive you. But I have to resolve my own life before I'm in a position to do that. I love you, and I'll miss you."

But I could only feel rage. To the bitter end, my mother was still the Queen. Treating me as spitefully as she had ever treated any of her subjects. I could not forgive her forcing me to choose between her and my *existence*. I needed my bravado to stay whole. So I stormed out of her kitchen and said to my family, "Come on, let's go," my lips pursed into a terse silence.

I started the U-Haul truck, released the brake, and slowly let out the clutch. The engine shuddered to a halt. *Fuck!* The brakes were frozen. At long last, would this cult *ever* let us go? It took an hour to locate one of our mechanics, who thawed the brakes with a propane torch. It was nearly dark when our caravan finally headed north on US 89, through near white-out conditions, into the blizzard of our unknown future.

---

[1] Hill, N. (1937). *Think and grow rich*. The Ralston Society.
[2] Givens, C. J. (1991). *Wealth without risk*. Simon & Schuster.
[3] Estés, C. P. (1992). *Women who run with the wolves: Myths and stories of the wild woman archetype*. Ballantine Books.
[4] Memory Alpha contributors. (n.d.). *Discommendation*. In *Memory Alpha, the Star Trek Wiki*. Retrieved from https://memory-alpha.fandom.com/wiki/Discommendation
[5] *Jonathan Livingston Seagull*, a novel by Richard Bach, tells the story of a seagull who is cast out from his flock for his unorthodox desire to perfect the art of flight rather than conform to the mundane life of scavenging for food. This seagull, Jonathan, driven by his passion and determination, embarks on a spiritual journey of self-discovery and enlightenment, proving that being true to one's self is more fulfilling than adhering to the expectations of others. Despite being branded an outcast, Jonathan's quest leads him to attain higher levels of existence and understanding, ultimately serving as an inspiration to those who hear his story.
Bach, R. (1970). *Jonathan Livingston Seagull*. Macmillan.

CHAPTER TWENTY EIGHT

Healing: Beyond Deprogramming

I don't recall how old I was when I first heard the term "deprogramming," but it was a dirty word. It meant "bad people" kidnapping our members and filling their heads with "lies" about my cult. From an early age there was a clear separation between "us" and the "outside world." My childhood home La Tourelle, our five-acre cult redoubt with its stone perimeter wall, stood out like a medieval relic in the wealthy Broadmoor neighborhood of Colorado Springs. One girl in my first-grade class told me the walls of my home were "made of poop." Which succinctly distilled our local reputation.

A few years later, I watched fundamentalist Christians protest my mother's public lectures, baffled by their accusations that we were satanic. When we moved in 1976 to the former campus of Nazarene University on Howard Street in Pasadena, the protests became a regular occurrence. "What are they so upset about?" I wondered. We didn't worship Satan. We believed in Christianity, worshiped Jesus, and prayed against satanic influences.

Then came November 18, 1978—the Jonestown massacre. Suddenly, every article about my cult mentioned Jonestown. Concerned parents of our members raised alarms, and that generated extensive press coverage. Beginning in 1979, my mother was featured in several Los Angeles newspapers, including the *Times* and the *Herald Examiner*. On April 2, 1980, stung by the negative publicity, we bought a full-page ad in the *Times* to "set the record straight."

My mother's crowning publicity "achievement" was landing a profile in the January 1979 issue of *Hustler* magazine, titled "Elizabeth Clare Prophet—Synthetic Guru of the '80s," by Gar Smith. She passed out xeroxed copies of the article—with the racy pictures and cartoons redacted—urging everyone to decree for the "judgment" of the author. It was shocking to me that my mother had appeared in a skin magazine. Even though it was thoroughly researched, the article was scathing and rife with sexual innuendo. Playing on her formal spiritual title of "Mother," Smith referred to our members as "Mombies."

Los Angeles Times, Full Page Advertisement, April 2, 1980

By then, my curiosity about the outside world had grown to the point where I was forced to wonder: *Was there something really wrong with us—or was the world wrong for persecuting us?* Both couldn't be true. I was genuinely upset that a national publication like *Hustler* was accusing my own mother of being a scam artist. But it also confirmed in my mind that my cult was growing large and important enough to warrant that level of attention, even though it was negative. And it planted a seed of doubt: Why would Gar Smith write such awful things? Could they be even a little bit true? I couldn't see how at the time—but I did wonder—what was I *not* seeing?

Religious freedom is meaningless unless it protects people's right to be wrong—and even to make drastic life changes based on those beliefs. The right to peaceably assemble means nothing if it doesn't protect people's right to form cults if they wish, and to worship gods of their understanding.

Still, parents can't help but worry. How should they feel when a child abandons college, a career, or a prospective spouse, cuts ties with friends and family, and becomes a different person? Both religious freedom and parents' rights to safeguard their adult children must be respected. But what happens when those imperatives clash?

Marilyn Malek of Duarte, California launched an intense publicity campaign after her son Bill joined my cult. She tried and failed to deprogram him. Like many ex-members I've interviewed, Bill had stumbled into my cult by chance: In 1978, he was a senior studying environmental engineering at UC Santa Barbara. After seeing one of our posters in a laundromat, he began attending our meetings. He showed his mother our literature, including the cult's code of conduct. "As soon as he came home with the church's code of conduct handbook, I knew that something was terribly wrong," said Mrs. Malek.[1] I can't blame her for feeling that way—draconian rules are a well-known hallmark of abusive cults. Bill claimed his mother "refused to accept him as an adult" and used falsehoods in a "personal vendetta" against my cult. The two faced off on a *60 Minutes* episode that aired in March 1982.[2]

I knew Bill Malek as "William" and worked with him on the shelter project for two years. A talented engineer, he designed the shelter's mechanical systems, including HVAC and a waste-heat recovery system. I remember him as smart and rational, but he chose not to apply his rational skepticism to our cult dogma. I felt a kinship with him in that choice. While solving engineering problems,

Cartoon of Elizabeth Clare Prophet, *Hustler* magazine, January 1979,

Marilyn Malek holds a picture of her son Bill Malek—
Monrovia News-Post February 28, 1982

it was easy to forget we were in a cult at all.

That's the dilemma posed by deprogramming. I sympathize with both William Malek and his mother. Marilyn had valid concerns about her son's disconcerting path, and William was equally justified in defending his right to live as he chose. But Marilyn crossed the line into criminality when she had her son kidnapped and held in a hotel against his will for days. Mrs. Malek now says she regrets the decision, and I should hope so. There's no life circumstance that justifies a parent kidnapping an adult child. It's false imprisonment, a universally condemned act.

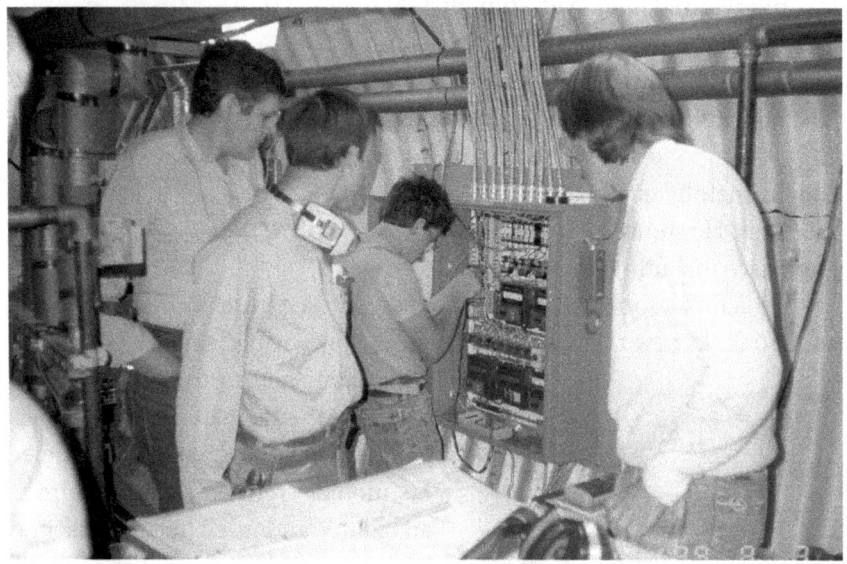

William Malek (right) inspects a mechanical system control panel in a shelter generator room under construction, August 1989

Coercive deprogramming is an anti-thought-reform methodology which originated with Theodore (Ted) Roosevelt Patrick, Jr., a controversial figure of the late 20th century. Patrick, who died in 2021 at age 90, was a high school dropout from Chattanooga, Tennessee. Starting in 1971, he conducted more than 1,600 anti-cult interventions, often using kidnapping and false imprisonment. His methods led to misdemeanor and felony charges, lawsuits, and jail time. While imprisoned in the early 1980s, he even deprogrammed fellow inmates.[3]

Patrick targeted not only destructive cults but individuals outside clear cult contexts. He tried to convince[4] a woman to divorce her husband, another to leave[5] her lesbian partner, and a third to re-enter[6] a conservative

Amish sect she had left. Motivated by money more than genuine cult concerns, these were grotesque civil rights violations that tarnish Patrick's legacy as a defender of freedom of thought.

Another coercive deprogrammer, former New York City cop Galen Kelly, operated on the East Coast from the 1970s to the 1990s. Kelly served 16 months in prison in 1992 for felony misprision related to a kidnapping case involving the Circle of Friends cult, although he was exonerated of the kidnapping itself.[7] By the 1990s, most deprogrammers abandoned such illegal methods and rebranded as exit counselors.

While cults are reprehensible, coercive deprogramming is indefensible. Survivors describe it as traumatic—a profound betrayal by their parents. Forced interventions rarely lead to self-reflection. It's the parable of the sun and the wind: coercive deprogramming is the wind that makes someone cling tighter to their "cloak," while the gentle persuasion of exit counseling, like the sun, encourages voluntary change.

At least some good came out of Ted Patrick's work, in spite of his terrible methods. He founded the Citizens Freedom Foundation (CFF) in 1971, which became the Cult Awareness Network (CAN) in 1978. The Cult Awareness Network (CAN) brought together a who's who of anti-cult activism, including Rick Alan Ross, Margaret Singer, Steven Hassan, Janja Lalich, Joe Szimhart, Cynthia Kisser, Dr. Louis Jolyon West, Patricia Ryan, Ron Loomis, and many others.[8] Ginni Thomas, wife of Supreme Court Justice Clarence Thomas, was also active in the anti-cult movement, later becoming notorious for her ties to QAnon.[9]

CAN was a sharp critic of the Church of Scientology. And Scientology sued the group dozens of times. Most cases were dismissed or reached summary judgments. CAN alleged that Scientology used lawfare to drain its resources, and countersued in *Cult Awareness Network v. Church of Scientology International, Inc.* The countersuit was dismissed, and the dismissal was upheld by the Illinois Supreme Court in 1997.

CAN was eventually forced into bankruptcy, by Jason Scott and the Life Tabernacle Church, who won a $5 million judgment in September 1995 over the kidnapping and attempted deprogramming of Scott by Rick Alan Ross.[10] CAN was not implicated in the kidnapping, but it did provide a referral to Ross. Critics argued that the jury might have targeted CAN due to its deeper pockets, given the high punitive damages awarded. After declaring bankruptcy, the organization disbanded, and in November 1996,

CAN's name, phone number, records, and files were purchased by Scientology-affiliated lawyer Steven L. Hayes. This was part of a broader move by Scientology to control the narrative surrounding the now-defunct organization. For several years, Scientology used the name, phone number and logo of CAN to direct anti-cult inquiries to its own offices.

CAN's referrals, and the tacit approval of coercive tactics that implies, was a fatal strategic flaw. I'm conflicted. Kidnapping adults is counterproductive, illegal, and damaging. Yet, at what point does a cult become so dangerous that outside intervention is justified? How can voluntary self-harm in the name of religion be curtailed? Should religious freedom shield cults from accountability for fraud and abuse? How do we reconcile Scientology's shutdown of CAN with the principle of free speech? Should wealthy religious organizations be able to use lawfare to silence critics—while enjoying First Amendment protection and tax exemptions? These are big ethical gray zones. I wish I had satisfactory answers. The tension between sincerely-held beliefs and fraud, as seen in *United States v. Ballard*, continues to trouble me, as does the broader conflict between sanctity and harm I've explored in this book.

CAN wasn't the only anti-cult organization. The International Cultic Studies Association (ICSA) was founded as the American Family Foundation (AFF) in 1979, and it remains active. ICSA offers publications, webinars, and annual conferences, and disavows coercive deprogramming:[11]

> An old model of forcibly deprogramming persons from controversial ideological organizations has given way to progressive, non-coercive models that emphasize dialogue within voluntary 'exit counseling' settings.[12]

Many exit counselors now follow a code of ethics.

> A subscribing consultant must inform the concerned party (or parties) that should a client be prevented from leaving the site of the consultation or physically restrained in any manner (unless legally sanctioned permission has been obtained), the consultant will terminate the consultation immediately.[13]

Why exit counseling? Why intervene in the lives of adults? Why not just let people believe what they want to believe? The most important reason is that everyone is born into a social fabric of family, friends and community, and cults tend to rip them out of that fabric. Those who join cults leave behind people who love them and miss them. They are making compromises to their personal boundaries—under intense peer pressure—that they would be unlikely to make on their own.

The goal of an exit counseling is to expose the member to an understanding of the manipulative nature of thought reform. And to demonstrate the falsity of the cult's beliefs, whatever they may be. Cult members will have gradually agreed to more restrictive conditions and will have given up more of their autonomy while believing they've done so of their own free will. The cult member may be psychologically unfit to leave on their own. Being reminded that they have a family who still loves them enough to stage an intervention might be the factor that tips the scale. Regardless of circumstance, any cult member is incurring steep opportunity costs by rejecting other life options. Each year that passes, it becomes harder to leave, and fewer choices remain. Too many cult members become lifers.

To explore current methodologies, I interviewed professional exit counselor Joe Szimhart, a veteran of over 500 interventions since 1980—about 30 of which involved coercion. Szimhart, born in 1947 to Hungarian refugees in a displaced-persons camp in Germany, immigrated to Pennsylvania in 1951. Educated in Catholic schools, he earned a BA in Fine Arts from the University of Dayton and later studied painting at the Pennsylvania Academy of Fine Arts. He lived in Santa Fe, New Mexico, from 1975 to 1993 and authored two books: *Santa Fe, Bill Tate, and Me: How an Artist Became a Cult Interventionist* (2019)[14] and *Mushroom Satori: The Cult Diary* (2013).[15] For the past 25 years, he's been a crisis caseworker at a psychiatric hospital.

Szimhart was successful in over 60 percent of cases but now conducts only about three interventions per year. In 2024, he knew of just four or five other people in the United States still offering exit counseling.[16] Even without coercion, initiating contact can involve trickery or extraordinary measures, which would breach ethical guidelines for licensed therapists.

It's a conundrum. Mental health professionals are well-suited to exit counseling, but their strict ethical codes prevent unsolicited approaches. Exceptions like the duty to warn, court-ordered evaluations, or public health emergencies do not apply to cult interventions. And certainly not if the cult member was tricked into showing up.

Traditional trauma-focused therapy is essential for post-cult recovery. But it's no help for people still in cults who haven't sought treatment. The best hope for concerned family members is either talking directly to their loved ones or finding someone still offering exit counseling services. In lieu of that, I'll present Szimhart's methodology in the hope that it might help people exit cults on their own, and perhaps provide a reference guide for families thinking about staging their own compassionate interventions.

For about a year-and-a-half in the late 1970s, Szimhart was a member of my cult. Disillusioned, he left and began exit counseling our members. That put him near the top of our enemies list, ensuring that he was on the receiving end of thousands of hours of decrees for his "judgment."

One of Szimhart's subjects in the late 1980s was Elise Farnell. Her mother lured her to a remote cabin near Salyer, California. After Szimhart arrived, Farnell agreed to speak with him. The situation grew complicated when it emerged that she was engaged to another cult member. Szimhart advised canceling the intervention, which almost never works without the significant other present. Farnell's mother wanted to press on.

Though Szimhart wasn't holding Farnell against her will, her mother threatened to sequester her "as long as it takes"—possibly even abducting her "to Europe"—a story she told on the Oprah Winfrey show. She became frightened, climbed out a bathroom window and plunged into the nearby Trinity River. Szimhart dove in after her, was swept away by the current, and narrowly survived hypothermia after being rescued. Farnell struggled to cross the river and also nearly lost her life. After she made it to the other side and called 911, police returned her to the cabin. Despite her mother's threats, she returned to my cult. The incident became the centerpiece of an anti-deprogramming seminar we held soon after. In 1989, I officiated Farnell's marriage. The couple stayed a few more years, leaving shortly before I did in the early 1990s.

I was angry with Szimhart, believing he had kidnapped my friend. I didn't realize that so far as he knew it was a voluntary exit counseling. Years later, I met up with him online and finally learned the truth. We've stayed in touch, and he's been kind enough to appear on my podcast twice, providing commentary on cults and Theosophy.

"Deprogramming is a misnomer," Szimhart said. "No one gets taken out of a cult like a prison break. That was the big mistake the government made at Waco with the Branch Davidians. Clients call me because someone has cut off communication after joining a cult or extremist group. I tell them, 'I can't get them out. I can offer information, and they can choose their way out. I'm just giving them choices.'"

Szimhart described making arrangements with the family, finding a neutral location, and getting the subject to show up. Ideally, several family members are present, both for moral support and to attend to food and physical comforts, since interventions can last three or four days. It can also help to have an ex-member present, someone the subject knows and trusts.

The subject must see the exit counselor as non-threatening. Szimhart cautioned, "The key is to gain rapport, get them comfortable with the idea that I understand what they're involved in. That I know their language. It's also very important that someone in the family still has a relationship with the subject, that there's a good bond that I can work with. I need leverage, or I can't do anything."

"Who the hell am I?" Szimhart asked. "I've got to sell myself. One of the first things I always said was, 'Well, I have an art career. I've adopted two daughters.' No one's afraid of an artist. I explain that I've studied comparative religions. I ask, 'Is it okay if we talk about the group you're involved in?' I always give the person power over me. I always say, 'If there's any point where you don't want to talk about this, if you want me to leave, I'll be out the door.'"

I was struck by Szimhart's cautious approach and ethical code. Unlike coercive deprogrammers, he maintains dignity, respect, and open-hearted communication. Balancing strategy with compassion to breach the walls of non-communication with familial love.

Szimhart continued, "One subject finally said, 'OK, I'm leaving the group, I'm quitting.' And the dad started crying, because this was six years he's been struggling with this, and he said, 'I don't know how you did that, you're a magician,' and I said, 'Listen, I couldn't have done a damn thing if you didn't love your son.'"

Successful exit counseling requires knowing why the subject is in the cult. What needs does the cult fulfill? Can you help them find better ways of meeting them? Are you willing to learn about cult dogma, to get inside the mind of your family member? Has the cult made testable claims that can be debunked? What do you know about thought reform?

Szimhart described four factors:

"It's a self-sealing social system. The first thing is called a *transcendent attraction*. The Army's transcendent attraction is you can become fulfilled defending your country. In Ascended Master groups, the ascension is the transcendent goal, because it solves the problem of death. In martial arts cults, they claim they can teach superhuman Kung Fu powers, you know, harm without touch.

"The second step is, you need an authority figure to make sense of the transcendent goal, to condense it for you. Your life goes into orbit around this force. 24/7 in your mind, psychologically, you're orbiting this group. The slogans, the chants, at breakfast, at lunch, in the clothes you wear, the rituals assigned by the leader.

"The third thing is what Robert Lifton brings up, the 'dispensing of existence.' It's the final of his eight themes of thought reform. What is real, and what is not? Who is saved, and who is not? Who is worthy of life, and who is not? What is superior, and what is inferior? Who are the Gnostics, and who are the Hylics? Hylics, meaning mud-people, the majority of the Earth, the unenlightened.

"The fourth hurdle is dealing with exit costs. People leave these groups with a variety of issues, depending on how long they were in. The leader might have married them off to a real jerk, and now they gotta go through a divorce. They might have invested hundreds of thousands of dollars they can't get back. Twenty-five percent of them—maybe more—actually have psychological problems like an anxiety disorder. The cult was containing an inner anxiety that now comes back."

I recognized my own struggles in Szimhart's four stages. Getting out of cult psychosis is a convoluted journey, and it's difficult to put those pieces together after the fact. The interview was a bit like therapy, as I reviewed my mental states from 30 years ago. It's knowledge I could have used, back then.

I pressed him, "Walk me through it—give it to me step-by-step." He emphasized that each person has different triggers, interests, and needs that are fulfilled by the cult. His job is to find opportunities where the subject may still be open to thinking outside the cult milieu, to exploring contradictions.

That knowledge helped him counsel a woman who was introduced to my cult through Baird Spalding's *Life and Teachings of the Masters of the Far East*.[17] Szimhart explained, "Someone lent her that book, and that got her on the Ascended Master path. So I pointed out that Spalding was not in India. That book is a fabrication! He didn't get to India until the 1930s, and he wrote that book in the late 1920s. She said, 'How do you know that?' I said, there was an eyewitness that traveled with him in India the first time. When confronted, Spalding said, 'Well, I traveled in my astral body,' and she had thought he was there physically. That one fact was enough for her to dismiss the whole damn thing."

The Spalding story reminded me of a spiritual fraud my mother committed—with my help. Saint Germain gave a dictation in which he said that abortions were acceptable only in cases of "rape, incest, or to save the life of the mother." Mother said she wanted to change the dictation to say that the only exception was "to save the life of the mother." That's one hell of a consequential edit! There were about a dozen recordings, in various audio and video formats. So Will Adams and I had to collect the tapes, make the edits on our digital editing system, and then re-record every tape—destroying the originals. All to create an even stricter cult scripture about abortion. I cynically did my job—even though I knew it was wrong. After the near-beer fiasco, I knew the dictations just said whatever she wanted to say.

Spiritual fraud is a predictable feature of any form of channeling. The reason why cons work, and why people fall for cults, isn't because their minds are weak. It's because the cult or con had the key that unlocked their specific mental lock at a specific time. And that involves the prospective member or mark being willing to absorb a particular falsehood that lowers their defenses. So evidence of fraud like Baird Spalding's fabrication or our tape-doctoring can be effective.

Every revealed truth has the same questionable provenance. From Joseph Smith's golden tablets[18] to Guy Ballard's tall tales of magic elixirs and hollow mountains in *Unveiled Mysteries*[19] to my mother's dictations—all rely on human sources.

I asked Szimhart how to neutralize each of the four factors, starting with the transcendent attraction. The power of transcendence is *ineffability*—it can't be pinned down. Vague notions and imaginary worlds benefit from a charismatic presentation involving a form of hypnosis, or what Szimhart calls "influence communication."

Szimhart continued, "Probably ninety percent of what your mother did is hypnosis. She had a captive audience. They're already interested in Ascended Masters before they even see her, so they're in that milieu. She's got that audience by the balls because they think the ascension is real. Not everyone agrees with everything she's saying, but they pick up bits and pieces they agree with. Audiences weed themselves out if they don't agree with anything at all.

"Stage hypnotists try to educate people. They'll say, 'Everybody lock your fingers together, I'm going to put you on an elevator, we're going down now.' Then they make a suggestion that when we come back up you won't be able to unlock your fingers. Ten to fifteen percent won't be able to unlock their fingers. Then he says, 'If your fingers are still locked, would you like to come up on stage?' People say yes. So now they've complied twice. Then he knows they're under the power of suggestion, and he can make them act like chickens. He can make them play invisible trombones. So this is what cult leaders do, they cast a wide net of the transcendent attraction, and some people stick around to go the next level."

"It's the same with altar calls. The foot-in-the-door: complying with small requests leads to agreeing to larger ones, reinforced by social pressure. First, people stand. Then they open hymnals, sing, and join others at the altar. By the time they're 'slain in the spirit,' they've complied so much they'll fake it rather than admit that the spirit didn't slay them."

I asked, "So it's a Darwinian self-selection?"

Szimhart replied, "Yes, and you can see this in the film *Captive Minds, Hypnosis and Beyond*. It's been used thousands of times by exit counselors.[20] You can see that everyone in the film is complying under the power of suggestion. You play the film, you pause and you talk, you stop and think."

"Sometimes people ask me at that point, 'Well what is the true religion?' And I say, 'You're asking me the question that got you in trouble in the first place.' A good philosopher knows how to ask good questions, it's not about the answers. What is heaven? Back up a little bit, learn how other cultures define the term, compare it with *nirvana*, take the time to relish this thing before you start swallowing the meal."

I said, "Well, nobody knows anything about heaven, right?"

Szimhart laughed, "But we know what other people say about it. Some things are more interesting, horrible, or aesthetically pleasing than others. We all die in doubt. I don't care who you are. You're going to die with some sense of 'I don't know what in the world is going on.' So I'm not going to doubt the whole abstraction. I'm going to doubt the way it's expressed, when people are going beyond testable reality. I'm trying to get people to think more about what's useful to them in their lives. What you can dismiss, you dismiss, like Baird Spalding was not in India. He's lying."

I asked, "So it's more about getting rid of certainty? Challenging pronouncements that go beyond testable reality?"

Szimhart replied, "Right, and that brings us to the second stage of orbiting the cult leader as an authority figure. When I worked with exit counseling members of Chung Moo Quan,[21] I used this film called *The Wave*, which was based on a real event that took place in 1967 in Palo Alto, California.[22] It was run by this teacher named Ron Jones. A two-week experiment in a high school. He tricked the kids. He put his class through a Nazi youth education program. Half the school ended up joining this thing. It caught on like wildfire. And then he had to call it off, and he was fired."

I watched the 2008 German version of *The Wave* and found it chilling. What's striking is the subtlety and speed with which authoritarianism takes root. The film begins with an anarchist teacher who puts students through a real-life version of autocracy to demonstrate its dangers. It starts with casual discipline and small rituals like marching, cultivating a sense of superiority over outsiders.[23] This transformation provides tangible benefits at each step. And it shows the mechanics of flipping the group's hive switch.

Such parallels between cults and Nazism are obvious. We might ask, "What's wrong with everyone wearing the same white shirt and jeans? Why not strengthen cooperation within a group by building pride in a strong identity? Isn't banding together to stop bullies a *good thing*?" Once more, cults and dictatorships can deliver benefits.

There's not much distance between getting high school students to wear white t-shirts and cults like Synanon or the Hare Krishnas convincing followers to shave their heads. The only difference is the degree of commitment. Totalitarian movements are built on the same subtle foundations, with simple hive-identity markers like swastikas, MAGA hats or flags. Exit counseling must flip the hive switch in reverse, encouraging people to value their individuality and family relationships. In population-scaled cults like MAGA, hive symbols are everywhere. Families, communities and even entire towns are all in it together. Which is a tough nut to crack, as history has proved.

Szimhart cautioned that authoritarian leaders get caught in their own traps. "You're becoming a guinea pig in your own experiment. Robert Lifton says that the engineers of totalism don't necessarily control the product. They create a monster, and they have to manage it. In spiritual cults, the leader claims he can dance, like that he can go to the Ascended realms and bring back special knowledge. Now people want the leader to dance. They want more information from El Morya or whoever, and now the leader is stuck. They have to keep coming up with something more exciting, so maybe they'll bring the Buddha into it, like your mother did."

In my cult, "progressive revelation" was central. People hung on every precise word of the dictations, which were published in written form in our *Pearls of Wisdom* newsletter. That's why I knew our dictation edit was so sinister—it would affect believers' lives in perpetuity. One popular feature of the *Pearls* was a section called "I AM the Witness," in which members gave testimonials of divine intervention.

It's as if my mother's certainty was a weakness that had to be overcome with social proof. These anecdotes were pivotal in maintaining my cult's "dispensing of existence." The implication of "I AM the Witness" was, "Look at how lost I would be if I didn't have the Ascended Masters!" It's a veiled threat—of no longer having access to the miraculous. Of being an ordinary human, forced to muddle your way through life.

If the teachings reflected universal "cosmic law," they would be accessible to anyone. Why the need for loyalty to a specific guru? Why did so many followers fear the messenger's wrath, as if her dismissal could jeopardize their souls? I asked Szimhart how he overcame such fear in his subjects. He said, "Generally, if I can show that the leader is human and has made some stupid errors, has lousy morals, or is poorly informed about what they claim, the fear just melts away. Some phobias take more time. For example, one young woman took maybe a year before she was comfortable wearing red or black clothing."

I laughed, recalling my experience with a black leather jacket. I came home to Montana from a trip to Los Angeles with a swanky soft bomber I had found on sale. It was exceptional, and the fit was perfect. I wore it everywhere. Then I got into a car accident. My mother blamed the jacket, "Sean, you can't wear that. It's an open door for dark forces, and you lost your protection as a result." I complained that the accident had nothing to do with my black jacket. She said, "You knew it was against our dress code and you bought it anyway." The next time I went to town, I sold my prize to a thrift shop. I remember feeling defeated at the pointless sacrifice. But how could I have been so naïve? There's no way she could allow her son, an ordained minister and vice-president, to walk around sporting a reminder that he didn't believe her teachings. That embarrassment had to be quashed like any other threat to her messengership.

What happened next was astonishing. She bought a jet-black mink coat. When I objected, she pulled back tufts of the fur to reveal that at the roots, it was dyed a dark shade of turquoise-green. If you squinted, you could just see the dark teal of the fur, in just the right light. But that damn coat was *black* to all appearances, and she knew it. If the color was OK for her, why did she take away mine?

Without fail, cult leaders engage in hypocrisy. Being able to set rules and not follow them is the crucial perk of power. But if such rules are spiritually valid, what would make the cult leader exempt? The only explanation is that the cult leader doesn't believe their own dogma—making them incapable of dispensing existence.

Szimhart connects dispensing existence to exit costs. Which tie the member's salvation to the cult's mission. "The exit cost is, well, this group and this mission is going to save the world, and if I leave, the mission will fail. The problem to me is, whether your particular version of reality—that you can't prove anyway—is being overvalued. Does it put you into an exclusive club? Does it mean that you look down on everybody else as being unable to ascend into heaven? You've now become very special. You've now become narcissistic."

I said, "So facing exit costs means realizing you're *not* special?"

"That's right," Szimhart said. "It's who you are in the real environment. The best revenge is recovery. And there will be a process of recovery. People need to know that they may have trouble sleeping, they may need medication, they might need to go to a psychiatrist or a doctor. But they will eventually get absorbed back into life. In many ways, learning to be a well-adjusted good citizen over time is the therapy. It has to be about being a good neighbor. If your religion is making you a bad neighbor, then you've got a bad religion."

---

[1] *Son's religious choice plunges local family into 'nightmare'.* (1982, February 28). *Monrovia News-Post*.

[2] "Both mother and son will air their views on a segment of *Sixty Minutes*, filmed last November and tentatively scheduled to be shown the first or second week in March." (Monrovia News-Post, February 28, 1982).

[3] Donovan, M. (Director). (2015). *Deprogrammed* [Film]. EyeSteelFilm.

[4] *Ted Patrick acquitted of abduction.* (1979, May 20). *Eugene Register-Guard*.

[5] *Cult opponent on trial in Ohio kidnapping case.* (1982, April 19). *The New York Times*.

[6] *Amish woman charges deprogramming.* (1990, November 30). *The Pittsburgh Press*.

[7] Gray, L. (1994, December 16). Closing the circle: *The last installment (maybe) in cult-buster Galen Kelly's war against the Circle of Friends*. *Washington City Paper*. Retrieved from https://washingtoncitypaper.com/article/289901/closing-the-circle/

[8] Rick Alan Ross founded the Cult Education Institute in 1996, originally known as the Ross Institute, to provide resources on cults and coercive groups (Cult Education Institute, n.d.). He authored *Cults Inside Out: How People Get In and Can Get Out* (2014), has performed over 500 interventions, consulted on thousands of cases, and served as an expert witness in numerous legal proceedings related to cult activities (Ross, 2014).

Margaret Singer co-authored *Cults in Our Midst* (1995) with Janja Lalich, exploring psychological coercion and cult influence (Singer & Lalich, 1995). She pioneered research on brainwashing and coercive persuasion, becoming a leading authority on the subject. Singer testified as an expert witness in several high-profile court cases, including those involving former members of Scientology and other controversial groups (Langone, 2006).

Steven Hassan, a former member of the Unification Church, was freed through deprogramming in 1976 (Hassan, 2015). He later founded the Freedom of Mind Resource Center (Freedom of Mind Resource Center, n.d.) and developed the BITE model of cult mind control, which outlines methods of behavioral, informational, thought, and emotional control used by coercive groups (Hassan, 2015). Hassan has assisted more than 1,000 individuals through exit counseling and detailed his experiences in *Combating Cult Mind Control* (Hassan, 2015).

Janja Lalich is a sociology professor specializing in indoctrination, cults, and coercive systems (California State University, Chico, n.d.). She authored *Bounded Choice: True Believers and Charismatic Cults* (2004), drawing from her experiences in the Democratic Workers Party, a Marxist-Leninist group (Lalich, 2004). Lalich has provided cult awareness training nationwide.

Joe Szimhart was a member of the Church Universal and Triumphant in the late 1970s but left after recognizing its cultic characteristics. Since 1980, he has worked as an exit counselor and cult interventionist, conducting interventions and consultations over the past three decades (Szimhart, n.d.). Szimhart has also authored several works, including *Mushroom Satori*, which explores themes of cult influence, psychological manipulation, and personal recovery (Szimhart, 2021). Retrieved from https://joeszimhart.com

Cynthia Kisser served as the Executive Director of the Cult Awareness Network (CAN) until its dissolution in 1996 following legal challenges from the Church of Scientology (Kent, 2001). Kisser played a key role in providing post-cult counseling resources and preventative education through CAN in Illinois (Ross, 1997). Retrieved from https://culteducation.com

Dr. Louis Jolyon West chaired the UCLA Department of Psychiatry and Biobehavioral Sciences beginning in 1969 and was a leading expert on psychological coercion and mind control (Marks, 1979). He published numerous studies on coercive persuasion and was consulted on high-profile cases, including that of Patty Hearst, where he examined the psychological effects of captivity and indoctrination (West & Martin, 1994). Retrieved from https://ucla.edu

Patricia Ryan, daughter of Congressman Leo Ryan who was killed during his visit to Jonestown in 1978, became a prominent anti-cult activist following her father's death (Kinsolving, 1979). She served as the first president of the original Cult Awareness Network (CAN), which provided support and resources for individuals affected by cults (Kent, 2001). Retrieved from https://culteducation.com

Ron Loomis was a president and Hall of Fame member of the Cult Awareness Network (CAN), presenting at over 120 campuses and traveling globally to share his expertise through workshops, panel discussions, and lectures (*Association of College Unions International*, 2020). He also served as the education director for the American Family Foundation and was a past president of the Association of College Unions International (ACUI), where he was recognized as a diversity advocate. Retrieved from https://acui.org/blog/2020/10/15/ron-loomis-past-acui-president-and-diversity-advocate-dies-at-82/

[9] Ginny Thomas, after leaving the Lifespring group—which she later described as exhibiting cult-like characteristics—joined the Cult Awareness Network (CAN) and became an active critic of controversial religious groups, participating in panels and organizing anti-cult workshops for congressional staffers in 1986 and 1988 (Farhi, 2022). Later, aligning with QAnon, Thomas was implicated in insurrection through text messages supporting the January 6, 2021, riot at the U.S. Capitol (Peters, 2022). Retrieved from Farhi, P. (2022, August 2). *Ginni Thomas: From anti-cult crusader to conservative firebrand*. The Washington Post. https://www.washingtonpost.com/; Peters, J. (2022, June 15). *Text messages reveal*

Ginni Thomas's role in insurrectionist rhetoric. The New York Times. https://www.nytimes.com/

[10] *Scott v. Ross*, Civil Action No. C93-2004WD, U.S. Dist. Ct. W.D. Wash. at Seattle (1995).

[11] International Cultic Studies Association. (n.d.). ICSA *home*. Retrieved from https://www.icsahome.com/

[12] Kent, S. A. (n.d.). Exit counseling and the decline of deprogramming. *International Cultic Studies Association*. Retrieved from https://articles1.icsahome.com/articles/exit-counseling-and-the-decline-of-deprogramming-kent

[13] Giambalvo. (n.d.). Ethical standards for thought reform. *International Cultic Studies Association*. Retrieved from https://articles1.icsahome.com/articles/ethical-standards-for-thought-reform-giambalvo

[14] Szimhart, J. (2019). *Santa Fe, Bill Tate, and me: How an artist became a cult interventionist*. CreateSpace Independent Publishing Platform

[15] Szimhart, J. (2013). *Mushroom Satori: The Cult Diary*. Aperture Press

[16] Ross, R. A. (n.d.). *Cult Education Institute*. Retrieved from https://culteducation.com/; Hassan, S. (n.d.). *Freedom of Mind Resource Center*. Retrieved from https://freedomofmind.com/; Ryan, P., & Kelly, J. (n.d.). *Cults 101 and Cult Mediation*. Retrieved from https://cultmediation.com/

[17] Spalding, Baird T. *Life and Teaching of the Masters of the Far East*. Devorss & Co, 1924

[18] Joseph Smith, founder of the Latter Day Saints movement, claimed that in 1827 he was directed by an angel named Moroni to a set of golden plates buried in a hill near his home in upstate New York. According to Smith, these plates contained the writings of ancient prophets from the Americas, which he translated into English to produce the Book of Mormon—a central scripture of the Latter Day Saints—and, upon completion of the translation, the plates were returned to the angel. *The Book of Mormon: Another Testament of Jesus Christ* (1830). Salt Lake City, UT: The Church of Jesus Christ of Latter-day Saints.

[19] Ballard, G. W. (1934). *Unveiled mysteries*. Saint Germain Press.

[20] Lasry, P. (Director). (1983). *Captive Minds: Hypnosis and Beyond* [Film]. National Film Board of Canada. https://youtu.be/WbURGXqpzNE

[21] Chung Moo Quan. (n.d.). *Chung Moo Quan, the Cult and The Con* [Video]. YouTube. https://youtu.be/OwxuyHh-52A

[22] Gansel, D. (Director). (2008). *The Wave* [Film]. Rat Pack Filmproduktion.

[23] This footnote contains SPOILERS for *The Wave* (Gansel, 2008): First the teacher established a casual air of discipline and conformity within the group—insisting that students maintain an erect posture and stand while speaking—while asking those who did not comply to leave, increasing the level of commitment. He then devised in-group bonding rituals, such as marching and a salute, created a uniform dress code, and introduced a status symbol in the form of a logo. Students promoted these symbols, established an external enemy—the punks and anarchists—and began flaunting their new norms, forming an exclusive club that attracted new recruits. The group came to the aid of individuals who were being bullied, creating a sense of empowerment and impunity. Later in the film, "traitors" within the group were exposed and delivered up for punishment. By the end, the teacher had absolute power with one exception: he could not control the fervent enthusiasm of his students, who did not want the experiment to end, effectively rendering him a prisoner of their expectations. The film concludes with a shooting, a suicide, and the arrest of the teacher (Gansel, D. [Director]., 2008, *The Wave* [Film]. Rat Pack Filmproduktion).

CHAPTER TWENTY NINE

A Clean Break?

There's no clean break from a cult. Like scar tissue from a broken bone, cults leave a mark. Breaking away resembles a divorce—sometimes literally becoming one. The initial euphoria of freedom can deceive you, masking the pain of separation and the work left to be done. Deeper layers of the cult's impact emerge as you build a new identity. You're not restoring who you were before the cult—that person is long gone.

It's Heraclitus' parable: You can't step into the same river twice, because you aren't the same person, and it's not the same river.[1] Like marriage, cults change you permanently. The longer you were involved and the higher your commitment, the more this is so. Rebuilding means incorporating the lessons you learned and reframing any cult traumas as necessary growth. If you cling to your cult-self, you risk returning (like I did after my Rumspringa)—or hopping over to another cult. Whether you feel fine or not, seek out a cult-aware trauma specialist as soon as you can afford it. The injuries of emotional trauma are deeper and less visible than you might think.

Important caveat: The same focus on purity and perfection that made you reject the larger world and retreat into your cult can also sabotage your recovery. The world you're re-entering is messy, and perfection is a myth. Focus on your core values and be satisfied when you stick to them imperfectly. Even those who see the perfection trap might chase impossible ideals or try to "win" therapy in a handful of sessions. Spoiler alert: I'm 30 years into therapy—sometimes regular, sometimes with long breaks. It's a personal journey that involves patience, self-care, and forgiving yourself for any setbacks. Some blocks vanish in a single session, but others require years of work.

Your efforts begin with reversing thought reform—through exit counseling if needed—finding better ethics and rejecting totalism, embracing dissent, deciding to leave, and handling the social fallout. Those are useful strategies to address non-violent cults—in an environment where you are physically unconstrained. That's most cults, mine included. While my cult endorsed the damaging practice of spanking children, we never saw serious systemic physical or sexual violence. But many aren't so fortunate.

Some cults cross into criminality, harming members, restraining them from leaving, or violently attacking ex-members and opponents. Not all cult violence is physical. There's social violence—shunning, shaming, intimidation, character assassination, rumor-mongering, legal harassment, stalking, or cyberstalking. Among the cruelest tactics is dividing families, weaponizing attachment to parents, spouses, or children.

Scientology wrote the playbook on hostile cults with its 1950s "fair game" policy—declaring that "suppressive persons" (anyone opposing them) can be "deprived of property or injured by any means.... tricked, sued, lied to, or destroyed." The policy includes dispensing existence through family "disconnection" and black propaganda campaigns to "destroy reputation or public belief in persons, companies, or nations." Though Hubbard officially canceled the term "fair game" in 1968 due to bad publicity, the behavior continues. Critics like Jenna Miscavige Hill, Leah Remini, and Mike Rinder have detailed these abuses in book-length exposés.[2]

Other cults make family disconnection central, defending against the cult's paranoia about "family mesmerism." This comes from the idea that the cult member should devote their life entirely to God (i.e. the cult), and family ties are a hindrance to their spiritual path. The goal is to monopolize the new recruit's time and resources. Ironically, some cults label *all families* as cults. Most families are absolutely not cults and can only be considered cults if they meet the strict qualifications of rigid authoritarian dominance, rejection of outside information, demand for total loyalty, and so on. Breaking up families without clear evidence of abuse is violence. Consider two examples:

Liana Shanti's online "Lemurian Mystery School" targets women combining pastel-QAnon conspirituality and alt-health regimes with virulent anti-vax and anti-trans rhetoric. Shanti offers expensive counseling sessions that often include baseless sexual abuse allegations against fathers and husbands—sight unseen. Like many cult leaders, she condemns psychotherapy. *The Daily Beast* describes her cult's impact:

> Many of these concerned ex-spouses and parents describe a similar pattern: A woman starts following Liana, their diet changes drastically, they begin giving themselves coffee enemas, and they go through a physical transformation. They become increasingly conspiratorial and isolated; they begin uncovering new memories of past abuse; they cut off their parents and separate from their husbands; they try to gain sole custody of their children and leave town.[3]

"Liana Shanti" is really Liane Wilson, a 51-year-old former timeshare salesperson who lives in Hawaii. Convicted of a felony in 2019 for concealing assets in a bankruptcy, Wilson was sentenced to five years' probation and barred from leaving the state. But she didn't need to travel to break up families, using her online counseling sessions to encourage women to flee across state lines—and even international borders—with their children. Wilson also promoted the wildly unhinged notion of vaccine contagion, encouraging members to disconnect from vaccinated family members. As if to check every box on the vindictive cult agenda, Wilson published the intimate confessions of members who fell out of favor—sometimes tagging their employers on social media.

White-nationalist, anarcho-capitalist, and "men's rights" podcaster Stefan Molyneux promotes a similar anti-family agenda targeting men. His Freedomain Radio community, widely regarded[4] as an online cult, advocates "deFOOing," severing ties with one's "family of origin." In 2008, Molyneux claimed, "Deep down I do not believe that there are any really good parents out there—the same way that I do not believe there were any really good doctors in the 10th century."[5] His dismissal of parenting as inherently flawed frames family as fundamentally toxic, encouraging total disconnection under the guise of self-improvement. He also denigrates therapy as "fraudulent" and mental illness as a "myth," undermining legitimate tools for addressing family issues.

Family relationships are rarely all good or all bad—there's almost always some positive glue holding even difficult families together. Moving out, relocating to another city, or setting firmer boundaries are valid steps short of cutting ties. For adult children who need to go "no contact," this should follow serious reflection and attempts at family therapy. Be extra wary of anyone claiming "special knowledge" and dismissing medical or psychological science.

Both Shanti and Molyneux exploit isolation, capitalizing on perfectionism to frame severing family ties as personal growth. But the manipulation of parent-child relationships reaches its most extreme form in the "troubled teen" industry—private prisons and wilderness camps masquerading as therapy for kids 11-17. Protected by political connections, claims of religious freedom, and deep pockets, these programs operate with minimal oversight.

There are two main types:

Reform schools sell "intense discipline," but they are actually prisons. While the abuse impacts teens, cult tactics are used to recruit their parents. Slick marketing convinces them to pay thousands of dollars per month to send their kids to "schools" they believe are staffed with skilled professional counselors. But most employ minimum-wage guards and no certified teachers or mental health professionals. There are virtually no academic classes. Using Synanon-based thought reform, these facilities isolate teens, breaking their will through beatings, torture, and solitary confinement. Food quality can be worse than adult prisons, and sexual abuse is common. *The Program: Cons, Cults, and Kidnapping* (Netflix, 2023)[6] explores the Academy at Ivy Ridge.

The "wilderness therapy" model employs similar punitive tactics, forcing kids into extreme physical and mental stress in harsh outdoor conditions. Teens can be denied food, and forcibly marched for long distances in extreme heat or cold. When they collapse from exhaustion, they face verbal abuse and physical punishment for "weakness." Sexual abuse has also been documented. These programs contrast starkly with legitimate outdoor programs teaching life skills in safe environments. *Hell Camp: Teen Nightmare* (Netflix, 2023)[7] lays bare the dangers.

Both types are trauma factories, responsible for dozens of teen deaths, suicides, and widespread CPTSD. Maia Szalavitz's *Help At Any Cost* (2006) exposes their methods as torture tactics borrowed from military prisons like Guantanamo Bay.[8] Parents are indoctrinated into signing waivers that allow goon squads to abduct their kids and contracts that restrict communication or withdrawal—sometimes for years. This industry remains federally unregulated, with widely varying state laws. Beyond physical harm, these programs create permanent rifts between parents and their teens. If you wouldn't torture your own child, why pay someone else to do it?

Many types of cults use criminal force or intimidation to prevent members from leaving. Ex-members have documented years of beatings, imprisonment, malnutrition, and rape. Children born into such cults don't understand their abuse is illegal or are too scared to escape. Law enforcement can be reluctant to prosecute religious organizations or their leaders, who deny the abuse—or claim that it's part of a "protected" religious ritual such as exorcism.[9] When cults are deeply entrenched in a small or rural jurisdiction, police or prosecutors may be members themselves or have close ties to the cult. Justice can be hard to come by. Here are some examples, with varying outcomes:

> **John Huddle** endured a grueling battle to break free from the Word of Faith Fellowship (WOFF) in Spindale, North Carolina, and escaped in 2008, leaving his wife and children behind. The organization faced numerous allegations of abuse, including forced "blasting" rituals, physical violence, and family separation. These claims are documented in Huddle's 2015 book *Locked In*.[10]
>
> **David and Louise Turpin** ran a family cult under twisted Pentecostal Christianity. They imprisoned their thirteen children ranging in age from 2 to 29. In 2018, their 17-year-old daughter escaped their home in Perris, California through a window and called 911. Police found horrific conditions—the children were malnourished and cognitively impaired, and some were chained to their beds. The Turpin parents pleaded guilty to torture, child abuse, false imprisonment, and cruelty to an adult dependent and were sentenced to life in prison.
>
> **Jehovah's Witnesses** engage in congregational discipline, including "marking" and "disfellowshipping," which requires other members, including family, not to associate with those cast out.[11] Those who fail to shun them can be punished in turn. Shunning is upheld by American and Canadian courts as an expression of *sincerely held* religious belief. But in 2021 Jehovah's Witnesses was fined €12,000 by a Belgian court. In 2022, the Supreme Court of Norway cut state religious funding for the cult over a shunning claim.
>
> **Carolyn Jessop** fled the polygamist FLDS cult in 2003. The cult engaged in a campaign of shunning, stalking, harassment and death threats. Her husband and the cult leadership filed false domestic abuse charges to retain custody of Jessop's eight children. She waged an expensive three-year legal battle against the well-funded cult and won custody of her children in 2006.[12]
>
> **John Post** walked out of the abusive Twelve Tribes cult in 1999, at 19. Fifteen cult members physically blocked his path, forming a human wall and telling him he would face "consequences" for leaving, including death. He forced his way past the group and escaped. Founded in Tennessee in 1972, the cult maintains 70 properties in the United States and operates throughout the world. Former members, including many children raised there, have reported widespread physical and sexual abuse.[13]
>
> **Coral Anika Theill**[14] was a "handmaid" or "helpmeet" in an abusive

"headship" marriage in the People of Praise cult from 1979 to 1984. Her husband then became a cult-hopper, bouncing from one fundamentalist Christian cult to another for 15 years. Theill was held by her husband's threat to retain custody of her eight children. She suffered marital rape, withholding of medical care, intimidation and constant threats. After legal battles in which she could not afford competent counsel, she lost custody of all her children in 1996, including a nursing infant. She told her heart-wrenching story in *BONSHEA*.[15]

The 700-member Gloriavale cult in New Zealand, near Lake Haupiri, was founded in 1969 by Neville Cooper.[16] He was jailed on sexual assault charges in 1995 and served eleven months. Cooper claimed "religious persecution." The cult faces chronic allegations of physical and sexual violence, and labor code violations. Gloriavale enforces strict gender-based oppression, limiting the roles of women. Members Rosie and Elijah Overcomer left with their children in 2014 after a years-long effort by the cult to separate their family.[17] Elijah was initially kicked out for dissenting against Cooper. Rosie was told Elijah didn't love her anymore. The cult denied Rosie contact with her husband, then told her she could only speak to Elijah if she demanded he obey cult leadership. When the couple finally left the cult, they were shunned by their community of 27 years.

These examples highlight the challenge of exposing insular cults that disguise their oppression as religious practice. It's even harder when family ties are involved, as with John Huddle, Carolyn Jessop, Coral Anika Theill, or the Turpin family. Polygamy is illegal, yet FLDS sidesteps the law by framing plural marriages as spiritual and unofficial. While they routinely violate statutory rape laws, prosecutions are rare because victims can be too terrified to testify. In Coral Anika Theill's case, the court system failed her, normalizing the patriarchal structures of "headship" and "helpmeet" that kept her trapped.

In the Turpin case, some might argue the parents were incompetent or mentally ill, unrelated to their Pentecostal beliefs. But what led them to isolate all 13 of their children? The common thread in abusive cults is their claim of doing "God's work," which they believe exempts them from accountability. The Turpins are serving life sentences. Their crimes weren't worse than those of other cults that beat, starve, imprison or rape their members. The Turpins faced punishment mostly because they lacked the sophistication, money and institutional structure to hide their crimes behind a religious pretext.

As with domestic abuse, the highest danger is during separation—when the cult attempts to reassert control. While most cult violence stops short of lethal force, some cases involve murder or attempted murder. In one case, a former member took revenge against his abuser. These tragic escalations include:

> **Yahweh Ben Yahweh**, leader of the black separatist Nation of Yahweh cult, was convicted in 1992 for plotting 14 grisly murders in Miami, along with charges of racketeering, extortion, and firebombing.
>
> **Thomas Drescher**, aka Tirtha Das, a disciple of the New Vrindaban Krishna (ISKCON) cult, murdered ex-member Steven L. Bryant, aka Sulochan Das, in 1986. Bryant had been working on a book exposing the cult, *The Guru Business*. The cult leader, Keith Ham, aka Kirtanananda Swami, was implicated but never formally charged.
>
> **Lance Kenton and Joe Musico**, members of the Synanon cult, attempted to kill attorney Paul Morantz in 1978 by placing a rattlesnake in his mailbox. The attack, orchestrated by Synanon's founder, Charles E. "Chuck" Dederich, led to Dederich pleading no contest to conspiracy to commit murder. He received probation due to poor health.
>
> **Ricky Rodriguez** was groomed as the future leader of the Children of God cult (now The Family International), and left the group in the late 1990s to expose its abusive practices. After years of post-cult trauma and lack of justice, he released a video manifesto in January 2005, murdered Angela Smith, his former nanny whom he accused of sexual abuse, and then tragically took his own life.

While extreme cases command attention, all cult trauma—including psychological manipulation and social control—leaves lasting damage. Healing begins with acknowledging the full weight of what occurred. Shunning is a big deal. Public shaming is a big deal. Attempts to separate your family are a big deal. Thought reform is a big fucking deal.

You were lied to. You were conditioned to believe that vital parts of your human nature were sinful, especially if you are a woman. Your boundaries were violated. You were convinced to reject the larger world. You followed a "leader" or "master," and you let them make important decisions for you. You were persuaded to donate time and money. You were taught to fear being cast out, and even to fear punishment after death. Part of healing is learning to forgive yourself for buying into all that. Non-physical trauma alters a person's sense of safety, self-worth, and emotional regulation. Unlike physical injuries, which heal with time and treatment, psychological scars linger and aren't obvious to others. They may not even be obvious to you.

---

[1] The parable attributed to Heraclitus, a pre-Socratic Greek philosopher from Ephesus who lived around 535–475 BCE, emphasizes the constant state of flux in the universe. Heraclitus famously asserted that life is like a river—the waters continually flow and change, and one cannot step into the same river twice. This metaphor underlines his philosophy that everything is in constant change and that

stability is an illusion. His teachings challenge the notion of permanence and highlight the importance of embracing change as the fundamental essence of the universe. Reference: Kahn, C. H. (1979). *The art and thought of Heraclitus: An edition of the fragments with translation and commentary*. Cambridge, MA: Harvard University Press.

[2] Hill, J. M. (2013). *Beyond Belief: My Secret Life Inside Scientology and My Harrowing Escape*. HarperOne; Remini, L., & Paley, R. (2015). *Troublemaker: Surviving Hollywood and Scientology*. Ballantine Books; Rinder, M. (2022). *A Billion Years: My Escape From a Life in the Highest Ranks of Scientology*. Hachette Books.

[3] Brown, J. (2023, March 3). *Inside Liana Shanti's Lumerian Mystery School*. The Daily Beast. https://www.thedailybeast.com/inside-liana-shantis-lumerian-mystery-school

[4] Sources supporting this claim include the Southern Poverty Law Center, which documents Stefan Molyneux's anti-family rhetoric and describes his Freedomain Radio community as cult-like (Southern Poverty Law Center, n.d.; https://www.splcenter.org/fighting-hate/extremist-files/individual/stefan-molyneux), and Counter Extremism, which further details his extremist activities (Counter Extremism, n.d.; https://www.counterextremism.com/extremists/stefan-molyneux).

[5] Hilpern, K. (2008, November 14). *You'll never see me again*. The Guardian. Retrieved from https://web.archive.org/web/20131223212938/http://www.theguardian.com/lifeandstyle/2008/nov/15/family-relationships-fdr-defoo-cult

[6] Netflix. (2023). *The Program: Cons, Cults, and Kidnapping* [Limited series]. https://www.netflix.com/watch/81616648

[7] Netflix. (2023). *Hell Camp: Teen Nightmare* [Film]. https://www.netflix.com/title/81449757

[8] Szalavitz, M. (2006). *Help at any cost: How the troubled-teen industry cons parents and hurts kids*. Riverhead Books.

[9] Martin, R. (2020, February 17). *Word of Faith's pattern of abuse 'got worse over time,' says 'Broken Faith' author*. NPR. https://www.npr.org/2020/02/17/806052660/word-of-faiths-pattern-of-abuse-got-worse-over-time-says-broken-faith-author

[10] Huddle, J. E., III. (2015). *Locked in: My imprisoned years in a destructive cult*. CreateSpace Independent Publishing Platform.

[11] Wikipedia contributors. (n.d.). *Jehovah's Witnesses congregational discipline*. Wikipedia. Retrieved from https://en.wikipedia.org/wiki/Jehovah%27s_Witnesses_congregational_discipline

[12] Jessop, C., & Palmer, L. (2007). *Escape*. Broadway Books.

[13] Bradbury, S. (2023, June 8). *"They are evil": Ex-Twelve Tribes members describe child abuse, control inside religious cult*. The Denver Post. https://www.denverpost.com/2022/03/03/twelve-tribes-cult-child-abuse/

[14] Theill, C. A. (n.d.). *Coral Anika Theill*. Retrieved from https://www.coralanikatheill.com/

[15] Theill, C. A. (2014). *Bonshea: Making light of the dark*. Coral Anika Theill.

[16] Wikipedia contributors. (n.d.). *Gloriavale Christian Community*. Wikipedia. Retrieved from https://en.wikipedia.org/wiki/Gloriavale_Christian_Community

[17] Odlum, G. (2024, March 11). *Rosie Overcomer shares her story about growing up in Gloriavale*. NZ Herald. https://www.nzherald.co.nz/kapiti-news/news/rosie-overcomer-shares-her-story-about-growing-up-in-gloriavale/WOX2TEFHMNEWNN2446JNHZF3M4/

CHAPTER THIRTY

Earthquake!

From one perspective, I was lucky to be born to my parents. I've led a privileged life. I grew up safe, with plenty to eat and a roof over my head. I wasn't physically or sexually abused—unless you count routine spanking or having a six-inch cannula shoved up my ass for a high-colonic. Compared to the horrific abuses so many others have endured in cults, my experience was tame. My cult exit was a best-case scenario: I had a car and was free to leave. No one followed me or tried to take my kids. Thanks to friends, I had a place to live, found a job quickly, and bought a house within five months. So why did the aftershocks keep coming?

Let's pick up where I left off as we caravaned away from the Ranch into a blinding blizzard in January of 1994. The storm was no joke, with visibility near-zero. We shouldn't have been driving, but we had to make our getaway. I worried about my family in that 1985 Subaru sedan. But I also knew Kathleen's long experience driving in Canadian blizzards under the tutelage of her oil-roughneck father, Gust Mattson. And I was confident I could manage the big diesel U-Haul, so long as I could see the road.

The quickest route to Los Angeles was through Yellowstone, which would save about three hours. But the park closes for the winter. So we headed north on US 89 to Interstate 90 west through the Bozeman pass, eventually through the Targhee National Forest to Idaho Falls. I had driven the route countless times, but never under such conditions. And in 1994, there was no phoning for help.

As we white-knuckled through the storm, I realized our departure was the perfect metaphor for my cult experience. From the frozen brakes that wouldn't let us go to the blinding snow of divine disinformation, and the dangers lurking around every corner like the Dweller on the Threshold, seven years condensed into one harrowing seven-hour journey.

We rolled into Idaho Falls around midnight and found a nondescript motel. I went out in the Subaru to buy a six-pack of *beer*—no more near-beer for us! Kathleen and I cuddled in bed and watched *Beavis and Butthead*. It was our introduction to 1990s culture. I was still caught up in my cult judginess and thought, "This show is disgusting, juvenile, and beneath me. I shouldn't be laughing." But I was!

Later that night, we marked our freedom by ravishing each other, with the renewed abandon we had felt since giving our notice in September. We had kicked the interloper God out of our bed and our minds. Stripping away the body armoring around forbidden parts and positions. Whoever came up with those damn sex rules didn't care about fairness. Missionary position isn't great for women. Men come every time. Women? Not so much.

Our bedroom liberation wasn't just about pleasure—it was an act of defiance against seven years of spiritual subjugation. Like other staff married couples, Kathleen and I had worn my mother's sexual straitjacket. The rules we were now breaking had been crafted to control us through shame, always wrapped in layers of cosmic significance. This meant that any sexual transgressions weren't just a risk to our own souls, they potentially endangered the spiritual sponsorship of our entire cult. We had taken these concerns very seriously. We hadn't killed our intense sexual passion right away—it was a gradual acceptance of the commitment we made. Compliance became a sort of mutual affirmation of our dedication to "the path" over our personal desires. Kathleen reflected, "I chose to be there, to be under the guru-chela relationship. It was really a training ground. You can consciously not believe something is wrong, but things go into your subconscious, you know, all the negative things Elizabeth said about oral sex."

There were reasons why my cult was so *fucked up* about sex. As I've discussed, from the cult leader's standpoint, it's authoritarian subjugation under whatever spiritual pretext they can cobble together. And as I've noted, it's difficult to control people who own their orgasms. But how could adults *agree* to let such an important part of their lives be controlled? Who would monitor bedroom compliance?

It's complicated. Most religious people believe God is always watching—and knows their sexual fantasies. That alone deters some people from breaking sexual taboos, even in their own minds. In my cult, admitting a desire for backdoor action, mutual masturbation, or oral sex would be seen as a serious breach. Renunciation of worldly appetites was foundational: transcending lust and sublimating impure desires. Our members believed these teachings were morally binding.

Any desire for unsanctioned pleasure could be viewed as betrayal of a partner's salvation. One of the inner teachings for permanent staff came from a secret tape called *Oral Sex and Clearance*. It recycled 1930s Mighty I AM dogma about wasting the life force. On the tape, Mother claimed oral sex drained so much light from people's bodies that they couldn't make their ascension. She discussed a married staff member's oral sex confession, after which she performed "clearance" calls to "bind" the "sex entities" and restore the couple's light.

She and the Ballards believed sexual pleasure depleted some *finite reservoir* of "life force," ending in spiritual or physical death. Consider this passage from *The I AM Discourses*:

> Gratification of the sex appetite… is the greatest avenue of waste that human beings have to contend with. This is what makes it impossible to hold fast to the "God Presence" long enough to attain the Mastery.… Perhaps one of the most unfortunate things in which human beings live is the man's so-called legal right to bind another individual in the sex activity, when the other wishes to rise out of it.… True Love never requires sex contact of any kind.[1]

This tangled thicket of puritanical guilt and fear also has antecedents in ancient South and East Asian traditions. Hinduism, Taoism, and Buddhism feature writings from the 3rd to 8th centuries urging seminal retention to conserve *prana, chi,* or *ojas*—terms for the "life force." These traditions propose that conserved "serpent" kundalini energy can rise from the base of the spine to the crown chakra, leading to enlightenment. This parallels the Western Esoteric goal of ascension. Both involve self-transcendence through renunciation of desire to attain a spiritually ideal state, and both deliberately conflate energy and life force between physical and spiritual domains. Like Mesmer's discredited "vital fluid," or "animal magnetism," these concepts lack any testable basis.

As I've discussed, purity and perfection can lead open-minded people to embrace authoritarianism, and assigning spiritual significance to the orgasm is an equally damaging misconception that leads to sexual repression. It's even invaded the language. A French term for orgasm, in use since 1882, is *la petite mort* or "the little death," which connotes an expenditure of the life force and a brief loss of consciousness.[2]

The stigmatization of orgasm and especially non-procreative sex is certainly a form of shame. But it also turns a wonderful aspect of life into an ugly source of control. It's easy to see how people might be convinced that if something is this powerful, and feels this good, there must be a downside to it. But science confirms the opposite. A 2023 study in *The Journal of Sexual Medicine* shows that regular sexual activity has significant health benefits:

> We present evidence associating increased sexual activity with decreased risk of many disease states. Populations with higher frequency of arousal and orgasms showed reduced rates of breast cancer, prostate cancer, obesity, vaginal atrophy, dyspareunia, dysmenorrhea, dysfunctional uterine bleeding, recurrent urinary tract infections, urinary stress incontinence, fecal incontinence, genitourinary symptoms of menopause, abnormal false pap smears, vulvar, labial, and vaginal obliteration, and cardiovascular disease.[3]

So long as people honor consent and take precautions, sex is overwhelmingly beneficial. It can be solo or with same-sex or opposite sex partners. The only negative consequence remains *spiritual*, based on divine commands, cultural taboos, or dubious ancient mythologies. Since spirituality can't be tested or disproved, it remains the primary "just so" story told to vilify sexual pleasure. Though attitudes have improved in some parts of the world, sexual shame infects a significant portion of the global population—far beyond those in cults.[4] It's without doubt among the worst superstitions of all time.

Our liberation was just beginning. The morning in Idaho Falls was sunny and clear. After the blizzard scare, Interstate 15 stretched ahead like an old friend—a single ribbon of concrete leading all the way to Los Angeles. We stopped in Baker, California. Over breakfast in a low-rent motel, Kathleen and I joked about Monroe Shearer, our former vice president who was rumored to be starting his own cult. I quipped that maybe *I* should be the one to start a new cult—given my uncertain job prospects in L.A. We both laughed bitterly—the idea was about as appealing as poking out my own eyes. By 1995, Shearer had founded *The Temple of the Presence*.

Rugged bluffs locally known as "The Twelve Apostles" overlook Chatsworth, California in the west San Fernando Valley.

We arrived at Tony and Patty Nottoli's home in Chatsworth on January 6, 1994—a placid Los Angeles suburb bisected by Topanga Canyon Boulevard—where horse property and a nature preserve borders light industry. Tony and I had been friends since age 10, and he and his siblings had left the cult after high school to build successful careers, dodging our doomsday boondoggle. They were living proof that a cult childhood doesn't have to derail your life—which was lucky for me. Tony towed my trailer from Montana, let me park it on his property with full hookups, and helped me unload the U-Haul into a storage facility. He and Patty rented us a room with kitchen privileges. We installed phone lines and set up our office—and we were in business. Everyone leaving a cult needs that kind of help to get back on their feet.

Eleven days later, at 4:31 AM on January 17, I was jolted from a dream. Barely awake, I thought someone was stealing our trailer. By the time I was fully alert, the 6.7 magnitude Northridge earthquake was over. Its epicenter was just six miles away—the worst quake to hit Los Angeles since 1971. But I had no idea what happened. The kids didn't even wake up.

I stumbled outside to minor devastation: fallen concrete block walls everywhere. Inside Tony and Patty's house, broken dishes littered the kitchen, along with a smashed china cabinet and fallen bookshelves. But the Nottolis were OK. Tony sprang into action. "Let's go," he said, and we jumped in his truck to fill the tank before gas stations ran dry. Sirens wailed as we passed fractured buildings and burning warehouses. We weren't the only ones looking for fuel, but Tony's quick thinking paid off.

The CA-14 to I-5 interchange collapse, following the 1994 Northridge earthquake.

As morning dawned, the city was in chaos. Three freeways had collapsed: the 14 to 5 interchange near Valencia, the 10 in Santa Monica, and the 118 which ran along the north edge of the San Fernando valley, near Chatsworth.

I had already been commuting on the 118 to Varitel Video in Studio City. After the quake, it took me an extra hour to get to work. My friend Brad and I were colleagues in the Varitel machine room back in 1985, and he was now the supervisor. Within days of my arrival in Los Angeles, he hired me for temporary work, which completely saved me at a critical time. There's nothing like getting that first post-cult paycheck. After the quake, I helped the Varitel crew clean up broken glass and fallen tiles, restore wiring, and test systems. Within a week, we were up and running.

California isn't normally too fazed by earthquakes, but Northridge was different: 57 dead, thousands injured, billions in damages. In spite of the tragedy, the city got back to work quickly, restoring collapsed freeways within months. But beneath the practical response lay a familiar undercurrent of religious judgment. The rest of America doesn't always view California's resilience as a success story. Whenever there's seismic activity on the left coast, there's always a frisson of superstitious schadenfreude: That the "Big One" is coming, and California might finally sink into the ocean as punishment for its sinful ways. I've heard this hostile dumbassery my entire life. We were still at La Tourelle in Colorado Springs when the 1971 Sylmar quake struck. I was only seven years old, but I recall the adults squawking with excitement, declaring it "God's judgment of Los Angeles."

In *Prophet's Daughter*, Erin described the same ugly superstition about a different earthquake. In November 1972, my father gave a dictation from the master "Helios," warning that God was going to cause a massive earthquake because the world was "just as wicked as in the days of Sodom and Gomorrah." What was he really upset about? A flourishing red-light district in Colorado Springs. It's just more religious projection: under messianic strict-father morality, inappropriate sexual pleasure warrants mass-death.

A month later, the December 1972 Managua earthquake killed between 4,000 and 11,000 people, injured 20,000, and left 300,000 homeless. People on our staff exchanged smug glances, considering my dad's prophecy confirmed. We were righteous! They were dead! All because a few people were getting hand jobs in massage parlors or masturbating in X-rated theaters thousands of miles away—according to that twisted logic. Erin pointed out that the victims were impoverished and struggling, hardly enjoying sodomite lifestyles.

Nicaragua sits on the Pacific Ring of Fire, where the Cocos and Caribbean plates collide. Did no one in my cult understand plate tectonics? That continents and oceans float on crusts of rock over a sea of magma? That earthquakes relieve plate pressure at random? It's basic fifth-grade Earth science. Predicting a catastrophic earthquake "soon" somewhere on Earth is one of the safest prophecies anyone can make.

With Northridge, my cult's delusions got personal—my mother told her followers *my anger had caused the earthquake!* As if human feelings could move trillion-ton tectonic plates! But here's what's worse: You may laugh it off, but recognize that if you have ten friends, two or three of them engage in such cult-like thinking. Apophenia about natural disasters is common. Studies suggest up to one third of the US and global population connects natural disasters to divine punishment.[5]

Sitting US Congresswoman Marjorie Taylor Greene (R-GA) tweeted on April 5, 2024, "God is sending America strong signs to tell us to repent.

Earthquakes and eclipses and many more things to come. I pray that our country listens." She might as well have been talking about witchcraft collapsing houses. Such ignorance is contemptible.

These broadly accepted apophenic forebodings mirrored my mother's world view. She routinely blamed catastrophic world events on anyone who had left the cult, or challenged her authority. Even minor disagreements were fraught with danger. In 1984, after her father Hans Wulf's death, she claimed his rage on the astral plane had caused the Bhopal disaster—a Union Carbide gas leak in India that killed 4,000 people.[6] The Northridge earthquake was just the latest event she would fold into her virtual narrative of cosmic cause and effect.

As I've previously discussed, this pattern of magical thinking had its roots in her early virtual retreats from reality, particularly her experiences with social isolation and sexual repression. As an adult, she vacillated between repression and transgression. As Erin documents in *Prophet's Daughter*, after discovering *The I AM Discourses* on my grandmother's bookshelf at the age of 18, my mother swore off sex, turning down a marriage proposal from her high school boyfriend, Dick Fontaine.[7]

It's all emblematic of the small world versus big world confusion I've referenced throughout this book, reflecting parts of my mother's psychology that were frozen at Piaget's pre-operational stage (age 2–7)—which is characterized by egocentrism. Even as an adult she failed to recognize that her personal experiences—whether a loss like her father's death, or internal sexual conflict—may have been seismic in her small world, but had no connection to the larger world.

In retrospect, the dual perspective is clear: Her world was both small and big. Small because our cult was insular, and she rarely received criticism—except negative press, which she mostly refused to read. This isolation kept her inner world too narrow to grasp that global events had nothing to do with her. Yet her world was undeniably big: she held international events and considered herself the world's spiritual leader. This duality reinforced her belief that everything involved her. If the world was so vast, and she was central to it, then she must be immensely powerful—and anyone opposing her equally powerful, capable of causing disasters or industrial accidents with their "energy." It's the only way I can make any sense of it. My mother wasn't stupid or crazy. She was trapped by her messianic identity.

Given all the batshit crazy behavior I've described in this book, that may seem hard to believe. But consider this: If my mother was who she claimed to be, and truly had spiritual sight, then her actions might have made sense. But there's no way to tell. Her visions came from her virtual world—the same impenetrable shield and coping mechanism she'd used since childhood. The rest of us could only take her word for what she saw—or what my sister Erin helped her see. She was a shrewd defender of that virtual reality, translating it into a powerful organization. She was politically astute, and aside from a few exceptions like the Mull trial fiasco, she fended off her enemies and challengers for decades. No stupid or crazy person could have accomplished that. Within her private cosmic realm, there were concrete realities she described, which featured an internally consistent logic that I came to understand. It's what made my cult attractive to so many people and breaking away from her cosmology so difficult.

Her virtual reality also had a profound impact on mundane business matters. During the shelter project in early 1989, we had a misunderstanding over an archival film restoration project she had approved in writing but forgot about. Sadly, I now recognize this was a symptom of her early-onset dementia. Out of frustration I defended myself, "If you can't remember what you signed, I don't know how I'm supposed to conduct our business." Most people would have said, "I'm sorry I forgot." Instead, she twisted up her face and mocked me: "Nyah, nyah, nyah!" And accused me of causing "a serious rent in the garment of our community."

Hearing the messenger of God use a schoolyard taunt was something I was unprepared for. She told me I had committed a grave sin. That night, she made the congregation decree and swing their swords for three extra hours to heal the "spiritual damage" I had caused. I was so mortified that I hiked alone up a nearby mountain, where I looked down on Ranch Headquarters and contemplated my careless words. The buzz of chanting from our main chapel carried up through the darkness. All those people were losing precious sleep correcting my "mistake."

I feel only sadness about such moments, and compassion. What must it have been like to *be* her? She was unraveling. My callous remark had triggered her fear of mortality, even if she was unaware of why her memory failed. She responded the only way she knew—spiritualizing her fear as an attack on her messengership that came through me. I had become, once again, a "tool of the sinister force."

The culprit was, of course, the same old perfectionist thinking: The messenger of God must be perfect, can never be wrong, can never forget. She was as unmerciful to herself as she had been to Robert Zimmerman, Kathleen and others she expelled, or the world itself when she called for nuclear bombs to descend. It was the same resolute intolerance I faced the day I left Montana. There was no room in The Prophet's world for error or weakness. Her larger-than-life role made vulnerability impossible. Had she taken off her armor, I might have hugged her and said, "Mother, how can I help you bear this burden?"

Apophenia—amplified by group reinforcement—is devastating. It doesn't just draw people into cults. It's everywhere in the mystical milieu permeating the Western Esoteric Tradition and New Thought[8] going back to Blavatsky, Mesmer, and Quimby. A twist on Descartes: "I think, therefore *it is so.*" No grounding in observation or logic, or what's real or testable. Just wild guesses, wishes, projections and gut feelings. It's also characteristic of superstition that sees signs and portents connecting the spiritual to the physical, assuming divine purpose behind random events—weaponizing irrational fear of nature to justify shame and repression. It's all highly dangerous nonsense.

---

[1] Ballard, G. W., & Ballard, E. W. (1935). *The "I AM" discourses.* Saint Germain Press.
[2] Wikipedia contributors. (n.d.). *La petite mort.* Wikipedia. https://en.wikipedia.org/wiki/La_petite_mort
[3] Dominguez-Bali, A., Santana, R., Basta, J., Belizaire, J., & Dominguez-Bali, C. (2023). Healthy ef-

fects of sex. *The Journal of Sexual Medicine*, 20(Supplement_1), 459. https://doi.org/10.1093/jsxmed/qdad060.431

[4] The percentage of people who believe that non-procreative sexual activities (such as oral sex, anal sex, masturbation, and same-sex activity) are morally wrong varies significantly across different societies, cultures, and religious groups. However, some relevant data can provide a general sense of these views: According to a 2021 Gallup poll, 69% of Americans believe that gay or lesbian relations are morally acceptable, while 30% believe they are morally wrong (Gallup, *Changing one's gender is seen as most contentious moral issue in U.S.*, 2021, https://news.gallup.com/poll/351020/changing-one-gender-sharply-contentious-moral-issue.aspx). This marks a significant shift from 2001, when only 40% found them morally acceptable and 53% considered them morally wrong (Gallup, *Moral issues: Historical trends*, 2001, https://news.gallup.com/poll/1681/moral-issues.aspx).

Regarding masturbation, attitudes vary widely across religious traditions. While some Christian denominations view it as morally wrong, others adopt a more permissive stance depending on doctrinal interpretations and cultural contexts. For instance, conservative evangelical groups often condemn masturbation as sinful, while more progressive denominations may view it as a normal part of human sexuality (*Wikipedia, Religious views on masturbation*, n.d., https://en.wikipedia.org/wiki/Religious_views_on_masturbation).

Globally, attitudes towards homosexuality vary widely. A 2019 Pew Research Center survey conducted across 34 countries found that acceptance of homosexuality ranged from 94% in Sweden to 7% in Nigeria. Many countries fell somewhere in between, with a median of 52% across the surveyed countries saying homosexuality should be accepted by society (Pew Research Center, *The global divide on homosexuality persists*, 2019, https://www.pewresearch.org/global/2020/06/25/global-divide-on-homosexuality-persists/).

[5] According to a press release from the Public Religion Research Institute (PRRI, 2011), about 29% of Americans believe that natural disasters, such as earthquakes and floods, are a sign from God or a form of divine punishment for human misdeeds (Public Religion Research Institute, 2011, https://www.prri.org/press-release/few-americans-see-earthquakes-floods-and-other-natural-disasters-a-sign-from-god/).

Paul, B. K., & Nadiruzzaman, M. (2013). Religious interpretations for the causes of the 2004 Indian Ocean Tsunami. Asian Profile, 41(1), 67-75. Retrieved from https://icccad.net/wp-content/uploads/2014/05/religious_interpretations_for_the_causes_of_the_indian_ocean_tsunami_1.pdf. The article documents how religious interpretations of the tsunami, particularly in Aceh, Indonesia, reinforced conservative social controls. Fundamentalist groups used the disaster to justify stricter enforcement of religious codes, especially regarding women's dress and behavior, while characterizing the tsunami as divine punishment for perceived moral transgressions.

[6] The 1984 Bhopal disaster, considered the world's worst industrial accident, occurred when over 40 tons of methyl isocyanate gas leaked from a pesticide plant owned by Union Carbide India Limited, exposing more than 500,000 people to toxic chemicals. Immediate fatalities were estimated at 3,800, with later estimates suggesting between 15,000 and 20,000 deaths over time, alongside long-term health effects for hundreds of thousands (*Wikipedia, Bhopal disaster*, https://en.wikipedia.org/wiki/Bhopal_disaster).

[7] Prophet, E. (2009). *Prophet's daughter: My life with Elizabeth Clare Prophet inside the Church Universal and Triumphant* (p. 76). Lyons Press.

[8] The New Thought movement originated in the United States during the late 19th century, emphasizing metaphysical beliefs, particularly the idea that positive thinking can create positive results. This philosophy has significantly influenced self-help and motivational literature, contributing to modern ideas of personal empowerment and the Law of Attraction (*Wikipedia, New Thought*, https://en.wikipedia.org/wiki/New_Thought).

CHAPTER THIRTY ONE

Seeking Normal

After the earthquake, I settled into my routine at Varitel. While I didn't yet have a permanent position, I was scheduled to work most nights from 5 p.m. to 1 a.m. Setting up edit bays, assisting editors, managing tapes, and making dubs kept me busy, with plenty of overtime. Working 45-50 hours a week felt like a vacation compared to my VP-level responsibilities with my cult. The job wasn't mentally taxing. Most importantly, my days were free—and so was I: free from worrying about making karma, free from the crushing burden of world salvation, and free from perpetual exhaustion.

I brought my Franklin Day Planner to work, journaling to sort through the madness I had left behind. I also strategized about buying a house for my family. Back in 1994, it was still possible for an average working stiff to afford a decent home in the San Fernando Valley, and I was determined to make that happen.

At first, I wasn't too social with my workmates. Culture shock made me uncomfortable—which is totally normal for anyone coming out of a cult. My former life was deadly serious: there was a world to save. The machine room was unfamiliar. It was full of camaraderie, joking, cussing and lewd talk. I worried about fitting in. After years of being around cult prudes, my coworkers were sharing graphic details of their sexual exploits. It didn't offend me, but I couldn't help wondering: Had I been living under a rock?

In some ways, I had. Six years in the Montana mountains left me clueless about '90s culture—music, TV, movies, fashion—even sports. At Varitel, there was always a game on a monitor. Sometimes we played Nerf basketball. I couldn't believe how much fun we had on the clock while still getting work done. The night crew was full of great people who gradually brought me up to speed and pulled me out of my shell. They could tell I was different, but they never disrespected me. Slowly, I relaxed into normalcy. It was a relief to be nobody. My world was finally appropriately small.

The Centrum Building, former location of Varitel Video, Cahuenga Blvd, Studio City, California, 2023

In time, I caught another break: one of the senior assistant editors quit, and I became Varitel staff. Having a steady paycheck and no world-saving responsibilities meant I could focus on a more modest mission: getting my family out of Tony's backyard. My full-time position qualified us to buy a house, and Kathleen was planning to open a home daycare and school. She had been refinishing miniature desks and chairs in Tony's garage, and our plan was coming together. During the day, we scoured the West San Fernando Valley for homes on busy streets where we could put up a daycare sign. We looked at about 30 houses, and there were bargains. The earthquake had driven some easily rattled people out of Los Angeles, dropping property prices by 20 percent. It was satisfying to benefit from earthquake superstition—instead of being its target.

In late March 1994, we found a foreclosure in West Hills on Valley Circle Boulevard, just a few miles south of Chatsworth. It was a tan 3+2 tract house from 1961, with a garage and a pool. Against five other offers, we bid $165,000—$500 over asking—and got it. The down payment came from my grandparents Hans and Frida Wulf, and from Kathleen's mother Lois Mattson. No help came from my mother or the cult.

There was earthquake damage—cracked walls and ceilings, and the previous owner had stripped the floors to bare concrete. Escrow couldn't close until everything was repaired. Using credit cards would jeopardize loan approval, so I had to pay in cash or do the work myself. A race against time began. By day, I worked on the house. By night, I clocked in at Varitel. One entire paycheck bought slate tile, which Tony hauled in his truck. We knocked out the install in two days—what a *mensch*—may life always be kind to him! My next paycheck covered half the carpet, and the shop owner financed the rest. We barely had money to buy food and gas. By the skin of our teeth, we passed inspection, and got our deed shortly after my 30th birthday, in May of 1994.

Our fixer-upper in West Hills, California, with our 1985 Subaru, c. 1994

But I was about to be blindsided. Too focused on work and stabilizing our home, family, and finances in Los Angeles, I missed the clear signs of it all crumbling. Kathleen was not OK. Leaving the cult had traumatized her in ways I didn't understand. She longed for an artistic life—like her brother Charles had on Vancouver Island. She missed her siblings, and she never saw them because I had dragged us back to Los Angeles. She felt trapped in the trailer with our kids. She later reflected, "When I signed up to have kids, I was in a community that supported families. We had help with meals and a school I was involved with. Chatsworth had none of that. All of a sudden, I'm landing in a trailer."

Since January, we had shared one car—the old red Subaru. Kathleen dropped me off and picked me up so she could explore the city while I worked. She found some semblance of the community she craved at Agape, a church in Santa Monica that held evening services. Patty's niece Ina was happy to babysit, and I supported Kathleen's adventures—at first.

Kathleen was often hours late, offering vague explanations like "I fell asleep." Fell asleep where? At Agape? I couldn't imagine her having an affair—after all we had survived. Tony and Patty assured me that she wasn't in Chatsworth. This was before cell phones, so I would sit in the lobby at Varitel until 3 or 4 a.m. like a chump, with no communication from my wife.

One night she was hours late *again*, and I reached my breaking point.

Fuming, as she turned onto the freeway, I demanded, "Where have you been going, and what have you been doing??"

"I fucking fell asleep, like I told you," she snapped. "I'm not going to talk about this in the middle of the night!"

I exploded, "Stop lying to me!!"

She jerked the wheel and the car careened across all five lanes of the empty freeway, and then back again, and then across again. We drove home in silence. The next day she apologized, and promised not to be late again.

I let it go. Things would blow over. On the surface, Kathleen seemed happy. Christopher was turning eight, and we had a small birthday party at the house we didn't yet own. But the cracks were widening.

We went to Home Depot to choose paint colors, but Kathleen seemed distracted and withdrawn. When I asked what was wrong, she said, "I just can't do this," and walked out.

I demanded answers.

"I can't be stuck in some meaningless life in suburbia with three kids," she said.

Dumbfounded, I said, "We just bought a house, partially with your mom's money! What are you talking about? We've been planning this for months, and *now* you tell me? What are you going to do?!?"

"I don't know," she said, leaving me in a state of consternation.

That night, everything came out. Kathleen had been sleeping with a musician she met at Agape. She wasn't moving into our house—instead she was headed for Mt. Shasta with her new man. Then came the bombshell: she had gone to a clinic, fearing she was pregnant. Her pap smear came back positive for cervical cancer. *What. The. Hornswoggled. Fuck?* The room spun around me. I couldn't have been more thunderstruck. Did

I even know this woman?

It was an emotional earthquake clean off the Richter scale. The affair was the least of it. Now she was leaving? Now she might die? How could I have been so disconnected from what my wife was going through? Even worse, I realized she no longer trusted me enough to share her burdens. Had I been that neglectful?

Kathleen hadn't just been stifling her sexuality in the cult—she had buried her longing for creative expression for twelve years. Then she found herself trapped in the suburbs. The musician from Agape connected her to the Los Angeles arts scene, becoming both muse and liberator from the cage she felt closing in. In that metaphor, I was her jailer.

I couldn't talk Kathleen out of her plan, because the life I had put together for us was not a life she could handle in her degraded condition. My ignorance about the lived experience of women with young children could have filled volumes. I was too caught up in my own cult exit journey. The nuts and bolts of buying a *house* had blinded me to the understanding that it was only Kathleen's wholeness that could make it a *home*. My strict-father morality was still such a big part of my identity that I was clueless to my wife cracking apart in front of me. I thought the emotional and physical labor she was doing to hold our family together was simply *her job*.

She reflected, "I was in the midst of a nervous breakdown, which you didn't even see or acknowledge. My body was breaking down. I was so weak and exhausted from moving and packing, and the constancy with three young boys. I knew we needed a home, and that's why I got the money from my mom. But I needed a break, and I wasn't sure how long that would be, or whether I was even capable of coming back."

Kathleen borrowed money from a friend and bought herself a car. As she packed and ran errands over the next several days she was around less and less. And then she was gone. It was a triple-decker shit sandwich. I found myself trying to juggle kids and work and figure out a way to afford a full-time nanny. But the numbers didn't add up. And I wasn't willing to entrust my kids to a stranger. So I broke down and called my mother. There was nowhere else to turn. She was the only family I had.

Given my dramatic exit, going back to my mother—hat in hand—was humiliating. But it further highlights the difficulty of leaving a cult: You might not have many outside friends or family you can count on in a crisis. I had already been lucky to have Tony and Brad, who helped me with housing and work. But caring for my kids was a much tougher problem. My sisters were spread across the country, busy with work and school and their own cult exit journeys. Finding someone trustworthy to care for three young children indefinitely—when I had no money to offer—would have been well-nigh impossible. I knew my mother had plenty of resources. So I had no choice but to make that call.

After her obligatory "I told you so's" about Kathleen, my mother agreed to take in her grandkids. I ignored her criticism of my wife, but it hurt. On top of everything, all she could do was rub my nose in my misfortune? I've never had such mixed feelings. But I needed her help, so I swallowed my pride. It was a big ask, and I was grateful. She assigned the Widmers—a staff couple I knew well—to care for my children. They were both teachers at the Ranch school. So I knew my kids would be well-fed and safe until I could afford to care for them again. I packed them up and sent them off with a cult member who was driving to Montana.

That is how I found myself not just out of my cult, but alone, in an empty three-bedroom house, in West Hills, California, in June of 1994.

Sean Prophet, West Hills, California, June 1994

CHAPTER THIRTY TWO

Alone

I had never been alone. For cult members, solitude is scarce—rituals, decrees, and work demand constant group participation. For me, it was scarcer still. When my mother wasn't around, I was the center of attention in every room. Conferences were the worst, with members stopping me with questions, or to give me messages to pass along to my mother. I had no answers, and didn't feel comfortable acting as a go-between, so usually I just listened. Over time, I learned to avoid eye contact, walk quickly, and say little. Kathleen described it as wearing a "cloak" of social boundaries in public. But it had a big downside: I forgot how to take it off. I developed severe social anxiety—a lasting side-effect of my cult years that I still haven't fully overcome.

When Kathleen and the kids left our new home, I was in shell-shocked panic. Who even was I? I was sad and humiliated and lonely and angry and depressed. I didn't know how to live with myself. The only place I felt vaguely human was at Varitel with my workmates. I was also struggling with my leftover sense of entitlement: I *deserved* to be happy. I *deserved* companionship. On some deep unconscious level, I still thought I *deserved* to be the center of attention. I can forgive you for thinking that as a former cult leader, being left alone is *exactly* what I deserved.

My entitlement was rooted in something deeper—the idolatry of cult leadership that had warped all my relationships. Every social connection I had formed had been artificial, based on who my mother was, not who I was. I didn't know whether the real world would accept me, which left me uncomfortable in my skin. I felt marked, as if people could read Kathleen's rejection on my face. I pulled back into my shell and started driving straight home after my shift, even when my workmates were headed for the bar. I dreaded weekends and waking up alone. My thoughts echoed through the empty rooms of what I had once hoped would be a happy home.

I was adrift on an ocean of solitude, having never learned to swim. For those deprived of it, time alone can feel like a luxury—but I wasn't equipped for it. As Hannah Arendt observed, solitude means being "together with yourself," while loneliness is being surrounded by others without meaningful connection—something I knew all too well. My years in the cult had left me uniquely unprepared for this challenge. Being sought-after, the center of attention, or at the beck and call of others had made privacy unattainable—and eroded my ability to find peace in my own company. It was like a muscle that atrophies—and mine was extremely weak.

I didn't know how to cook, do laundry, or clean—tasks Kathleen or personal staff had always handled. At 30, I was a former cult VP and father of three who'd never mastered the basics of living. I could manage budgets and bark orders but in terms of self-care I was only half a man, like a drill sergeant who'd never bounced quarters or spit-shined my own boots. And I was broke. After putting every penny into the house, my budget—based in part on Kathleen's planned day-care income—was shot. One day I went to the ATM to take out $20, and my balance was $13.

After a few weeks of self-pity, I rallied. I took weekend shifts and extra overtime. I went to Home Depot and picked out neutral gray paint colors that mirrored my cloudy ennui—but felt somehow comforting. I blasted music at all hours. I painted every room, rebuilt the sagging kitchen cabinets, and stumbled through the basics of cooking and cleaning. I learned how to keep my pool from turning green and took solo swims. I unpacked boxes from Montana, put up pictures, bought a pair of Doc Martens, and got a little more in tune with '90s fashion. I drove to Yosemite, camped, and hiked. Each of these steps helped strengthen my solitude muscle. The rhythms of physical work—painting, repairs, yard maintenance—gave structure to my empty hours and slowly rebuilt my confidence. In mastering these small domains, I began to see myself as capable of larger changes.

Growing stronger in my solitude, I faced a deeper realization: I could no longer wait to see what Kathleen might do. Regardless of my marriage, I was determined to move forward. I had worked too hard to get where I was. Outside the cult, what was my role as a human being? How did I fit into the world? What should I expect of myself? Beyond paying bills, working on the house, and staving off weekend depression, what was my purpose? I needed to define my own hero's journey on a manageable scale, while I barely comprehended the psychological cult exit costs that lay ahead.

Through this fog of uncertainty, one truth anchored me: I was still a father to three young sons, a purpose that never ends. But even that wasn't enough. I needed to frame a scaled-down journey that would end with my death. At 30, you wouldn't think mortality could loom so large. To learn to live, I had to admit I would eventually die—forever. Replacing the lofty aspiration of *ascension to God* with a finite life is not to be taken lightly. After leaving any religion or cult, the struggle to accept your mortality can impinge on your every thought. I needed a plan to navigate this new reality. I sat down at my computer and made a map—a chart of my own presence, plotting my course through life. I put it up next to my bathroom mirror, and I looked at it every morning:

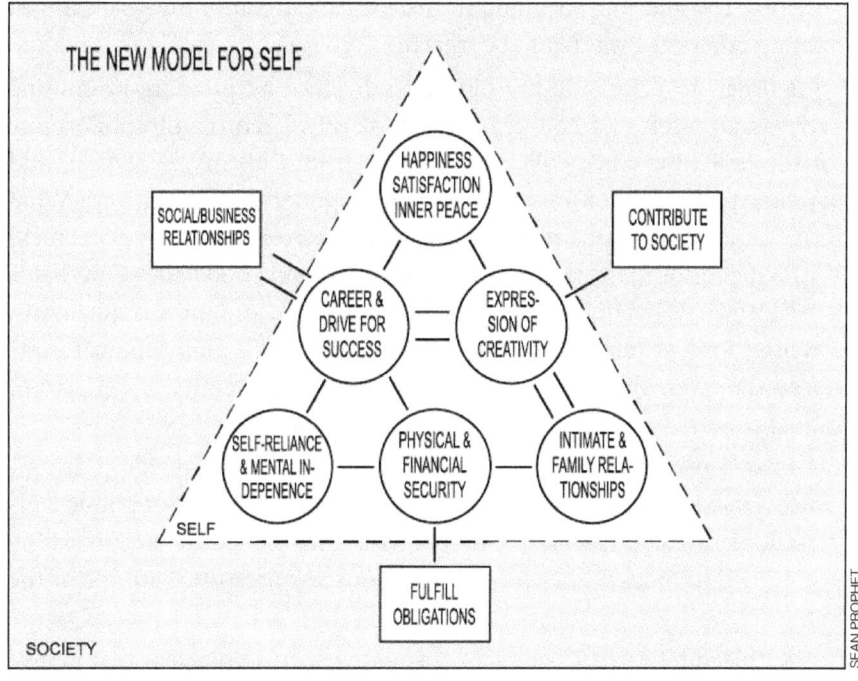

What's *not* on my chart spoke volumes: No God or Jesus. No divine anything. No flowery colors, halos, rays, beacons, clouds, flames, or mountains. When it comes to how you live, none of those things matter. I had to strip my life down to the bare facts—a chart as stark as the questions I was trying to answer: Who was I? Me and society—a social animal among billions. What relationships did I need to sustain myself and raise a family? What obligations did I owe? What could I contribute? How could I build a reliable foundation for my future self?

My post-cult moral inventory led me to an insight: ethics have nothing to do with God-belief or religion—which often conceal worse ethics through shadow repression. A moral person "handles their business" with integrity, and respects others. They contribute to their community, value truth and reality, maintain mental independence, and honor their own values while avoiding Dark Triad traits, manipulation, and delusional thinking. I hadn't yet discovered *The Moral Landscape*, but I was on my way.

The implications were liberating. I asked myself, what more do you need to be a good human? Meaning? "Bollocks," I thought. With all due respect to Dr. Lorne Dawson, I no longer felt any need to belong to a group larger than myself, unless it was my family or all of humanity. No cults, no religions. I would find meaning in the ethical pursuit of my goals and in treating others as I wanted to be treated.

I began to dismantle my old cult-self piece by piece, re-examining every assumption that had defined my identity. I returned to philosophy for the first time since college, diving deep into history, evolution, and psychology. Each book raised increasingly fundamental questions: What forms of economic and political organization create the best outcomes? Without gods or masters, how do we define human good and evil? What is love? Justice? What does it mean to live a good life, and more importantly, a well-examined one? These questions weren't mere philosophical exercises—they were lifelines pulling me toward a new identity, and a path of introspection I'm still walking today.

First, I needed to sort out my family. Despite my growing independence, I still loved Kathleen and wanted our family whole. But phone conversations revealed her path: she frequently mentioned divorce, insisting she needed to focus on her recovery without any pressure from me or the kids.

Kathleen reflected: "The main reason I wanted a divorce is that I knew you would put yourself on hold. Even if I told you to go out and experience life and people, you wouldn't. I needed to heal psychologically, mentally, and physically, but I needed to do that my way and alone. You thought I was crazy not to get medical help. I just couldn't fight that."

Her refusal to seek cancer treatment frustrated me. Did she have a death wish? I tried to insist on medical treatment, but she was adamant. She would rather leave me than fight that battle. Making our separation official felt like admitting defeat, but in August I filed for divorce, which released me from responsibility for her well-being. We kept it simple and drama-free, working through shared custody and property division with an intermediary attorney and paralegal. The judge's approval started a six-month countdown to finality.

That September, my mother arranged a trip to Seattle with the boys. Despite my growing independence, I couldn't resist the chance to see them. The situation was less than ideal. I was once again tied to my mother and the cult—because she had my kids.

We spent several days aboard a member's $2 million yacht, where my sons melted my heart and reconnected me with fatherhood.

Sean Prophet and sons Christopher, Nathaniel, and Laurence, Tacoma Narrows Bridge, September 1994

The trip was a grand adventure, with crabbing and delicious meals. Still, it was a little awkward, since my mother was trying to set me up with the yacht owner's daughter—a divorced woman my age with two kids. I wasn't remotely over Kathleen, and while the daughter was pleasant, she wasn't interested either.

It was also jarring for me to enjoy such opulence while I was barely earning enough to survive. I felt small knowing that I wasn't pulling my weight as a father—still dependent on my mother's largesse. The boys asked when they were coming home, and I couldn't honestly tell them. Leaving them to return to Los Angeles ripped my heart out all over again.

After my trip, Kathleen left Mt. Shasta and rejoined our kids in Montana. That was progress—she was no longer with her lover. She later explained, "It was agonizing to leave my kids, but I had fallen into reactive emotions with them. As a trained Montessori early childhood teacher, I knew too much about how emotional reactivity can harm kids psychologically. I needed to heal and find myself for them. The primary reason I went to Mt. Shasta was to heal my body, mind, and soul—to learn to love myself and my life again." In Montana, a gynecologist worried she had waited too long to treat her cancer and might need a hysterectomy. But her biopsy came back clean—her cervix had healed and she was cancer-free. It seemed like a miracle. Had the alt-health treatments worked? Had she been misdiagnosed? Or was she just beyond lucky?

That summer and fall, I reclaimed parts of myself. My aloneness was *hellish*, but it forced me to confront my entitlement and adjust to reality. I started weekly therapy, which helped me see that my struggles weren't solely about Kathleen. Being micromanaged in my cult, denied my authentic voice, and subjected to thought reform had short-circuited my adult personality development—that should have occurred in my teens and twenties.

These insights clarified my social anxiety and discomfort with solitude. My therapist assured me that retracing those missed steps could lead to a stronger future partnership—whether with Kathleen or someone else. Gradually, I stopped fixating on what others had done to me or what I "deserved" and began to focus on my growth. For the first time since Kathleen left, I could see a narrow path to happiness.

I can't stress enough the importance of taking this step toward emotional maturity. As long as you remain stuck in the mindset of "this thing was done to me," no progress is possible. That holds true for leaving a cult, an abusive relationship, business deals gone bad, a failed marriage, or any setback. The key is reframing the experience: "This didn't happen to me personally—it would have happened to anyone in similar circumstances," and, "I'm learning how to make better choices moving forward." It's not about blaming yourself or excusing what happened. It's about depersonalizing the trauma and letting go of narratives that cast someone else as the villain who "ruined your life." You can pay a therapist a lot of money to talk you through this over a long period of time—or you can take my word that it works.

CHAPTER THIRTY THREE

Reconnection and Disconnection

Just when I had accepted my marriage was over—Kathleen called me. It was late November, and she was coming to Los Angeles. Could she stay at the house for a few days? Could she store some belongings there? "Absolutely," I said. There was no chance I would be vindictive. I reminded myself that *I* had sent her away when she was pregnant with Christopher, and she forgave me. We had both hurt each other in ways that were tough to forgive, and yet I couldn't contain my joy that, at least for now, she was coming home.

A few days later, Kathleen arrived, looking amazing. She was impressed with all the work I had done on the house, saying it felt like… home. We cooked together, talked for hours, and she shared stories about her time in Mt. Shasta. She reminded me so much of the woman I fell in love with in 1984—full of energy and sparkle. I didn't dare ask about her long-term plans. But she was warm, present, and said she had missed me.

Eventually, we ended up in the sheets, reconnecting as if no time had passed. It was a passionate moment we both needed, breathing new *life* into each other—and with it, a glimmer of hope for a future I thought was gone. Afterward, we took a selfie in the backyard, and I implored her, "Please stay and make this a home for our family." And she did.

Kathleen later explained to me that her Mt. Shasta companion was a good friend but not someone for a long-term relationship. They had both been at a crossroads in their lives. She reflected, "I still really loved you, and I wanted to be with my boys. When we started talking, we reconnected in a unique, beautiful, and authentic way. I had reframed and healed so many things, and so it just felt totally right."

There was only one thing left to do: Get. Our. Kids.

We drove to Montana just before Christmas, spending a casual holiday at the snow-covered Ranch, watching my mother delight in her grandkids opening presents. Gone was the fear and tension of the year before. Our family was together, and our boundaries were clear. Her attitude toward us had changed. Was it the barest beginning of—respect?

Sean and Kathleen Prophet, West Hills, California, November 1994

We arrived back in Los Angeles a full year after we had driven off into that blizzard. And we had survived a bitter course I could never have foreseen. But we were *home*, and *really out* of the cult. The pattern of divorce following a cult exit appears so often that I now warn others to expect it. We beat the odds, but the residual cult hangover nearly ended us. Kathleen's breakdown and my insensitivity to her needs were aftereffects of toxic cult archetypes. For her it was the long-suffering sacrificial mother, inattentive to her body and emotions. For me it was the patriarchal strict-father, pawning off physical and emotional labor onto my wife.

What saved us was my full acceptance of the situation. Gut-wrenching as it was, Kathleen needed that break—including the affair—for our family to survive. If I had clung to resentment over her "cheating," or harbored any nonsense tied to strict-father morality about her "duty," it would have been over. That kind of purity and perfectionism is the same cult mindset that caused our rift.

I've seen far too many people wreck their families over wounded pride. The key is owning your part and choosing your battles. The storm of emotions and psychological shifts you'll face after leaving your cult poses a grave risk to even the strongest families. Both partners need extraordinary love, tolerance, and understanding, as well as a deep capacity for forgiveness.

This realization didn't just apply to my marriage—it helped me confront another lingering obligation: the remnants of my relationship with my mother and the cult. I needed to set even stronger boundaries that would protect the healing my family had achieved. So on January 6, 1995, I wrote my mother a letter to formally withdraw my church membership and cancel my subscription to the weekly *Pearls of Wisdom*. Now that she no longer had my kids, I was free to speak my mind.

I thanked her for caring for my kids and acknowledged her Christmas gifts. Then I stated my growing alienation from the cult's absolutism—its rigid "thou shalts" and "thou shalt nots," its suffocating guilt, its fear of loss of ascension. I let her know I had decided to cancel the *Pearls of Wisdom* because receiving them forced me to confront painful contradictions between my choices and her teachings. I told her I had found a different path, working to understand the universe rather than focusing on God or doctrine or special knowledge. "Please accept me as your son, the way that I am," I wrote. "I accept you as my mother, the way that you are, and I do love you very much."

My mother never answered the letter. But the *Pearls* stopped. While I drew strong boundaries, I remained tethered to old beliefs—still clinging to a deistic[1] view of God, still hesitant to name what my former church had become. I wasn't nearly ready to write this book, but my 30-year-old self had taken a big step away from idolatry.

The letter marked a turning point which reminded me of something crucial: I wasn't alone. My journey was one thread in a much larger tapestry of cult exits. Everyone walks this path differently. As I've listened to others who left my cult, I've heard echoes of my own journey—along with insights I wish I had gained sooner. The following quotes are from ex-cult friends, most of whom I knew very well—some since my childhood. I'm grateful to them for sharing their stories, which help illuminate the struggles of cult recovery, and the many paths toward healing.[2]

Donald Trowbridge: The circumstances of our exit really are very meaningful for us. Because it really started with our family becoming the central concern of our lives, and it became more and more of a conflict. When your family starts, you really feel like you've got something and you really have something to live for. The whole mission had become so complex and scary that it was just getting beyond us, and it was really the antithesis of the love and family life we were trying to create. I say, "I need to talk to Elizabeth." So I go on in and "Hi Elizabeth," and she said "Well, what's going on?" I said "You asked if we had any issues, and I just want to be honest, yeah I do." She said, "Well"—I mean it was very quick—"Well, Donald, I don't know what more we can do for you. We've given you everything." Never got to see her again, just got called into the accountant, Jim, and, "You've got two days, you're out of here." So it began a whole process of reintegrating with our family and society, and that took many years.

Stan Holt: A year-and-a-half or two years after leaving, I started to question the existence of the masters, the viability of the messengership, and the community. There was a period of anger, disillusionment, feeling cheated, that I'd been duped, and that it had been a fraud. On the other side of that I started to come out of it and realize, "Hey wait a minute, look at what came out of that. I met my wife there, we were married, my son was born there, the best friends that I've ever made all date to that period of time." Ultimately, the reason I was there was because of community. That was really the legacy. I've come to a feeling of, I think—I was there until I no longer needed to be there—I needed to be there until I learned those things. One of them was to recognize the validity of my own needs as a human being. Looking at it that way allows me to be at peace with the almost 20 years I spent there.

Mark Filipas: It took a long mental process and a good handful of personal experiences of discipline and things that just struck me as not being right, but still trying to justify it in my own head, like, "OK, let's go on with this, maybe there's a spiritual message here." But ultimately after about nine years in Montana—it was around the same time a lot of other people left—we were completely disillusioned. It was very hard to extricate yourself from the Montana community, and a big reason was lack of money. We really didn't get paid. We had room and board provided. We had to save up money, it took us a while. So there was a good two or three years at the end when we kind of had to walk the walk, but secretly there was a lot that we didn't believe in anymore.

Jessicah Filipas (daughter of Mark Filipas): My father—he would completely and honestly answer any question I had. My mother is a different story, she really doesn't enjoy talking about it. I think it's just a part of their lives that they don't really think about any more. And I can remember my parents had obviously been planning on leaving the church for several years. But were not telling their friends, were not speaking about it. They couldn't risk being excommunicated with no means of making a living. I remember when they told me, "We're going to leave Montana, and we're going to go to Portland, but don't tell any of your friends." And I remember thinking, "Well, why can't I?" I was eight years old, I wanted to talk to my friends, I wanted to say goodbye. The shelter cycle was really hard on the entire community, definitely my parents. What affected them most and especially my mother as far as reluctant-ness to speak about it is the embarrassment, I guess you could say, or the kind of guilt for raising your child in a community where you didn't really have a lot of control over anything. I think for those eleven, twelve years of their life, they were in it and they gave everything they had to the church, and to the mother. But once they left that, I think they both had a lot of "what the fuck was I thinking?" And that sort of turned into I don't really want to talk about this with anyone ever again.

Anna Maletta: I think I had a period of being angry after I left at first, thinking about all the things that maybe were abusive that I allowed to happen to myself. But I realized that I was probably just as abusive to others. It was kind of like a domino effect. Everybody kind of was interwoven into the whole dysfunctional way that the community had been set up. So I think I had to let my anger out. I think everybody needs to let that shadow part out. A lot of us really felt that we were repressing a certain part of our humanity. You cannot change certain darknesses that are part of your creativity. Part of our inner workings of humanity. I mean you just can't get rid of all of that with the "violet flame." Or, thinking that some prayers you're going to do is going to exorcise you of sexual thoughts. It was not good in that respect. I've had to learn to let out things that had been repressed for so long and reclaim my own personal self.

John Waid: Personally, withdrawing from the church—it was as if someone had died. Someone more dear to me than anyone I had personally ever known. Because I'm giving up a dream. And now, twelve years later, I realize that it has nothing to do with that. It's all inside of you. And there's nothing outside of you. If you get in touch with your own reality, then you don't need the external reality. Very few people are capable of making their own way. They don't have the courage to face the fear of stepping into the void that exists inside of them. Because they're going to free fall. And then all of a sudden one day you wake up and you discover that free fall is what it is. All the crutches, all the religion, all the opiates, will not stop the free fall. We're free falling. We've been doing it since there was cognitive thought in any of us. And we'll continue to do that. And continuing to be angry about your experiences with the church are preventing you from getting to the base of your fury. Of your anger. You're railing against something that occurred in the past. But today is all you have. And if you will simply get hold of today—even if you have to revisit every single event that's causing you this anger—to get to the point where you're neutral.

John Waid's words struck a chord: "Withdrawing from the church—it was as if someone had died." The relationship to cult ideology, ritual, and sociality mirrors human attachment. The cult milieu—its concepts, personalities, and behaviors—becomes a companion.

This isn't just a metaphor. Modern research shows that our brains process religious figures—whether Jesus, Allah, Yahweh, or Ascended Masters—exactly as they process human friendships.[3] Psychologists call these "parasocial relationships"—bonds of intimacy without interaction. You might find this truth unsettling, even blasphemous. Yet our brains treat these idols the same as flesh-and-blood companions, which explains why leaving them feels like a death or breakup.

Consider how people mourn celebrities they've never met. The line between fandom and worship blurs across cultures. Santa Muerte and Santeria devotees pray to Marilyn Monroe. Vietnamese and Bolivian folk religions venerate Elvis Presley, Che Guevara, Michael Jackson, and Vladimir Putin. The Love Has Won cult worshiped Saint Germain, Robin Williams, John Lennon, and Donald Trump.

My cult followed this pattern. We worshiped the mythical King Arthur alongside George Washington and Joan of Arc. We transformed my father Mark Prophet into the Ascended Master Lanello. Understanding these parasocial bonds explained their persistence.

When I grasped this framework, it recast my departure. It wasn't betrayal—it was outgrowing relationships that had served their purpose. If you see yourself in this—your bonds to gods, gurus, or sacred communities—know that these spiritual connections shaped you as truly as any earthly love. Their loss carves real wounds.

Take the time to grieve.

---

[1] Deism is a theological belief that posits the existence of a supreme being who created the universe but does not intervene in its operations. Emerging during the Enlightenment in the 17th and 18th centuries, deism emphasizes reason and observation of the natural world as the primary means to understand the divine, while rejecting supernatural revelations and miracles. *Wikipedia, Deism*, https://en.wikipedia.org/wiki/Deism.

[2] Personal interviews with Donald Trowbridge, Stan Holt, Mark Filipas, Jessicah Filipas, Anna Maletta, and John Waid, 2007–2012.

[3] A study by Jordan Grafman and colleagues at the National Institute of Neurological Disorders and Stroke found that religious beliefs activate the same brain regions involved in understanding the emotions and intentions of other people, suggesting that the brain processes the concept of God similarly to how it processes social interactions. *Cognitive and neural foundations of religious belief*, 2009, https://doi.org/10.1073/pnas.0811717106

CHAPTER THIRTY FOUR

The Faith I Lost

"So much for being the Buddha, then." Those cutting words from fellow cult member Cole Braunley haunted me. I had announced my departure at the age of 29, and people like Braunley began to treat me as an outcast. Just a few months away from leaving, I was hopelessly confused. Was I really leaving? Had I ever been a "Buddha?" Would I lose my cosmic titles? Let's revisit the theology I escaped to understand how I went from princeling in the court of the Ascended Masters to atheist five years later. My upbringing was steeped in mythologies of my cosmic importance. My parents indeed told me I was the physical incarnation of one of the "nine planetary Buddhas" destined to save Earth.

Reflecting recently on the "nine planetary Buddhas" story, I assumed it came from authentic Buddhist tradition. As a child, I embraced my "Buddha-hood" wholeheartedly, believing it connected me to something ancient and profound. But now I can't find anything to back it up. Burmese Buddhism mentions nine planetary gods—Surya, Chandra, Mangala, Budha, Brhaspati, Shukra, Shani, Rahu, and Ketu—and nine examples of "Buddha potential." But nothing connects them to Earth's salvation. The idea likely stems from Theosophy or Mighty I AM folklore, heavily embellished by my parents. The closest analogy I can find is Maitreya Buddha, the fifth and final Buddha of this *kalpa* in Buddhist eschatology, meant to follow Gautama.

I held other spiritual titles: the mantles of "Lanello," "Sanat Kumara," and "Rex." They shaped how I saw myself and how others viewed me. They were meant to make me feel important. But they were also a cage. My future was full of spiritual expectations like "being the Buddha," making walking away unthinkable—until it wasn't.

Members of my cult shared a spiritual identity represented by the chart of "Your Divine Self." We also called it the "Chart of the Presence," referring to the "I AM Presence," a concept inherited from the 1930s Mighty I AM cult. Our chart is similar to theirs, except we added the middle-figure mediator of the "Holy Christ Self" to align with Christianity. I was so taken with this chart that during my mother's *Nightline* interview in May 1990, I placed a miniature version behind her head to ensure Ted Koppel's audience of millions would see it. The chart is foundational to our faith and imbued with a kind of magic. Every chapel centers its altar on what we considered to be the image of God. Members carry copies in their wallets, and they hang framed versions in their homes and offices.

Chart of *Your Divine Self* (left) popularized by The Summit Lighthouse c. 1960, derived from an earlier work called *Chart of the Mighty I AM Presence*, (right) created c. 1930 by the Mighty I AM cult

ABC News *Nightline*, Ted Koppel interviews Elizabeth Clare Prophet, ...with the Chart of the Presence visible in the background... May 17, 1990

It's more than a symbol. The chart encapsulates our theology.[1] It depicts a trinity of Self, akin to the Christian Trinity of Father, Son, and Holy Spirit, but with hierarchy: the I AM Presence at the top, the Holy Christ Self in the middle, and the human self stuck at the bottom. My cult uses dozens of metaphors to denigrate human nature, holding disdain for the lower chakras beneath the heart, suppressing the "electronic belt" of human "substance" tied to base emotions and desires. Yet to believers, the chart offers a clear, comforting depiction of divine order.

The ultimate goal is for the lower figure to transcend human nature with help from the Holy Christ Self and reunite with God as the I AM Presence through the ritual of the ascension. This resolution of the soul's journey through karma and suffering aligns with the Western Esoteric Tradition. It resonates across cultures because everyone's heard some version of the hero's journey. Departure, struggle, purification, reunion—the monomyth of Eastern and Western religions and fiction: The Prodigal Son, *The Odyssey*, The Mahabharata, Dante's *Divine Comedy*, The Legend of Mu Lan, *The Lord of the Rings*, The Labors of Hercules, and *Star Wars*.

While I still believed, God was like the air I breathed—essential, omnipresent. The Ascended Masters overshadowed me through their *presence*, though they never spoke directly in my mind as my friend Will Adams once claimed. I never heard voices. Instead, I believed sufficient devotion would allow the masters to *guide* my thoughts and actions—like a mind-meld—their thoughts to my thoughts. When they spoke through my mother, I felt like the luckiest person alive, watching cosmic history unfold from a front row seat. Sometimes I sat on her side thrones—adjutant to the Messenger. Other times, I saw myself as an imperfect vessel, suppressing human questioning to ask, "What would my Mighty I AM Presence do?" I felt enveloped in a divine bubble—protected, loved, and special. The seduction was simple: inside that bubble, I could never be wrong.

I now recognize such certainty as perilous. Back then I saw everything through the lens of destiny and my role within it. I believed I was a vital link in the lineage of saints and luminaries. But it was a free pass to validate my every thought and belief. Nietzsche's insight is revelatory: God represents the ultimate projection of the human will to power.[2] Such hubris paves the way to corruption, leading in the most extreme cases to vicious totalitarian regimes. The Third Reich's slogan, "Gott mit uns" ("God with us"), was emblazoned on their coat of arms. The late Roman and Byzantine empires cried "Nobiscum Deus," Imperial Russia echoed "Съ нами Богъ!"—all effectively meaning the same thing: "Whatever we're doing is God's work." It's now impossible for me to see the concept of God as anything but a device for marshaling corrupt, militaristic power.

The German coat-of-arms during the Third Reich which reads "Gott mit uns," or "God with us."

While I was still involved, I didn't recognize those pitfalls. As an ordained minister, I craved my ascension. I longed to commune with the masters, experience God's infinity, explore the universe, and understand its mysteries. I wanted to be immortal, not just because I was greedy for more life. To miss such an opportunity for understanding would be like not boarding the ultimate starship, bound for First Contact with Cosmic Beings. I wanted to move beyond space and time. I fantasized about fulfilling the Styx lyric from *Man of Miracles*[3] I had heard in college, but for real:

> He was a man of miracles,
> riding golden meteorites,
> ruler of distant galaxies,
> born of the northern lights!

"Ruler of distant galaxies." *Ruler?* Like many others in my cult, my fantasy was also centered on *power*. It reminds me of Mormon theology, in which members of The Church of Jesus Christ of Latter-Day Saints believe they'll one day rule their own planets. Like Mormon "exaltation," my cult believes that by becoming one with our "I AM Presence" through the ascension, we can become all-powerful. In terms of sheer grandiosity, there's little difference between the two belief systems.

Everything I read—and everyone I knew in my cult—reinforced those dreams. We weren't just becoming gods. We were returning to our true home in the cosmos. By contrast, Earth is small, insignificant, and fleeting—a means to a greater end. Maya. Samsara. Illusion. There was a time I would have gladly traded my life for even a moment at the feet of cosmic beings such as Sanat Kumara, Lady Venus, or Alpha and Omega. And that's a terrifying thought.

My de-conversion wasn't linear. Countless small realizations chipped away at my belief. To understand the weight of that transformation, it's important to reflect on the cognitive dissonance that sustained my former state. Despite my rebellion, I was deep into the theology. I'm living proof that it's possible to doubt and believe at the same time—as most people of faith do. I pored over the King James Bible. I studied Hinduism, Buddhism, Kabbalah, and Catholic saints. I chanted mantras, sang Bhajans, and devoured esoteric classics like *Unveiled Mysteries, The Magic Presence, Isis Unveiled, A Dweller on Two Planets, The Secret Doctrine, Brother of the Third Degree,* and *Autobiography of a Yogi.*

Reflecting on my spiritual greed is humbling. How could I have been so pompous, so dismissive of humanity? How could I have felt so superior? How did I get lost in such a state of sci-fi delusion? It's hard to say. Indoctrination and socialization are effective. And what a self-congratulatory fantasy it was! I see now that during my most devout years, I was no different from the "uglets" I had mocked as a teenager. They flaunted their spiritual pride to boost their social standing in my cult, but I didn't need to parade my devotion—I had already arrived. Yet I was just as fanatical as they were. We were all chasing the same God-smack opiate fantasy. I buried myself in religious studies, growing more intoxicated—always hungry to chase my next high. I had immersed myself in the world's religions. I had lived them, and I had taught them.

From outside, my cult's theology appears both overwrought and childishly simplistic. But to believers, it's deeply resonant, offering cosmic struggle and redemption along with answers to existential questions. Untangling my beliefs took years. By the time our "shelter cycle" ended, whatever had driven me to believe my mother's apocalyptic predictions—and prepare to survive them—had begun to fade. The subsequent near-beer dictation confirmed her messages were human. After leaving Montana, I slowly began to doubt the existence of God and the Ascended Masters, but I hadn't rejected them completely.

One question haunted me: If we were doing God's work, why had we gone so horribly wrong? We billed ourselves as the highest and best representatives of God, the *Church Universal and Triumphant*, posing as the only true spiritual authority on Earth. We believed we were destined to supplant the *Church Militant*, loosely represented by the Catholic Church. Yet there was no triumph in what we had become. The Catholic Church has endured for two millennia despite its deep corruption. In just 32 years, from 1958 to 1990, we went from would-be world saviors to would-be world destroyers. Powerless to manifest judgment on the world, we instead shattered our own community.

My cognitive dissonance peaked as my rational understanding clashed with my fading spiritual beliefs. Which led to an epiphany. One day after work, probably in 1998, I was in a Burbank parking lot when clarity struck. My brain, after years of spinning its wheels like a slot machine, finally hit triple sevens. A jackpot of silver-dollar thoughts dropped into my coin hopper all at once. Smiling slightly, I shook my head with a mix of bewilderment and relief: "You know? It was all bullshit. Just plain BULLSHIT." The prophecies? The Ascended Masters? The dictations? God? No—*everything*.

My parents had drilled these fictions into my head when I was too young to distinguish reality from make-believe. Even as I saw the harm and saw through my mother's manipulations, I couldn't shake it off—until now. Such is the power of childhood indoctrination.[4] But there was no basis to *any* of it. It was just as those cynical newspaper reporters had always claimed: I had grown up in a bad *Marvel Comics* movie, full of imaginary superheroes.

I felt a rush of euphoria, tinged with sadness for my lost naiveté and anger at having duped myself. My thoughts raced: "If that's true, what else has to be true?" Parts of my identity were still on guard—and they were panicking. How could I accept that my whole life in the cult was a lie? Those devout sub-personalities didn't want to lay down their arms and face my sunk costs. But the logic was inexorable. My mind had delivered its revelatory opus—practically gift-wrapped—and there was no going back.

Why did it take so long? Why had I returned to the cult? As ex-member John Waid observed, "It was tough to give up on that cosmic dream." Now I would have to rebuild my worldview—stripped of all myths. My new journey would be just as rigorous as my former religious studies, applying science to the existential problems I had once solved with theology. Having gone to college for electrical engineering, I had a running start. I began to devour popular science books, including *The Selfish Gene*,[5] *Chaos*,[6] *Cosmos*,[7] and *A Brief History of Time*.[8] But why didn't my engineering courses lead me to atheism right away?

I struggle to convey just how much my mind resisted this transition. Many people think atheists are hasty, arrogant and disrespectful of religion. That our views are ill-considered and based on rebellion, denial or negation. That we're looking for an excuse to commit immoral acts or free-riding on Christian morality. That we haven't read the Bible enough. Or that we're devil worshipers or that we hate God. But are you kidding me? I never decided—or even planned—to become an atheist. I clung for dear life to the preciousness of my beliefs, long after they were indefensible.

I resisted rejecting God and the *Marvel* menagerie of Ascended Masters with every ounce of willpower I could muster. I stayed loyal to all the gods I knew—until my formerly hated "carnal mind" left me no choice. My nemesis became my savior. At first, the realization burned. Those stories had shielded me from uncertainty, given me a sense of purpose, and made me feel like my life was written into the fabric of the universe. But as my illusions shattered, so did their chains. For the first time, I could see the cosmos for what it truly was—not some divine stage with me at its center, but a vast expanse governed by rules, which I could learn to understand. Without divine fear and cosmic drama, I found something I hadn't expected: liberation.

Cognitive dissonance played a key role in my confinement. I kept science and theology far apart—like matter and antimatter that would annihilate each other on contact. Science explained how things worked—cars starting, rockets flying, phones transmitting voices. Religion addressed existential questions like, "What happens when you die?" Renowned paleontologist and evolutionary biologist Steven Jay Gould called this separation *non-overlapping magisteria*: science dealt with the "how," religion with the "why." That compartmentalization is how I could spend my days designing electrical systems that obeyed the laws of physics and then go to a service that evening, where my mother was impossibly channeling beings from other galaxies.

Gould tried to suggest that science and religion could coexist. But we can't reconcile them. Once science proves its utility through testable explanations, magical thinking must dissolve. We're left with one cosmos containing all that exists. We're left with what's explained, what remains unexplained, what's possible, and what can be dismissed. This principle of parsimony, or Occam's Razor, is attributed to the 14th-century philosopher William of Ockham: "The best explanation is the one with the smallest number of entities" or that makes "the fewest assumptions."

Grandiose spiritual ideas violate this principle. Take the Renaissance esoteric notion from Paracelsus—adopted by my cult—that nature is guided by invisible entities called "elementals." These stem from Empedocles' ancient concept of the four basic elements: Fire, Air, Water, and Earth. Paracelsus personified these as Salamanders (fire), Sylphs (air), Undines (water), and Gnomes (earth).

New Years' Eve bonfire in the desert, Nipton, California, c. 2018

We can respect ancient philosophers while acknowledging that modern science renders their ideas obsolete. They lacked the tools to uncover the inner workings of matter and energy. So they devised living metaphors and taxonomies to organize their observations. Fires can resemble living beings, and it's easy to see how they might have inspired the concept of Salamanders. But now we know that fire is a chemical reaction—rapid oxidation. If you see a dragon in the bonfire photo above, it's *pareidolia*, not proof of elementals.

Fire needs fuel, oxygen, and ignition. A tree's metabolism, from absorbing carbon to photosynthesis, is explained by well-understood biochemical reactions—no "tree deva"[9] required. We don't need to disprove tree devas because they add nothing to our understanding. What's more likely: that photosynthesis depends on an invisible, undetectable being, or that it relies on natural processes? The simpler, proven explanation wins every time.

The question isn't, "Do you believe in elementals?" or even "Do you believe in God?" It's whether you accept a rules-based universe with laws that can't be violated. Gods, miracles, nature spirits, and superheroes live outside this framework. A passive deistic God may fit within the cosmos we observe, but it makes no difference to humanity. In a rules-based universe, the structure of divine fear and punishment crumbles, along with prayers for healing the sick, finding jobs, or securing parking spaces. Everything converges to cause and effect.

Recognize that in a rules-based universe, God is no more *necessary* to our existence than a tree deva is to a tree, or a salamander is to a fire. No one can prove God doesn't exist, and that's an improperly framed question. Science doesn't rule things out of existence. It rules them in, to the extent its principles explain what we observe. We're all free to coexist without dueling interpretations of divinity. By combining science with the principle of parsimony, we dispense with supernatural explanations.

---

[1] There are three humanoid figures in the chart. The top figure, the "I AM Presence," represents God. But the I AM Presence is a unique fraction of God personally tied to you, which is why it's called "Your Divine Self." You're surrounded by seven concentric rings of color, pierced by 41 beams of white light shooting out from the center: white, yellow, pink, violet, purple, green, and blue, known as the "Causal Body." This chart, originally designed by May DaCamara in 1935 for the "I AM" Activity, featured only two figures—the "I AM Presence" and the individual in the physical realm—and differs from the later version adopted by the Church Universal and Triumphant, which included the third figure, the "Holy Christ Self." Details on DaCamara's original chart are provided by the *Material and Visual Cultures of Religion* project at Yale University: https://mavcor.yale.edu/conversations/object-narratives/chart-magic-presence

These are the "seven rays" that my parents considered to represent different "god-qualities." Each ray has an associated Archangel, Chohan, and Elohim, derived from Theosophical teachings. The seven rays are described in the Wikipedia entry on the topic: https://en.wikipedia.org/wiki/Seven_rays The rays in turn derive from the physical color spectrum of light (with the notable exception of red, brown, black, orange, or chartreuse—which my parents considered to represent dark, human "misqualified" energy).

The middle humanoid in the chart looks like the familiar Christian image of Jesus, with a yellow halo, floating on clouds. It's appropriately called the "Holy Christ Self." That's also you, but a less divine and more human version of you, more understanding and closer to your day-to-day existence. The Holy

Christ Self is considered the mediator between a judgmental Old-Testament style God and the human. The Christ Self is more loving and forgiving of your sins, just like the biblical (New-Testament) Jesus. The bottom humanoid figure represents you as a physical person. It's also pictured with a halo, wearing a robe, arms outstretched, standing in a pillar of violet-tinged flames. At the center of the lower figure is the "three-fold-flame," composed of pink (for love), yellow (for wisdom), and blue (for power). This teaching is outlined in *The Chart of Your Divine Self*, available at the Mark Prophet website: https://www.markprophet.org/Teachings/Chart-Divine-Self.html In the background of the chart is a mountain, symbolizing the upward trek toward "self-mastery," and a beacon of light from "The Summit Lighthouse," calling seekers home to their God.

[2] The will to power, as conceptualized by Friedrich Nietzsche, suggests an intrinsic drive toward dominance and mastery. In the context of religious belief, this drive can manifest in the pursuit of aligning one's actions with what is perceived as the "will of God." This alignment often serves as a means for individuals and institutions to assert authority and influence, positing their interpretations of divine will as justification for their dominance or leadership roles within societies. The identification with a higher, divine will allows for a form of transcendence of individual power, where the pursuit of power and influence is sanctified as a higher moral or spiritual duty. This dynamic can be observed in various historical and contemporary contexts, where religious leaders or groups wield significant social, political, and even military power, framed as the execution of a divine mandate. The concept underscores how deeply human the desire for power is woven into the fabric of spiritual and religious life, driving individuals and groups to seek dominance under the guise of fulfilling a divine purpose. Friedrich Nietzsche explores this interplay between power and religion in On the Genealogy of Morality, where he discusses how religious institutions manipulate moral concepts to exert control over individuals. The full text is available at https://en.wikipedia.org/wiki/On_the_Genealogy_of_Morality

[3] DeYoung, D., Young, J., & Brandle, R. J. J. (1974). *Man of Miracles* [Song]. On *Man of Miracles*. Wixen Music Publishing.

[4] In two studies, 5- and 6-year-old children were questioned about the status of protagonists in realistic, religious, and fantastical stories. Results showed that children from religious backgrounds were more likely to judge protagonists in religious stories with divine intervention as real, while secular children judged them as fictional. This trend extended to fantastical stories, where secular children were more likely to differentiate fiction from reality. The study highlights the influence of religious exposure on children's ability to distinguish between fact and fiction. Full study available at https://doi.org/10.1111/cogs.12138

[5] Dawkins, R. (1976). *The selfish gene*. Oxford University Press.

[6] Gleick, J. (1987). *Chaos: Making a new science*. Penguin Books.

[7] Sagan, C. (1980). *Cosmos*. Random House.

[8] Hawking, S. W. (1988). *A brief history of time: From the Big Bang to black holes*. Bantam Books.

[9] A tree deva, in Theosophy and New Age movements, is a nature spirit regarded as the divine essence or guardian of a tree, embodying its life force and spiritual essence. More on devas in Theosophy can be found at https://en.wikipedia.org/wiki/Deva_(Theosophy)

CHAPTER THIRTY FIVE

Who Am I?

The Tao Te Ching observes, "Good fortune follows upon disaster. Disaster lurks within good fortune."[1] A pithier modern take is, "You can't tell good news from bad news while it's happening to you." The journey toward self-awareness is much the same: a lifetime of fumbling in the dark, often oblivious to the long-term implications of our experiences. Sometimes, we reach plateaus of understanding, only to revise them later. For those committed to introspection, analysis is never complete. Decades after the fact, I'm still unearthing the deeper impacts of my cult experience.

Identity investment is the beating heart of all cults, driving political polarization, tribalism, and the culture wars. Over time, your beliefs fuse with your sense of self, becoming indistinguishable from who you are and how you see the world. When I left my cult, the changes gave me whiplash. Some came quickly, like updating my wardrobe and enjoying long-denied activities. But the deeper work of untangling my identity took time.

Leaving a cult causes social, mental, and moral shock. You absorbed cult frameworks over time, and your moral sense will need recalibration. The cult jargon you normalized is indecipherable to outsiders. Residual cult sanctimony can surface unexpectedly through judging things you once accepted and accepting things you once judged. Such disorientation will make you feel like you don't quite fit. Without redefining who you are outside the cult, everything else will remain a struggle. How easily you reintegrate depends on how far you strayed from consensus reality—and how the moral and political systems of your new environment contrast with the ones you left behind.

Cults are broadly authoritarian, including "pastel-QAnon" and female-led versions, which still rely on strict-father morality, purity, and perfectionism. These frameworks align with the Loyalty, Authority, and Sanctity moral foundations, which foster cohesion and commitment. As I rebuilt my identity, I saw how these elements had shaped both my cult life and political worldview. Two tests helped map my evolution.

Developed in 2001, the Political Compass Test plots beliefs along left-right and authoritarian-libertarian axes,[2] while 8values measures views on equality-vs-markets, nation-vs-globe, liberty-vs-authority, and tradition-vs-progress.[3] These tests evoke the moral foundations later identified by Jonathan Haidt. Had I taken them in 1990 before leaving my cult, my answers would have revealed that I was a *right-wing authoritarian* and *capitalist fascist*—someone with a strong belief in God, hierarchical social organization, and America as a divinely inspired nation. I voted Republican and held restrictive views on sexuality, staunchly supported free enterprise, and dismissed the concerns of minorities and the poor. Anyone who couldn't make it in America without government help was morally defective, in my view. This corresponds to Kohlberg's stage 4 of moral development: law-and-order.

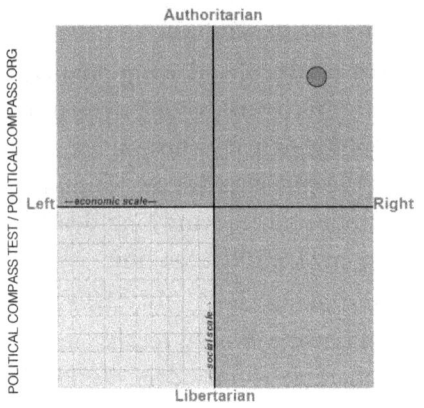
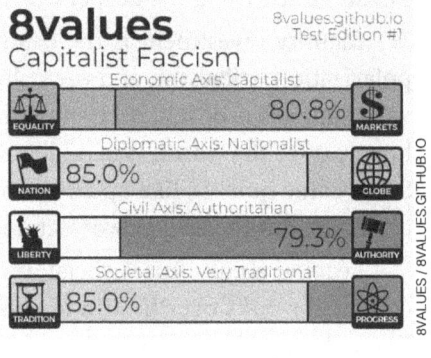

Sean Prophet's in-cult political compass   Sean Prophet's in-cult 8values test

Today, the same tests place me as a *left-libertarian* or *libertarian socialist* with a global focus, rejecting most traditions, including the false allure of "ancient wisdom." My current political identity aligns more closely with Kohlberg's stage 5: the social contract. This transformation was a struggle

380

that took nearly a decade, with several twists and turns. Membership in a hierarchical cult system not only maps onto authoritarianism and nationalism but also fosters a desire to impose such a system on others. This creates a stubborn identity hangover—which I experienced in full.

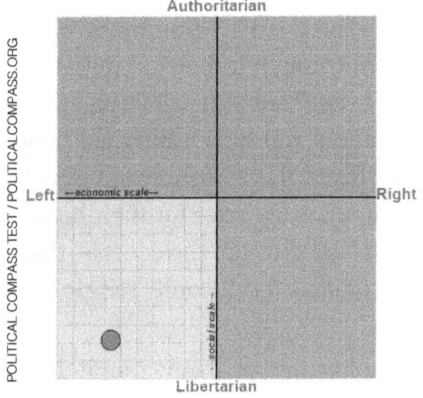

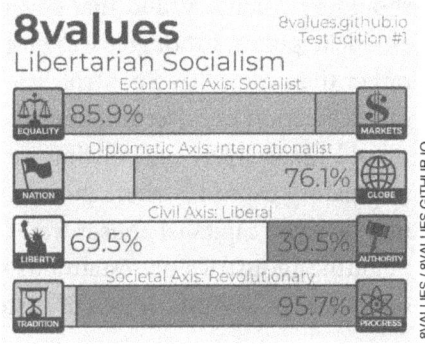

Sean Prophet's present-day political compass

Sean Prophet's present-day 8values test

The Republican Party has long been the party of hierarchy and religion—a variation on the "divine command" ethics I had worked so hard to escape. After leaving my cult, I rejected the GOP because most 21st-century Republicans embrace Christian theocracy. Beyond tax cuts and privatization, it's their central focus. This was true long before MAGA-Jesus or Project 2025. Modern Republicans remain determined to impose Christian morality through government power. They aim to control family, religion, education, media, the arts, business and government, while still refusing to treat women as equals. This Seven Mountain Mandate, published in 1975, is firmly rooted in the Holy City from the Book of Revelation and the conservative moral hierarchy.[4]

After leaving my cult, my views on sex, drugs, race, and homosexuality liberalized, though I retained conservative beliefs about economics and human nature. I was in that liminal space for recovering fascists between Kohlberg stages 4 and 5, often labeled "fiscally conservative, socially liberal." Seeking to explore and solidify my post-cult identity, I founded a blog in 2001 called *Black Sun Journal*, which focused on Jungian psychology, cult recovery, and atheism.[5] I connected with other right-libertarian and anarcho-capitalist bloggers. It felt logical. I had just rejected religious hierarchy, and my friends drew parallels between gods and governments. Both hierarchies are rooted in tradition and accepted with insufficient scrutiny.

I began to lean toward anti-statist views. Like Neil Peart in his early years, I studied Ayn Rand—admiring "prime movers" like her characters Dagny Taggart, John Galt, and Howard Roark. I believed all transactions should be voluntary, and that governments shouldn't set minimum wages. Social policy, I thought, was best handled through individual initiative rather than centralized control. The "nanny state" felt authoritarian, and I saw regulation as governments picking winners and losers. I argued they should focus solely on policing force and fraud. I was concerned about "regulatory capture," where industries manipulate agencies for their benefit. I believed capitalist abuses were best resolved through the courts—that polluting industries or restaurants selling tainted food would self-police out of fear of lawsuits or loss of customers.

I had never signed a "social contract" obligating me to any moral duty beyond reciprocity. Helping others was *my choice*—no one had the right to demand charity. I saw altruism as the enemy, influenced by Ayn Rand's 1964 anthology *The Virtue of Selfishness*.[6] I recorded several audio essays for a friend's podcast, denouncing compassion in one and defending bloodsport in another. Yikes. Looking back, my naive hot takes evoke shades of the Roman Empire—or the hypercapitalist dystopia of *Altered Carbon*.[7]

I had found my new anarcho-capitalist tribe, and it was cultish. We believed our principles stemmed from pure logic and reason. But dissenting posts straying from core ancap beliefs often drew lengthy—and sometimes angry—rebuttals. Still, we thought we were applying the same skepticism that led us to question God's existence to challenge the existence of governments.

It was my first time discussing political philosophy within a radically skeptical framework. While I was well-versed in undergrad sociology, history, and philosophy, I had never challenged the idea of government itself. "Consent of the governed" felt weak if not everyone consented. Why should I pay taxes? I had no voice in how my money was spent. Why should I bail out someone collecting a government check? Why fund a war I don't support? Why get a building permit to construct a house on my own property? I was channeling Republican isolationist and anti-government tropes. But my ancap friends gave me a superior rationale beyond partisanship.

One day I heard a radio report on the cost of the American carceral system. A sociologist noted that incarceration rates for college graduates are four times lower than for those without degrees and argued that enrolling low-income students could reduce crime and shrink the carceral system enough to graduate additional students for free.

That's when I woke up.

Universities and prisons use similar facilities, and we choose which to build. I was jolted into recalling my sociology and poli-sci courses which favored an outcome-based approach, and a social contract. My ancap friends considered the concept of "schools over prisons" borderline blasphemous. They claimed college was "too expensive," or a "fraud," that it "indoctrinates" people, that a lot of poor people "aren't smart enough" for college. But I had already begun to tune them out.

Right-libertarianism appeals primarily to young, straight, white, male professionals who've never faced serious illness or misfortune. I fit that demographic to a tee, and at the time, it made perfect sense to me. No one enjoys taxes or government bureaucracy. But within a year or two, I rejected anarcho-capitalism after reconsidering its core principle: limiting government to policing force and fraud. Because even that requires spending on bureaucracy, cops, prisons, and courts. Why not solve problems at their source instead?

I was becoming more socially conscious. I began to embrace the necessity of systemic solutions. I came to see taxation as the foundation of civilization, without which the ultra-wealthy would establish a feudal system on the backs of the poor. Building permits and property taxes fund public infrastructure. Food safety standards and public health agencies save lives. Regulatory capture can be fought with ethics rules and tighter controls on lobbying. Environmental regulations curtail externalities and force companies to pay their true costs. Tax I "pay" is money that was never legally mine. Minimum wages reduce wage slavery and fuel economic growth. What right-libertarians deride as the "nanny state" is crucial for achieving best outcomes.

Are we prepared to tell our fellow Americans, "You ate poorly, so you deserve to die of a heart attack?" I came to see that in advanced, wealthy, modern democracies everyone has a right to health care, regardless of financial means or lifestyle choices. Even in selfish terms, I would rather tolerate some welfare fraud than step over people sleeping on the street. The only way to ensure a social safety net is to accept that *there will be waste*. Efforts to eliminate waste in social spending will always harm those on the margins who need help. Why not err on the side of help?

I came to believe that the social safety net should include middle-class people, 60 percent of whom live paycheck-to-paycheck and can't cover a $1,000 emergency. Many of us are just a few months away from homelessness if we lose a job, face addiction, or suffer a serious injury. Once homeless—mental health declines, life expectancy plummets, and the odds of regaining stable housing or employment are slim. Right-libertarians don't live in the real world—where bad things happen to good people. So I moved left. It wasn't just political. It was moral. I moved into Kohlberg stage 5—signing the social contract.

My residual cult sanctimony had stunted my moral development, and I wasn't alone. Right-libertarian thinking is ultra-seductive. My dalliance had an explanation: I was reeling from the messianic burden of saving the world through prayer and proselytizing. I needed to shed that weight and live in my small world of self-interest. My boundaries had been violated, and my spiritual responsibilities had been limitless. So to find balance in my new identity, I shrank my circle of concern to the point of narcissism—as expressed in the Pink Floyd song "Money": "I'm-alright-Jack-keep-your-hands-offa-my-stack."[8]

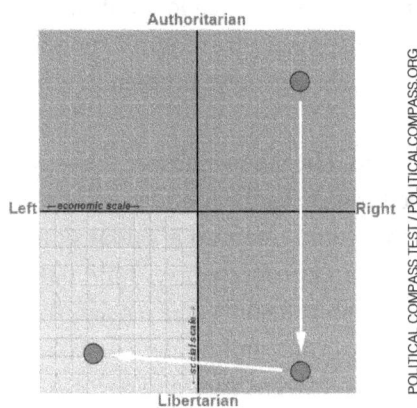

Sean Prophet's path from right-authoritarianism, to to left-libertarianism.

After Kohlberg stage 5 comes stage 6, which imposes the even greater ethical burden of managing the human condition.[9] This involves recognizing *The Moral Landscape*: there are no perfect solutions, no absolute good or evil, and moral dilemmas are everywhere. There's no way to avoid getting blood on your hands—only compromises that choose between better and worse ways that blood can be spilled. Sustaining this awareness requires the capacity to love humanity—despite its horrors. Stage 6 demands commitment to universal ethical principles, autonomous moral reasoning, and a duty to justice that considers all perspectives. It also involves a fearless reckoning with history and an inventory of privilege. Perhaps fewer than one percent of people reach Kohlberg stage 6. It's a tall order—one I strive for, even if I don't succeed.

"Socialism" shouldn't be controversial, but it's practically a curse-word for many Americans. It's time to confront the stark consequences of the unregulated capitalism championed by right-libertarians, versus the benefits of more socialistic systems. This is no mere academic disagreement. It's a battle over resource allocation—a contest on which the future of billions of lives depend. Where you stand on this conflict determines where you fall on *The Moral Landscape*.

Democratic socialism delivers high living standards and robust worker and environmental protections, while still leaving plenty of room for free-market capitalism. When right-wingers push fear-porn about socialism, they usually cite failed *left-authoritarian* states like Russia, Cuba, or Venezuela. (Although under Putin, Russia has become right-authoritarian.) More socialistic *left-libertarian* nations like Denmark, Finland, Sweden, Norway, and the Netherlands have high GDPs, long life expectancies, and top happiness rankings: 2nd, 4th, 7th, 8th, and 5th globally.[10] The US, while spending 19 percent of GDP on public goods, lags behind Nordic nations, which allocate 23 to 31 percent. With lower social spending, the US ranks 15th in happiness and

Nation	Social Spending (%GDP)	Happiness Rank	Life Expectancy
Denmark	28.1	2	81.6
Finland	31.6	4	82.4
Netherlands	23.9	5	82.2
Sweden	26.1	7	83.3
Norway	27.6	8	83.1
United States	19.3	15	79.1

Age-adjusted mortality rates by county, darker areas represent higher mortality.[11] Source: countyhealthrankings.org

has a life expectancy two to four years shorter than Nordic countries. Is it "the greatest nation in the world?" Not by these metrics.

Even within the US, "red" Republican-led states are far stingier with public services than "blue" Democrat-led states. According to Jeremy Ney of Harvard, life expectancy diverges by up to *20 years* between the best and worst counties, with the highest mortality rates concentrated in the South and rural areas. As a general rule, blue states and urban areas have better health outcomes.[12]

The 2023 study *Missing Americans: Early Death in the United States—1933–2021* found that before 1980, US mortality rates were lower than those of peer nations.[13] But after 1980, excess deaths surged, peaking at over 1 million annually during the Covid-19 pandemic—13 million in total. The political theorist Friedrich Engels referred to this phenomenon as "social murder."[14]

So what happened around 1980? US economic policy became more capitalist. President Reagan's tax and service cuts in 1981 were exactly the kind of moves my anarcho-capitalist friends applauded—but they want-

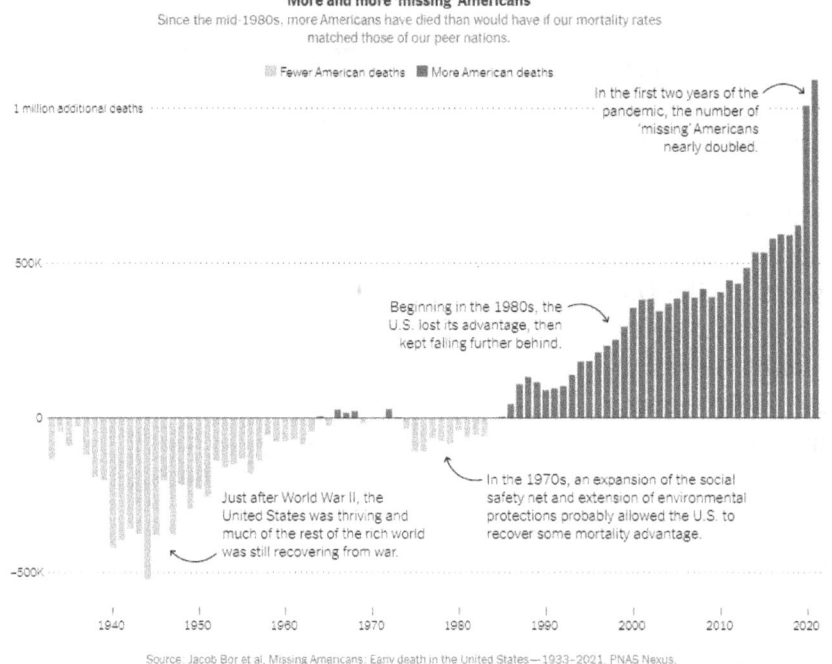

ed even more. Their goal was eliminating taxes and government services *entirely*. This would kill more Americans each year than died in the Civil War—a lot more. Yet that's where ancap ideology leads. The Orwellian "Department of Government Efficiency" or "DOGE commission," formed under Trump's second administration and led by right-wing billionaire Elon Musk echoes these extreme ideas.

Worker productivity has more than tripled over the past century, yet wages have stagnated for 50 years, channeling much of that gain to investors and the wealthy. The productivity-wage gap emerged in the early 1970s. Contributing factors include the decline of labor unions, deindustrialization, and globalization, but the primary cause is the failure to raise the US federal minimum wage along with productivity growth. Had this alignment been maintained, the minimum wage would now approach $30 per hour. Instead, it's been stuck at $7.25 since 2009, with a purchasing power that has declined by nearly half since its 1968 peak of $12.50 in current dollars.

The American working class has seen a sharp decline in living standards. Today, the average worker struggles to afford rent at 30 percent of their income, even while holding a full-time job. In cities like Cleveland, Detroit, or Tucson, a living wage[15] for a household with two adults—one working and one caring for children—ranges from $28-43/hour. In New York City, it's $37-53/hour, and in Los Angeles, $36-55/hour. Meanwhile, the federal minimum wage remains $7.25/hour.

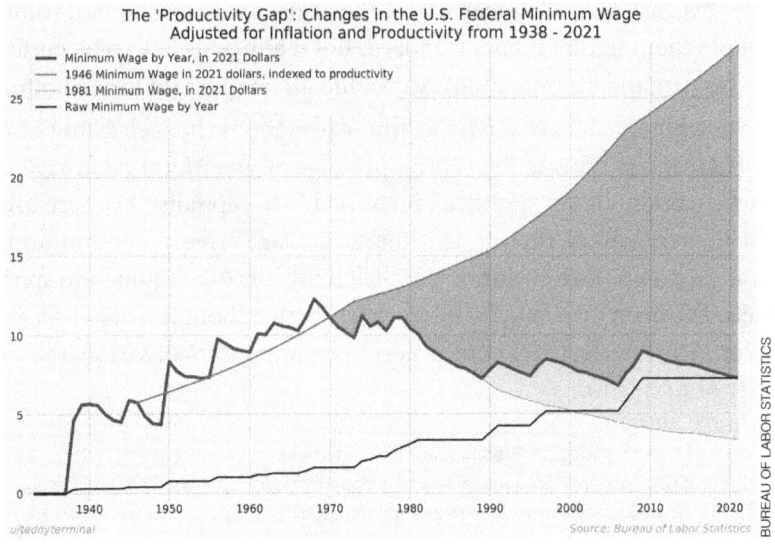

Armed with these facts, we can now return to *The Moral Landscape*. As you should recognize, politics *is* morality. There's a direct progression from God-belief to the cultish strict-father morality of the conservative moral hierarchy, which leads to policies that harm the common good and spread poverty and early death. This doesn't mean all God-believers accept the conservative moral hierarchy, or that all conservatives vote Republican—just most of them.

There have always been liberal God-believers, some of whom have cited their faith as a driver for social justice, like Martin Luther King Jr., Malcolm X, Rabbi Heschel, Dorothy Day, and Desmond Tutu. But the evidence shows that in the U.S., God-belief trends toward right-wing authoritarianism and capitalistic fascism, while secularism leans toward left-libertarianism. Everyone rejects some religious dogma, and generally, the more dogma you reject and the more you embrace science, the more liberal and socialistic you become.

Striving for moral progress can draw criticism, especially from those whose identities are invested in preserving immoral, unearned hierarchies. MAGA cult members never tire of mocking liberals with accusations of being "woke," "virtue-signaling," or "hypocrisy." It's true—those who strive for better values sometimes fail to lead by example. Some liberal elites are just as highly insulated from the concerns of the working class as conservative elites. But at least they support policies which promote justice and equality. People of all political persuasions can be afraid to demand better ethics, because they may fear that if they raise their ethical bar, someone will hold them to that higher standard. But if any of us had to be perfect in order to demand accountability, we would all be in a race to the bottom.

So, who am I? I am a person who cares about the well-being of conscious creatures. This is the central premise of *The Moral Landscape*. The transformation of my political identity from capitalist fascism toward right-libertarianism, then to left-libertarianism, represented moral progress at each step. This evolution paralleled my loss of religious and spiritual beliefs. I've been on a lengthy quest to feel better about the man I see in the mirror. Am I perfect? Of course not. Even in matters of virtue, there's no purity or perfection.

---

[1] Laozi. (2015). *Tao Te Ching* (D. Hinton, Trans.). Counterpoint.
[2] *The Political Compass* provides a model to analyze political ideologies based on both economic and social dimensions, offering a nuanced view beyond traditional left-right spectrums. More information

can be found at https://www.politicalcompass.org/

[3] *8values* is an online political quiz that maps users' political positions across four axes: economic, diplomatic, civil, and societal. More information can be found at https://8values.github.io/

[4] The *Seven Mountain Mandate* is a conservative Christian movement that advocates for believers to influence seven key areas of society: religion, family, education, government, media, arts and entertainment, and business. More information can be found at https://en.wikipedia.org/wiki/Seven_Mountain_Mandate#

[5] *Black Sun Journal* is a blog published since 2001 by Sean Prophet. https://www.blacksunjournal.com

[6] Rand, A. (1964). *The virtue of selfishness: A new concept of egoism*. Signet.

[7] *Altered Carbon* is set in a dystopian future where human consciousness can be digitized and transferred into new bodies, called "sleeves." This technology, primarily accessible to the wealthy elite, intensifies social inequalities. The presence of profitable bloodsport, where the rich exploit the poor and disposable "sleeves" for violent entertainment, further highlights the brutal and morally decayed nature of this hypercapitalist society. More information can be found at https://en.wikipedia.org/wiki/Altered_Carbon_(TV_series)

[8] Waters, R. (1973). *Money* [Song]. On *The dark side of the moon*. Pink Floyd Music Publishers Ltd.

[9] Stage 6 of Lawrence Kohlberg's moral development theory is defined by adherence to universal ethical principles like justice, equality, and human rights. Individuals at this stage engage in autonomous moral reasoning, critically evaluating ethical dilemmas based on internalized values rather than societal norms. They are committed to justice, often willing to challenge laws or social expectations if they conflict with these principles. Kohlberg believed few individuals reach this stage consistently, citing figures like Martin Luther King Jr. and Mahatma Gandhi as examples. More at https://en.wikipedia.org/wiki/Lawrence_Kohlberg%27s_stages_of_moral_development

[10] OECD (2020 or latest available) https://www.oecd.org, *World Happiness Report 2023* (United Nations) https://worldhappiness.report, World Bank (2021) https://data.worldbank.org

[11] This interactive map displays age-adjusted mortality rates by county, with darker areas representing higher mortality. Source: countyhealthrankings.org. The map is available at https://esrimedia.maps.arcgis.com/apps/Media/index.html?appid=64eee75d4b274d939d7d52ed7c457b1d

[12] Ney, J. (2021). *Making inequality visible: An interactive map of America's economic opportunity*. Harvard Kennedy School. Available at https://www.hks.harvard.edu/faculty-research/policy-topics/poverty-inequality-opportunity/jeremy-ney-mpa-2021-making-inequality#

[13] Bor, J., Stokes, A. C., Raifman, J., Venkataramani, A., Bassett, M. T., Himmelstein, D., & Woolhandler, S. (2023). *Missing Americans: Early death in the United States—1933–2021*. PNAS Nexus, 2(6), pgad173. https://doi.org/10.1093/pnasnexus/pgad173

[14] *Social murder* refers to the concept introduced by Friedrich Engels to describe the preventable deaths resulting from societal and political neglect, particularly due to poverty and poor living conditions. More information can be found at https://en.wikipedia.org/wiki/Social_murder

[15] *The MIT Living Wage Calculator* provides data on the minimum income needed to meet basic needs by region in the United States. More information can be found at https://livingwage.mit.edu

CHAPTER THIRTY SIX

A Quiet Life

> I have a foreboding of an America in my children's or grandchildren's time—when the United States is a service and information economy; when nearly all the manufacturing industries have slipped away to other countries; when awesome technological powers are in the hands of a very few, and no one representing the public interest can even grasp the issues; when the people have lost the ability to set their own agendas or knowledgeably question those in authority; when, clutching our crystals and nervously consulting our horoscopes, our critical faculties in decline, unable to distinguish between what feels good and what's true, we slide, almost without noticing, back into superstition and darkness...
>
> —Carl Sagan, *The Demon Haunted World: Science As A Candle In The Dark, 1996*

The years 1995 to 2001 were the most quiet and carefree of my life. It wasn't just liberation from my cult. Despite the impeachment circus and a handful of serious international crises like the Kosovo Conflict and the Rwandan Genocide, the William Jefferson Clinton presidency was a tranquil and prosperous time for the United States. That is, when compared to the pure political insanity and pitched cultural battles of the present day. In the late-'90s, I often enjoyed the luxury of not thinking about politics at all. And I didn't see any downside to that blissful indifference. I had yet to read or understand the prescience of Sagan's warning—written in 1996. I was focused on my career and my family, both of which were finally on track. My financial worries were behind me, and my decisions were finally my own.

West Hills is a medium-upscale suburb of Los Angeles, offering exactly the kind of normalcy Joe Szimhart recommended to cure my post-cult angst. My little corner of LA was idyllic, and I got to know my neighbors: My kids attended well-funded, safe public schools, and crime was nearly non-existent except for occasional graffiti. Gorgeous public parks and hiking trails were just a short walk away.

Echoes of the cult milieu still made noise in my head, but the direct blare had ceased. There was practically nothing to worry about—well, except for my post-cult nuclear war nightmares. But we all led charmed lives under *Pax Americana* during the decade between the end of the Cold War and 9/11. In 1992, Francis Fukuyama declared the "end of history" in a fit of myopia.[1] He wasn't alone. Intellectual circles became flooded with wishful thinking that the lull in global tensions was permanent. In 1997 *Wired* magazine published an article titled "The Long Boom," predicting 25 years of world peace and endless growth—just a few years before the dot-com crash.[2] America was completely unhinged with optimism, as has often occurred in our history during interregna before calamitous eras.

Sean Prophet with sons Christopher, Nathaniel, and Laurence, atop Castle Peak, El Escorpion Park, West Hills, California c. 1996

As previously noted, my cult identity was right-authoritarian. From the time I turned 18 in 1982, I consistently voted Republican. But in 1996, I cast my first all-Democratic ballot. It was the easiest decision ever. Bob Dole wasn't going to "Bob Dole" me into Bob Doling. But it wasn't about his age or weirdness—or even climate change, which barely registered for me in the '90s. I knew there was vague concern about future impacts of fossil-fuel emissions, but not enough to connect it to my vote. What made me choose the Democrat was purely the Christian Nationalism factor. On that basis alone, no Republican could ever get my vote again.

Living in California and working in entertainment, I found myself in a liberal bubble. When Fox News launched in 1996, I barely noticed. I tuned out the incendiary right-wing talk that exploded across AM radio after Reagan's FCC repealed the Fairness Doctrine in 1987. Far away from red-state evangelical lunacy and the politics of racism, I naively believed the whole nation was shifting toward a scientific, secular, egalitarian perspective—just as I was. It was another childlike mistake, seeing *my* small world as *the* world. I was blind to the forces of reaction, quietly coalescing outside my view.

I still struggled with diversity, particularly around sexual orientation. After rejecting my cult's broad bigotry against "fallen ones," I avoided most conscious bias. But subconsciously, I was still stuck in my "birthright" as a white, cisgender, heterosexual male. In my cult, I was used to hearing cruel jokes and gay slurs that distorted my view of the LGBTQ+ community. I had believed homosexuality was a mental illness and that any struggles—including HIV—were the victims' fault for rebelling against "God's laws."

Around 1995, I befriended a gay Black coworker at Varitel. His kindness and contagious joy helped reduce my lingering homophobia. But one day, I asked if he "turned gay" because he had "bad luck with women." It was a tactless, ignorant question. I had never learned that people are born gay. My friend opened my eyes to the full humanity of gay people, and I will always be grateful to him. He had denied his sexuality for many years and had once been married to a woman. His misery had driven him to the brink of suicide until he finally accepted his nature. His revelation humbled me and gave me empathy. How could I have passed such harsh judgment on anyone? What other cult nonsense lingered in my mind?

I sought more new experiences to gain fresh perspectives. Kathleen and I attended as many rock concerts as we could afford—Rush, Jethro Tull, Nine Inch Nails, Dream Theater, and Yes, to name a few. We took our sons to see Rush twice on the Test for Echo tour in '97, once in Los Angeles and again in Phoenix. Our children all became accomplished musicians. I credit those early concert experiences and Kathleen's excellent tutelage. Nine Inch Nails had a significant impact on me, too. We had worked on Trent Reznor's videos at Varitel, and I had been shocked by their dark, graphic imagery. But after attending his shows and hearing his interviews,

I recognized Reznor as a shadow-warrior—an evocative artist with an integrated dark side and a strong conscience.

At one Jethro Tull concert at Universal Amphitheater, I learned it was definitely possible to smoke too much weed—I was so stoned I basically missed the second half of the show. I also endured a bout of pot-paranoia, along with a super-weird culty flashback that I was trapped on the astral plane. The music was off-key, my vision was distorting, and I had a disturbing, almost psychedelic experience. Oops. That's concert-etiquette-101 I should have learned as a teenager: Don't get too high.

I came to recognize the concert experience as almost mystical—a peak connection to humanity—especially the Rush shows. Cynically, I know it's just show business. But concerts are far more than that. People pay huge sums for tickets because there's no other way to access that collective experience. It far surpassed anything I had ever felt on the altar listening to my mother's dictations. Concerts are more nourishing, transcendent, and immersive. Because they're rooted in virtuoso performance—not flowery, thin-gruel cult fakery. Unlike spiritual grifters, musicians respect their audiences. They know people are there to experience that tribal connection of mass ritual. For music and nothing else. I don't think there's a better *religious* experience. Crucially, no one's selling salvation. Religions demonize rock concerts, raves, and festivals as satanic because they simply can't compete.

During the late 1990s, I was determined to advance my career and sit in the editor's chair. Encouraged by my mentor David Webb, I quit Varitel and moved to Pacific Media Post, a smaller Burbank shop. I'm deeply grateful to Mel Harrison and Neil Weiner for hiring me. Their trust allowed me to form vital relationships with producers and directors and take the next step in my career. The fraught professional dynamic with my mother gave me excellent client skills: No real-world client could be as demanding as the messenger of God. One day a client was furious over a mistake. I knew how to be non-reactive—there was plenty of time to fix it. Making FedEx was a walk in the park compared to the impossible spiritual deadlines I had faced in my cult. My slowly healing trauma had given me a kind of super-power: a career advantage I could never have predicted.

It was a pivotal time in television, as the industry transitioned from video tape and million-dollar suites to Avid's computer-based editing. I adapted quickly, but Pacific Media Post did not, and it went bankrupt within 18 months. Fortunately, I had built strong client relationships and was soon working at numerous facilities, sometimes in several locations within a single week. I finally had a cell phone, and it was always ringing. I was in the loop. The irregular hours sometimes clashed with family life, but I had more time with my kids than I did in the cult. But that was all small-world stuff compared to the rude awakening we were all about to receive with the turn of the new millennium.

The true beginning of the 21st century was 9/11—not January 1, 2000. The world was suddenly introduced to the mass cult violence of Wahabist jihad. And it's grown less rational and less free almost every year since.[3] Sometimes it feels almost hopeless. I'm not hopeless that individuals can escape cults—you absolutely can. But from 1995 to 2001 I remained blind to the prevalence of cult-like thinking. I thought I had escaped to a mostly sane world. 9/11 shattered that illusion. Suddenly, a terrifying number of people were using messianic language just like the Ascended Masters. It wasn't only jihadists. Christians joined in too, from the homophobic extremists of Westboro Baptist Church to widely accepted figures like Pat Robertson and Jerry Falwell, who both declared 9/11 was God's judgment on the United States.

Westboro Baptist Church members hold anti-gay hate signs pronouncing God's judgment on the United States of America, Portland, Oregon, 2015

Beyond these messianic doomsayers, vast numbers of people failed to understand one of the most heavily documented events in modern history. Worldwide, 9/11 "truthers" echoed the conspirituality I grew up with. Global polls showed most people rejected or questioned Al-Qaeda's responsibility, with many blaming the US government, Israel, or unnamed others. Few even mentioned the Saudi connection, which remains the focus of an ongoing civil lawsuit brought by 9/11 victims' families. Within the US, widespread belief that the government ignored warnings about 9/11 became a proxy for deeper institutional distrust. That distrust has since engulfed pockets of the left and the entire Republican Party, along with its media allies, straining America's grip on reality. Conspiratorial thinking leaves us unprepared to respond to foreign aggression, biological threats like Covid-19, and existential crises like climate change. Carl Sagan's 1996 warning in *Demon-Haunted World* foresaw this exact danger.

Cult leaders—and politicians—tailor their messages to what followers want to believe, because that's the path to money and power. Truth doesn't sell. And it often provokes fury, like an addict fighting to protect their fix. People cling to comforting lies as if their survival depended on them, and the harder truth is to face, the more they attack truth-tellers and double down on desperate diversions.

The 1999 film *The Matrix* plowed fertile existential ground about the nature of truth and reality.[4] While it doesn't directly address cults, it remains one of the most insightful films on the topic, symbolizing the unexamined lives of those cocooned in comforting illusions. Morpheus warns Neo that anyone still plugged into the Matrix can be taken over at any time by an agent. That is to say, anyone who isn't prepared to face reality for what it is—as opposed to what they want to believe—is potentially an agent—symbolizing cult-like thinking. The "steak dinner" scene breaks down this moral collapse:

> Agent Smith: "Do we have a deal, Mr. Reagan?"
> Cypher: "You know, I know this steak doesn't exist. I know that when I put it in my mouth, the Matrix is telling my brain that it is juicy and delicious. After nine years, you know what I realized? Ignorance is bliss."

Cypher's deal betrayed Morpheus in exchange for a new identity, free of any memory of his real life. The film feels prophetic, foreshadowing 21st-century reality denial. Perhaps the Wachowskis intended a broader warning to the West—which was triumphant and complacent during the false peace of the 1990s, and blissfully unaware of internal divisions and rekindled global tensions after the Cold War. The film's caution is distilled in Morpheus' chilling line: "Welcome to the desert of the real."

The Matrix is also an allegory for an Earth destroyed by the combustion cult of fossil fuels, the most dangerous cult of all time. Its acolytes deny science and worship money with millenarian zeal. Even more than religious zealots—the combustion cult has concrete, physical power to end civilization. It's therefore even more dangerous than MAGA, while being central to MAGA's agenda. On April 11, 2024, twenty of its high priests—including executives from ExxonMobil, EQT, Venture Global LNG, Cheniere Energy, and the American Petroleum Institute—were feted by Trump at Mar-A-Lago. He solicited a $1 billion bribe in campaign contributions, promising to roll back climate and environmental regulations.[5] The first day of his second term in office, he signed executive orders delivering those high priests a substantial return on their investment.[6]

I've spent two decades studying energy and climate—issues fraught with titanic *sturm und drang*. Despite the chaos, the global scientific consensus debunks every facet of combustion-cult doctrine. Making that detailed case is far beyond the scope of this book. Renewable energy is cheaper, more reliable, and would save millions of lives each year.[7] None of that will happen so long as the combustion cult is welcome in the halls of the world's governments.

The climate-combustion conundrum brings me back to my analogy about moving Mount Everest. Human nature is even harder to change than "the world." Deniers gonna deny. People are in love with their internal combustion engines, and corporations will always wring out the last dollar every single quarter, despite long-term ruin. Politicians will continue to pander to their paymasters. People will have to learn this lesson the hard way. I've realized that accepting what I cannot change is key to whatever happiness may still be possible. Which is not easy to stomach—especially now.

Our lives are about to get a lot less quiet. As I type these words, I am living through the unprecedented 2025 Los Angeles fires—an up-close and personal cost of climate change that's destroyed over 12,000 homes—and counting. My sister Tatiana, and several other people I know, have already lost everything they owned. I can only warn my readers about the escalating, deadly consequences of our current path: We're now at 1.6 degrees Celsius of temperature rise above pre-industrial conditions. If we don't change how we produce and consume energy, we can expect to be at 2.5 to 3 degrees Celsius by the end of this century. We can scarcely imagine the devastation in store. Unlike prior millenarian false alarms, climate change threatens our civilization in a measurable, testable way. The punishment for our Promethean abuse of combustion since the start of the Industrial Revolution won't be meted out by Zeus—but through the laws of planetary physics.[8]

[1] Fukuyama, F. (1992). *The end of history and the last man*. Free Press.
[2] Schwartz, P., & Leyden, P. (1997, July 1). *The long boom: A history of the future, 1980-2020*. Wired. https://www.wired.com/1997/07/longboom/
[3] Freedom in the World 2024 finds that global freedom declined for the 18th consecutive year in 2023. The breadth and depth of the deterioration were extensive—political rights and civil liberties diminished in 52 countries and improved in only 21. *Freedoms denied as world enters consequential year of elections*. https://freedomhouse.org/article/freedoms-denied-world-enters-consequential-year-elections
[4] *The Matrix*. (1999). Directed by Lana Wachowski & Lilly Wachowski. Warner Bros.
[5] At a private meeting at Mar-a-Lago, the former president said fossil fuel companies should donate to help him beat President Biden. Friedman, L., & Thrush, G. (2024, May 9). *At a dinner, Trump assailed climate rules and asked $1 billion from big oil*. The New York Times. https://www.nytimes.com/2024/05/09/climate/trump-oil-gas-mar-a-lago.html
[6] On his first day in office, President Donald Trump signed several executive orders benefiting the fossil fuel industry. These actions included declaring a national energy emergency to expedite fossil fuel production, withdrawing the United States from the Paris climate agreement, and temporarily halting offshore wind lease sales in federal waters. These moves aligned with Trump's broader agenda to prioritize fossil fuel development over renewable energy initiatives and environmental protections. *Trump signs slew of sweeping energy executive orders*. Axios. https://www.axios.com/2025/01/21/trump-energy-executive-orders

Trump signs order directing US withdrawal from the Paris climate agreement. AP News. https://apnews.com/article/trump-paris-agreement-climate-change-788907bb89fe307a964be757313cdfb0

Trump temporarily halts leasing and permitting for wind energy. AP News. https://apnews.com/article/wind-energy-offshore-turbines-trump-executive-order-995a744c3c1a2eddb30cacf50b681f13
[7] Jacobson, M. Z. (2020). *100% clean, renewable energy and storage for everything*. Cambridge University Press.
[8] A 2.5 to 3 degrees Celsius temperature rise by the end of this century would have devastating consequences for humanity. Heatwaves, extreme weather events, sea-level rise, and ecosystem disruption would lead to widespread loss of life, property damage, and displacement. According to the World Bank (Rigaud et al., 2018, https://openknowledge.worldbank.org/handle/10986/29461), by 2050, climate change could force over 140 million people to migrate within their countries in sub-Saharan Africa, South Asia, and Latin America alone. The Global Commission on Adaptation (2019, https://gca.org/reports/adapt-now) estimates that a 2°C temperature rise could lead to a 30% decrease in global crop yields, potentially causing food shortages and famine for millions. A study published in *Nature Climate Change* (Mora et al., 2017, https://doi.org/10.1038/nclimate3322) projects that a 3°C warming scenario could expose an additional 1.5 billion people to life-threatening heat events by 2050. The economic toll of climate change is staggering, with potential global economic losses up to $600 trillion by the end of the century if the Paris Agreement's temperature goals are not achieved (Phys.org, 2020, https://phys.org/news/2020-04-paris-climate-goals-failure-world.html). These figures underscore the urgent need for action to mitigate the worst impacts of climate change and protect the lives and livelihoods of billions of people worldwide.

CHAPTER THIRTY SEVEN

I've-Got-Mine-Ism

During the late 1990s, I stayed in touch with ex-cult members I knew in Los Angeles and occasionally attended their social events. Kathleen and I hosted Thanksgiving dinner one year for about 30 ex-members, including some from out of town. The nostalgia was fun, and it briefly rekindled a sense of the community I had left behind. But at some of these gatherings, I noticed subtle tells in conversation—signs that some ex-members hadn't fully absorbed the lessons I had been forced to learn.

Some clung to hierarchical, purity and perfection-based beliefs. Others revered the teachings or idolized my mother, excusing her hypocrisies or insisting she never truly wanted nuclear war. Some voiced criticisms, but if *I* made strong statements that cut to the core of why things had gone terribly wrong, they rushed to the cult's defense. This wasn't about truth but rather a reflexive need to justify their invested years. Some even gaslit me, dismissing events I had witnessed, or claiming I was lying about my own mother.

It became so uncomfortable that I distanced myself from the group. Many lacked clarity, and some were whitewashing history. This pattern, I learned later, is so common among ex-members of abusive cults that it has earned its own name, coined by Matthew Remski: *I've-got-mine-ism* (IGM)—where individuals who had a positive or neutral experience refuse to acknowledge the group's abuses, choosing instead to protect their own memories.[1]

IGM emerges from our evolutionary hardwiring—primal tribal responses that must be dismantled to achieve post-cult clarity. For any community to survive, it must provide basic safety, food, shelter, and mutual care. Think of the rule in an airborne crisis: "Put your oxygen mask on first, then help your child." You can't contribute to a community if you're dead.

This creates a pernicious psychological cul-de-sac: "The community kept me alive, therefore it was good." To our primate brains, even a bad group seems preferable to no group, which amplifies the terror of leaving any cult. But let's be clear: basic subsistence isn't worthy of praise—any functional community would have kept you alive. There's a crucial distinction between the *fear* of being alone, the *feeling* of being alone, and actually *being* alone. In the modern world, complete isolation is nearly impossible. Unless you're in a remote undeveloped region, there's always some infrastructure to keep you alive, and always some untapped community you can count on. Once you recognize this, you can see how you would have been better off literally *anywhere* else that treated you better than your cult did.

Understanding interdependence frees you to assess cult life honestly. The results are damning. Everyone in my cult—*me especially*—helped enable my mother's abusive behavior. We squandered the life savings of hundreds, maybe thousands of people. Plus at least ten thousand person-years of unpaid labor—sucked down our cult black hole. How many lost lives does *that* add up to? Our community took everything and gave back only the barest minimum: cheap food, cheap housing, and subsistence-level stipends. This hits hardest for idealistic people who gave the best years of their lives. But we have to face facts: We all contributed to the collective delusion and to the collective abuse. Every member, without exception, empowered the cult to harm more people and do more damage than it could have without our time, money and talents.

The power of this collective denial becomes painfully clear when we examine the children of Synanon, who endured horrific abuse and parent-child separation in the 1970s and '80s. Their stories show how IGM warps memory and reality. In *Born in Synanon* (Paramount+), Cassidy Arkin, raised at Synanon through age six, revisits her childhood. Through the arduous process of documentary filmmaking, she reached the unvarnished conclusion that it was not the utopia she remembered. "Synanon was the only place I felt where I was loved wholeheartedly," she said. "It was this beautiful memory, but it was also an illusion." Her mother, Sandra Rogers-Hare, embodies this same conflict: "Terrible things happened. It's hard to accept that. You're not going to talk me out of being loyal to my experience in Synanon. I lived in a community, and when we left it, I missed the community." Christian Wells, another survivor, captures the frustration of watching others maintain their denial: "A lot of them see through the lens of what Synanon was to them. And it's hard to break that down… the whole thing was just abusive, and they really don't get that."

This denial does more than protect comfortable illusions—it harms other survivors. Ex-members who guard their pristine memories of a divine leader become shields for ongoing abuse. They won't admit their idol did serious wrong or even committed crimes. Worse, they attack victims who come forward as disgruntled or lying. This pattern extends beyond cults into popular culture. For instance, despite overwhelming evidence, many refuse to believe Michael Jackson sexually abused children simply because they love his music. And there are many such examples. The MAGA cult demonstrates this loyalty dynamic in its most extreme form—no crime is too great for them to justify, no victim too innocent to throw under the bus in service of preserving their illusions.

This selective memory has always frustrated me, both inside and outside my cult. Yes, even abusive cults have positive qualities. Synanon saved lives and helped thousands of addicts find sobriety and purpose. But at what cost? Meaningful experiences and relationships, however genuine, cannot validate a cult's BOMP, justify its abuses, or absolve members of their shared responsibility. The path to redemption for any cult requires implementation of a robust self-correcting mechanism to hold the group accountable—and genuine atonement for prior failings. Few cults ever take this step.

Healing demands brutal honesty about our roles. As part of the inner circle upholding my mother's leadership, I bear direct and personal responsibility for enabling her abuses. I definitely got mine—including financial and personal advantages denied to other members. But every member and ex-member shares responsibility to some degree—no one's responsibility is 0 percent. Understanding our collective complicity means moving beyond the simplistic victim-perpetrator narrative to confront the complex dynamics of cultic pathology.

Consider the parallel of toxic domestic relationships: It's tempting to simply point to the partner who commits physical violence and declare "It's his fault, he's the perpetrator." Yet the reality often reveals a more nuanced picture—the "victim" may be caught in patterns of codependency and avoidance, unable to set appropriate boundaries, which can trigger the "perpetrator's" rage. *Important caveat*: This isn't about justifying violence or blaming victims—it's about understanding the full spectrum of dysfunction. A codependent person lacks boundaries and communication skills. A person with anger management issues lacks emotion-regulation skills. Once it has led to violence, we often lose this dual perspective.

Blame gets us nowhere. Growth comes through emotional awareness, clear communication, and effective boundaries. These tools improve post-cult mental health and prevent future exploitation. I urge members and ex-members to re-examine their roles—what did you add to the toxic dynamic? Remember: without members, there can be no cult. This recognition brings with it a moral imperative to leave any abusive cult you find yourself in. We must view cultic social dynamics as a system rather than a collection of isolated individuals. True healing begins when you acknowledge your own place within that system.

While most ex-members struggled with their complicity, one voice cut through the fog of denial. Among all my interviews, ex-cult member Anna Maletta stood alone in her clarity about her role. Her words capture the essence of collective responsibility:

> I think I had a period of being angry after I left at first, thinking about all the things that maybe were abusive that I allowed to happen to myself. *But I realized that I was probably just as abusive to others.* [emphasis added] It was kind of like a domino effect. Everybody kind of was interwoven into the whole dysfunctional way that the community had been set up.

This interweaving of abuse and responsibility mirrors the complex experience of surviving a battle. Like veterans, cult survivors share both trauma and triumph. The bonds forged with your "war-buddies" feel sacred, even knowing that your collective actions enabled violations and harmed others. This cognitive dissonance can paralyze you unless you're willing to face three central truths:

1. The decision to join the cult was a life-altering mistake.

2. The opportunity cost of the life not lived outside the cult is staggering.

3. Any benefits you received came through mutually consensual oppression.

These truths become clearer when you stop comparing cult life to a vacuum and instead consider the alternate paths your life might have taken. Without the cult, your journey would have unfolded differently—leading to different friends, relationships, spouses, children, and experiences. This isn't mere speculation. It's a crucial recognition that meaningful connections form wherever humans gather. Your cult could have been centered on anything—a self-help philosophy, a religion, yoga, free love, or medieval battle reenactments—and you still would have had rich experiences. Cults are simply villages, and like any village, the social benefits flow from the humanity of its members, forged through shared experience—not from the cult's teachings or leadership. In fact, these connections formed *despite* the cult structure, not because of it, and always carried the distorting influence of third-party control.

So, to find closure, it's important to keep in mind all three perspectives:

1. "There were great people, positive benefits, and things I enjoyed."

2. "It was a harmful system, and even though at times I was coerced, I was also complicit."

3. "I could have had a whole different life, which might have been better or worse."

Withdrawing from ex-cult events didn't end my community involvement. I still felt compelled to follow and contribute to online discussions through email chains and forums. Some interactions proved valuable, offering space for candor, clarity, and healing. When I posted "mea-culpas" about my role as cult vice-president and shared sharp criticisms of the organization, many appreciated my willingness to speak honestly about our shared trauma.

Yet a persistent undercurrent of hostility ran through these exchanges. Given my years as vice-president of an abusive cult, this wasn't surprising—I could never undo the damage I caused or come out with clean hands. The attacks I received revealed distinct patterns of unresolved cult programming:

The first group lashed out with unhinged rage: "You Prophets are all a bunch of privileged brats, I don't care if you're out now, I don't want to hear your damn apologies, you stole everyone's money—where's the money? I hope you all rot in hell!"

The second group gave patronizing lectures: "You're throwing the baby out with the bathwater, the teachings were good, your mother made some mistakes, but you're overreacting. You're still the same fanatic you were when you were an ordained minister, you just flipped your belief system."

The third group made spiritual threats with familiar cult terminology: "You're ungrateful for everything you were given. We raised you and paid for your education. You owe us. You're making terrible karma. You've become a 'fallen one' now, and you won't get away with it! You'll pay for your betrayal of El Morya—when you go through the second death!"

Members of a fourth, less hostile but equally exhausting group forwarded conspiracy chain emails, recommendations for wacky books, photocopied pamphlets, and bizarre health scares. These messages flooded my email, postal mail, and *Black Sun Journal* blog for years, foreshadowing today's social media madness.

One stalker in the early 2000s took his harassment to new extremes. He bombarded me with emails and messages, creating fake accounts when I blocked him. Letters and packages flooded my mailbox. He bought a domain name using my name and built an impostor site filled with spiritual slander, threats, and lies. The site ranked high in web searches, spreading its toxic message to anyone who looked me up. It was gross, and insane. But there was nothing I could do about it.

In desperation, I agreed to meet this chucklefuck at Denny's, hoping to negotiate the removal of his site or at least get him to stop using my name. Like most stalkers, he saw this engagement as validation. When I told him I had no interest in debating spiritual concepts with cult members such as himself, he countered, "Fine, I'll take down my site if you take down *Black Sun Journal*." Right. His entire goal was for me to silence myself.

His fanatical cult programming proved impervious to rational argument. Hours at that Denny's table couldn't shake his obsession with controlling my identity and speech. He presented me with a laser-carved altar he'd made in his woodshop, dedicated to my family. I refused it. Days later, it arrived in my mailbox. I returned it. Growing more desperate, he sent the package again with a photo of a $100 bill inside, trying to tempt me to open it. I returned that too. Finally, I did what I should have done from the start—cut off all contact and ignored him. Live and learn.

---

[1] "I've got mine-ism" in the context of cults refers to a phenomenon where individuals who have had positive experiences within a cult show reluctance or outright refusal to acknowledge or criticize the abuses and negative aspects that may have occurred within the same group. This mindset stems from a personal sense of fulfillment or benefit derived from their involvement, leading to a dismissive attitude towards the experiences of harm or exploitation reported by others. It embodies a prioritization of one's own positive experiences over the collective well-being of all members, including those who have suffered. This attitude can contribute to the perpetuation of harmful practices within cults, as it downplays the significance of abuses and hinders collective acknowledgment and action against misconduct. *The unbearable smugness of "I've got mine-ism" amongst cult and ex-cult members* https://matthewremski.com/wordpress/the-unbearable-smugness-of-i-got-mine-ism-amongst-cult-and-ex-cult-members/

CHAPTER THIRTY EIGHT

Neocons

America's descent into cult nation status didn't start with MAGA. It began when the Supreme Court handed the presidency to George W. Bush on December 12, 2000. The next day, I was working at the Filmgarden production company in Studio City when Al Gore conceded. People left their offices and edit bays to watch him speak. Time seemed to freeze. When the speech ended, everyone wept openly. I was devastated. We were watching the door close on evidence-based leadership.

History will mark Gore's defeat as a pivotal victory for the combustion cult and a global turning point. America lost a critical decade in the fight against climate change. Gore, who understood the stakes better than anyone, still gave a dignified, presidential concession. He nobly put country over party, despite winning the popular vote and losing Florida by just 537 votes. (Contrast this with Trump's refusal to concede in 2020 and the ensuing "Stop the Steal" chaos.) Studies like the Florida Ballots Project[1] suggest a full recount might have handed Gore a narrow victory. But the fix was in at the Supreme Court.

George W. Bush became the first radically anti-science American president. Just as Trump did in 2017 and 2025, Bush went right to work for his combustion-cult paymasters on day one of his presidency. In 2001, he pulled the US out of the Kyoto Protocol, censored EPA climate reports, overruled scientific reviews under the Endangered Species Act, and gutted Clean Air Act standards for power plants. He restricted stem cell research and closed several EPA libraries, crippling access to critical environmental data. He rolled back Clinton-era energy-efficiency standards on air conditioners that could have cut bills by 30 percent and closed five coal-fired power plants. This sabotage cost American ratepayers $10 billion and added over 100 million tons of CO2 emissions in just five years. He delayed light-bulb efficiency standards required by the Energy Policy Act of 1992, which didn't go into effect until 2012. This systematic dismantling of scientific institutions and evidence-based policymaking created a template that would later be perfected under Trump.

The Bush administration marked the beginning of a dangerous fusion between religious fundamentalism and state power. His Office of Faith-based and Community Initiatives was created in 2001, and the No Child Left Behind Act of 2002 directed public funds to religious organizations. Faith-based initiatives allowed religious organizations to receive federal grants without separating their religious activities from their social services—allowing the use of public funds for proselytizing and discrimination in hiring practices. Meanwhile, school vouchers drained resources from public education, funding private religious indoctrination instead. It was a key triumph for Christian Nationalism and a harbinger of its growing influence.

After 9/11, Bush led America into two wars. The first, in Afghanistan, began as immediate retaliation for Osama bin Laden's attack on the Twin Towers and the Pentagon. It became America's longest war, lasting nearly 20 years, killing 243,000 people, including 2,459 US service members, and costing $2.3 trillion. The second war, in Iraq, started on March 20, 2003, lasted over eight years, killed 134,000 Iraqi civilians and 7,888 US personnel and contractors, and cost $3.9 trillion. Both wars left a devastating legacy: veterans with high rates of PTSD and suicide, and nations in chaos.

The 9/11 attacks required a military response. But Iraq never attacked the United States. The pretext for the Iraq war included false reports of weapons of mass destruction and bogus linkages between Iraqi President Saddam Hussein and Al-Qaeda. Like many Americans, I initially accepted the WMD narrative. But it was the same reality-denying groupthink I had faced in my cult. The cronyist feeding frenzy by the oil, arms, and mercenary industry—spearheaded by then Vice President Dick Cheney through corporations like Halliburton/KBR, Blackwater, and at least a dozen other security contractors—showed complete indifference to truth or democratic values. It was neoconservative money-grubbing at its finest. And a giddy national orgy of first-person-shooter sadism videos, set to a rock and roll soundtrack, glorifying the death and destruction we rained on that country and its people. The United States wasn't in Iraq on any mission of liberation.

What was the strategic result?

Twenty years on, the Iraq War strengthened Iran by eliminating its largest adversary, turning it into a regional bully that has flirted with fielding nuclear weapons. The war also helped create ISIS, which seized control of vast areas in Iraq and Syria and declared itself a "caliphate." Under US supervision, Iraq's 2005 Constitution enshrined Islam as the sole source of law. Despite democratic elections and a representative government, Iraq remains authoritarian and theocratic, rated "Not Free" with just 29 out of 100 on the Freedom House scale. Iran-backed Shia factions dominate its politics, and in 2024, its parliament passed a new law criminalizing LGBTQ+ relationships and gender transition.

Afghanistan fared even worse. After the Trump administration's Doha Agreement and 2021 withdrawal under Biden, the Taliban erased 20 years of progress—particularly for women, who had gained education and career opportunities under the 2004 western-backed Constitution. Now they face harsh persecution again, including public floggings and stonings. By 2023, Afghanistan rated "Not Free" with an abysmal 6 out of 100 on the Freedom House scale.

This is the legacy of the combustion cult and the George W. Bush presidency: arrogance, corruption, and authoritarianism at the highest levels. Wars costing over $6 trillion—and hundreds of thousands of civilian lives—only entrenched US dependence on oil, worsened climate change, and delayed the shift to renewable energy. The Bush administration ignored Carl von Clausewitz's strategic principle, "War is politics by other means." Its brittle victories in Iraq and Afghanistan culminated in strategic defeat, reshaping regional politics and turning Iran into a hegemonic power. Yet the Bush White House remained defiant. Senior Advisor Karl Rove famously declared, "We're an empire now, and when we act, we create our own reality... We're history's actors... and you, all of you, will be left to just study what we do." That's cult-speak 101. The phrase "we create our own reality" is especially damning.

What could have been achieved with the $6 trillion squandered on Iraq and Afghanistan? Early adoption of electric vehicles, a large-scale transition to solar and wind power, reduced air pollution, tens of thousands of lives saved annually, and a revitalized economy and infrastructure. The US would have been a global renewable energy technology leader, a role we've now ceded to China. The combustion cult and military-industrial complex got everything they wanted. When cults seize power and distort reality as Bush, Cheney, and Rove did, reality always loses big. The ripple effects extend far beyond any individual believer or decision maker.

There are qualitative differences between people who falsely claim the Earth is flat and those who insisted that Saddam Hussein was hiding "weapons of mass destruction." But they both reject evidence in favor of belief. The flat Earth claim is grassroots ignorance which may seem comical, in comparison to a false pretext for war. But it maps directly onto the climate-change denial of the combustion cult, the election denial of the MAGA cult, and the vaccine denial of the conspirituality cult. These forms of reality denial reinforce and legitimize each other, creating an ecosystem where truth becomes whatever serves power. The size of the cult and the severity of its consequences may vary. But the mechanism is the same. Reality-seeking must be uniform across all domains, or it's cherry-picking. If you only seek the reality-checks you want, then you're choosing to reshape reality in your own fantasy image.

"Creating your own reality" forms a nexus between New Age philosophies like New Thought and its Law of Attraction, conspirituality, and the freeform lies of rogues like Trump and Rove. "I think, therefore, *it is so.*" Or, "I want, therefore, *it is so.*" These tools have been weaponized by right-wing deniers to erode scientific and institutional credibility, and to elevate subjective beliefs over evidence. When faced with overwhelming proof of human-caused climate change, some politicians dismiss it as a "social construct," co-opting postmodernist rhetoric. This mindset also embraces the false relativism that all viewpoints are equally valid. Such approaches deny that mind-independent reality can be understood through empirical observation and logical analysis. The "recoil argument," as cited in Simon Blackburn's 2005 book *Truth: A Guide*,[2] exposes the contradiction—that relativism (and bastardized postmodernism) relies on the very concepts of truth and reality it seeks to dismantle.

Right-wing attacks on institutions in the United States also rely on the very structures they aim to destroy. When conservatives decry the "deep state" or "liberal elite," they implicitly affirm their power even as they undermine public trust. Dismissals of climate science or vaccine efficacy can involve cherry-picking data or citing fringe studies published in the same academic journals they label as corrupt. This selective use of postmodernist tactics sows doubt and confusion while exploiting the remaining credibility of scientific institutions whenever it's convenient.

Their favorite broadside against science is the replication crisis, a legitimate issue where some studies, particularly in social sciences, are based on flawed or fabricated data and cannot be replicated.[3] While this is a serious concern, addressing it requires improved scientific rigor *within institutions*—not rhetorical Molotov cocktails from bad-faith agitators indifferent to scientific accuracy. Reforms already underway include preregistration of studies, more open science practices, publication of negative or null results, replication grants, and enhanced peer review. This demonstrates how genuine reform differs from cynical attacks on truth itself.

Why are cults of all shapes and sizes reliably abusive, hierarchical, anti-science, anti-intellectual, morally bankrupt, and authoritarian? Because, aside from enriching their leaders, cults are engineered refuges for people who've rejected empirical reality. Cult leaders and dictators alike weaponize sanctity, violence, and totalitarian power to suppress the humanistic imperatives of ethical realism and freedom of thought. They oppress dignity, replacing the rule of law with a reign of terror. These dynamics underpin the tight relationship between cult structures, leadership behavior, and what political theorist Corey Robin calls The *Reactionary Mind*.[4] You won't overcome your cult trauma—or safeguard yourself against falling prey to another cult—until you uproot every last one of your internalized reactionary beliefs, even those you may still regard as an essential part of your identity.

There are two major categories of reactionary ideas from which all others flow. The first is Robin's definition of conservatism as "a meditation on—and theoretical rendition of—the felt experience of having power, seeing it threatened, and trying to win it back."[5] The second is the "divinely ordered" conservative moral hierarchy, with God or the cult leader at the top. Rush Limbaugh's 1993 bestseller, *The Way Things Ought to Be*, exemplifies this worldview, defending white-Christian-male-dominated social hierarchy and American military power.[6] Beneath this veneer, this philosophy boils down to "might makes right." Its logical endpoint is the erosion of democratic accountability and the rise of dictatorship.

A sharp critique posted under a pseudonym in a comment on the *Crooked Timber* blog in 2018 aptly summarizes this: "Conservatism consists of exactly one proposition, to wit: There must be in-groups whom the law protects but does not bind, alongside out-groups whom the law binds but does not protect."[7] It's the antithesis of equality under the law. Power would be worthless if leaders were bound by their own rules. Hypocrisy is a feature of all totalistic systems, not a bug.

Cults are reactionary, and reactionary thinking is universal among their leaders and followers. This stems from evolutionary instincts prioritizing caution, tribalism, and adherence to familiar patterns. While not inherently conservative in a political sense, these pre-thought reactions resist change, favoring ideas like "things that stay still are safer than things that move," "when in doubt, don't," or "the old way is better than a risky new way." Conditioned responses like xenophobia, sexual shame, and homophobia operate as reflexes, bypassing the lengthier process of examining evidence and making values-based decisions.

The primary purpose of cults is to reinforce such evolutionary math—to form a bulwark against any attempt to reverse longstanding power relations or move toward an egalitarian social structure. They suppress democratic self-organization or independence of thought within the cult. Rank-and-file members aren't allowed in the pulpit, and cult leaders never put their dogma to a vote.

Robin notes:
> Conservatism is the theoretical voice of this animus against the agency of the subordinate classes. It provides the most consistent and profound argument as to why the lower orders should not be allowed to exercise their independent will, why they should not be allowed to govern themselves or the polity. Submission is their first duty, and agency the prerogative of the elite. [8]

I've described shedding my unconscious sense of superiority over LGBTQ+ people through a friendship with a gay man, and my political evolution from hard-right authoritarianism to left-libertarianism. These steps of moral progress are an essential part of your cult exit journey. But it's not enough to declare mental independence from a cult leader. You must fully divest yourself of any sympathy for *unearned hierarchy*, the essence of every cult. Hierarchies depend on categories like special knowledge, chosen people, saints, gods, the saved, the elect, and the anointed. These imply their opposites: lesser humans—sinners, fallen ones, heretics, devils, the Hylics or mud people—not far from dehumanizing terms like "vermin."

Banish such thoughts from your psyche, including unconscious judgments against others for their race, gender, gender identity, sexual orientation, promiscuity, nationality, age, weight, body type, fashion choices, or economic status. Replace these conditioned reactions with reasoned distinctions based on behavior—the values people espouse and the social outcomes they embrace. Everyone is equal in their humanity, even those with poor values. We're not excluding them from the human tribe. Instead, there are two goals:

1. Curtailing their power to cause harm.

2. Extending a hand, inviting them to reap the mutual benefits of better values.

Although America has made significant progress since the Civil War—abolishing slavery, granting civil rights, and women's suffrage—the shadows of old hierarchies persist across society, particularly in employer-employee dynamics and the domestic sphere. What are the two most abusive cult-like structures in America's recent past that have fallen? The plantation and the strict-father patriarchal household. Reactionaries have fought fiercely—from the Civil War to opposition to the Equal Rights Amendment—to preserve both. Why? Robin explains:

> Politicians and parties talk of constitution and amendment, natural rights and inherited privileges. But the real subject of their deliberations is the private life of power. 'Here is the secret of the opposition to woman's equality in the state,' Elizabeth Cady Stanton wrote. 'Men are not ready to recognize it in the home.' Behind the riot in the street or debate in Parliament is the maid talking back to her mistress, the worker disobeying her boss. That is why our political arguments—not only about the family but also the welfare state, civil rights, and much else—can be so explosive: they touch upon the most personal relations of power.[9]

What drives Trumpian totalitarianism? White reaction against equality for Black Americans and immigrants, and men's backlash against women's rights. Strip away the economic and cultural anxiety, the daily posturing, and conspiracy theories, and MAGA's core goal is restoring the plantation and patriarchy. Preserving historical race and gender hierarchies underpins every MAGA judicial ruling and policy decision—and none of it aligns with free and fair elections. Christian Nationalist meddling in education and the outrage over "wokeness," "illegals," affirmative action, trans people, and abortion are divisive ploys to grow Trump's cult, entrench inequality, and subvert democracy into permanent minority rule. Totalistic cults demand rigid hierarchy.

"Order is heaven's first law."[10]

[1] "Analysis of ballot reliability from the 2000 U.S. presidential election. NORC at the University of Chicago, The New York Times, The Wall Street Journal, The Washington Post Company, Tribune Publishing, CNN, Associated Press, St. Petersburg Times, & The Palm Beach Post. (2001). *2000 Florida Ballots Project* [Data set]. Inter-university Consortium for Political and Social Research. https://doi.org/10.3886/ICPSR36207.v1

[2] Blackburn, S. (2005). *Truth: A guide*. Oxford University Press.

[3] The "replication crisis" refers to a significant issue in the scientific community where researchers find that the results of many previously published studies are difficult or impossible to replicate or reproduce. This crisis predominantly affects the fields of psychology, biomedical sciences, and social sciences, but its implications extend across various scientific disciplines. A key aspect of this crisis is that it exposes problems with research practices such as small sample sizes, selective reporting of results, and publication bias, which prioritizes novel and positive findings over negative or null results. In response, the scientific community has taken steps to address these issues by promoting open science practices, improving peer review processes, encouraging the publication of replication studies, and advocating for changes in the criteria for publication. The crisis has led to increased scrutiny of research methodologies and has spurred a movement towards greater transparency and reliability in scientific research. Wikipedia. (n.d.). *Replication crisis*. https://en.wikipedia.org/wiki/Replication_crisis

[4] Robin, C. (2018). *The reactionary mind: Conservatism from Edmund Burke to Donald Trump* (2nd ed.). Oxford University Press.

[5] Robin, C. (2018). *The reactionary mind: Conservatism from Edmund Burke to Donald Trump* (2nd ed., p. 4). Oxford University Press.

[6] Strongly defending free market capitalism and depicting business/corporate leaders as rightful holders of economic and political power. Portraying economic hierarchy as natural and earned. Advocating for traditional Christian family values and gender roles, with men as heads of households. Opposing feminism as a threat to this proper order. Defending American exceptionalism and the U.S.'s dominant global military and economic position as justified and necessary. Dismissing critiques of U.S. power as unpatriotic. Harshly criticizing social welfare programs as rewarding the undeserving and allowing deviation from traditional work ethic and self-reliance. Warning against multiculturalism and immigration as dangers to America's rightful European-derived cultural character. Decrying political correctness and cultural relativism as existential threats to upholding traditional moral standards and hierarchies. Limbaugh, R. H. (1993). *The way things ought to be*. Pocket Books.

[7] Crooked Timber is a collaborative blog featuring contributions from academics and intellectuals, offering commentary on politics, culture, and society. Crooked Timber. (n.d.). *Home*. https://crookedtimber.org/ Wikipedia. (n.d.). *Crooked Timber*. https://en.wikipedia.org/wiki/Crooked_Timber

[8] Robin, C. (2018). *The reactionary mind: Conservatism from Edmund Burke to Donald Trump* (pp. 7–8). Oxford University Press.

[9] Robin, C. (2018). *The reactionary mind: Conservatism from Edmund Burke to Donald Trump* (p. 10). Oxford University Press.

[10] Pope, A. (1734). *An essay on man* (Epistle IV, lines 49–52).

CHAPTER THIRTY NINE

Dénouement

My mother's reign as the messenger of God was not thwarted by her cognitive decline, nor her failed war prophecy, nor the gun deal, nor even when she lost the Mull case. Her fate was sealed in March 1981 when she unwisely filed suit against Mull in the first place. On April 2, 1986, her mistake came full circle, putting us on a path to quite literally bury our cult in the mountains of Montana. That day she stood on the altar of the Chapel of the Holy Grail at Camelot—with perfectly coiffed hair, wearing a purple blouse and white skirt—completely out of options. We had lost. She gave an opening invocation, then sang "Christ Arose," and "How Great Thou Art," before softly reading the verdict:

> We the jury, in the above entitled action find for the cross-defendant, Gregory Mull, and against the cross-complainant Church Universal and Triumphant and Elizabeth Clare Prophet for compensatory damages in the amount of $521,100 and against Church Universal and Triumphant for punitive damages in the amount of, $521,100, and against Elizabeth Clare Prophet for punitive damages in the amount of $521,100.

My mother observed, "this amount apparently did not translate to the plaintiffs as a victory, they were expecting much greater damages… this judgment will not destroy us." Edward Francis presented his trial report, telling our congregation, "We are very grateful for the outcome as it now stands, because what could have happened is that we could be standing here discussing the end of the church."

Instead of acknowledging her colossal blunder in suing Gregory Mull and rejecting Levy's settlement offer, my mother shifted blame onto our membership. She warned that "every Keeper of the Flame worldwide" would now be held accountable for how they "interface with every new person who comes through the door." The church's behavior had been on trial, she claimed, so "every act of ourselves, every word we speak" might "ultimately come to trial and be judged."

Elizabeth Clare Prophet, moments after she read the jury verdict in *CUT v. Mull*, April 2, 1986, Camelot, Malibu CA

But did she hold *herself* to account?

It was a desperate gambit to deflect attention from the elephant in that room—her conduct had cost us millions that we didn't have. She planned to raise it from members. According to her self-defined "law of the one," *they* were responsible to pay her bill:

> We can see then that as we are a part of this body, whatever is charged against one of us (in this case it happens to be me)… all of us then have a share in that burden. The burden of the Lord, the burden of his light, and the burden of that world karma that the Lord also carries. It's an amazing lesson to me of the guru-chela relationship. That there is a oneness whereby we do bear one another's burdens… We are expanding from this moment and going forward, and we have been delivered by Almighty God from the very, very worst that could have possibly happened to us today. So praise God for the sun that is shining. Praise God! Praise God![1]

The congregation chanted "Hail, Guru Ma!" and sang a devotional song called "Mother, Dear Mother." Yet, beneath the surface of their adulation, practical realities loomed: These were staggering financial consequences. Posting an appeal bond would cost one-and-a-half times the judgment, or $2.34 million. Reflecting on the Mull trial with what remained of her ample bravado, my mother clung to her illusions of righteousness, "One out of twelve jurors was apparently converted to our cause, though we prayed for them all." It was wishful thinking. USC sociology professor and jury foreman Carole Snow had deflected the fatal blow. But it was no endorsement. Rather, it reflected Snow's humanistic sense of fairness, and her principled approach to deliberation.

Soft-spoken in public, my mother was dour in private. The money wasn't the half of it. What stung is that her spiritual authority—and El Morya—had been rebuked in a court of law. The verdict deepened my mother's internal conflict, as her public humiliation clashed with her infallible self-image. This curdled into a vengeful divine rage that began to leak its way into her ever-more-apocalyptic dictations.

In *Prophet's Daughter*, Erin connected our mother's escalating prophecies of doom to our mundane difficulties, including the denial of building permits for our Camelot expansion, and the fallout from the *CUT v. Mull* verdict. Edward spoke plainly that day about how close we had come to a corporate death sentence, while my mother spiritualized the trial as a battle with "serpents." But we hadn't beaten any "serpents," and we didn't survive because of our prayer vigils or expensive attorneys. We survived only because one juror stood up for what she thought was fair.

On July 3, 1986 El Morya announced the sale of Camelot. It marked a point of no return, committing us to withdraw to "The Inner Retreat." In September, mother lectured once again about "The Four Horsemen of the Apocalypse." At Thanksgiving, I recall my dread as I attended our last hurrah at the Los Angeles Airport Hilton and Towers. In a dictation, Saint Germain warned us to vacate the coasts of the United States, which sealed my decision to quit my job, relocate to Evanston, Illinois, re-enroll in Northwestern University, and rejoin my cult as an ordained minister in early 1987.

In April 1989, the California Court of Appeal affirmed the Mull verdict. It found that there had indeed been errors involving the admission of irrelevant testimony, but they were not reversible errors. Erin details some of these in *Coercion or Conversion*, which included allowing testimony about our decrees, the silver futures scandal and my mother's affair with Randall King.[2] But the appellate court wrote that my mother's conduct toward Mull was "reprehensible," "despicable," and "shameful." Several attorneys have told me that it's highly unusual for appellate courts to weigh in with commentary. In order for them to have done so, they must have considered the facts of the case to have been extraordinarily severe. We appealed again to the California Supreme Court, then again to the US Supreme Court, both of which declined to hear our case. The damages were paid.

With decades of hindsight, I can't help but wonder if Snow's measured approach in that jury room was a blessing or a curse. While the $1.56 million judgment allowed us to survive, it's hard not to consider the counterfactual: A $30 million verdict. Instead of having the option to sell Camelot and move our headquarters, my cult would have faced the seizure of all of our properties, including our Montana ranch. Erin speculated that a larger damage award might have merited closer scrutiny on appeal. But what about the appeal bond? It would have been $45 million. Which would have exceeded our net worth. It would have spelled the end of my cult, which would have gone into receivership, with all assets liquidated. There would have been no bomb shelters, no gun deal, no prayer for world judgment, and no fuel spill.

That entire history would have *vanished*.

My mother might have tried to start again with a new business entity, claiming "religious persecution" and capitalizing on the sympathy of her worldwide membership. Or she might have found a more productive use for her time. Without properties or infrastructure, members would have scattered, and her prospects for cult leadership would have been bleak. Had she made prophecies of nuclear war, they would have remained obscure.

If there were no cult for me to rejoin at the end of 1986, I would have kept my job at Composite Image Systems, giving me a seven-year head start on my television career. I would have gained my mental and financial independence in my early twenties, and I would have been able to raise my family at a much better standard of living. When I think about that colossal fork in the road, I wish we *had* been destroyed. It would have been a better outcome for all of us.

I don't think Mull deserved $30 million. But such an award would have punished my cult for its decades of ill-gotten gains and ended its consensual exploitation of thousands of vulnerable people. In hindsight I would rather have made even Mull's attorney Lawrence Levy fabulously wealthy, instead of allowing our dangerous self-destructive arc to continue. Even though it would have been shocking and traumatic, it would have been the lesser of evils.

Because my mother's career of abuse did not end in 1986. Over the next five years, thousands of her disciples, including me, wasted untold amounts of time and resources on our millenarian folly. I don't blame Carole Snow. She acted with integrity according to her principles. But it's a tough object lesson about unintended consequences, where cults are concerned. I have to wonder if Snow regretted her efforts after she learned about my cult's "shelter cycle," gun deal, and fuel spill?

Was it really a *good thing* that we sank $25 million and hundreds of person-years into a useless bunker in Mol Heron Canyon? What of our larger membership, who spent perhaps twice that amount on their private shelters? What was the total price of Snow's rescue? It's difficult to quantify. Taking a wild guess, roughly $75 million in 1990 dollars went to bomb shelters and supplies, with perhaps another $100 million in opportunity costs. In today's money, that might approach half a billion dollars.

We'll never know what might have been.

It's fitting to give my sister Tatiana Prophet the last word on *CUT v. Mull*. In a 2007 interview, she described canceled classes and all-day prayer vigils for the trial during her senior year of high school. As my siblings and I faced our long-term disillusionment, it slowly dawned on us all that our mother was a very different person than she claimed to be:

> I was dragged through some pretty heavy-duty lawsuits. Where the truth was not really represented. It was hidden. It was massaged. It was violated. And when I find out that a lot of these things were true that were brought up in these lawsuits, you know I'd like my time back when I prayed for my mom. I'd really like that time back. And you know it's not like 'Oh, you should stick by your family.' No! She shouldn't have done those things. They are a fact. You don't treat people like that. I don't care who you are. You just don't treat another human being like that. So that is the truth. There are many people who were abused by her. Verbally. Psychologically. And emotionally.
>
> She did raise me to uphold the lofty goals of justice, freedom, justice for the underdog, truth… Some who are still part of the church have criticized me for not allowing my mother to be human. This goes beyond that. This goes to hypocrisy. Because she was holding people to a standard that she could not uphold herself.… I think that because she was a public figure, her actions in her life should be viewable—should face the light of day. I think that people would probably allow her to have a sexual liaison. But I don't think that they would look as kindly on it when it was kind of endemic, periodic. It was pervasive… People want to know who she was. And her personal life is part of that.
>
> I also think—people might even bring up the Ten Commandments, the commandment of 'Honor thy father and thy mother.' And it's like, I love my mother, and I honor her. I honor what was honorable… But I worship truth. That is my only god. As a journalist—but also my siblings and I—I believe that we all are of the same mind. We really hold truth above everything. That's all we really have in this world.

Neither Tatiana's candor nor my counterfactual musings can change history. Nor can they heal the broken dreams of our members. After I left my cult, I only saw my mother a few more times before she died. But I did find closure. It was the late 1990s when I made a special trip to the Ranch. Mother and I went for a walk near the bank of the Yellowstone River, where we had our last substantive conversation—one that's burned into my memory. She began by telling me that she recognized that she had been hard on me in the years before I left. And that she was very sorry. Then she made a more generalized apology—an astounding re-evaluation of her life and leadership.

> I realize I've abused power. I've hurt many people. I've been doing a lot of reflection and spiritual work, and I understand why this happened. When I was embodied on Atlantis as a high priestess 10,000 years ago, I made the same mistakes. I manipulated my followers for personal gain. In this life, it was my mission to right those wrongs.
>
> I was given the opportunity by El Morya and the Lords of Karma to come into a spiritual community and lead it properly. But I fell into the same traps. I failed in my mission. I realize it's too late for me to make amends to everyone.
>
> Sean, I want you to tell people what I said. Tell as many people as you can. Help me to pay the karmic debt I've incurred.

It was earth shattering. I never expected my mother to admit that she could be wrong—about anything. Her infallibility was drilled into my brain since childhood. Including claims that her dictations were "99 percent accurate." She had even announced in a dictation from "Padma Sambhava" that she had balanced 100 percent of her karma—casting herself as a Bodhisattva: a spiritual adept who could attain "nirvana" at any time, but remained in human form out of compassionate dedication to humanity.

Erin wondered if the apology was a ploy to regain my loyalty? Maybe so. As revealed in *Prophet's Daughter*, the Atlantis embodiment wasn't mother's idea. It traced back to Erin's "seer" work I discussed previously, which mother had accepted as true. None of that mattered. By then I was an atheist, having especially rejected anything to do with past lives. I didn't know at the time that the story came from Erin. But to me it was yet another example of spiritual folklore—a kind of cop-out.

I knew the apology was only the barest beginning of what it would have taken for my mother to become a mentally healthy and supportive parent. Still, within her virtual world, the Atlantis anecdote was the best she could muster. It was an important milestone. On some level she took accountability. I understood her meaning, and I'm profoundly grateful for it. Most adult children of dysfunctional parents don't get closure. While I certainly recognize how difficult it must have been for her to own up to her mistakes, it's impossible for any apology to repair the harm her unchecked power caused to so many—including herself.

The next time I saw her was on her 60th birthday in 1999. She still recognized me. In 2000, we had a small family reunion at Erin's home in Bozeman. When I arrived, I tried to give her a hug. She was surprised and stepped back, asking, "And, who are you?" At first, I thought she was joking. I had not known her memory loss was so severe. I couldn't fathom the woman who gave me life and loomed so large as the messenger of God was now unable to recognize her firstborn son. We all reminded her we were her children and posed for a photo. But who can say whether she understood? Her Alzheimer's was only getting worse.

Elizabeth Clare Prophet (center) with her five children, left to right, Tatiana, Erin, Seth, Moira, Sean, Bozeman, Montana, October 8, 2000.

I said goodbye to her in 2007, in her basement apartment in Bozeman. By then, she was under full-time nursing care. Erin and I each held one of her hands. We played her favorite music and sang songs to her, as to a child. She made eye contact with me a few times and managed a few labored smiles, responding most strongly to the music. But it was just a bare minimum of awareness. She tried to speak, but couldn't form the words. For much of the hour-long visit she had her eyes closed, or stared into space with her mouth open. Her pitiful condition hit me hard: The person I had known as my mother was gone.

Two years later, on October 15, 2009, I got the call from Erin. Our mother had died. I was on deadline, with no time to reflect. I took a moment to walk out of my edit bay and stand outside my building. Staring down at the clumps of grass growing up through cracks in the sidewalk, and up at the passing traffic on Santa Monica Boulevard, I felt numb.

My mother's passing forced me to confront the stark duality of our relationship: the tenderness and love of my earliest years, eclipsed by the rigid messianic identity that later defined her. And it took a long while to sort that out. I feel more emotion now and a huge lump in my throat as I reflect on her death. What makes me saddest? No one gets to choose their parents, and we all only get one mother. But I can't help but wonder what life would have been like for us without our cult? When I was a small child, my love for her was pure, innocent, and limitless. She was my world. And within that world, she loved me back with her whole heart and treated me with absolute tenderness. I've never felt anything like it.

Sean and Mother c. 1966

As I grew up, circumstances stole any chance for us to maintain a secure attachment. Or to develop a healthy, emotionally mature relationship—which was gradually steamrolled into oblivion by her singular mission focus. Decades later I finally recognize that beneath my stale, cold anger about how things turned out, that's what still hurts most: I deeply, deeply miss our love. And above all I miss what it might have blossomed into. It's an ache that will never be assuaged—like mortality.

Through her circumstances of birth and a series of fateful decisions driven by fascination with her virtual world, my mother deprived herself of a normal life. She had brief snippets of it: When she was a child, she played the piano and clarinet, and as a young adult she enjoyed tennis. She was once a cafeteria cashier, and held more consequential jobs at the United Nations, the Association of American Railroads, and the *Christian Science Monitor*. There was her brief marriage to Dag Ytreberg, trips to London and Paris, dancing, singing songs around a campfire, attending a performance by Thelonius Monk, and an exchange year when she studied in Switzerland and hitchhiked across Europe.

I'm glad she met my father at age 22, or I wouldn't be alive. But I also find it tragic that she cut herself off from life. I think about the turning points in her youth, when she could have gone in a different direction. But she was laser-focused on her all-consuming quest to find the God of her lifelong virtual visions. And it seems no one could have deterred her. She did ponder some valuable questions at the age of 19 in a 1958 letter to her mother she wrote while studying at Antioch College—experiencing a moment of clarity that was all-too-brief.

She began, "What are my values? How much of this life is it humanly possible to overcome? Would I be true to myself if I compromised my ideal to meet the demands of this life? Would I be truly happy if I gave up part of these truths which are so dear to me for society, custom, tradition?" These thoughts were sparked by her interactions with Lester Berman, a fellow student she described as "brilliant" but also the "personification of the devil." Berman, an atheist, challenged her beliefs, accusing her of avoiding reality. "By refusing to acknowledge evil and loving everyone I was escaping this world instead of facing it," he told her. Their debates were lively and contentious, and despite their opposing philosophies, she enjoyed his company. "He presented a challenge. I was at the point where I thought my ideas were radically fanatic and so I listened to him."

One weekend, she and Berman joined other students for dinner and a campus beer party, where she drank four mugs of beer and had a wonderful time. The night before, she had laughed and danced with abandon. While she found these new experiences liberating, they left her conflicted. She felt her transient happiness was a betrayal of her faith, contrasting it with the eternal joy of her spiritual ideals.

One snowy night, she walked alone beneath the stars and forced herself to imagine a universe without God. She described the attempt as deeply unsettling, feeling a vast emptiness and isolation. "The sense of the void and the nothingness that would exist without God's presence was truly, to me, proof in itself that there was a God"—which drove her to return to her lifelong certainty in her faith, declaring she had "passed these tests without knowing they were being administered."

My mother chose—poorly—to follow her virtual reality. She didn't pass anything. Instead she locked herself into a lifetime of struggle with imaginary enemies, and walled herself off from human connection. It's poignant that my mother came *so close* to recognizing her predicament, and then decided to retreat into her safe space. She was asking precisely the right questions, at precisely the right age: "What are my values?" "Am I a fanatic?" Between the lines she was asking, "Have I closed myself to the world without learning anything about it?"

Here was Berman—a man she admitted was brilliant, but he was also the personification of the devil? *But she liked him!* So why not take the opportunity to challenge herself further—and learn what he knew? I can only conclude that it was easier to detach and feel superior. She declared that he was "fun," but then decided that having fun was turning her back on God, who she imagined would be jealous, like a jilted lover. Why couldn't she do both? The answer is as mundane as it is heartbreaking: Her parasocial relationship with God subtracted the negative of her social anxiety. As long as she felt more connected to God than to human beings, she never had to risk rejection.

During her meditation on a "cosmos without God," she felt "suspended alone." Sadly, I believe her feeling of aloneness had everything to do with her exclusion from community in grade school and high school. Yes, she had friends, but her virtual inner life kept her out of the mainstream social scene. As an adult, she built a cult of thousands of people, yet she still withdrew into divine superiority, re-creating the same dynamic of insulating herself from rejection. It's the crowning irony of her life: As an adult, her vaunted position never allowed her to have a single close friend. Because friendships can only be with *peers*. None of her chelas could fill that role because reciprocity is ruled out by the guru-chela relationship. She knew the score. The saddest words I ever heard her say were, "El Morya doesn't allow me to have friends."

Ever since I learned about my mother's crisis of faith at age 19, I've had a fantasy about having a frank conversation with her—perhaps over a few beers—during her intellectual ferment at Antioch. As Erin wondered in the final pages of *Prophet's Daughter*, what if I could have told my mother exactly where her path would lead? Could I have persuaded her to make a different choice? I'm not sure anyone could have. It seems her die was cast by the age of four, the moment her mother convinced her that she had seen a past life on the Nile River. What if her mother had said, "Betty Clare, it's just a daydream. That's your imagination giving you fun toys to play with." Those words from my grandmother could have changed history.

Despite her commitment to strict hierarchy and her arch-conservative views, my mother maintained a parallel set of egalitarian values. In *Preparation for My Mission*, she said, "When I would hear kids at school talking against Jews and Negroes and East European immigrants, I would remember. All my friends were welcome at our house. We understood what it was like to be singled out and ostracized through guilt by association."[3] She held that sense of basic fairness and empathy throughout her life, despite the paradox of what often manifested as calculated cruelty.

I know it may be difficult to accept, but within my mother's virtual reality I believe she tried to do what she thought was best for her family, her community, and the world, *according to her understanding*. That was true even when her perspective was fatally flawed—including when she crucified Gregory Mull in Saint Germain's office and later decided to sue him. It also extends to that awful day when she led Erin and me—along with her entire community—in the prayer for world destruction. Looking at both cases in retrospect, it's become clear to me that she always sincerely believed she was doing God's work.

The doctrines she embraced made her do terrible things. Through the psychological purgation of writing this book, I've now come to realize that despite her flaws my mother never stopped loving me in her own way. And I can allow myself to love her still. She is not the villain of my story. She gave me many gifts. And it's impossible for me not to have compassion for her personal struggles on a deeply human level. Something during her formative years drove her to retreat from reality. Had she broken through to self-honesty with Lester Berman's help, there's just so much useless pain we could have all avoided. Instead of chasing phantoms, she might have become an executive, a politician, a doctor, an attorney, or a humanitarian. She had the intelligence and leadership qualities to accomplish any goal she set her mind to—and a work ethic second to none.

The core nemesis of my life—and my mother's too—has always been the sincerely-held spiritual beliefs that infected her mind. As much as I abhor them, I can't help but grieve for the woman she might have grown into without them. These virtual tall tales built my cult and consumed my mother. They drove her to lie, to forecast doom, to abuse people and cast them aside, to manipulate, to squander resources, to use her dictations for political purposes, and worst of all to believe that using her spiritual authority to call for global genocide was her only option.

They nearly consumed me.

I chose not to go to her funeral, which turned out to be an idolatrous cult-fest. And how else could it have been? Cult leaders don't just die. Their death is always imbued with exaggerated significance, enshrining an ongoing presence in the lives of members. When my mother unplugged dad's life support in 1973, before his body was even cold, she and Randall and several others at the hospital had already seen virtual visions of his ascension, and installed him as an Ascended Master.

But in 2009, no one dared step forward to do the same for her. They had already been without a spiritual leader for a decade, and the cult's caretaker board was too weak and conflicted to seize her mantle. They did canonize her—after a fashion. Even in life they had made her into a god, and now their invention belongs to them. As much as I wish I could rewrite her story—or mine—I've come to accept that some chapters will remain unfinished.

Other Ascended Master organizations picked up the slack. They've since taken to calling my mother "the Ascended Lady Master Clare" or "Clare de Lis." David Lewis of The Hearts Center cult now claims to speak for her, in dictations he calls "HeartStreams." He used my parents' names and identities to kick off a $5 million fundraising campaign in 2021 called "The Heart-Mind Miracle Initiative" which proposed building "centers of light" in Montana, Arizona, California, and Texas.

The persistence of such movements underscores the enduring appeal of virtual realities and the human yearning for spiritual certainty. The history of my cult is repeating itself to the letter. Turnabout is fair play, I must admit. I'm sure David Lewis also sincerely believes he is doing God's work—just as my mother spoke for my father as "Lanello," for Guy Ballard as "Godfre," and for Edna Ballard as "Lotus." It's how succession works with Ascended Master cults: Like Dread Pirate Roberts in *The Princess Bride*, each messenger usurps the identity of their predecessor, while justifying themselves under the guise of their virtual reality. And new generations of seekers keep lapping it up.

---

[1] Prophet, E. C. (1986). [*Unreleased VHS video footage*]. Church Universal and Triumphant.

[2] Prophet, E. (2018). *Coercion or conversion? A case study in religion and the law: CUT v. Mull v. Prophet* (pp. 137–141). Linden Books.

[3] Prophet, E. C. (2009). *Preparation for my mission* (E. L. Prophet & T. M. Prophet, Eds., p. 51). Summit University Press.

Afterword

I've held nothing back, protected no one, and considered nothing sacred—except the search for truth. For those who feel as I do, it's a tough time to be alive. Yet there is hope. Perhaps not for our civilization in the near term. Too many of us have rejected truth and embraced cult-like thinking, committing us all to relearning the painful lessons of history. Our governments have abandoned fairness, justice and equality, leading us backward.

Yet there is hope.

Each of us can commit to a better path. We can each reject dogma, superstition, and conspiracy. We can each resist lies. We can be the glue that binds our civilization back together. When our friends and loved ones are ready, we can share what we've learned.

We can each reject the allure of purity, perfectionism, and hierarchy. We can each renew the social contract—moving into Kohlberg stage 5—recognizing that our superpower is cooperation. Our most powerful tool is empathy: Taking the perspective of those far removed from our own. Our salvation, if it comes, will be hard-fought through finding unity in shared human values. Through embracing *The Moral Landscape*—putting science at the center of ethics and governance, where it belongs.

That will never happen through blind loyalty, authority, or sanctity. And never through wealth or leaders with inferior values. When we're in crisis, no God, or strongman, or cult leader, or king pretending to be God will ever save us.

We are our only hope. So never give up.

If you've made it to the end, you've realized this book isn't really about cults—it's about power. I just happened to grow up in a cult, so that was my introduction to unchecked power and shared delusion—the hallmarks of fascism. To re-emphasize a repeated message of this book, these patterns recur in every human context. From governments to cults to relationships. Millenarianism spans all domains, as a reflection of our collective struggle with mortality. When anyone shouts about the end of *the* world, look into *their* world, and you'll find trauma, chaos, and fear of death. The more power such a traumatized person accumulates, the more dangerous they become.

This makes accountability our central priority. And it depends entirely on well-designed institutions that can deliver good results even when run by flawed people. Human perfectibility might be our most destructive myth. Smarter people are better at manipulation, and at hiding their agendas. We'll never find a philosopher-king or queen, because unaccountable power warps the mind.

So we must hold ourselves accountable, and claw back accountability in our families, friend groups, social systems, and governments. It will require courage, self-honesty and psychological healing on a mass scale—a heavy lift.

There are no panaceas. And I'm not crazy enough to believe I can change the world with a book. My hope instead is to spark reflection that might help individuals avoid the traps of power, cults and cult-like thinking. And that might lead to small improvements.

Cult Films, Series, and Documentaries

Disclaimer: This list has been compiled from online sources and is provided as a reference guide to a sampling of cult-related content. It's not intended to be a comprehensive list, nor does it represent a specific endorsement of the accuracy or point of view of any film, documentary, or series.

Bad Faith (2024) Amazon Prime
The Family (2019) Netflix
Wild Wild Country (2018) Netflix
Leah Remini: Scientology and the Aftermath (2016) A&E
Filthy Rich (2020, 2022) Netflix
The Vow (2020) HBO
Heaven's Gate: The Cult of Cults (2020) HBO
Keep Sweet: Pray and Obey (2022) Netflix
The Way Down: God, Greed, and the Cult of Gwen Shamblin (2021, 2022) HBO
The Program: Cons, Cults, and Kidnapping (2023) Netflix
Jonestown: The Life and Death of Peoples Temple (2006) PBS
Bikram: Yogi, Guru, Predator (2019) Netflix
Bad Vegan: Fame. Fraud. Fugitives (2022) Netflix
My Scientology Movie (2015)
The Anarchists (2022) HBO
Born in Synanon (2023) Paramount+
Jonestown: Paradise Lost (2007) History Channel
The Wave (2008)
How To Become A Tyrant (2021) Netflix
Deprogrammed (2015)
Behind the Curve (2018) Netflix
Twin Flames Universe (2023) Amazon Prime, Netflix
Stolen Youth: Inside the Cult at Sarah Lawrence (2023) Hulu
Kumaré (2011)
The Source Family (2012)
Captive Minds: Hypnosis and Beyond (1983) National Film Board of Canada
Hell Camp: Teen Nightmare (2023) Netflix
Love Has Won: The Cult of Mother God (2023) HBO
Murder Among the Mormons (2021) Netflix
How To Become A Cult Leader (2023) Netflix
The Deep End (2022) Freeform
Shiny Happy People (2023) Amazon Freevee
Blessed Child (2019)

Acknowledgments

I thank my parents, Mark and Elizabeth Prophet, for bringing me into the world, providing a rich foundation of experiences that encouraged my reflection and, perhaps in spite of themselves, inspiring a deep reverence for truth. They equipped me with the comprehensive education I needed to eventually see through my indoctrination. This book is, in part, an effort to fulfill my mother's final lucid request: that I publicize her belated remorse for her abuse of power. I don't know if it's possible for any book to make meaningful amends, but perhaps it may help future seekers be more cautious about idolizing cult leaders.

I'm grateful to my siblings—Erin, Moira, Tatiana, and Seth—for their perseverance. Growing up in our family presented unique challenges and rewards, and each of us has had to make our own peace with our past. My sister Erin deserves particular mention for earning her Ph.D. in religion from Rice University in 2018, and for blazing the literary trail with *Prophet's Daughter (2009)* and *Coercion or Conversion (2018)*. Her research, background material, critique, and perspective have been invaluable. My sister Tatiana also made generous contributions, including her research into our grandparents, her interviews with our mother and me, and her work on *Preparation for my Mission (2009)*.

I'm especially grateful to Kathleen Prophet for her irreplaceable input on the project, and for her willingness to relive some of the difficult moments in our family life. And to Robert Donaldson for his friendship and his stalwart support of Kathleen and our family. I thank my adult children, Christopher, Nathaniel, and Lilyette Prophet for their support and resilience.

I also acknowledge my father's first wife, Phyllis Prophet, and their children, Rebecca, Beth, Dan, Marcia, and Allison, who endured a different set of challenges during the early years of my cult.

Many friends and acquaintances encouraged me over the years to write my "cult book," which often felt like an unwelcome, daunting assignment. Assignment complete! I thank my 3M friends Mark Gregg, Mandy Calvano, and Misty Howell, along with Steve Woodward and Nancy Johnston, for goading me into action. I'm also grateful for the work of Matthew Remski, Julian Walker, Derek Beres, and Jim Stewartson, whose research has deepened my understanding of conspirituality and fascism. Coral Anika Theill's harrowing escape from a family cult likewise inspired me.

To my friend and mentor Price Pethel, thank you for recognizing my predicament when I was a young man, and for offering your wisdom and guidance. I'm grateful to my agent George Elder and his wife Beth Elder, who helped bring this book to fruition, and worked tirelessly to help refine my ideas. George also connected me with Amika Press and my brilliant editor John Manos, whose encouragement and insights greatly enriched this work.

Special gratitude to William Hamby, LCSW, for his close collaboration on exploring cult psychology, perfectionism, and moral development, and for his thoughtful Foreword. And much love to Selma Filali Baba, for reading my unfinished manuscripts and for her unwavering support as I launched this project.

Thanks to Joseph Conarkov for his clarifications on Buddhism. I also appreciate several unnamed beta readers who provided valuable feedback, and everyone else who offered moral and practical support.

Special thanks to Joe Szimhart for his interview on exit counseling and discussions on the Mighty I AM cult and Theosophy, and to Christophe Difo and Joe Occhipinti, former co-hosts of *The Radical Secular*, for their friendship and wisdom. Thanks to Peter Jacobs and Jillian Skye Jacobs for their support, which made this project possible.

Much appreciation to Mouna Moumni for her diligence on the cover artwork and to Andrea Elder for the cover design.

While I am deeply grateful to everyone who helped bring this project to completion, errors and omissions are mine alone, and I apologize for any that may have slipped through.

www.ingramcontent.com/pod-product-compliance
Lightning Source LLC
Chambersburg PA
CBHW071234160426
43196CB00009B/1050